COMMUNICATING AT WORK

PRINCIPLES AND PRACTICES FOR BUSINESS AND THE PROFESSIONS

FOURTH EDITION

RONALD B. ADLER

Santa Barbara City College

McGRAW-HILL, INC.

New York   St. Louis   San Francisco   Auckland   Bogotá   Caracas
Lisbon   London   Madrid   Mexico   Milan   Montreal   New Delhi
Paris   San Juan   Singapore   Sydney   Tokyo   Toronto

COMMUNICATING AT WORK
Principles and Practices for Business and the Professions

Copyright ©1992, 1989, 1986, 1983 by McGraw-Hill, Inc.

Credits and Acknowledgments appear on pages 455–456, and on this page by reference.

1 2 3 4 5 6 7 8 9 0 DOC DOC 9 0 9 8 7 6 5 4 3 2

ISBN 0-07-000454-4

This book was set in Meridien by Ruttle, Shaw & Wetherill, Inc.
The editors were Hilary Jackson and Jean Akers;
the production supervisor was Janelle S. Travers.
The cover was designed by Wanda Siedlecka;
cover photo by André Baranowski.
The photo editor was Debra P. Hershkowitz.
R. R. Donnelley & Sons Company was printer and binder.

Library of Congress Cataloging-in-Publication Data

Adler, Ronald B. (Ronald Brian), (date).
    Communicating at work: principles and practices for business and the professions / Ronald B. Adler. — 4th ed.
        p.   cm.
    Includes bibliographical references and index.
    ISBN 0-07-000454-4
    1. Business communication.   2. Interpersonal communication.
I. Title.
HF5718.A33   1992
658.4'52—dc20   91-33939

ABOUT THE AUTHOR

Ronald B. Adler is Associate Professor of Communication at Santa Barbara City College, where he specializes in organizational and interpersonal communication. He is the author of *Confidence in Communication: A Guide to Assertive and Social Skills* and coauthor of *Understanding Human Communication, Interplay: The Process of Interpersonal Communication* as well as the widely used text *Looking Out/Looking In.* Professor Adler is a consultant for a number of corporate, professional, and government clients and leads workshops in such areas as conflict resolution, presentational speaking, team building, and interviewing.

CONTENTS

CHAPTER 12   VERBAL AND VISUAL SUPPORT IN PRESENTATIONS   320

CHAPTER 13   DELIVERING THE PRESENTATIONS   356

PREFACE

"The more things change, the more they stay the same." This saying is an apt characterization of this fourth edition of *Communicating at Work.*

On one hand, this book retains the strong link between scholarship and the "real world" of business and the professions that has been so successful in the past. Every chapter reports on the work of researchers in a variety of disciplines, but the constant emphasis is on how scholarship can help readers communicate more effectively. Throughout the book, numerous examples drawn from real business and professional situations show how effective communication can help get any job done in a more productive, satisfying way. A diverse array of quotations and comments from people in business and the professions illustrate the importance of communication and offers suggestions about how to handle specific communication challenges. In addition, each chapter ends with a Communicator Profile: a first-person account from an experienced business or professional person offering insights and suggestions on how the principles in this book apply in day-to-day situations.

As in the past, this edition of *Communicating at Work* should be helpful to virtually every business communicator. Readers who are just beginning their careers will learn the basic communication principles that are necessary for success in any career. Experienced communicators who have already spent time in the world beyond the classroom will find that the book provides information that will help them improve the communication skills they have already developed.

FEATURES OF THE NEW EDITION

Although the successful elements of preceding editions of *Communicating at Work* are retained here, this new edition contains new information that should make it even more helpful for communicators. In addition to an overall updating of research, several key changes are apparent:

- Chapter 2 has been revised to include communicating in the culturally diverse world of the 1990s. Besides surveying the changing nature of the work force, the chapter offers suggestions for how to communicate more effectively with others whose backgrounds may vary widely.
- The information on small-group communication has been consolidated into two chapters in order to make it clearer and more useful. Chapter 8 discusses how communication operates in working teams, and Chapter 9 focuses on the skills necessary to lead and participate in effective meetings.
- The two most important types of presentational speaking have been given separate treatment. Chapter 14 outlines specific suggestions for informative speaking and provides an annotated transcript of a typical informative presentation. Chapter 15 is now devoted exclusively to persuasive presentations. It offers an expanded list of strategies for organizing and presenting messages designed to influence others.
- A new Appendix provides a summary of formats for presenting written communication. Although *Communicating at Work* focuses on face-to-face interaction, students need models for how to present the paper-and-ink materials that accompany their oral messages. This Appendix will provide a useful tool for ensuring that written documents meet the same professional standards as the student's speech.

Besides these prominent changes, every chapter contains new or updated material designed to give readers a current, useful guide to communication on the job. For example:

- Chapter 1 offers an expanded discussion of the differences and merits of oral versus written communication that will help readers decide whether to deliver a message in person, in writing, or both.
- Chapter 4 contains a new section on "Listening to Criticism" that offers advice on how to respond constructively and nondefensively to the inevitable attacks that occur in every job. It also contains a self-test to help readers identify their own listening strengths and weaknesses.
- Chapter 5 offers an expanded discussion of various methods of handling conflicts.
- Chapter 6 discusses the ethics of interviewing and contains an annotated interview plan that will help readers develop an interview strategy that accomplishes their goals.
- Chapter 7 provides both new information on giving feedback in performance appraisal interviews and more detail on strategies for coping with illegal questions in selection interviews.
- Chapter 8 emphasizes the interdependence that is a feature of most working groups. It describes the stages in problem-solving groups, and discusses leadership emergence—an important topic in teams without a designated leader.
- Chapter 12 describes the advantages and potential pitfalls of computer-assisted design in creating visual aids for presentational speaking.

In addition to these improvements in the text itself, several ancillaries that accompany the text will help both students and their professors use *Communicating at Work:*

- A new Instructors' Manual, written by Lawrence W. Hugenberg of Youngstown State University, provides a wealth of teaching and testing strategies.
- A computerized test bank contains over 650 examination questions.
- A videotape developed by Carol Shuherk of the University of Southern California presents a variety of speakers delivering informative and persuasive presentations.

ACKNOWLEDGMENTS

The changes in this edition are due in great part to the helpful suggestions of the following people: Phyllis B. Bosley, Towson State University; Robert Greenstreet, East Central University; John Haas, University of Tennessee at Knoxville; Linda S. Henderson, San Francisco State University; Lawrence W. Hugenberg, Youngstown State University; and Sandra M. Ketrow, University of Rhode Island.

In addition, the thoughts of reviewers from previous editions of the book continue to be useful. Thanks to Bette Brunsting, Central College; David C. Burke, Bob Jones University; Russell T. Church, John Carroll University; Joyce E. Crouch, Morehead State University; H. C. Eichmeier, Clinton Community College; Lois Einhorn, State University of New York at Binghamton; Robert Hirsch, Arizona State University; Robert L. Husband, University of Illinois; Nancy Israel-Perry, University of Michigan—Dearborn; Gary L. Kreps, Indiana University—Purdue University at Indianapolis; Janet K. Larsen, University of South Dakota; Kaylene A. Long, Louisiana State University; Clarice P. Lowe, Texas Southern University; Karin McCallum, The University of Texas at Arlington; Jean Michulka, University of Texas at El Paso; Charles R. Newman, Parkland College; Terry A. Pickett, Iowa State University; David J. Robinson, Youngstown State University; June H. Smith, Austin College; Barbara Strain, San Antonio College; Everett E. Walde, District One Technical Institute—Eau Claire; and G.A. Yeomans, University of Tennessee.

Finally, thanks are due to all the publishing professionals who made this revision possible. The entire team at McGraw-Hill—Hilary Jackson, Jean Akers, Fran Marino, and Roth Wilkofsky—were models of effective, positive communication. Robin Adler's speed and diligence in manuscript preparation kept the project moving. Ann Bennett's interviewing and writing skills produced a diverse and interesting crop of Communicator Profiles. Carol Flechner's copy editing was thorough and accurate. Angie Grandbouche's indexing skills helped make the material accessible to readers. If every team was as competent and personable as this group, communicating at work would be much less of a challenge.

Ronald B. Adler

PART I

BASICS OF BUSINESS AND PROFESSIONAL COMMUNICATION

CHAPTER | 1

After reading this chapter, you should understand:

■ The prevalence and importance of communication on the job
■ Settings in which on-the-job communication occurs
■ The four functions of on-the-job communication
■ The elements and characteristics of the communication process
■ The differences between oral and written communication channels

You should be able to:

■ Identify the types of communication and the settings that now play or that will play the greatest role in your career
■ Use the communication model in Figure 1-1 to diagnose organizational problems you have experienced
■ Apply your understanding of the communication process to increase the chance that you will successfully achieve a communication goal
■ Choose the best channel to send a given message

COMMUNICATING
AT WORK

THE IMPORTANCE OF COMMUNICATION

There is no denying the importance of job-related knowledge. Whether you are an engineer, accountant, computer programmer, machinist, contractor, medical professional, or any other kind of worker, succeeding on the job requires specialized information and skills.

But specialized knowledge alone isn't enough to guarantee success. Whatever job you choose, communication skills will also be vital. Employers recognize this fact. An impressive collection of research identifies communication as the most important factor in successful job performance. For example, Table 1-1 lists the results of a survey of 1,000 personnel managers in the United States. The respondents identified the top three skills for job performance as involving communication. Other important attributes—including technical competence, work experience, academic background, and recommendations—all lagged behind.[1] In another poll, business and government executives named oral communication as the single most valuable skill an employee could have, followed by written communication and interpersonal skills.[2] Communication skills are valuable throughout a career. Subscribers to the *Harvard Business Review* rated "the ability to communicate" the most important factor in making an executive "promotable," more important than ambition, education, and capacity for hard work.[3] A twenty-year study that followed the progress of Stanford University M.B.A.s revealed that the most successful graduates (as measured by both career

TABLE 1-1   Factors Most Important in Helping Graduating College Students Obtain Employment

RANK/ORDER	FACTORS/SKILLS EVALUATED
1	Oral (speaking) communication
2	Listening ability
3	Enthusiasm
4	Written communication skills
5	Technical competence
6	Appearance
7	Poise
8	Work experience
9	Résumé
10	Specific degree held
11	Grade point average
12	Part-time or summer employment
13	Accreditation of program
14	Leadership in campus/community activities
15	Participation in campus/community activities
16	Recommendations
17	School attended

From Dan B. Curtis, Jerry L. Winsor, and Ronald D. Stephens, "National Preferences in Business and Communication Education," *Communication Education* 38 (January 1989): 11.

advancement and salary) shared personality traits that distinguish good communicators: a desire to persuade, an interest in talking and working with other people, and an outgoing, ascendant personality. As students, these achievers developed their communication skills by choosing courses in areas such as persuasion, selling ideas, negotiation, and other forms of speaking.[4]

Although the need for face-to-face skills may seem less important in today's high-tech world, the opposite is true. Without human skills, technology will overwhelm an organization. Cornell University researchers discovered that, in the changing workplace, computers and other kinds of sophisticated equipment are now performing routine jobs, leaving workers to handle the human challenges of improving the organization and responding to customers.[5] After studying the needs of four Silicon Valley manufacturing firms, educational psychologist Russell Rumberger discovered that what employees needed was "oral literacy—the ability to communicate, to work in teams and to shift rapidly as the work changed."[6]

Most successful people recognize the role communication skills have played in their career. In a survey of college graduates in a wide variety of fields, most respondents said that communication was vital to their job success. Most, in fact, said that communication skills were more important than the major subject they had studied in college.[7] In one survey of business-school alumni, oral communication skills were judged as "mandatory" or "very important" by 100 percent of the respondents—every person who replied.[8]

The importance of communication is not surprising when you consider the staggering amount of time people spend communicating on the job. Most experts state that the average business executive spends 75 to 80 percent of the time communicating—about 45 minutes out of every hour.[9] One survey of almost a hundred companies revealed that 80 percent of the businesspeople responding conducted interviews, 78 percent gave instructions to subordinates, 76 percent gave oral reports, and 75 percent spoke with clients.[10] Communication is just as important in other fields. Lawyers, teachers, and salespeople (the most common entry-level job in many industries) obviously need to be able to communicate effectively. Health-care professionals work with colleagues and patients. Computer programmers interview clients to learn their needs and to explain how programs work. Even research scientists must frame grant proposals that communicate the need for a project and must be able to report the results clearly to others.

The importance of communicating effectively on the job is obvious. But the discussion so far hasn't even addressed the fact that communication skills often make the difference between being hired and being rejected in the first place. In a study of the help-wanted sections of 160 Sunday newspapers, nearly 6,300 classified ads specifically asked for applicants with communication skills. Oral communication and selling were most frequently mentioned, followed by writing, counseling, recruiting, interviewing, and supervisory skills.[11] A survey of 154 employers who recruit on college campuses showed that one of the three most preferred areas of study was oral and written business communication. (The other two were accounting–personnel management and human behavior in organiza-

---

One can lack any of the qualities of an organizer—with one exception—and still be effective and successful. That exception is the art of communication. It does not matter what you know about anything if you cannot communicate to your people. In that event you are not even a failure. You're just not there.

Community organizer Saul D. Alinsky, *Rules for Radicals*

---

tions.) When 170 well-known business and industrial firms were asked to list the most common reasons for *not* offering jobs to applicants, the most frequent replies were "inability to communicate" and "poor communication skills."[12]

TYPES OF ON-THE-JOB COMMUNICATION

Communication on the job takes many forms, including formal speeches, job interviews, meetings, even casual conversations. It may be between colleagues at the same level, between managers and subordinates, between people in the same company or people in different companies, between suppliers and customers, and so on. While communication may take many forms, we usually study business and professional communication according to its setting, whether it is external or internal, and its purpose.

SETTING

The *setting* of communication refers broadly to the number of people involved. Although many principles of effective communication apply to all settings, there are some important differences.

Dyadic communication involves two people communicating on an individual level. Some dyadic communication is informal—for example, two co-workers talking casually during a coffee break or managers chatting informally with subordinates about a project. Other dyadic communication is more formal and may include one person giving instructions to another, two department heads meeting to solve a problem, or a manager and subordinate negotiating a pay raise or increase in responsibility. A special kind of dyadic communication is *interviewing*—for example, a job interview or a performance appraisal.

Small-group communication involves a few more people, usually between three and ten. Our study of small groups will focus specifically on people who are meeting to accomplish some task—for example, in committees, task forces, and quality circles. A great deal of decision making in businesses and other organizations is accomplished in small-group meetings.

Public speeches and presentations involve more formal, prepared, and usually rehearsed communication in which one person does all or most of the talking. Usually, it involves one person speaking to a group, but the classification also includes other communication, such as a salesperson's presentation to a single client. Reports, briefings, training sessions, and ceremonial speeches are all examples of public speeches and presentations.

EXTERNAL AND INTERNAL COMMUNICATION

Some organizational communication is *external*—that is, it is between people who are within the organization and people who are outside it. It includes such activities as salespeople talking with customers, a purchasing agent's negotiations with a potential supplier, a small business's application to the city council for a zoning variance, and a public-relations speech to a community group.

Other communication is *internal*, between people who work within the same company or organization. Internal communication includes communication within a department (for example, conversations between co-workers, or between managers and subordinates, and informal problem-solving meetings within a department) and communication between people in different departments (for example, a corporation lawyer consulting a product manager, an official statement about company policy, a sales meeting, and a chief executive officer's annual speech to employees).

FUNCTIONS OF COMMUNICATION

Most on-the-job communication serves at least one of four purposes. Of course, many instances of communication serve two or more of these purposes at the same time.

To Tell   Communication that presents information is common in most jobs. Sometimes this means explaining how to do a job—for example, how to fill in a purchase requisition to order supplies, how to use the computer terminal to see whether an order has been shipped, or how to approach potential customers about a new product your company has developed. Sometimes you need to explain what is going on in your organization—for example, you may have to report your progress on an assignment to a client or explain to new employees how work is trafficked through your department.

To Sell   Whereas telling deals almost exclusively with facts, selling also involves feelings and attitudes. You don't have to have the word "sales" in your job title to be a salesperson. In fact, everyone needs to be a persuasive communicator at one time or another. Convincing the boss that you deserve a raise or more responsibility calls for selling. So does getting approval for a new project, motivating employees to work their hardest, and convincing a supplier that you need the shipment *today*. It doesn't take much imagination to see that the success or failure of a career depends on the ability to persuade others.

To Learn   The ability to understand others might be less obvious and dramatic than telling or selling skill, but it is no less important. Take a moment to recall the most effective on-the-job communicators you've known, and you'll see that they were almost certainly good listeners.

To Decide   As you advance in your career, the number and importance of decisions you face will grow. What is the best approach to the new job? How can we handle these people? Where should we put the resources we have? Even the highest decision makers in the biggest companies don't make judgments like these on their own. They trade ideas with others, testing and evaluating. In other words, good decisions require good communication.

THE NATURE OF COMMUNICATION

It is easier to recognize the importance of communication than it is to define the term. A close look at what happens when people try to communicate can offer clues about why some attempts succeed and others fail.

ELEMENTS OF THE COMMUNICATION PROCESS

No matter what the setting or the number of people involved, all communication consists of several elements. Although the process of communication is more than the total of these elements, understanding them can help explain what happens when one person tries to express an idea to others.

Sender   The communication process begins with a *sender*, the person who transmits a message—a sales manager making a presentation to a client, a computer programmer explaining a new program to a co-worker, or an after-dinner speaker introducing a guest.

Message   The *message* is the idea that a sender wants to convey. For example, a sales representative's message may be that a certain product is worth buying, and a manager's message to her secretary might be that a report needs to be typed in a particular format and completed by a certain deadline.

Encoding   The sender must choose certain words or symbols to express an idea. This activity is called *encoding,* and it occurs every time someone creates a message. The words that a speaker chooses to deliver a message can make a tremendous difference in how that message is received. A sympathetic manager might help employees understand that a personnel layoff has nothing to do with their competence and might convince them that the company expects to call them back as soon as business picks up. Likewise, an installer who explains how a new piece of equipment operates can influence how satisfied the users will be.

Channel   The *channel* (sometimes called the *medium*) is the method used to deliver a message. As a business communicator, you can often choose whether to put your message in writing as a letter or memo, a mailgram or telegram. You can deliver it electronically via computer linkup. Or you can communicate it orally, either over the phone or in person.

Receiver   A *receiver* is any person who notices and attaches some meaning to a message. In the simplest of circumstances, a message always reaches its intended receiver with no problems. In the confusing and imperfect world of business, however, several problems can occur. The message may never get to the receiver. It might be delivered but lie buried under a mountain of papers on the recipient's desk. If the message is oral, the listener might forget it. Even worse, a message intended for one receiver might be intercepted by someone else. A bystander might overhear your critical remarks about a fellow worker, or a competitor might see a copy of your correspondence to a customer. These problems make it clear that you need to be sure your messages are received by the intended receiver and no one else.

Decoding   Even if a message does get to its intended receiver intact, there is no guarantee that it will be understood as the sender intended it to be. The receiver must still *decode* it, making sense out of the words or symbols. Decoding is not always accurate. Your friendly joke might be taken as a deliberate offense, or a suggestion might be misinterpreted as an order. The request for "next year's figures" might mean the next fiscal year, not calendar year. It is a mistake to assume that your messages will always be decoded accurately.

By now, it might seem that communicating is like inoculating: a sender encodes a message and injects it via one or more channels into receivers who then decode it. This view is not only simplistic, it is downright wrong. It implies that the responsibility for succeeding or failing to get a message across rests only with the sender. While some types of messages, such as letters and radio broadcasts, do have one-way flow, a linear model does not completely or accurately describe most types of face-to-face communication. Usually most successful communication depends on the skill and commitment of all the parties involved.

Feedback   Receivers don't absorb messages like sponges; they respond to them. Consider audience questions during a talk or the way a customer glances at the clock during a sales presentation. Imagine the tone of voice an employer might use while saying, "I'll have to think about your proposal." Behaviors like these show that most communication is a two-way affair. The discernible response of a receiver to a sender's message is called *feedback*. Some feedback is nonverbal—smiles, sighs, and so on. Sometimes it is oral, as when you react to a colleague's ideas with questions or comments. Feedback can also be written, as when you respond to a co-worker's memo. In many cases, *no* message can be a kind of feedback. Failure to answer a letter or to return a phone call can suggest how the noncommunicative person feels about the sender. When we add the element of feedback to our communication model, we begin to recognize that in face-to-face settings people are simultaneously senders and receivers of information. This explains why these two roles are superimposed in the communication model pictured in Figure 1-1.

Noise   It might seem that, with enough feedback, the mental images of sender and receiver will match: the message received will be identical to the message

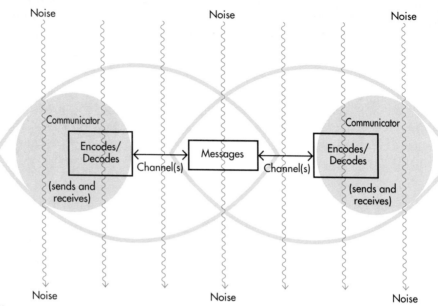

Figure 1-1   Communication model.

sent. Your own experience shows that this doesn't always happen. One of the greatest sources of communication failure is *noise*—factors that interfere with the exchange of messages. *Physical noise*—external sounds that distract communicators—falls into this category, but there are other types of external noise that don't involve sound. For example, an overcrowded room or a smelly cigar can disrupt concentration. A second kind of noise is *physiological*. Hearing disorders fall into this category, as do illnesses and disabilities that make it difficult to send or receive messages. Recall how hard it is to pay attention when you are recovering from a night on the town or have the flu. The third type of noise is *psychological*, consisting of forces within senders that interfere with understanding. Egotism, defensiveness, hostility, preoccupation, fear—all these and more constitute psychological noise.

Environment   A second source of misunderstandings is the fact that every communicator inhabits a unique *environment*. Environments aren't simply physical locations; they also include the personal history that each individual brings to a communication transaction. While we certainly have some experiences in common with a communication partner, we also perceive a situation in a way that is unique. Consider, for instance, the environmental difference between men and women, managers and subordinates, Anglos and members of ethnic minorities, wealthy and needy people, experienced and inexperienced workers.

COMMUNICATION PRINCIPLES

The communication model pictured in Figure 1-1 is not yet complete—like a still picture of a live event. All the elements are present except action. Several characteristics describe the dynamic nature of the communication process.

Communication Is Unavoidable   A fundamental axiom of communication is "One can't not communicate." As you will learn in Chapter 3, we send a rich stream of nonverbal messages even when we are silent. Facial expression, posture, gesture, clothing, and a host of other behaviors offer cues about our attitudes. The impossibility of not communicating means that we send messages even by our absence. Failing to show up at an event or leaving the room suggests meanings to others. Because communication is unavoidable, it is essential to consider the unintentional messages you send.

Communication Is Irreversible   At one time or another, we have all wished we could take back words we regretted uttering. Unfortunately this isn't possible. Our words and deeds are recorded in others' memories, and we can't erase them. As the old saying goes, people may forgive, but they don't forget. In fact, often the more vigorously you try to erase an act, the more vividly it stands out. This means you should weigh your words carefully. An offhand comment or a critical remark uttered in the heat of conflict can haunt you long afterward.

Communication Is a Process   It is not accurate to talk about an "act" of communication as if sending or receiving a message was an isolated event. Rather, every communication event needs to be examined as part of a continuing, ever-changing process. Suppose, for example, your boss responds to your request for a raise by saying, "I was going to ask you to take a *cut* in pay!" How would you react? The answer probably depends on several factors. Is your boss a joker or a serious person? How does the comment fit into the history of your relationship—have your boss's remarks been critical or supportive in the past? How does the message fit with ones you have received from other people? What mood are you in today? All these questions show that the meaning of a message depends in part on what has happened before. Each message is part of a process: it doesn't occur in isolation.

Communication Is Not a Panacea   Although communication can smooth out the bumps and straighten the road to success, it won't always get you what you want. If the quality of communication is poor, the results are likely to be disappointing. This explains why some problems grow worse the longer they are discussed. Misunderstandings and ill feelings can increase when people communicate badly. Even effective communication won't solve all problems: there are some situations in which the parties understand one another perfectly and still disagree. These limitations are important to understand as you begin to study communication on the job. Boosting your communication skill can increase your success, but it isn't a cure-all.

GUIDELINES FOR SUCCESSFUL COMMUNICATION: A FIRST LOOK

Every chapter of *Communicating at Work* contains suggestions for boosting the effectiveness of on-the-job communication. The information you have read so far provides an initial set of guidelines that can improve your success even at this early point. At the same time, these guidelines preview some important topics that are covered in the remainder of the book.

CHOOSE THE MOST CREDIBLE SENDER

Research shows that people are often more impressed by *who* delivers a message than by the content of the message itself. Communication researchers term this factor *source credibility*.[13] They have found that receivers are likely to accept a message that comes from a source they respect, while they will reject the same idea when it comes from a less believable source.

This fact means that you should think carefully about who ought to do the communicating in an important situation. Are you the best person to make the suggestion? To deliver the criticism? To make the request? If not, who is?

CHOOSE THE OPTIMAL RECEIVERS AND CONSIDER THEIR NEEDS

Just as a message can be delivered by more than one sender, it can be aimed at more than one receiver. In many cases, an idea that will be rejected by one person or audience is likely to be accepted by another.

If the department head whose approval you need for an emergency equipment purchase is in meetings all day, for example, you can ask her assistant to get her signature when she stops by her office between meetings. Although company policy might seem to specify who should receive a given message ("All messages to the sales force must be routed through the regional sales managers and distributed through the marketing department"), you may find that the actual choices are greater—for example, you might make some quick telephone calls to individual sales representatives to give them an urgent piece of information they will be happy to get. A person who works in an organization needs to be careful with this technique, however. For instance, routinely making purchases without the required management approval or going to your boss's boss to propose a special project you know your boss would refuse will eventually get you labeled as insubordinate and a troublemaker.

When official policy dictates who should receive a given message, you can still make some strategic choices about when and how to approach that person. Just as it's a better idea to ask for time off when you have just been praised for putting in long, hard hours on a project than when you have just been reprimanded for coming in late, you may get a more careful hearing for a new idea if you can speak to your boss when he or she is not rushing to meet a deadline or to get to a meeting.

DEVELOP MESSAGES STRATEGICALLY

Once you have decided who should present the message and to whom, the message should still be tailored to the person who will receive it. For example, a product manager may make several presentations of a new product. When she presents it to management, she will focus on market demands and profitability; when she presents it to the sales force, she will focus on how to present the product to customers to earn the greatest commissions; when she presents it to customers, she will focus on how the product meets their needs better or more cheaply than the product they are using now.

STRUCTURE MESSAGES CLEARLY

Many communicators shoot from the lip, blurting out ideas without much planning. Making yourself understood is hard enough when a message is clear; when it is garbled, long-winded, or obscure, the chance of success shrinks to almost nothing. Despite this fact, people who should know better often rattle off ideas in a meeting or conversation with only the barest preparation. Paradoxically, messages that are the simplest to understand often owe their success to careful planning. Just as the best athletes make hard feats look simple, the best communicators are the people who make complex ideas easy to follow.

STRIVE TO REDUCE COMMUNICATION NOISE

While it's impossible for you to eliminate physical, physiological, and psychological noise, you can reduce them. One way to reduce noise is to pick the best time and place to communicate. Whenever possible, choose a setting that won't distract you or the other person. Making a sales pitch on the hottest day of the year after the air conditioner has broken down isn't a good idea. Neither is barging into the boss's office five minutes before a deadline and asking, "Mind if we talk?"

Timing also means being sensitive to your own emotional state and that of the other people involved. If you're boiling over with anger, it might be best to delay facing people until you have cooled down. If the person you are communicating with has feelings about you that might interfere with the success of your interaction, it might be best to work on resolving them before addressing the business at hand.

TAKE ADVANTAGE OF FEEDBACK

Sometimes people volunteer feedback by telling you outright what they think of your behavior. At other times you may have to ask for it. Even *no* response to your request for information is a message in itself.

The problem with much feedback is its ambiguity. Does the boss's lack of response to your proposal mean that she's thinking it over or that you'd better drop the idea? Is a fellow worker's assurance that your work looks great sincere, or is it a way to avoid hurting your feelings? Whenever possible, the best way to reduce this kind of uncertainty is to seek clarification:

"Just to be sure you understand those instructions, why don't you tell me what you're going to do."

"I wanted to check back and see if you had any questions about the proposal I sent you last week." (Notice the diplomatic wording that reminds the other person to look at the proposal.)

"You mentioned in your memo that you want to get together to discuss the new campaign. Do you want to do it now or wait until after the holiday?"

As you will learn in Chapter 3, communicators often deliberately try to make their reactions vague and hard to read. Despite this tendency, a determined effort to seek feedback can usually boost your knowledge of what others think of you.

ORAL VERSUS WRITTEN COMMUNICATION

As a business communicator, you often can choose how to deliver a message. You can put your ideas in writing as a letter, memo, or report. You can deliver them electronically via computer network or facsimile. Or you can communicate orally either over the phone or in person.

Deciding which communication channel to use isn't a trivial matter. Sometimes a written message succeeds where an oral one fails; at other times talking to the recipient in person will produce results that the printed word can't match. An understanding of these two channels will help you make the best choice about how to deliver your important messages.

ORAL COMMUNICATION

All types of spoken communication share a number of characteristics. Whether you speak face-to-face or over the phone, whether you have an informal talk with a workmate or deliver a formal presentation to a roomful of VIPs, several features distinguish the spoken word from the same message in written form.

Advantages of Speaking   One obvious feature of oral communication is its speed. Once you make contact with your audience, there is no time lag between the transmission of a message and its reception. This is especially valuable when time is of the essence: if you need a price or have to have the funds in an account released *now*, putting your request in a letter or memo won't be much help.

A second advantage of oral communication is the control it gives you as the speaker. You might spend hours drafting a memo, letter, or report only to have the recipient scan it superficially or not read it at all. In a conversation, however, you have much more command over the receiver's attention. The listener at least has to pretend to pay attention—and if you use the speaking skills described in the following chapters, your messages ought to be clear and interesting enough to capture the attention of your audience.

British prime minister Lloyd George had a low opinion of professional diplomats and their belief that notes and memoranda were the best means of clarifying issues. "Letters are the very devil!" he said on one occasion. "If you want to settle a thing, you see your opponent and talk it over with him. The last thing you do is write him a letter!"

Gordon A. Craig, *Diplomatic Problems of Our Times*

Another enormous advantage of oral communication is that it permits instantaneous feedback. When you speak directly to one or more listeners, you can respond to questions as soon as they arise—an impossible feat in written communication. You can rephrase or elaborate when your listeners seem confused, and you can speed up if details aren't necessary. You can revise hurriedly if you see you have used the wrong word and offended or confused your audience.

Because of the tremendous amount of feedback available in oral communication, it has been termed a "richer" communication channel than the written word.[14] Face-to-face interaction is the richest type of communication since it provides both visual and vocal cues about the other parties (see Figure 1-2). A telephone conversation lacks the visual feedback that often reveals how your message is getting across. The telephone still communicates vocal cues, however—tone of voice, pauses, interruptions, and so on. Telephone conversations also make it harder to hold the attention of your listener. Recall, for instance, all the fingernail cleaning and paper-clip sculpting you have done while unsuspecting speakers have rattled on.

The drawbacks of telephone communication are offset by one tremendous advantage: it often lets you contact a receiver who would be impossible to reach in person. You can touch base with someone halfway around the world in less time than it takes to catch an elevator to the next floor. The telephone can even help you get through to busy people who are nearby. Office hermits who barricade

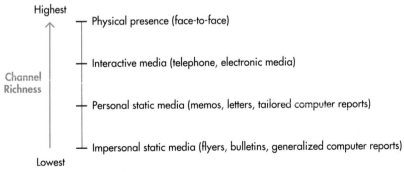

Figure 1-2   Richness of communication channels. (Adapted from R. H. Lengel and R. L. Daft, "The Selection of Communication Media as an Executive Skill." *The Academy of Management EXECUTIVE* 11, 1988, p. 226.)

themselves behind closed doors will often drop everything when the telephone rings—or at least answer it grudgingly.

Disadvantages of Speaking Despite its advantages, oral communication isn't a perfect medium. Possibly the greatest disadvantage of speech is its transience. All communication is fragile, but the spoken word is especially prone to being forgotten or misunderstood. Listeners quickly forget much of what they hear—half of a message almost immediately and half of the remainder two days later. Thus, a customer might forget three of the five product features you mentioned, or your boss might forget exactly *why* you need more staff support and only recall the dollar amount you requested.

Even if they remember an oral message, listeners are likely to distort it. Chapter 2 will describe the problem of serial transmission—the way a message changes as it passes from one person to another. Some details drop out with each telling. Facts and figures change. Receivers may even invent variations on the truth, just to make the story more interesting or to make it fit their own idea of what ought to have happened. The farther the message travels in space and time from its original sender, the greater the chance of distortion.

WRITTEN COMMUNICATION

Letters, memos, and other written messages have a different set of advantages and drawbacks than their spoken counterparts.

Advantages of Written Messages Unlike speech, written communication is permanent. Once your words are down on paper, they are saved for future reference—either to your delight or your undying embarrassment and chagrin. While people may have trouble accurately recalling what you said a few hours ago, they can refer to your written remarks years later. Even if the receiver has lost or forgotten your message, you can always supply a copy from your files.

Along with its permanence, written communication can be easier to understand than speech. Readers can study complex passages as many times as necessary, a luxury they do not have when the same message is delivered orally. They can take a break if their interest wanes and, after a cup of coffee or a quick stretch, come back to what they were reading refreshed and ready to go on.

Perhaps the greatest advantage of written communication is that you can compose it in advance. You can take as much time as necessary to shape a message just as you want it, pondering every word if necessary. You can try out several versions on test readers to anticipate the reactions of your real audience, and you can make changes until you get the desired response.

Finally, written messages are less likely to be botched in the transmission. Even the best-rehearsed oral presentations can go awry. You can misplace an important set of papers, forget to mention a key idea, or come down with a sudden cold on the big day. Furthermore, the spontaneity that makes spoken communication so effective can backfire. Your attempt to improvise might sound

On a recent morning at Amoco Corp.'s Tulsa Data Center, writing consultant Lee Johns leads 18 students in the first of five early-morning classes. She asks participants to explain what they do when they receive a two-page memo. "If I get two paragraphs, I read all of it. If I get two pages, I read some of it. If I get a three-page letter, I lay it at the bottom of the pile," answers one.

Cynthia F. Mitchell, "Firms Seek Cure for Dull Memos," *Wall Street Journal*

confusing or lame, and the joke you thought would make the perfect ice-breaker might fall flat. Every speaker has thought, hours after a conversation, "If only I'd said . . . " When you communicate in writing, you have time to choose exactly the right words.

WHICH CHANNEL TO USE?

As Table 1-2 shows, both oral and written communication have advantages and drawbacks. Despite these pros and cons, there are guidelines that will help you decide how to deliver your message most effectively. Following these guidelines can produce dramatic results. In one survey, managers who were identified as "media sensitive"—those who matched the channel to the message—were almost twice as likely to receive top ratings in their performance reviews when compared to less media-sensitive peers.[15]

In general, oral communication is best for messages that require a personal dimension. Oral channels are also best for ideas that have a strong need for visual support—demonstrations, photos or slides, and so on. Spoken communication is

TABLE 1-2   Differences Between Oral and Written Communication

ORAL COMMUNICATION	WRITTEN COMMUNICATION
More personal	More formal
Greater control over when and how thoroughly message will be heard	Little control over if, when, and how thoroughly message will be read
Immediate feedback	Delayed or nonexistent feedback
Transitory, off the record	Permanent record
Effective for relatively simple ideas	Effective for detailed, complex ideas
Most effective for messages with visual or hands-on elements	Less effective for visual or hands-on messages
Most effective when seeking immediate, emotional response (motivation, sales, and so on)	Most effective when seeking delayed, thoughtful response
Possible loss of accuracy when message passes through several people	Ensures accuracy when message is passed from one person to another
Requires listener and speaker to be in same place at same time	Does not require reader to be in same place at same time as writer
Much nonverbal information available	Little nonverbal information available

also especially useful when there is a need for immediate feedback, such as question-and-answer sessions or a quick reply to your ideas.

Written communication works best when you want to create a relatively formal tone. It is also the best medium when you must choose your words carefully. Writing is better than speaking when you want to convey complicated ideas that are likely to require much study and thought by the receiver. You should also put your message in writing when you want it to be the final word, with no feedback or discussion. Finally, writing is best for *any* message if you want a record to exist. In business and the professions, sending confirming letters and memoranda is common practice, as is keeping minutes of meetings. These steps guarantee that what is said will be a matter of record, useful in case of later misunderstandings or disputes and in case anyone wants to review the history of an issue.

In many cases, it is wise to send a message using both oral and written channels. This kind of redundancy captures the best of both media, and it works in a variety of settings:

- Distribute a written text or outline that parallels your presentation.
- Follow a letter or memo with a phone call, or call first and then write.
- Send a report or proposal, and then make appointments with your readers to discuss it.

You won't always have the luxury of choosing the communication channel. But when you do, the right decision can make your message clearer and more effective.

SUMMARY

No matter what the job, communication is both a frequent and a critically important process. It occupies more time than any other activity and often makes the difference between success and failure for the organization as a whole and for its individual members.

On-the-job communication is sometimes internal and sometimes external. It can occur in dyadic, small-group, or public settings. Whatever the context, communication serves at least one of four functions: telling, selling, learning, or deciding.

Communication, as the term is used in this book, is a process in which people who occupy differing environments exchange messages via one or more channels and often respond to each other's messages through verbal and nonverbal feedback. The accuracy of communication can be diminished by physical or psychological noise, which can exist within either the sender, receiver, or channel. Communication is an unavoidable, irreversible process. Although it is vitally important, it is not a panacea that can solve every personal and organizational problem.

Attending to the fundamental elements of the communication process can improve the chances of success: choosing the most credible sender, picking the optimal receivers and attending to their needs, developing messages strategically and structuring them clearly, minimizing communication noise, and taking advantage of feedback to clarify confusing messages.

Business communicators should choose wisely among delivering a message face-to-face, by telephone, or in writing. Each of these channels has both advantages and drawbacks. The best medium depends primarily on the nature of the message.

ACTIVITIES

1. Think of the last time you were involved in the following types of on-the-job communication:

    Internal
    External
    Dyadic
    Small-group
    Public

    Which of these types do you encounter most often on the job? Which would you most like to improve your skill in? *Note:* If you are not now employed, answer this question in terms of a job you expect to hold in the future.

2. Interview someone who has a job that interests you. Determine what amount of time your subject spends communicating in one form or another. What percentage of that time is spent in each of the following activities: telling, selling, learning, deciding?

3. Think about a situation you have experienced in which communication went wrong. Diagnose the problem by finding the location or locations in which the trouble occurred:

    a. *Sender*   Did the wrong person *send* the message?
    b. *Message*   Was the message unclear? Were there too many messages?
    c. *Channel*   Was the most appropriate channel chosen?
    d. *Receiver* Was there no receiver at all? Was the message poorly formulated for the person(s) at whom it was aimed?
    e. *Feedback* Was feedback adequate to ensure understanding?
    f. *Noise*   Did physical, physiological, or psychological noise distort the message?

4. Imagine that you want to propose a change in the policy of your college bookstore for buying back used textbooks from students. Answer the following questions:

    a. Who would be the best person(s) to send the proposal to?
    b. Who would be the optimal receiver?
    c. What factors should you consider when developing the message containing your proposal?
    d. Via what channel(s) should the message be delivered?
    e. What types of noise might reduce the effectiveness of your message? How might they be minimized?

5. Explain which communication channel is best for each message:

    a. Complaining to your boss about a difficult co-worker

b. Asking for a few days of leave from work to attend a special reunion

c. Training a new employee to operate a complicated computer program

d. Notifying the manager of a local business that you still haven't received the refund you were promised

e. Reminding your busy, overworked boss about a long overdue reimbursement for out-of-pocket expenses

f. Apologizing to a customer for a mistake your company made

g. Getting your boss's reaction to the idea of possibly giving you more responsibility

Communicator Profile

Linn Kastan, President
Red Line Engineering, Inc.
Newbury Park, California

The best advice I can give about communicating is to have patience. Know at the start that your ideas won't always be accepted or understood the first time around. Keep calm and figure out a better way to deliver the message.

Red Line Engineering produces a line of state-of-the-art bicycles. Our products are sold all around the world and are used in every country except the Soviet Union. Our headquarters is in California, where we handle administration, sales, and distribution. We have manufacturers in Australia, New Zealand, Japan, and Taiwan. As you can imagine, geography alone makes good communication a must for us.

I spend 100 percent of my time on the job communicating. All day long I have the phone in my ear, sit across the table from someone, or read and write letters and memos. As president, I deal with a wide variety of people both inside and outside the company: manufacturers, designers, bankers, distributors, and our administrative staff.

A typical day involves all types of communication. This morning I spent an hour on the phone trying to convince my buying agent in New York to persuade his associate in Japan to pay more attention to a customer in South Africa. I drafted a letter to our distributors to convince them that our new bicycle color schemes will be successful, so that they will feel as enthusiastic about the line as we do. I met with our newsletter writer (who also is a Hollywood columnist) to show him that material for twelve-year-old boys requires an approach quite different from the one he uses for housewives. I spent lunch making small talk with Japanese business executives. And to close out the afternoon, I met with an employee who was convinced that she deserved a large raise.

I believe that effective communication is absolutely essential for a successful operation. Our bicycles are excellent, but without clear communication in situations like the ones above, we never could have developed them, or manufactured them economically, or found ways to distribute them. The same thing applies to any business. After all, an organization is a group of people working together, and you can't work with someone if you don't understand one another or get along.

Some of the communication challenges we face involve just getting an idea across clearly. This is especially tough when people come from different cultures or speak different languages. It's hard, for example, to explain to a Japanese quality control board that our bikes need to meet standards unlike ones they use for domestic customers. Their bikes may need to carry loads of groceries over cobblestone streets, but ours have to stand up to acrobatic stunts by daredevil teenagers, and the engineering requirements are quite different.

Sometimes getting an idea across is just as hard when two people speak the same language. It's not easy, for instance, to convince a hard-nosed banker that the deals we make with overseas suppliers on the basis of a handshake are just as solid as the ones they pinpoint in legal documents. The bankers routinely expect the worst from people and often get it. We expect the best from the people we choose to do business with, and we're seldom disappointed.

It's even more difficult to communicate on personal matters. For example, it's hard to find ways of saying "I can't talk now" or "I don't like that idea" without discouraging people from speaking out in the future. We're a reasonably small, happy group here, and it takes a lot of careful communication to keep everyone feeling good about one another and the company.

The best advice I can give about communicating is to have patience. Know at the start that your ideas won't always be accepted or understood the first time around. Keep calm, and figure a better way to deliver the message. And pay special attention to timing. Your idea may get a bad response if you barge into someone's office and demand a hearing; but if you choose a time and place that makes the other person more receptive, you just may get through.

CHAPTER | 2

After reading this chapter, you should understand:

- How organization charts and flow charts describe formal communication channels
- The functions, problems, and guidelines for downward, upward, and horizontal communication
- The composition and functions of informal communication networks
- The way organizational cultures are formed and perpetuated, and their influence on communication within organizations
- The types and dimensions of cultural diversity represented in the changing work force
- How the changing nature of the work force affects on-the-job communication

You should be able to:

- Construct a simple flow chart for organizational tasks with which you are familiar
- Evaluate the effectiveness of upward, downward, and horizontal communication in an organization and suggest any necessary improvements
- Identify the informal communication networks in an organization, describe their functions, and evaluate their effectiveness
- Describe how you can cultivate informal networks in an organization with which you are familiar
- Describe the culture of an organization and suggest ways it could be improved by changing communication practices
- Identify the culture of an organization that interests you and determine if you would feel comfortable and work well within it
- Describe the cultural and demographic profile of the work force to which you belong and describe how you can apply the guidelines in this chapter to communicate more effectively with your co-workers

COMMUNICATION
SYSTEMS AND
CULTURES

When Carol Teinchek and Bruce Marshall first started Sundown Bakery, the business was fairly simple. Carol ran the shop up front, while Bruce ran the bakery and ordered supplies. In the evenings, after the shop closed and before Bruce began the all-night baking operation, they discussed which items were selling well and which were not, how they needed to set prices in order to make a profit, what new items they might try out, and so on. If a customer complained, Carol and Bruce figured out the solution together.

When the business began to grow, Carol hired two part-time clerks to help out in the shop. Marina had moved to the country two years ago from El Salvador, and Kim was a newly arrived Korean who was working his way through college. Bruce hired Maurice, a French-Canadian, as an assistant. Despite their different backgrounds, the owners and employees of Sundown often thought of themselves as a family. They celebrated birthdays and holidays together, and shared the ups and downs of one another's personal lives.

The ovens were soon running twenty-four hours a day, supervised by Maurice, who was now master baker, and two assistants on each of three shifts. Marina and Kim were supervising the shop since Carol was usually too busy managing general sales distribution to spend much time with customers. Bruce still spent three or four hours a day in the bakery whenever he could get out of his office, but still spent most of that time coordinating production and solving problems with Maurice.

The growth of Sundown Bakery led to some important changes. First, the lines of communication—the patterns of who communicated with whom—had become more complicated. For example, Carol rarely heard directly from customers about their likes and dislikes. Now, shoppers talked to the clerks and managers, who might pass those reactions on to Carol, who shared them with Bruce, if he was available. If Carol and Bruce decided to offer a new product line, the information was passed to the master baker and then to the assistant bakers.

The expanding size of Sundown led to a change in the personality of the company. The family feeling that was so strong when Sundown was a small operation was less noticeable. The new employees didn't know Bruce and Carol well, and, as a result, there was less give-and-take of ideas between the owners and workers. Bruce and Carol wanted to keep the lines of communication open, but the task was harder.

Another challenge grew out of the changing character of the employees. Sundown now employed workers from seven different countries. José, who was born in Brazil, confessed to Bruce that he felt uncomfortable being managed by Carol. "It's nothing personal," he said. "But where I come from, a man doesn't take orders from a woman." The Sundown employee profile was different in other ways. Two of the assistant bakers were gay; one of the sales clerks got around by wheelchair.

The challenges at Sundown Bakery are similar to those facing any organization. The need to manage information efficiently grew as the company expanded. The personality of the company—the organizational culture, as it is called—also became a bigger concern. And, finally, the different backgrounds and characteristics of the employees made the potential for communication both more rewarding and more difficult.

This chapter will deal with the same issues faced by Sundown Bakery—and, indeed, by every organization. It will explore the nature of communication systems and show how exchange of information is a vitally important issue. It will introduce the notion of organizational cultures, explaining how every organization has a personality, and the importance of that character to the success and satisfaction of its members. Finally, the chapter will describe the changing nature of the work force and show how communication can be more effective among an increasingly diverse body of workers.

ORGANIZATIONAL COMMUNICATION SYSTEMS

All organizations—Sundown Bakery, General Motors, a basketball team, the staff of an insurance agency, the local Red Cross chapter—are information processors. They absorb information, process it, and turn out some sort of finished product. Although the goal varies from one organization to another, the principle is the same.

As an organization grows, its needs to develop a system for managing information. Consider Sundown Bakery. When Carol and Bruce were the only two people in the business, they spoke to each other about all operations. As more employees entered the business, however, it was no longer practical for each of them to exchange information with every other person. As a result, communication pathways developed that directed the flow of information throughout the organization, just like an intricate system of veins and arteries directs the flow of blood throughout the human body.

You can appreciate the need for these information pathways if you consider how confusing unregulated communication would be in an organization. Sundown Bakery now consists of 17 people. If each were free to pass information to every other person, each employee would be sending and receiving information—possibly conflicting information—from 16 other people. In fact, there would be 136 possible 2-person combinations. In an organization with 200 members, there would be 19,900 possible combinations—clearly an unwieldy number.

It is obvious that organizations need some system for structuring who will communicate with whom. These systems are called *networks*—regular patterns of person-to-person relationships through which information flows in an organization.[1] Two kinds of networks exist: formal and informal.

FORMAL COMMUNICATION NETWORKS

Formal networks are systems designed by management to dictate who should talk to whom to get a job done.[2] In a small organization, networks are so simple that they may hardly be noticeable; in a larger organization, networks become more intricate. Figure 2-1 shows how the ordering process in a store might change as the business grows.

Graphic descriptions like Figure 2-1 are termed *flow charts*—pictorial representations of how people and tasks must interface in order to complete a project. Flow charts are more than a bureaucrat's toy; they provide a clear guideline of how to communicate in order to get a job done. As organizations grow larger and tasks more complex, flow charts become more useful. Figure 2-2 is a flow chart that shows the development of a new product.

Organizational charts—sometimes called tables of organization—also represent formal networks. But whereas flow charts describe who communicates with whom on a particular job, organizational charts describe who has authority over whom. For example, while the flow chart in Figure 2-2 shows that Hans Muller and Terry Kwan work together on documentation and drawings, the organization chart in Figure 2-3 reveals that Muller reports to his boss, Herman Flores, while Kwan reports to Bill North.

The connection between flow charts and organization charts isn't as confusing as it might seem. People from different departments work together daily in most organizations, and flow charts provide a kind of road map that guides them through complicated tasks. And since someone is always ultimately responsible

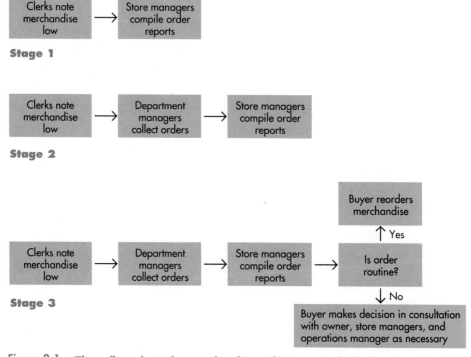

Figure 2-1   Three flow charts for merchandise ordering procedures showing the difference between a small organization (top) and larger organizations (middle and bottom).

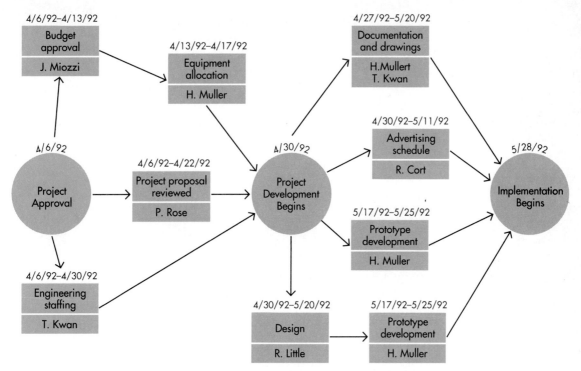

Figure 2-2 Flow charts become more valuable on complex projects; they provide a road map that makes it easier to visualize how people and resources fit together. As the example above illustrates, flow charts show how the scheduling of various tasks must be coordinated. Note that milestones (the most important events) are represented in circles. Each task (represented by a box) lists the human resources needed and the time involved.

for getting a job done well, an organizational chart helps to show where that responsibility lies.

Downward Communication   Information circulates through formal communication networks in several directions. One of those directions involves downward communication, which takes place whenever a supervisor sends a message to one or more subordinates.

Types of Downward Messages   There are several types of downward communication.[3]

- **Job instructions.** Directions about what to do or how to do it. "When you restock the shelves, put the new merchandise behind the old stock."
- **Job rationale.** Explanations of how one task relates to other tasks. "We rotate the stock like that so the customers won't wind up with stale merchandise."

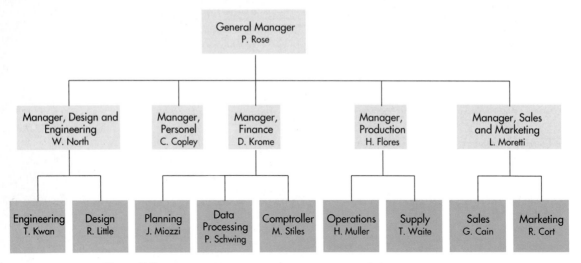

Figure 2-3   Dynacom Systems, Inc., organizational chart.

- ■ **Procedures and practices.** Information about rules, regulations, policies, and benefits. "Don't try to argue with unhappy customers. If you can't handle them yourself, call the manager."
- ■ **Feedback.** Information about how effectively a person is performing. "You're really catching on fast. If you keep up the good work, you'll be an assistant manager by the end of the year."
- ■ **Indoctrination.** Information aimed at motivating employees by impressing the organization's mission upon them and specifying how they should relate to it. "People can buy the stuff we sell at other places, but we can bring them in here by giving them what they want quickly and pleasantly. If we do that, we'll all come out ahead."

Most managers would agree—at least in principle—that downward communication is important. It is hard to argue with the need for giving instructions, explaining rationale, describing procedures, and so on. Like their bosses, employees recognize the importance of downward communication.

A recent study at General Electric revealed that "clear communication between boss and worker" was the most important factor in job satisfaction for most people. GE was so impressed with the findings of this study that it launched a program to encourage managers to communicate more and more directly with their employees, including holding informal meetings to encourage interaction.[4]

This desire for feedback is probably so strong because supervisors rarely provide enough of it. As two researchers in the field, Daniel Katz and Robert Kahn, put it: "The frequent complaint . . . by the individual is that he does not know where he stands with his superiors."[5] Many companies do take a more enlightened approach to feedback. Ed Carlson, former president of United Airlines, is generally credited with turning the company from a loser into a winner during his tenure. Part of his success was due to keeping United's employees—all of them—aware of how the company was doing. "Nothing is worse for morale than a lack of information down in the ranks," he said. "I call it NETMA—Nobody Ever Tells Me Anything—and I have tried hard to minimize that problem."[6] True to his word, Carlson passed along to the field staff information on United's operations that was previously considered too important to circulate.

Problems with Downward Communication   Even the best organizations often don't use downward communication as effectively as possible. In some cases there isn't enough information, and in others the messages that do travel down aren't clear or complete. These problems fall into several categories.

- **Lack of awareness.** Some managers don't know about all the types of downward communication. Giving instructions is natural enough, but such functions as explaining organizational rationale and giving feedback aren't so obvious. For example, a marketing assistant may need to know *why* the inventory must be checked weekly (to make sure an item is not permitted to go out of stock when large, unexpected orders are shipped) before he will do it willingly and reliably.

- **Insufficient or unclear messages.** Even when a boss knows about a certain type of downward communication, nothing guarantees that the message will be a good one. It might be too brief, lacking enough detail to make it clear. Or it might be too vague to be useful. For example, a message stating that "all expense reports for trips must be submitted promptly every week" may seem clear to the finance officer who issues it, but it may be confusing to the people who receive it. Does "every week" mean Friday of the week in which expenses were incurred, or is it all right to wait until Monday? Does the sales manager who goes out of the office on three-week appraisals of the field staff somehow have to put together expense accounts in motel rooms, or can it wait until the trip is over? What about the production manager who goes out to the factory to keep track of the production that's done on overtime over the weekend?

- **Message overload.** Sometimes the problem is not too little information, but too much. There can be *too many* messages, making it difficult to pay attention to any of them. Messages can also be *too long*, disguising important information in a sea of details. Or they can be *too complicated* to understand. One manager captured the frustration of information overload when interviewed about his communication problems:

> Communication problem? I'll tell you my biggest communication problem. Just look at this desk! Reports, computer printouts, telephone messages, letters, journals, telegrams. My biggest communication problem? I'm overloaded. I'm getting so —— much information from so —— many

people I can't see the top of my desk! I'm drowning in paper; drowning in information.[7]

Ironically, when asked to describe his second biggest communication problem, the same manager replied, "I never know what the —— is going on around here." These remarks show that overloading people with too much information can be like overloading a pack horse: you run the risk that none of the goods will be delivered.

- **Serial transmission.** As information passes from one person to another, it becomes less accurate. You probably saw this happen as a youngster if you played the game "telephone." One person in a circle whispered a message to the adjacent person, who did the same to the next player. The process continued until the message traveled back to the first sender, who compared it with the original. In the game the difference between old and new messages usually gets a few laughs, but in organizations the results are not so funny. The problem of serial transmission is especially great in "tall" organizations that have several levels of authority (see Figure 2-4). One remedy for information loss due to serial transmission is to put a message that has to travel through several hands (and heads) into writing. A second antidote is to ask for feedback from the receiver as a means of verifying understanding.

Upward Communication   Upward communication occurs when messages flow from subordinates to superiors. Many leading businesses attribute their success to the emphasis on upward communication in their organizations. Sam Walton, head of Wal-Mart, the fourth largest retailer in the United States, claims that "our best ideas come from clerks and stockboys."[8]

Types of Upward Messages   Upward communication can convey four types of messages.[9]

- **What subordinates are doing.** "We'll have that job done by closing time today."
- **Unsolved work problems.** "We're still having trouble with the air conditioner in the accounting office."
- **Suggestions for improvement.** "I think I've figured a way to give people the vacation schedules they want and still keep our staffing up."
- **How subordinates feel about each other and the job.** "I'm having a hard time working with Louie. He seems to think I'm mad at him." Or "I'm getting frustrated. I've been in the same job for over a year now, and I'm itching for more responsibility."

Benefits of Upward Communication   These four categories suggest several benefits of upward communication.

- **It gives feedback on how accurately downward messages have been received.** One company discovered that the summer-hours pro-

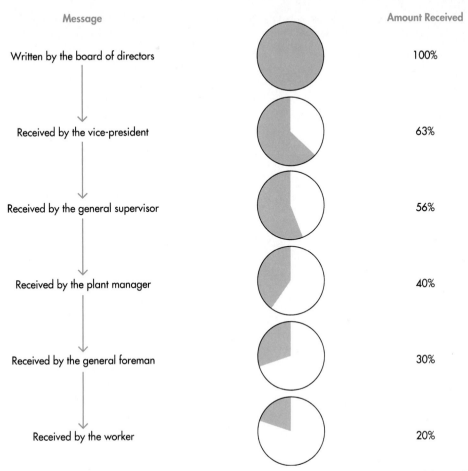

Message		Amount Received
Written by the board of directors		100%
Received by the vice-president		63%
Received by the general supervisor		56%
Received by the plant manager		40%
Received by the general foreman		30%
Received by the worker		20%

Figure 2-4   Effects of serial transmission on a message communicated downward through five levels of management. (From Ray Killian, *Managing by Design . . . For Executive Effectiveness.* New York: American Management Association, 1968, p. 255. Reprinted by permission.)

gram, initiated to permit people to work late four days a week and go home at noon on Friday, had been taken as a requirement. As a result of feedback from the employees, management was able to reassure the people who preferred to spend more time in the evening with their families that the company had no objections to their following the traditional schedule.

■ **It indicates how well management decisions are being received.** For example, a manager who declares that extra work must be distributed among the available staff instead of hiring temporary help should know whether the staff resents the extra work or prefers it to training and supervising temporary staff.

- **It can increase acceptance of management decisions.** Good listening boosts support. "They always let me have time off when I need it, so I guess I have nothing to complain about if they ask for overtime sometimes." "They don't always agree with me, but they do give my ideas a serious hearing. I can live with that."
- **It can prevent new problems and diagnose old ones.** One company that relied heavily on free-lance help discovered that secretaries resented the time they spent filling out lengthy forms for each free-lance assignment, especially since the information was always the same. After checking the insurance and tax requirements that supposedly mandated the form, the firm discovered that requirements could be met by stamping each invoice "Fee for free-lance services performed off company premises."

These advantages benefit both subordinates and superiors, and this explains why one survey showed that organization members find upward communication to be the most important and satisfying kind of on-the-job interaction.[10] Surprisingly, the survey produced a second finding: employees find participation in upward communication extremely difficult.

Problems with Upward Communication   Three factors create problems with upward communication.

- **Risk.** Employees have much to gain by opening up to the boss, but there is a chance of big losses as well. Expressing frustration with your present job might earn you a promotion, but you might also get fired. This fear of being punished for communicating upward is highest in two sorts of organizations: those with truly unsympathetic management (it's smart to keep quiet in these) and those in which managers are uncommunicative. In the second case, employees have no way of knowing whether supervisors will support the kind of open communication that sooner or later becomes necessary. The lesson for managers is clear: ask your subordinates—sincerely and clearly—for information about themselves, their jobs, and the organization, and use that information once you have it. That approach will win the trust of employees and cause more messages to filter upward.
- **Distortion.** One fact of organizational life is that negative information is less likely to be communicated upward than positive information.[11] This makes sense. Reports that a project is going badly, for example, might make the boss unhappy, and the bearer could wind up—fairly or not—being associated with the unpleasant message. In ancient Greece, messengers bringing bad news were slaughtered, and subordinates seem to fear that this practice hasn't entirely disappeared. However, no such problem exists with good news. Subordinates are usually glad to let the boss know how well they have done, sometimes exaggerating the degree or quality of their brilliance. Thus, managers run the risk of

getting shortchanged on bad news and overdosed on favorable reports—hardly an accurate picture of what's going on.

Distortion isn't entirely the fault of subordinates. Since many managers dislike bad news, they often twist it or screen it out. This is especially true when the bad news reflects poorly on the manager's skill. If a manager hears that the workers are unhappy with his great idea, he might chalk up their reaction to stupidity (theirs, of course) or ignore the negative report and plunge ahead with the idea, even if it isn't very good.

■ **Status differential.** Many bosses are members of the "I talk, you listen" school of management. They have the idea that listening to the factual reports of subordinates is all right but that ideas and opinions should only flow downward. This is a shame since the best ideas about how to improve an operation often come from the workers who are closest to it.

Most of the responsibility for improving upward communication rests with managers. The place to begin is for managers to announce their willingness to hear from subordinates. A number of vehicles facilitate upward messages: an "open door" policy, grievance procedures, periodic interviews, group meetings, and the suggestion box, to name a few. Informal types of contact can often be most effective; chats during breaks, in the elevator, or at social gatherings can sometimes tell more than planned sessions. But no method will be effective unless a manager is sincerely interested in hearing from subordinates and genuinely values their ideas. Just talking about this isn't enough. Employees have to see evidence of a willingness to hear upward messages—both good and bad—before they will really open up.

Horizontal Communication   Horizontal (sometimes called "lateral") communication consists of messages between members of an organization with equal power. The most obvious type of horizontal communication goes on between members of the same division of an organization: office workers in the same department, co-workers on a construction project, and so on. In other cases, lateral communication occurs between people from different areas: accounting calls maintenance to get a machine repaired, hospital admissions calls intensive care to reserve a bed, and so on.

Types of Horizontal Messages   Horizontal communication serves five purposes.[12]

■ **Task coordination.** "Let's get together this afternoon and set up a production schedule."
■ **Problem solving.** "It takes three days for my department to get reports from yours. How can we speed things up?"
■ **Sharing information.** "I just found out that a big convention is coming to town next week, so you ought to get ready for lots of business."

- **Conflict resolution.** "I've heard that you were complaining about my work to the boss. If you're not happy, I wish you'd tell me first."
- **Building rapport.** "I appreciate the way you got that rush job done on time. I'd like to say thanks by buying you lunch when it's convenient."

Factors Inhibiting Horizontal Communication   Despite the importance of these five functions, several forces work to discourage communication between peers.[13]

- **Rivalry.** People who feel threatened by one another aren't likely to be cooperative. The threat can come from competition for a promotion, raise, or other scarce resource. Sometimes rivalry is for an informal role. For example, two office comedians might feel threatened each time the other gets a laugh; that could inhibit their cooperation.
- **Specialization.** As the work a person or division does becomes more technical, others in the organization have a harder time understanding it. The computer experts in the marketing department of a manufacturing firm might be able to improve the company's sales, but if the sales manager doesn't understand technical computer jargon and the marketing experts are unable to translate their knowledge into simple terms, a joint effort doesn't have much of a chance.
- **Lack of motivation.** Everyone agrees about the importance of communicating more, but often no strong motivation to do so exists. Field representatives selling the same product lines for the same company could probably improve their sales techniques and increase revenue for the whole company by talking to one another; but if the company encourages them to compete with one another, they may be reluctant to share ideas.
- **Information overload.** Sometimes people are too busy to talk to one another, even though they recognize the need. One of the most common apologies in any organization is "Sorry I didn't get back to you sooner, but I've been swamped with work." Management needs to realize that if it wants people to communicate more, it has to provide the time.
- **Physical barriers.** Sometimes geography can be stronger than good intentions. Colleagues who work in different areas aren't as likely to keep in close contact as those who rub shoulders every day. Although there are memos and telephone calls, these often don't work as well as a face-to-face chat. The relationship between proximity and communication brings us to another area of study: the effect of environment on communication.

INFORMAL COMMUNICATION NETWORKS

So far, we have focused on networks that are created by management. While flow charts and tables of organization can describe some of the ways people interact in organizations, they don't tell the whole story. Alongside the formal networks,

1. The editor of religious books and the publisher both attend the Second Avenue Christian Science Church

2. The editor of cookbooks is a close personal friend of the publisher of the periodical division and recently influenced her to promote another friend to manager of educational journals.

3. The editor of fiction and the editor of travel books bypass the assistant publishers to enlist the aid of the publisher of the book division in getting raises.

4. The producer of feature films is engaged to the editor of *The College Librarian*

5. The director of the film division and the publisher of the periodical division disagree with the publishers fiscal policies and and collaborate against him.

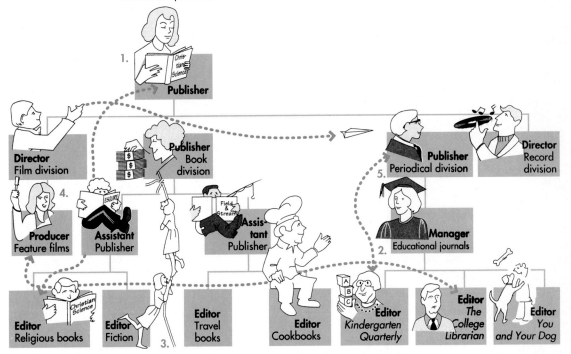

Figure 2-5   An informal communication network. Social relationships not recognized by the organization can influence decision making. (Adapted from *Business Today.* New York: Random House, 1979, pp. 102–103.)

every organization also has informal networks—patterns of interaction that follow neither the lines of authority described in tables of organization nor the functions that flow charts picture.[14] Figure 2-5 illustrates the difference between communication patterns in formal and informal networks.

Informal communication takes many forms and involves different sorts of people, as a few examples will demonstrate:

> Staff members in a large office overhear a co-worker mention the upcoming layoff of several dozen people in their factory. They learn the news almost a week before it is announced officially.

Two newly hired management trainees meet at a company party and discover their common interest in using computers to solve their respective problems on the job. They begin meeting for lunch regularly and sharing information.

An aspiring young executive strikes up a friendship with the secretary of a senior manager. Whenever the junior executive has an important presentation for the manager, she asks the secretary to look it over in advance and suggest any improvements. As a result, the younger person's work consistently meets with approval from the boss.

The Importance of Informal Networks   Some observers consider informal contacts like these to be the primary means of communication within an organization. Two well-known analysts flatly assert that as much as 90 percent of what goes on in a company has nothing to do with formal events.[15] Recognizing this fact, some corporations encourage informal networks. For example, Andrew S. Grove, president and chief executive officer of Intel Corporation, feels that cultivating the "frank, casual communication" and free flow of information common in a small company is vital to keeping a large corporation functioning smoothly.[16] There are several reasons why informal networks are so important.

Amount of Information   Informal networks carry a tremendous amount of information. In one study, researchers analyzed the communication of general managers over periods of six months to a year. They found that the managers spent a great deal of time with people who were not direct subordinates, superiors, or peers—people with whom, according to the official chain of command, they had no need to deal. Many of these people seemed relatively unimportant to outsiders: secretaries, lower-level subordinates, and supervisors with little power. Despite their unrelated job descriptions and low official status, successful managers all seemed to cultivate these contacts.[17]

Speed   Since they are not forced to follow official channels, these informal sources often provide information much faster than official methods. While a memo announcing a new policy is being typed and duplicated, a series of telephone calls from one person to another can spread the news throughout an organization. In one case, Keith Davis reported that 46 percent of management personnel learned about a colleague's newborn child within thirteen hours after it was born—less time than it would take to type a memo, send it to the reproduction department, and distribute it through interoffice mail.[18]

Accuracy   Informal contacts often provide more accurate information than official channels. Terrence Deal and Allen Kennedy give an example:

> The official announcement from the CEO may be that the vice-president resigned to pursue other interests. But half a day after the announcement goes out, the network has circulated the unofficial "truth": the vice-president missed his sales budget for the third year in a row—performance that is not tolerated in this company.[19]

Research has demonstrated that informal networks are consistently accurate—between 80 and 90 percent according to many studies.[20] Informal messages are relatively accurate because their face-to-face nature allows more clarification than the written, one-way, serially transmitted messages that come via formal channels. However, as the emotional impact of a message grows, the chances of its being distorted increase. Also, it is sometimes the case that information first introduced into the grapevine isn't true and, as a consequence, inaccurate information will be transmitted. Despite these qualifications, news that travels via informal channels usually suffers less distortion than formal messages do.

Membership in Informal Networks   Informal networks develop for several reasons. Some are based on physical proximity. Despite their distance on an organizational chart, some people communicate simply because they spend time close to one another. The office workers who overheard the layoff information fall into this category. Other networks form around the shared career interests of their members, as in the case of the management trainees who used computers. Finally, some networks (like the ones pictured in Figure 2-5) are based on personal friendships. Sometimes these friendships would exist even if there were no working relationship between the members. In other cases, the friendship is more of a means to an end for one or both of the parties.

Informal networks can involve two partners or scores of individuals. Some informal networks are almost as large as the organization itself. Large informal networks are often referred to as the *grapevine*. (This term originated during the Civil War, when telegraph lines were strung from tree to tree, resembling grape runners.) Our example of the plant layoffs shows how the grapevine operates. You can imagine that each of the office workers who heard that news would tell others in the plant. Those people would, in turn, pass along the news until the information was common knowledge. Figure 2-6 illustrates a typical pattern of information flow in a grapevine.

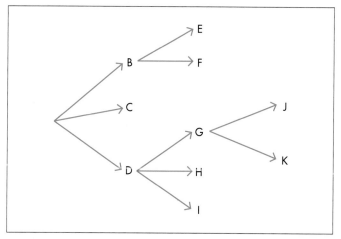

Figure 2-6   Information flow in a typical grapevine.

Functions of Informal Networks   Not all informal messages are idle rumors. As the following examples show, informal communication can serve several useful functions.

Confirming   Some informal communication confirms formal messages. You have probably heard this sort of confirmation yourself: "The boss is really serious about cutting down on long-distance calls this time. I heard him yelling about it when I walked past his office."

Expanding   Informal communication can fill in the gaps left by incomplete formal messages. You might say to an experienced co-worker: "The invitation to the office party says 'casual dress.' What does that mean—jeans and tee shirt or sport coat and tie?"

Expediting   Informal networks can often deliver messages more quickly than can official channels. Canny job hunters, for example, often use personal contacts to learn about openings within an organization long before the vacancies are published.

Contradicting   Sometimes informal networks contradict official messages. You might learn from a friend in accounting that the deadline for purchases on this year's budget isn't as firm as it sounded in the comptroller's recent memo.

Circumventing   Informal contacts can sometimes help you bypass official channels that are unnecessarily cumbersome and time-consuming. Your tennis partner who works in duplicating might sneak in an occasional rush job for you instead of putting it at the end of the line.

Supplementing   Sometimes even management realizes that informal communication can get the job done better than can the more formal variety. Paradoxical as it seems, many companies elevate informal communication to an official policy by encouraging open, unstructured contacts between people from various parts of the organization. A description of Hewlett-Packard's approach to problem solving characterizes this style, which has been termed MBWA, "management by wandering around."

Enlightened organizations do everything possible to encourage constructive, informal interaction. Corning Glass deliberately installed escalators in its new engineering building to boost the kind of face-to-face contacts that are less likely in elevators. 3M sponsors clubs for any groups of employees who request them, realizing that this sort of employee interaction is likely to encourage new ideas that will help the company. Other firms mingle workers from different departments in the same office, convinced that people who rub elbows will swap ideas and see themselves as part of a company-wide team.

A review of the six functions in this section shows that informal communication can operate in two ways. In poorly run companies, it is a kind of survival

At HP [Hewlett-Packard] it's a tradition that product design engineers leave whatever they are working on out on top of their desk so that anyone can play with it. Walking around is the heart of their philosophy for all employees, and the trust level is so high that people feel free to tinker with the things their colleagues are inventing. . . . HP also talks about the "next bench syndrome." The idea is that you look around you to people working at the next bench and think of things that you might invent to make it easier for them to do their jobs.

T. J. Peters and R. H. Waterman, Jr., *In Search of Excellence: Lessons from America's Best-Run Companies*

mechanism used by employees to get around unproductive policies and practices. In well-managed organizations like Hewlett-Packard, Corning Glass, and 3M, informal networks are simply another tool that management uses to make life more pleasant and efficient. Whichever type of setting you work in, the lesson is clear: it's vitally important to encourage and use informal networks as supplements to official channels.

Cultivating Informal Networks   Developing a strong informal communication network is not all coincidence. Several steps can help you to develop these important links.

Seek Exposure to People at All Levels of the Organization   Sometimes the best informants are people with low official status. A telephone operator or receptionist, for example, may have a better idea of who talks with whom than anyone else in the organization. Secretaries are exposed to most of the information addressed to their bosses, and they usually serve as gatekeepers who can give or deny access to them. Custodial and maintenance people travel around the building and, in their rounds, see and hear many interesting things. Besides, a friendly repairperson can fix a broken widget now instead of insisting that you file a work order that probably won't get attention for six weeks.

Treat Everyone in the Organization with Respect   As you will soon read, perhaps the most important factor in an organization's morale is the degree to which its members feel valued. Besides the fact that thoughtfulness and courtesy are simple good manners, they can make the difference between your developing a network of friends or a network of enemies. Remember birthdays. Ask about children. Discuss hobbies. And, above all, be polite and pleasant.

Ask Questions   When you discover a knowledgeable information source, ask for explanations of events. The simple question "What's going on here?" can generate more information than can a stack of policy manuals and managerial briefings. The other key question to ask is "Who can help me?" Your personal contacts can often direct you to the person or persons who can give you the information you need or support your efforts.

Don't Flaunt Informal Shortcuts   Almost no one totally follows the book—even the managers who wrote it. Nonetheless, it's asking for trouble to act in ways that blatantly violate official procedures. You might know that your boss's boss would authorize extra money for you to attend an out-of-town meeting, even though your department's travel budget is shot. If you think the only way to get the trip approved is to go over your immediate boss's head, be discreet. You might, for example, offhandedly refer to your interest in the meeting to the top boss while walking to the parking lot or coming in the front door in the morning, also mentioning that it's too bad the travel funds are gone. If the boss says "No problem," be sure to report the good news to your immediate superior, stressing the luck involved. If your boss thinks you've made an end run around his or her authority, you'll soon regret it.

ORGANIZATIONAL CULTURE

Just like individuals, organizations have personalities. Some are casual, energetic, even zany; others are formal, slow-moving, and serious. Social scientists call this personality an *organizational culture*—a relatively stable picture of the organization that is shared by its members. In everyday language, culture is the insiders' view of "the way things are around here."

Like human personalities, organizational cultures that appeal to one kind of person repel others. Many people abhor bureaucracies, with their clearly defined job hierarchies and voluminous rules; others feel most comfortable in that sort of setting. Some people welcome the chaotic disorganization and constant change that often characterize new companies in emerging fields; others feel more at home in organizations with clearly defined jobs and products. Some people like a working environment in which employees are one big family; others prefer to keep their working and personal lives separate.

Choosing a culture is choosing a way of life. Deal and Kennedy cite an example of how cultures—and their effects—can differ:

> Take an up-and-coming executive at General Electric who is being wooed by Xerox—more money, a bigger office, greater responsibility. If his first reaction is to grab it, he's probably going to be disappointed. Xerox has a totally different culture than GE. Success (and even survival) at Xerox is closely tied to an ability to maintain a near frenetic pace, the ability to work and play hard, Xerox-style.
>
> By contrast, GE has a more thoughtful and slow-moving culture. The GE culture treats each business activity seriously—almost as though each activity will have an enormous impact on the company. Success at GE is a function of being able to take work seriously, a strong sense of peer group respect, considerable deference for authority, and a sense of deliberateness. . . . But these same values might not be held in high esteem elsewhere.
>
> Bright young comers at GE could, for example, quickly fizzle out at Xerox— and not even understand why. They'll be doing exactly what they did to succeed at

GE—maybe even working harder at it—but their deliberate approach to issues large and small will be seen by insiders at Xerox as a sign they "lack smarts."[21]

Cultures aren't limited to large corporations. Every organization has its own way to doing business and treating people. Anyone who has worked for more than one restaurant or retail store, attended more than one college or university, belonged to more than one team, or volunteered for more than one worthy cause knows that even when the same job is being performed, the way of doing business can be radically different. Furthermore, the culture of an organization can make all the difference between a satisfying and a disappointing job. Research shows that employees are more satisfied and committed to their jobs when their values match those of their supervisors and the organization.[22]

Creating and Maintaining Organizational Cultures   Whether the culture is created deliberately or evolves without a grand design, the earliest phase of an organization's life is the best time to set the tone for its lifelong culture. Early events are enshrined in stories that can take on the quality of legends.[23] One of the most famous of these tales is told at IBM about former chairman of the board Thomas Watson, Jr. Watson was barred from entering a high-security area of one of the company's plants because he was not wearing the proper identification badge. Rather than firing the assertive guard who blocked his entry, Watson acknowledged the policy and waited at the gate until the proper identification was found. The story confirms a policy central to IBM's culture: everybody at the company obeys the rules.

An organization's culture takes on a life of its own. Customs and rituals develop that perpetuate a company's values. Some of these practices are as simple as changing labels. Employees are called "crew members" at McDonald's, "hosts" at Disney Productions, and "associates" at J. C. Penney, reflecting those companies' shared belief that every worker plays an important role in the corporation's success. Caterpillar employees have been known to celebrate the introduction of new earth-moving machines by hosting day-long events in which the huge pieces of equipment are dressed in costume. Company-sponsored events can also foster an organization's culture. At Tupperware, the president and senior managers spend fully one month a year at celebrations honoring top salespersons and managers.[24]

Practices like these both reflect the company's culture and continue to shape it, but they are nothing more than useless gimmicks unless they are backed up by day-to-day policies. The "employees count" orientation at Hewlett-Packard is backed up by a no-layoff policy that began in the 1940s and has continued through the toughest of economic times. When business dipped during the 1970 recession, HP personnel—from the founders down—took a 10 percent cut in pay and hours rather than lay off staff. HP's faith in its employees also shows in its "open lab stock" policy, which encourages engineers to take home equipment for their personal use. Enlightened managers are convinced that practices like these build a corporate culture that pays dividends in increased loyalty and productivity.[25]

Not all cultural traditions are so positive. In some organizations, negative customs perpetuate an unhappy state of affairs. Complaining can become a part of a company's culture: bitter employees may spend time over coffee ridiculing management and criticizing the company. So can coercion: supervisors often try to prod unproductive workers by issuing more and more rules, feeding the flames of unhappiness that they are trying to extinguish. Unavailability is sometimes an organizational trait as well: managers who dislike and fear subordinates often barricade themselves in offices, cutting off communication with the rank-and-file employees, who, in turn, feel increasingly alienated.

Building Positive Cultures Through Positive Communication   Since cultures play such a fundamental role in the life of an organization and its members, the question is how to create the kind of culture that will work best. When Allen Kennedy, co-author of the landmark book Corporate Cultures, was asked what ingredient was used to build and maintain strong cultures, he responded:

> The answer, pure and simple, is through effective communication—to employees, customers, shareholders, public officials, and the public at large. The companies and organizations that do the best job thinking through what they are all about, deciding how and to whom these central messages should be communicated and executing the communication plan in a quality way, invariably build a strong sense of esprit within their own organization and among the many constituents they serve.[26]

The following list outlines six ways to improve both communication climate and productivity. If you are a manager, the list can suggest ways to improve the climate of your organization. If you are a subordinate, the list will help you understand why your job is—or isn't—rewarding.[27]

1. **Job autonomy.** Do employees have the freedom to manage themselves without having continually to report to higher management?

2. **Achievement rewards.** Are the accomplishments of employees acknowledged and rewarded? The best systems make it possible for all employees to gain rewards through financial remuneration, symbolic tokens, and public recognition.

3. **Emotional support.** Does management show a genuine interest in the well-being of employees by seeking out and responding to their concerns? A study by Woodruff Imbermann, a Chicago business consultant, revealed that:

> Companies who make some attempt to talk with workers have fewer strikes. In many nonstrike companies, for example, managers and workers sit down regularly to discuss such irritants as broken windows or poor heating. Similarly, companies that try to minimize the personal disruption and sacrifices that overtime imposes on workers—by a gesture as simple as sending workers a box of candy or a potted plant—have fewer problems than companies that do nothing.[28]

4. **Opportunities for growth.** Does the company give workers the chance to develop their skills? Does it encourage education and training by giving employees time off and perhaps even paying some tuition for courses, and does it let employees try out what they have learned?

5. **Risk tolerance.** Does management allow employees to experiment and innovate without fear of punishment?

6. **Conflict tolerance.** Does the company recognize that disagreement is not necessarily a sign of disloyalty? Does it encourage an open exchange of ideas? Does it listen to constructive disagreements without threatening reprisals?

Organizational Culture and Career Planning Even if you are not in a position to help shape an organization's culture at this stage in your life, the concept still has major implications for your career. As a prospective employee, you might be tempted to select a company on the basis of its most obvious characteristics. What is the starting salary? How are the working conditions? What are the chances for promotion? If you consider only these factors, you could wind up with an impressive title and income—but miserable.

When you are thinking about going to work for an organization, make an effort to pin down its personality, just as you would if you were choosing a mate. After all, you are likely to spend more hours per year at work than you will with a spouse. You can get a sense of a company's culture in five ways:[29]

Study the Physical Setting An organization's physical plant says something about its personality. Even though most organizations don't make statements by *building* their environment, they do say something about themselves by *choosing* the space in which they operate. In Chapter 3, you will see that one axiom of personal nonverbal communication is "You can't avoid communicating"—that is, everything one does or does not do sends a message for others to interpret. The same principle holds for organizations. For example, choosing to locate in a high-rent or low-rent district might say something about the prosperity of the organiza-

---

At Allgemeine Rechtsschutz AG, a West German insurance firm, employees will have unmistakable evidence of their standing on the corporate ladder when a new $2.8 million headquarters opens in Düsseldorf at the end of the year. Each story will be occupied by a progressively higher echelon of workers, from 360 typists and clerks on the ground floor to president Heinz G. Kramberg alone at the top on the twelfth floor. Kramberg says he ordered the staircase design to "encourage ambition and provide a visual image of our organization structure."

"Stairway to Success," *Newsweek*

tion, its concern with thrift, the public it wants to serve, or even its competence. Likewise, the physical condition of the facilities makes a statement. Is the workplace clean or dirty? Are workers' areas personalized or standardized?

Power relationships can also become apparent when you look at the amount and location of existing space given to various groups. Environmental consultant Fred I. Steele illustrates this point:

> My work as a consultant to personnel departments has made it very clear to me that members of most organizations feel the personnel function to be of low potency and importance. The personnel offices are usually cramped, very inelegantly furnished (read "drab" if you like), and located in out-of-the-way or "leftover" space. The symbolic significance of this is all the greater because in many systems the personnel department is visited more frequently by both current and prospective employees than any other department. The setting of a personnel department should be quite carefully designed; in fact it is usually not, in keeping with its low status in the system.[30]

Read What the Company Says About Itself   Press releases, annual reports, and advertisements can all be revealing. Companies with strong values are proud to publicize them. An emphasis on only profit and loss raises doubts about the company's concern for its personnel. Pride about innovation, service to customers, and commitment to the community all are clues about an organization's culture. Of course, noble statements may only be lip service to praiseworthy values. Use the other suggestions in this section to see if a company practices what it preaches.

Test How the Company Greets Strangers   How are you treated when you visit a company or deal with its employees? Do they seem happy or grumpy? Are they willing to deal with you promptly, or are you left cooling your heels? Do they seem helpful, or do they seem unconcerned with your needs? A walking tour of the working areas can help give a feel for the organization's personality. "Vibrations" may not be a scientific term, but companies do have them.

Interview Company People   Strike up conversations with employees. See what they say about the company. Even rehearsed answers can be revealing: the apparent enthusiasm and sincerity with which they are delivered offer a clue about whether employees believe in the company line.

An employment interview is probably not the best place to explore these subjects. It's hard to imagine an employer who would do anything but praise the company in this setting. Talking with employees off company premises can yield information not gathered in a job interview. Even if you don't learn much about the organization as a whole, you'll get a good picture of the kind of people you will be working with.

Learn How People Spend Their Time   During your interview and observations, find out what kinds of activities occupy employees' time. A surprising amount of effort might go into activities that are only remotely related to getting the job

done: dealing with paperwork, playing office politics, dealing with balky equipment, or attending one meeting after another. The *way* a company goes about its business reveals more about its culture than the kind of work it does.

COMMUNICATION BETWEEN CULTURES

In past generations, most workers—at least most Americans—could spend their entire career without encountering people from different backgrounds. But those days are past. The world is entering a period in which cultural diversity is a fact of everyday life. Consider the statistics. Today, American-born white males constitute only 45 percent of the U.S. work force; over the next few years, that figure will decline to 39 percent. In the period from today until the year 2000, women, minorities, and immigrants will constitute 84 percent of the new entrants into the American work force. By the turn of the century, minorities will make up 25 percent of the population of the United States. English will be the second language for more than half of California's population. Sometime in the next century, whites will become the minority of the population in the United States.[31]

Changing demographics mean that more and more Americans are working with people who come from different backgrounds and thus have different customs and attitudes. This growing cultural diversity has the potential for disaster or benefit. For those companies and individuals who can take advantage of the richness of cultural diversity, the opportunities are great. Stona Fitch, vice-president of manufacturing for Procter & Gamble, says, "The first companies that achieve a true multicultural environment will have a competitive edge. Diversity provides a much richer environment, a variety of viewpoints, greater productivity. And, not unimportantly, it makes work more fun and interesting." Kevin Sullivan, vice-president of human resources at Apple Computer, echoes the idea: "When you are surrounded by sameness, you only get variations on the same."[32]

For those who cannot or will not face the changing scene, the dangers are unavoidable. "Trying to run an international or multinational company in a competitive environment without the creativity, resources, and skills of that size of a workforce is undercutting your company's ability to be successful," says A. Barry Rand, president of U.S. marketing operations for Xerox. Judith Katz, a corporate consultant in San Diego, states flatly, "Managers that haven't learned to manage diversity by the year 2000 will be incompetent."[33]

The realities of the changing workplace make it essential that every business communicator learn to deal effectively with cultural diversity. The remainder of this chapter will help achieve that goal. It describes the variety of cultures that workers are likely to encounter and offers advice on how to communicate most effectively with people from different backgrounds.

TYPES OF CULTURAL DIVERSITY

The culturally diverse workplace of the 1990s differs from that of earlier generations in two ways. First, it is made up of people from different national backgrounds. Instead of the mostly European ancestry that was the norm in past years, in most places there will be a larger number of workers from around the world, especially from Asia, the Caribbean, and Latin America. In addition to national backgrounds, more and more managers and employees represent different groups that have always been present, though less visible in the host nation. The most obvious example in this category is women. The percentage of female employees in the United States has skyrocketed in a single generation so that today over 45 percent of all workers and 20 percent of managers are women. The ethnic balance of native-born Americans is also changing. Instead of being concentrated in a few mostly low-status occupations, Hispanic-Americans and African-Americans are far more visible in every field today. Likewise, workers who are physically challenged are entering the work force in greater numbers than ever before.

DIMENSIONS OF CULTURAL DIVERSITY

Some cultural differences are obvious. A meal cooked by your host in Tokyo or Rio isn't likely to resemble dinner at home. Likewise, it doesn't require an expert to recognize the potential problems when one person can only speak English and the other French or when a wheelchair-bound customer arrives at an office that is not equipped for access by the physically challenged. Along with obvious differences like these, there are less visible but equally important characteristics that distinguish members of one culture from another.

Norms   Chapter 8 explains how norms—unwritten rules of behavior—affect communication in small groups. But norms operate on a society-wide level, too, affecting both obvious issues like table manners and clothing, and more subtle but equally important issues. For example, what is the proper balance between bluntness and tact? How much friendliness is appropriate, and what is too much? What is the proper way to handle disagreements? Differing norms have the potential of creating misunderstandings between members of different national cultures. Consider, for example, the different rules about time. The punctuality that is prized by North American and northern European businesspeople is disregarded in Latin American cultures, so that an American visitor might feel deeply (but unnecessarily) offended by having to wait to be admitted to a Mexican counterpart's office. The use of personal space also varies from culture to culture.

The instant use of first names is particularly obnoxious to many foreign business people. Although the Japanese may be an extreme example, it is fair to say that in that country first names are used *only* among family members and intimate friends. Even longtime business associates and coworkers shy away from the use of first names. Small wonder that when a foreign businessman is introduced to Marv, Cedric, Mary, or Bill, his greetings often turn into a muffled and embarrassed silence.

Arthur M. Whitehill, *Business Horizons*

Whereas Americans are comfortable standing at arm's length while conducting business, Middle Easterners prefer to stand much closer. It is easy to see how an American and an Arab talking business might both be offended. The American could view the Arab as pushy, while the Arab might see his conversational partner as being cold and aloof. Differences like these present challenges for smooth communication, especially when the parties are not aware of the differences in cultural norms. Table 2-1 lists some key differences between U.S. and Japanese work-related norms.

When norms change, the potential for problems can be high. Women know this well. Traditional standards of feminine behavior have been an invisible barrier to women in the workplace. The stereotypical model of male behavior has been forceful and decisive. By contrast, women were expected to be deferential and unassertive. Until recently, these stereotypes made it almost unthinkable in many circles to hire women for jobs in management. (The same stereotypes raised suspicion about the abilities of men who were considered too "soft.") But as the genders have begun to equalize, women have slowly but steadily expanded their presence in traditionally male positions. Although most people, both male and female, now acknowledge that gender should not be a barrier to employment in any job, old stereotypes die hard. In some circles, a woman who strongly asserts her position still runs the risk of being labeled "bitchy," and a male who defers to a female manager may be seen as unmasculine. But recognizing obsolete norms is one way to overcome these old customs.

Cultural Values   While most cultural norms are easy to recognize, another sort of difference is more subtle but potentially just as important. This second category involves the different ways cultures view the nature of work and personal relationships that affect the way business is done.

One survey of 160,000 employees in 60 countries revealed four ways in which the worldviews of one national culture can differ from another: individualism versus collectivism, power distance, uncertainty avoidance, and "hard" versus

TABLE 2-1   Some Differences in U.S. and Japanese Work-Related Norms

	UNITED STATES	JAPAN
Status differentiation	High status differential: dress, office space, compensation, etc.	Less status differential than in United States
Individualism versus collectivism	Individual initiative prized, rewarded	Emphasis on consensus
Decision making	Top-down decision making	Bottom-up decision making; decisions discussed and approved at all levels
Reason for working	Work is means to ends including status, money, promotion	Work is end in itself

Adapted from Thomas E. Harris, "East Manages West: Japanese Organizations in America," paper presented at the annual meeting of the Speech Communication Association, San Francisco (November 1989).

"soft." These cultural dimensions are extremely important. The study showed that they were better indicators of work-related values and attitudes than age, sex, profession, or position in the organization.[34] As Table 2-2 shows, a national culture can be described in terms of these four dimensions.

Individualism Versus Collectivism   Members of an *individualistic* culture are inclined to put their own interests and those of their immediate family ahead of social concerns. Individualistic cultures offer their members a great deal of freedom, the belief being that this freedom makes it possible for each person to achieve personal success. *Collective* societies, however, have tight social frameworks in which members of a group (such as an organization) are supposed to care for one another and for the group. In collective societies, members are expected to believe that the welfare of the organization is as important as their own.

Interestingly, the research disclosed a strong relationship between individualism and a country's wealth. Rich countries like the United States, Canada, Australia, and Great Britain are very individualistic. Poor countries like Pakistan and Colombia are very collectivist.

TABLE 2-2   Examples of Cultural Differences of Selected Nations

INDIVIDUALISM	COLLECTIVISM
United States	Colombia
Australia	Venezuela
Great Britain	Pakistan
Canada	Peru
HIGH POWER DISTANCE	**LOW POWER DISTANCE**
Philippines	Austria
Mexico	Israel
Venezuela	Denmark
Yugoslavia	New Zealand
HIGH UNCERTAINTY AVOIDANCE	**LOW UNCERTAINTY AVOIDANCE**
Greece	Singapore
Portugal	Denmark
Belgium	Sweden
Japan	Hong Kong
"HARD"	**"SOFT"**
Japan	Sweden
Austria	Norway
Venezuela	Yugoslavia
Italy	Denmark

Adapted from S. P. Robbins, *Organizational Behavior*, 4th ed. (Englewood Cliffs, N.J.: Prentice-Hall, 1990), p. 488.

Power Distance   Some cultures acknowledge the fact that power is distributed unequally—that some members have greater resources and influence than others. In these cultures, differences in organizational status and rank are clear-cut. Employees have a great deal of respect for those in high positions. Other cultures downplay differences in power. Supervisors and managers may have power, but it is not flaunted or honored. In countries with low power distance, employees are comfortable approaching—and even challenging—their superiors. Egalitarian countries with low power distance include Israel, Denmark, and Austria. Some nations with high power distance are the Philippines, Mexico, and Venezuela.

Uncertainty Avoidance   The world is an uncertain place. International politics, economic trends, and the forces of nature make it impossible to predict the future with accuracy. Some cultures (for example, Singapore and Hong Kong) are comfortable with this fact. Their acceptance of uncertainty allows them to take risks, and they are relatively tolerant of behavior that differs from the norm. Other cultures (for example, Japan, Greece, and Portugal) are uncomfortable with change. They value tradition and shun changes. Organizations in these cultures are characterized by more formal rules and less tolerance for different ideas. Employees have relatively low job mobility, and lifetime employment is common.

"Hard" Versus "Soft"   The original research labeled these characteristics "high masculinity" and "high femininity," but this terminology is both sexist and potentially misleading. *Hard societies* (Japan is a prime example) are less concerned with personal relationships than with the acquisition of money and material possessions. By contrast, *soft societies* like Sweden and Norway emphasize personal relationships, concern for others, and the overall quality of life. Material well-being is important but is not viewed as the most important goal in life.

How does the United States measure against these cultural dimensions? Out of 40 countries studied, the United States was the most individualistic. It was below average on power distance, meaning that Americans are not especially intimidated by status differences between authorities and subordinates. The U.S. work force scored well below average on uncertainty avoidance: its members are willing to take risks and are tolerant of different behavior and opinions. Americans scored well above average on the dimension we have labeled "hard," meaning that they value a direct, assertive communication style and take a results-oriented bottom-line approach to doing business.

When these characteristics are compared to those of other cultures, it is easy to see why patterns of communication that have worked well with traditional American organizations don't always succeed with a culturally diverse work force.[35] Consider, for example, the use of work teams. It should come as no surprise that they are successful in highly collectivized countries like Japan; likewise, it is understandable that they have met with mixed results in the United States, the culture of which is more individualistic. On the other hand, the low power distance of U.S. culture suggests that teams composed of people from various levels of authority can work well, while such mixed groups would not work in countries like India, where the gap between members of different social levels is great.

Cultural diversity also suggests that the best approach to leadership will vary from one culture to another. As you will read in Chapter 9, the best leadership style will change according to the situation—and one important situational variable is the cultural background of the people who are to be led. For instance, workers in cultures with high power distance—Latin Americans are a prime example—are likely to respond better to an autocratic top-down approach than those in more egalitarian cultures such as New Zealand, the United States, or Israel.

Cultural differences also explain why techniques that motivate members of one culture might not work in another setting. Traditional motivational theory is based on Abraham Maslow's claim that people are most concerned with satisfying basic physiological needs. Once these basic needs are met, people will, in turn, move on to satisfy higher-level needs in the following order: safety, love, esteem, and self-actualization. Whatever value this theory has with American culture, it does not seem to fit other cultures as well. In cultures that avoid uncertainty, security needs would be among the most basic. Countries with "soft" cultures like Sweden, Norway, and Denmark would view social needs as more important. The stress on achievement (a form of self-actualization) that is so fundamental when motivating U.S. employees makes sense according to Maslow since it fits neatly with two American cultural characteristics: a willingness to accept a moderate degree of risk and the "hard" orientation of concern for performance. The same stress on achievement would not work in a "soft" culture that emphasizes personal needs and avoids uncertainty.

Don't assume that this information is only important in international business. In the changing American work force, the chances are growing that a work team will be composed of members who don't fit the traditional American profile. It's fair to expect new arrivals to the United States to accommodate to the dominant culture; but it's also reasonable to expect mainstream Americans to recognize—and profit from—the different cultural perspective of new arrivals.

COMMUNICATING ACROSS DIVERSITY

Communicating with others from different backgrounds isn't always easy. Some of the responsibility for building bridges rests with management, and a growing number of businesses are taking this job seriously.[36] But you don't need to join a corporate training program to benefit from cultural diversity. Table 2-3 lists attitudes and behaviors that can promote more satisfying, productive relationships among members of different cultures. These principles can be summarized in four categories.

Learn About Different Cultures and Subcultures   Many cultural problems are not caused by malice, but by a lack of knowledge. Trainers in cultural

TABLE 2-3 Attitudes and Behaviors That Block or Promote Intercultural Relations

ASSUMPTIONS THAT BLOCK AUTHENTIC RELATIONS

Assumptions Majority Makes
- Differences should not affect performance
- Minorities will always welcome inclusion in the majority culture
- Open recognition of differences may embarrass minorities
- Minorities are using their situation to take advantage of the majority
- "Liberal" members of the majority are free of discriminatory attitudes
- Minorities are oversensitive

Assumptions Minorities Make
- All members of the majority have the same attitudes about minorities
- There are no majority members who understand minorities
- Majority members are not really trying to understand minorities
- The only way to change the situation is by confrontation and force
- All majority members will let you down in a "crunch"

BEHAVIORS THAT BLOCK AUTHENTIC RELATIONS

Behaviors of Majority Culture
- Interruptions
- Condescending behavior
- Expressions of too-easy acceptance and friendship
- Talking about, rather than to, minorities who are present

Behaviors of Minority Culture
- Confrontation too early and too harshly
- Rejection of offers of help and friendship
- Giving answers majority members want to hear
- Isolationism

ASSUMPTIONS AND BEHAVIORS THAT PROMOTE AUTHENTIC RELATIONS

- Treating people as individuals as well as members of a culture
- Demonstrating interest in learning about other cultures
- Listening without interrupting
- Taking risks (for example, being first to confront differences)
- Expressing concerns directly and constructively

- Staying with and working through difficult confrontations
- Acknowledging sincere attempts (even clumsy ones) to understand and support members of other cultures
- Dealing with others where they are, instead of expecting them to be perfect
- Recognizing that interdependence is needed between members of majority and minority cultures

Adapted from Philip R. Harris and Robert T. Moran, *Managing Cultural Differences,* 2nd ed. (Houston: Grid, 1987), pp. 245–247.

sensitivity cite examples of how mistaken assumptions can lead to trouble.[37] In one West Coast bank, officials were dismayed when Filipino female employees didn't cooperate with the new "friendly teller" program. Management failed to realize that in Filipino culture, overtly friendly women can be taken for prostitutes. A Taiwanese executive who was transferred to the Midwestern offices of a large company was viewed as aloof and autocratic by his peers, who did not understand that Asian culture encourages a more distant managerial style.

Misunderstandings like these are less likely to cause problems when mainstream workers understand each other's cultural backgrounds. As Paulette Williams, formerly senior manager at Weyerhaeuser's nurseries in Southern California, put it, "If you don't learn how other people feel, you can hurt them unintentionally."[38]

View Diversity As an Opportunity   It is easy to think of cultural differences as an annoyance that makes it harder to take care of business. Dealing with others who have different attitudes or customs takes patience and time—both scarce commodities in a busy work schedule. But with the right attitude, cultural diversity can stop being just a necessary cost of doing business and can become an opportunity.

People with differing backgrounds can bring new strengths to a business. Women, for instance, are generally more skilled than men at reading nonverbal cues.[39] This makes them ideal members of a negotiating team, where they may be especially skilled at interpreting how the other people are feeling. Workers from diverse ethnic groups can offer new insights into how customers or other workers with similar backgrounds can be reached. A Hispanic supervisor, for example, may be especially effective at motivating and training other Hispanics, and a Korean team member can give new insights into how a Korean-managed competitor operates.

Don't Condescend   It's easy to view people who are different as inferior. A new employee who was hired in part because of his or her ethnic identity might seem less qualified than mainstream workers. Your first reaction to a physically challenged colleague might be sympathy or pity. Immigrants who are learning English as a second language might sound less intelligent than native speakers. Even white males, members of the traditional majority, might seem like members of the "good-old-boy club," undeserving of respect since their success seemingly owes more to personal connections than to merit.

Despite the tendency to sell others short because they belong to one cultural group or another, it is better to regard each person on his or her personal merits. One way to develop respect is to recognize the special talent and energy it takes for members of minorities to succeed in a new environment. By imagining the difficulties *you* would face if you had to accommodate to a new society, you might appreciate the challenges faced by others.

Even though you may make allowances for those who are in a new situation, don't insult them by assuming that they are incapable of doing a good job. Even well-intentioned patronizing does a disservice. As one African-American employee of a major American firm put it, "So often, if a black is blowing it, the white manager is afraid to tell him."[40] This sort of kid-glove treatment is not good for anyone since it generates resentment from other employees and denies the employee in question the chance to learn and to prove himself or herself able to grow.

Barbara A. Walker, manager of international diversity at Digital Equipment Corporation, has learned—along with others at the company—that in order for organizations whose workforces are diverse to be fully effective, people at those firms need to confront and discuss their feelings about diversity in the workforce.

Management realized that the company had an unwritten rule against talking about the issues of race and gender. "The prevailing view," says Walker, "was that open and frank conversation on these issues, particularly in the presence of minorities and women, was taboo in polite conversation. But if people couldn't talk to each other, they couldn't learn from each other."

Once they became aware of the taboo against discussing differences among people, Digital's managers set out to destroy it. Top managers at the company were encouraged to meet in small groups to discuss the "undiscussable." Gradually, employees at other levels of the organization—of both genders and all ethnicities and races—were included in the discussion groups, which came to be known as Core Groups. Together, the employees struggled to acknowledge, understand, and eliminate the stereotypes and prejudices they held about each other.

The work was arduous . . . but the realization came at last: The best way for people to work effectively with each other was to recognize and celebrate, not deny, each other's differences. Stereotypes, they learned, grow out of ignorance; thus learning about their differences was the surest way to eliminate stereotypes.

Barbara Mandrell and Susan Kohler-Gray, "Digital Equipment Corporation: A Pioneer in Diversity," *Personnel*

Talk About Differences   Subjects like cultural, sexual, or ethnic differences can be so threatening that many people try to pretend they don't exist. They fear that bringing up these subjects can be embarrassing or that they will seem prejudiced. But since most differences are apparent, pretending not to notice them may appear phony or insincere.

Experts agree that ignoring differences can be just as dangerous as emphasizing them. The key to success is to recognize that cultural diversity can be positive and that understanding others who are different can enrich you and your organization. If you approach others with this attitude, you are likely to be well received.

The demographic profile of the marketplace is changing dramatically. The percentage of white males entering the work force is declining, while the number of women, ethnic minorities, employees from overseas, and physically challenged workers is on the rise. The diversity of employees and customers increases the diversity of norms and values that every worker is likely to encounter. These changes will require a shift in both attitudes and skills in order to maintain productivity and good working relationships. It will be necessary to learn about different cultures and subcultures, view diversity as an opportunity, avoid condescension, and discuss differences openly.

SUMMARY

All organizations need to process information. Some do this well and some poorly, and the difference often results from the way an organization is structured.

Formal communication networks—which can be pictured in flow charts and organizational charts—are management's way of establishing what it believes are necessary relationships among people within an organization. Formal communication flows in several directions: downward from superiors to subordinates, upward from subordinates to superiors, and horizontally among people of equal rank. Formal communication structures are necessary as a business grows and its tasks become more complex, but they must be handled carefully to avoid problems.

Unlike formal relationships, informal communication networks consist of interaction patterns that are not designed by management. Informal networks can be based on physical proximity, shared career interests, or personal friendships. An informal network can be quite small or a large grapevine that connects many people. Informal networks serve many purposes: they can confirm, expand upon, expedite, contradict, circumvent, or supplement formal messages. Because these functions are so useful, it is important to cultivate and use informal contacts within an organization.

Every organization has a distinct culture—a relatively stable picture of the organization's personality shared by its members. Cultures are usually shaped in the organization's early days, often by its earliest leaders. Everyday customs and rituals both reflect the culture and continue to shape it.

When evaluating an organization, a prospective employee ought to make sure that the culture is comfortable and positive. Good salary and working conditions are not enough to guarantee job satisfaction if the company's personality doesn't suit the employee. First-hand observation and informal contacts with current employees are good ways to analyze an organization's culture.

As American society becomes increasingly diverse, the ability to communicate with members of other cultures becomes a business necessity. Diversity has many faces: gender, physical ability, language, and ethnicity are a few. Diversity manifests itself in a greater variety of norms and cultural values such as individualism versus collectivism, power distance, uncertainty avoidance, and "hard" versus "soft" priorities.

Communicators who succeed in a diverse workplace must educate themselves to different cultures and subcultures. Viewing diversity as an opportunity instead of a problem is another important attitude. Treating people from different cultural backgrounds with respect is essential. Finally, being willing to acknowledge and discuss cultural differences will help communicators understand and appreciate one another.

ACTIVITIES

1. To what formal communication networks do you belong? Find out by drawing a flow chart for a project or a procedure you are or have been involved with, using the guidelines in Figure 2-1. Some possibilities you might consider, in addi-

tion to jobs you have had, are church groups, a volunteer organization you have been involved with, a sorority or fraternity fund-raising project, the process of registering for courses, and so on.

a. Start by drawing a box representing yourself and the task you perform.
b. Next, picture the people and tasks that connect with your work so that your chart includes every step in the project.
c. Add the days or time periods each task should take so that your chart shows the length of time the project or procedure should take.

2. Recall the last manager you worked for, the leader of a project you have worked on, or the leaders of an organization to which you belong.

a. Which kinds of downward messages listed on pages 27–28 did your manager most commonly send? If some types were lacking, what were the consequences of their absence?
b. Did the downward messages your manager sent suffer from any of the problems described on pages 29–30? If so, what could the manager have done to improve their quality?

3. Think about your own upward communication. Do you send and receive all four types described in this chapter? If not, why? What could be done to improve the quality and quantity of your upward communication?

4. Think of a major communication problem you have experienced at work or in school. Does the responsibility for the problem rest with you? Your boss? Both of you? Use the information on upward and downward communication in this chapter to suggest ways of improving your communication in the future.

5. Think of the person who is your most important horizontal communication partner on the job.

a. Use the list of functions on pages 33–34 to decide what kinds of messages you send and receive most often.
b. Do you send and receive enough horizontal messages of each type? If not, what are the consequences?
c. Which problems in the text describe the reason for your lack of effective horizontal communication? What can you do to improve these areas?

6. Diagram the informal organizational networks you belong to. To how many networks do you belong? How closely do these informal relationships resemble the formal networks of which you are a member?

What is the basis of the informal networks you have pictured: physical proximity, shared career interests, or personal friendships?

What functions do your informal connections serve? Do they confirm, expand upon, expedite, contradict, or circumvent information carried through formal channels? Would you be better off if you increased the scope of your informal networks? If so, how could you do this?

7. Identify an organization you might like to work for someday or one that interests you.

a. Describe why you chose this organization.
b. Use the guidelines on pages 43–45 to identify the organization's culture.
c. Decide whether the key elements of this culture are formally identified and promoted. Are these formal elements the key to maintaining the culture, or are there informal, everyday practices that are more important?

d. Based on your findings, explain whether or not you would enjoy working there.

8. Identify the demographic profile of an organization that interests you. You may choose to focus on your present place of work, or you may decide to explore an area in which you hope to work in the future. Using personal interviews or published information, identify the present cultural composition of the organization's members and its clientele. Compare this profile with the work force and clientele five years ago and its expected composition five years from now. What changes in cultural trends do your findings reveal? How might these changes affect the organization's way of doing business?

9. Identify the culture or subculture that you are most likely to encounter in the next few years of your work. Based on interviews and library research, identify the norms and values of that group, and describe how they differ from your own. Use the information on pages 50–53 to describe how you can communicate with members of this group in productive, satisfying ways. If you currently work with one or more members of the group, focus your description on how you can modify your behavior with these individuals.

Communicator Profile

Kathy Kobayashi, Marketing Director
McDonald's
Santa Barbara, California

American society has become more diverse, so we've recruited employees who reflect the ethnic balance of the neighborhoods we serve. Right now we have so many employees whose first language is not English that we actively need to recruit an English-as-a-first-language employee to maintain balance.

The local NAACP needed 100 eggs, so we donated them. An important part of my job is to be aware of situations like this, because it's McDonald's national policy and a big part of our corporate culture to be involved in the communities we serve. Like many other McDonald's, we affiliate ourselves with local schools. For the past twenty-two years, we have provided all the lunches for the 800 participants and volunteers in the Special Olympics here. We don't just lend support by donating food; we belong to the "Adopt-a-School" project, and we contribute funds to a program that encourages teachers who want to try out new ideas.

Another big part of the McDonald's culture is standardization. Our customers keep coming back because they know that they can count on some important things whenever they enter one of our restaurants anywhere in the world. For example, Big Mac will taste the same no matter where you buy it. Likewise, you can count on a spotless kitchen, clean restrooms, and a pleasant area to eat. You should never have to wait in line for more than three minutes. Any food that is not bought in ten minutes is supposed to be thrown away. Our customers don't come to McDonald's for surprises, and we work hard to be sure they will get what they expect and want.

This sort of standardization doesn't happen by accident. We have manuals that cover virtually every step of running a restaurant. There are classes for all levels of employees and at least 500 training videos. McDonald's even has a university, called Hamburger U., where you actually get a diploma! All of these things help create the distinctive McDonald's culture, and they help build a sense of morale as well.

In recent years, the company has recognized that flexibility is just as important as standardization. In some ways, our new flexibility is straightforward: whatever you want on your chicken sandwich or on your salad or on your Big Mac you can ask for. That might not seem like much, but until recently it wouldn't have been possible. Other kinds of adaptability are less obvious but just as important. American society has become more diverse, so we've recruited employees who reflect the ethnic balance of the neighborhoods we serve. Right now we have so many employees whose first language is not English that we actively need to recruit an English-as-a-first-language employee to maintain balance.

One way to assure that our policies are honored is by rewarding excellent personnel who embody the McDonald's image. They train other employees. People who set good examples are actually called "stars," and they serve as lobby hosts, run birthday parties, and provide information on store tours. Becoming a star is important to most of the people who work for us because it shows that the company rewards people who honor and strengthen the McDonald's culture.

We also try to maintain other principles of Ray Kroc, the founder of McDonald's. He was famous for the handshake deal: his word was as good as gold, and we aim to be just as dependable. His sayings are still learned and repeated by employees. Right now I have one of them in mind: "When you're green, you're still growing; and when you're ripe, you rot." We never want to get that ripe!

PART II

PERSONAL SKILLS

3

After reading this chapter, you should understand:

- The potential for misunderstandings that arises from equivocal statements, highly abstract language, and excessive jargon
- The occasions when ambiguity and judicious use of jargon are desirable
- The kinds of biased and trigger words that are likely to arouse undesired emotional reactions
- The difference between powerful and powerless language
- The characteristics of nonverbal communication
- How nonverbal variables such as voice, clothing, facial and body expression, time, space, and physical environment can reflect liking, involvement, and power relationships

You should be able to:

- Identify and provide alternatives for excessively vague or jargon-filled language
- Describe when judicious use of ambiguity and jargon is desirable
- Detect biased and emotion-laden language and replace it with more neutral terms
- Use powerful forms of language as appropriate in business and professional settings
- Identify your own nonverbal behavior that helps or hinders your effectiveness on the job and develop alternative behavior as necessary
- Identify and form tentative interpretations of the nonverbal behavior of others you encounter in job-related settings

VERBAL
AND NONVERBAL
MESSAGES

Although they are neighbors and see each other almost every day, Bob and Carolyn rarely speak to each other. Ever since their partnership broke up, the hard feelings have made even casual conversation painful.

"We both should have known better," Bob lamented. "It was such a simple misunderstanding. We went into the partnership agreeing that we would be 'equal partners,' but now I can see that we had different ideas about what being 'equals' meant. I saw each of us taking charge of the areas that we did best: I'm good at marketing and sales, and Carolyn knows product design and production backwards and forwards. So it made sense to me that, while we were each equally responsible for the business and deserving an equal share of the profits, we would each make the final decisions in the areas where we were experts."

"That's not what I meant by 'equal partners,'" stated Carolyn flatly. "Bob wasn't willing to take responsibility for the hard work of production. He kept saying 'that's where you're the expert.' And he didn't have any faith in my ideas about sales and marketing. He wanted to make those decisions himself, whether or not I agreed. To me, being equal means you have just as much say as the other person in every part of the business."

In hindsight, both Bob and Carolyn realized that there had been signs of trouble from the beginning of their partnership. "Even before we opened for business, I could tell that Carolyn was unhappy," sighs Bob. "I always saw the venture as a chance to make a fortune. But whenever I'd get excited and talk about how much money we could make, Carolyn would clam up and get this grim look on her face."

Carolyn also remembers early, unspoken signs of trouble. "I've always wanted to have a business that my kids could be proud of," she says. "But when I'd talk about that, Bob wouldn't have much to say. Even though he never said so, at times I got the feeling that he was laughing at my high ideals."

This story illustrates the importance of paying close attention to verbal and nonverbal messages. The ill-fated partnership between Bob and Carolyn could have been avoided if they had paid more attention to the unspoken but powerful nonverbal clues that warned of trouble. And examining more carefully just what an "equal" partnership meant could have helped them avoid the clash that finally led to their breakup.

How well you communicate your ideas will make the difference between success and failure. Expressing yourself effectively will boost your chances for a positive reaction, while a bungling delivery will torpedo even the best ideas. This chapter will look at the two channels by which you communicate: your words and your nonverbal behavior. In the following pages, you will gain a healthy respect for the advantages of using these channels effectively and the pitfalls of using them poorly. By the time you have finished this chapter, you should recognize that significant problems can lurk in even the simplest statements, and you will discover some ways of avoiding or overcoming such problems. You will also become more aware of the wordless messages that each of us constantly sends and receives.

VERBAL MESSAGES

Words are the vessels that carry most of our ideas to others. We sometimes forget, though, that they are only vessels and often imperfect ones—they are not the ideas themselves. Sometimes the message they carry is incomplete or even entirely different from our intended meaning. At its least complicated, misunderstandings involve words being interpreted differently from the way we intended them. Even a simple statement like "Let's talk next Tuesday at one P.M." can lead to problems. You might mean "Let's meet next Tuesday," while the other person interprets the remark to mean "Let's discuss the matter over the phone." It is easy to see how even a small misunderstanding like this can lead to lost time and feelings of irritation. Some problems with language go beyond simple misunderstandings.[1] As Table 3-1 shows, the listener can understand the meaning of every

TABLE 3-1 *Even Simple Messages Can Be Misunderstood*

WHAT THE MANAGER SAID	WHAT THE MANAGER MEANT	WHAT THE SUBORDINATE HEARD
I'll look into hiring another person for your department as soon as I complete my budget review.	We'll start interviewing for that job in about three weeks.	I'm tied up with more important things. Let's forget about hiring for the indefinite future.
Your performance was below par last quarter. I really expected more out of you.	You're going to have to try harder, but I know you can do it.	If you screw up one more time, you're out.
I'd like that report as soon as you can get to it.	I need that report within the week.	Drop that rush order you're working on and fill out that report today.
I talked to the boss but at the present time, due to budget problems, we'll be unable to fully match your competitive salary offer.	We can give you 95 percent of that offer, and I know we'll be able to do even more for you next year.	If I were you, I'd take that competitive offer. We're certainly not going to pay that kind of salary to a person with your credentials.
We have a job opening in Los Angeles that we think would be just your cup of tea. We'd like you to go out there and look it over.	If you'd like that job, it's yours. If not, of course you can stay here in Denver. You be the judge.	You don't have to go out to L.A. if you don't want to. However, if you don't, you can kiss good-bye to your career with this firm.
Your people seem to be having some problems getting their work out on time. I want you to look into this situation and straighten it out.	Talk to your people and find out what the problem is. Then get with them and jointly solve it.	I don't care how many heads you bust, just get me that output. I've got enough problems around here without you screwing things up too.

Source: *Organizational Behavior: Theory and Practice* by S. Altman, E. Valenzi, and R. M. Hodgetts, copyright © 1985 by Harcourt Brace Jovanovich, Inc. Reproduced by permission of the publisher.

word perfectly and still interpret a message in a way that is completely different from its intended meaning.

CLARITY AND AMBIGUITY

Since the most basic language problems involve misunderstandings, we will begin our study of language by examining how to prevent this sort of miscommunication. We will also look at times when a lack of clarity can actually be desirable.

Use Unequivocal Terms to Avoid Misunderstandings Equivocal words are those with more than one meaning:

> A shipment ordered for Portland goes to Oregon instead of Maine.

> Responding to a telephone message, you call the wrong Ms. Jones.

> In an employment interview, you respond to the interviewer's question "What are your goals?" by speaking for several minutes about your desire to become a divisional manager within five years, only to find that the interviewer really wanted to know what you are seeking from life.

Semanticists illustrate the problems inherent in equivocal language by telling the story of a newly hired clerk who was taking her first order for personalized stationery. She asked the customer whether the name should be put in the upper right or upper left corner of the page. After a moment's thought, the customer asked that the name be placed in the middle. The clerk dutifully sent off the order with these instructions, and the stationery arrived shortly with the customer's name printed "in the middle" of each sheet, exactly as ordered— equidistant from the top, bottom, and each side of the page.

The results of equivocal misunderstandings usually aren't amusing—at least not to the people involved. Anyone who has botched a job, missed a meeting, failed to meet a deadline, or fumbled some other important business event due to an equivocal mixup knows the grief that even simple misunderstandings can cause.

The key to avoiding equivocal misunderstandings is to double-check your understanding of any terms that can possibly be interpreted in more than one way. When you agree to meet "Wednesday" with someone, mention the date to be sure that you're both thinking of the same week. When your supervisor says your ideas are "okay," make sure that the term means "well done" and not just "adequate."

Use Lower-Level Abstractions When Clarity Is Essential Any object or idea can be described at various levels, some very general and others quite specific. Consider the following example:

problem

equipment problem

breakdown of copying machine

automatic paper feeder does not work

sheets jammed in paper path

Low-level abstractions are highly specific. They refer directly to objects or events that can be observed. High-level abstractions cover a broader range of possible objects or events without describing them in much detail.

High-level abstractions can create problems because they are often subject to a wide variety of interpretations. For example,

"Straighten up the area."	A quick cleanup or a spit-and-polish job?
"We need some market research."	A short questionnaire for a few of our biggest customers or lengthy personal interviews of thousands of potential customers?
"Keep up the good work!"	Which parts of the work are good?
"Bring me a list of your costs on this job."	General categories of costs or an itemization of every expenditure, including postage and my secretary's overtime? A handwritten list for discussion purposes or a formal report?
"Give me your honest opinion."	Speak my mind completely or only answer the questions you have specifically asked? Be diplomatic or blunt?

The need for clarification seems obvious when you read examples like these. In everyday life, however, it's easy to assume you understand another person without needing to ask for more specifics. We often learn that our language was too abstract only after the damage has been done.

So far we have been talking about the value of using low-level abstractions. But there are times when high-level abstractions are handy. For one thing, they are time-savers; they let us describe the "office staff" without naming Gladys, Sidney, Ida, Jerry, and all the others specifically. Or we can refer to "the orders for last month" without detailing each one. In addition, very specific language can sometimes create so many verbal trees that your listeners won't be able to see the forest. For instance, referring to "the Eastern-region sales force" saves your listener from having to figure out that that's what Bruce, Emily, Sam, Hilda, George, Fay, and Gary are. Similarly, itemizing each mechanical problem in a plant may obscure the fact that each of these problems is related to outdated, worn-out machines.

Since both abstract and specific language have their advantages, it is often best to use both. One way to achieve maximum clarity is to begin explaining your proposal, problem, request, or appreciation with an abstract statement, which you then qualify with specifics:

"I'm worried about the amount of time we seem to be spending on relatively unimportant matters [abstract]. In our last meeting, for instance, we talked for twenty minutes about when to schedule the company picnic and then only had fifteen minutes to discuss our hiring needs [specific]."

"Management has asked me to encourage you to share any ideas you have about how we could improve our operation [abstract]. We're especially interested in ways to reduce our transportation costs and to reward employees who have made specific contributions [specifics]."

"I'd like to take on more responsibility [abstract]. Until now, the only decisions I've been involved in are about small matters [still abstract], such as daily schedules and customer refunds [more specific]. I'd like a chance to help decide issues such as buying and advertising [specific requests]."

One common type of overly abstract language is the use of excessively broad terms. Consider a few examples:

all	each	any	never	nothing
every	always	none	no one	nobody

When faced with a statement containing one of these words, an astute communicator will politely question its use by echoing the phrase with stress on the universal quantifier:

A: Our needs never get considered around here.
B: *Never?*
A: I can't understand anything he's saying.
B: *Anything?*
A: All the staff support the proposal.
B: *All* of them?

In most cases, questions like these will encourage the other person to use more specific language. Sometimes, though, overly broad statements are implied rather than used outright:

THE STATEMENT	THE IMPLICATION
"The customers aren't happy?"	"None of the customers is happy."
"He doesn't understand me."	"He doesn't understand anything I'm saying."

"That's a bad idea."   "There's nothing good about that idea."

When faced with this sort of obscurity, make the overly broad term explicit:

"*None* of the customers?" or "What are the customers unhappy about?"

"He doesn't understand you *at all?*" or "What doesn't he understand?"

"You think the idea has *no* value?" or "Why is it a bad idea?"

So far we have been talking about how overly vague language can confuse listeners. But abstract speech can also confuse the sender. How many times have you promised to get back to callers "soon" without having a clear idea of whether you'd call them back later that day, in three days, or in three weeks? Have you ever grumbled about bad working conditions or a supervisor's unfairness without being able to state exactly what you are complaining about or without clarifying your own thoughts, which in turn will make you a better communicator?

Use Jargon Judiciously   Every profession has its own specialized vocabulary. People who order office supplies talk about "NCR paper" and "Three-up labels." Computer users talk about "CD-ROM drives" and "image-compression boards."

In most cases, terms like these serve a useful purpose. For one thing, they save time. It is quicker, for instance, for an accountant to use the term *liquidity* than to say "the degree to which an asset can be converted into cash." In the same way, *CPM* is a handy term that advertisers use to stand for "the advertising cost to make a thousand impressions." A specialized vocabulary is particularly vital when the subject matter is technical and complex. The phrase *sleeping pill* simply won't do for physicians, nurses, and other health professionals because it says nothing about the dosage, the particular drug, or the circumstances under which it should be used. Similarly, geologists can't discuss their findings by talking about *rocks*.

Most business professionals agree that it is important to learn the jargon of

---

According to Talleyrand, writing some 200 years ago, language was given to man to conceal thought. This would certainly appear to be the case in the twentieth century.

A former senior official in the Department of Defense, Gerald Dineen, met this problem head-on, pointing out, "We go to Congress and tell them that our WWMCCSS has got to have a BMEWS upgrade, our Fuzzy Sevens have to be replaced by PAVE PAWS, we want to keep our PARCS and DEW in operation, we have to harden the NEACE, and we have to improve our MEECN with more TRACAMO and begin planning to replace AFSATCOM with Triple-S . . . and then we wonder why no one understands."

Norman R. Augustine, *Augustine's Laws*

your field as quickly as possible.[2] Doing so can speed up the exchange of information and make you appear competent and well informed. A certain amount of jargon has its value for outsiders as well. Speakers who sprinkle their comments with jargon will appear more credible to some listeners. This principle has been referred to as the "Dr. Fox hypothesis."[3] The name honors Dr. Myron Fox, who spoke to an audience of psychiatrists, psychologists, social workers, and educators on "Mathematical Game Theory As Applied to Physical Education." Despite the high-blown title, the talk—and Dr. Fox himself—was a fraud. Fox was an actor whom researchers had coached to deliver a lecture of gobbledygook and double-talk: a collection of terms from a *Scientific American* article mixed with jokes, non sequiturs, contradictory statements, and meaningless references to unrelated topics. When couched in a mass of high-level jargon, however, Fox's meaningless remarks were judged to be important. In other words, Fox's credibility came more from the language he used than from his ideas.

The Dr. Fox hypothesis suggests that jargon does have its place as a credibility-builder. Notice, however, that while incomprehensible language may *impress* listeners, it doesn't help them to *understand* an idea. Thus, if your goal is to explain yourself (and not merely to build your image), the ideal mixture may be a combination of clear language sprinkled with a bit of professional jargon.

Problems arise when insiders use their specialized vocabulary without explaining it to the uninitiated. A customer shopping for a computer might be mystified by a dealer's talk about RAM and ROM memory, transparent software, and disk storage capacity in bytes and bits. When the same information is translated into language the buyer can understand—number of pages of information that can be stored on a disk, for example—a sale is more likely. One study among accountants, for instance, showed that management at many large and small companies were not using methods for reducing expenses, even though the methods were "readily available, easily installed and at little cost." One important reason was described as "the language barrier which has grown up between the technologist and the accountant," in which each is "content to largely talk among its members in terms only they can understand." In other words, the technical people and the accountants in many of these organizations used their own jargon to the extent that they could not understand each other and work together to reduce costs.[4]

Jargon-free speech is especially important when dealing with people who are not familiar with the English language or the culture. For example, phrases like "getting a handle," "thrown a curve," or "coming from left field" might seem perfectly clear to a native-born American, but they could stump even a fluent speaker who was raised elsewhere.

Use Ambiguous Language When It Is Strategically Desirable   Vague language can be a sign of deliberate deception, as an old joke shows. A reporter warned a state senator, "Sir, your constituents were confused by today's speech."

"Good," the senator replied. "It took me two days to write it that way."

While vagueness can signal an ethical lapse and while straight talk and clear

Through indirectness, we give others an idea of what we have in mind, testing the interactional waters before committing too much—a natural way of balancing our needs with the needs of others. Rather than blurt out ideas and let them fall where they may, we send out feelers, get a sense of others' ideas and their potential reactions to ours, and shape our thoughts as we go.

The beauty and pitfalls of language are two sides of the same coin. A word spoken, a small gesture, can have meaning far beyond its literal sense. But subtle signals can be missed, and meaning can be gleaned that wasn't intended and that may or may not be valid. Our power to communicate so much by so few words inevitably entails the danger of miscommunication.

Deborah Tannen, *"That's Not What I Meant": How Conversational Style Makes or Breaks Your Relationships with Others*

language are usually admirable goals, there *are* occasions when deliberate vagueness is the best approach.[5] Vague speech can achieve two useful goals.

To Promote Harmony   A group of workers who have been feuding over everything from next year's budget to funding the office coffee supply can at least reach consensus on abstractions like "the need to work well together" or "finding solutions we all can live with." While vague statements such as these might seem meaningless in light of everyday conflicts, they do provide a point upon which everyone can agree—a small but important start toward more cooperation.

To Soften the Blow of Difficult Messages   Business communicators face the constant challenge of delivering difficult messages: "This work isn't good enough." "You let me down." "We don't want to do business with you anymore." While statements like these may be honest, they can also be brutal. Ambiguous language provides a way to deliver difficult messages that softens their blow and makes it possible to work smoothly with the recipients in the future. For example,

BRUTE HONESTY	STRATEGIC AMBIGUITY
"This work isn't good enough."	"I think the boss will want us to back up these predictions with some figures."
"You're so disorganized that it's impossible to tell what you're driving at."	"I'm having a hard time understanding that last idea. Can you run it by me again?"
"I don't want to work with you."	"Right now I don't see any projects on the horizon. But if that changes, I'll let you know."

As these examples show, the challenge is to find a way to be ambiguous without being dishonest or misunderstood.

EMOTION

Language has the power to stir intense emotions. It can motivate, inspire, and amuse audiences. Unfortunately, it can also generate negative feelings: antagonism, defensiveness, and prejudice. You can prevent these negative outcomes by following two guidelines.

Avoid Biased Language Emotional problems arise when speakers intentionally or unintentionally use biased language. To understand the nature of biased language, we need to define two terms: denotation and connotation. The *denotative* meaning of a word is the literal definition devoid of any interpretation. The *connotative* meaning refers to the emotional associations that can accompany a term. Some words have little or no connotative dimension: *a, of, the, ignition, look,* and *liquid,* for example. Other words have associations far beyond their dictionary definition. You can see this for yourself by considering the following words: *cancer, sex, love, Internal Revenue Service.* One scholar recommends a quick test to discover whether a word has a connotative dimension.[6] Ask yourself where the term would fall on a good-bad scale. If an answer occurs to you, the word has connotative meaning; if not, it is probably purely denotative.

Problems arise when speakers use terms that seem to be objective but actually conceal an emotional bias. Consider, for example, the range of words you could use to refer to a twenty-five-year-old man who disagrees with your proposal: *gentleman, fellow, guy, young man, kid,* or *person.* All of these are denotatively accurate, yet each one paints a different picture in the listener's mind.

When faced with connotatively biased language, it's wise to recognize that the speaker is editorializing. Tactfully suggest another term with the opposite connotation:

"I wonder whether the idea is a gamble or a reasonable risk."

"I can understand how Bill may seem long-winded to you, but I'm sure he believes he's being thorough."

"Before judging Susan's behavior, I need to decide whether she's wishy-washy, as you suggest, or if she's just being open-minded."

Beware of Trigger Words Some terms have such strong emotional associations that they act almost like a trigger, setting off an intense emotional reaction in certain listeners. Trigger words can refer to specific people (your boss, the president), groups or categories of individuals (union stewards, the personnel department, customers with complaints), issues (right-to-work laws, affirmative action, flexible scheduling), or other topics (sexual harassment, Japanese imports, company travel regulations).

A term that seems innocuous to you can trigger an avalanche of emotions in someone else. Such words usually bring up intense feelings—either good or bad—that transport a listener out of the present into a mental or verbal tirade related to past experiences.

What is the best way to deal with trigger words? The first thing to realize is that, like others, you almost certainly have your own trigger words. You therefore ought to begin by recognizing them, so that when one comes up you'll at least be aware of your sensitivity and thus avoid overreacting. If, for example, you are very sensitive about your tendency to make careless errors when calculating even the simplest mathematical problems, you probably ought to think twice before getting defensive over a colleague's remark such as "Let's double-check those figures, just to be safe." It could be an innocent remark.

What about coping with the trigger words of others? If you are aware of the semantic triggers that set off other people, you can sometimes avoid using those terms. It's just as easy to refer to adult females as "women" as to call them "girls" since the latter is so offensive to many people.

Sometimes, however, you will discover too late that an apparently innocent term is a trigger word. The best reaction when faced with such an emotional response is to let the other person get the strong feelings out of his or her system. At that point, you can choose a more agreeable term and proceed with the discussion.

POWER

Few words are more interesting to most businesspeople than "power." The ability to influence others is one of the most important attributes a communicator can possess. Research has revealed that certain language patterns add to or subtract from a speaker's ability to shape others' thoughts and behaviors.[7] There is no question which of the following statements exhibits "powerful" language and which is "powerless":

"I'm sorry to interrupt. I hate to say this, but I, uh . . . I'm not sure we can have the shipment ready by April second. That schedule is a little tight for our staff. We could have it done by the sixteenth, okay?"

"We can't have the shipment ready by April second. That schedule is just too tight for our staff. We can have it ready for you by the sixteenth."

As the first statement illustrates, several features characterize powerless language:

Hedges	"I'm a *little* worried about . . . " "*Maybe* we should . . . " "I *guess* the best plan is . . . "
Hesitations	"The, *uh,* important point is . . . " "*Er,* couldn't we, *um* . . . "

Overly polite forms	*"I'm very sorry* to interrupt, but . . ." "Yes, *sir, . . .* "
Tag questions	"That price is awfully high, *isn't it?"* "Let's try to settle this problem now, *all right?"*
Disclaimers	*"This is probably a crazy idea,* but . . . " *"You may not like what I have to say . . . "*

These features suggest that powerful language is relatively brief and straight-forward, whereas less powerful speech is full of terms that suggest uncertainty. Many of these powerless features are simply bad habits. Others reflect a lack of self-confidence. Whatever the reason, they seem to say, "I'm not sure of myself. Don't take what I'm saying too seriously."

The consequences of using powerless speech can be serious.[8] Speakers who sound uncertain or hesitant lose credibility in the eyes of others. If your speech is full of hedges and disclaimers when you respond to your boss's questions, your answers will not have the ring of authority. Besides making you sound less credible, powerless speech can lower your attractiveness. Hesitations and stam-mering during a job interview, for example, can obscure the content of good answers. Finally, powerless speech is less persuasive than more fluent, confident speech. The product you are selling might be just what the customers need, but if you do not appear to believe in it or in yourself, your customers will probably have doubts about it.

Although more powerful language is often desirable, it isn't always the best type of speech. In some cases, an atmosphere of equality and trust is more important than power. For example, a sales representative might want to encour-age a friendly, informal relationship with a potential client. Likewise, a manager might want to encourage the freewheeling ideas of subordinates. In cases like these, it may be best to use less powerful language.

Despite its influence, language isn't the only way to assert power. Clothing, posture, gesture, distance, and many other nonverbal factors also affect the influence we exert over others. In the remainder of this chapter, we will examine such nonverbal communication.

NONVERBAL COMMUNICATION

Words are not the only way we communicate. You can appreciate this fact by imagining the following scenes:

Your boss has told the staff that he welcomes any suggestions about how to improve the organization. You take him at his word and schedule an appointment to discuss some ideas you have had. As you begin to outline your proposed changes, he focuses his gaze directly on you, folds his arms across his chest, clenches his jaw muscles, and begins to frown. At the end of your remarks, he rises abruptly from his chair, says "Thank you for your ideas" in a monotone, and gives you a curt handshake.

You are on a committee interviewing applicants for the job of customer relations representative. You notice one résumé that seems far superior to the others: the candidate received almost perfect grades at a top-flight university, had a similar position with a leading company in a distant city, and came with enthusiastic letters of recommendation. During the interview, you notice that she rarely looks you in the eye.

Despite the expense, you have decided to have a highly regarded CPA handle your tax matters. While waiting for the accountant to appear, you scan the impressive display of diplomas from prestigious universities and professional associations. The accountant enters and, as the conversation proceeds, he yawns repeatedly.

Most people would find these situations odd and disturbing. This reaction would have nothing to do with the verbal behavior of the boss, applicant, or accountant. In each case, though, the person's nonverbal behavior sends messages above and beyond the words being spoken: the boss doesn't really seem to want to hear your suggestions; you wonder whether the job applicant would in fact be good at dealing with customers, despite her credentials, or possibly even whether those credentials are genuine; and despite the CPA's reputation and credentials, you wonder whether he is interested enough in your case to give you the time and attention you want. Nonverbal communication plays an important role in all types of business and professional interaction.

What is nonverbal communication? If *non-* means "not" and *verbal* means "words," then it seems logical that nonverbal communication means communication that does not use words. Actually, this definition is not totally correct. As you will soon learn, every spoken message has a vocal element coming not from *what* we say, but from *how* we say it. For our purposes, we will include this vocal dimension along with messages sent by the body and the environment. Our working definition of nonverbal communication, then, is those messages expressed by other than linguistic means.

Common sense might suggest that most of the messages we send and receive are verbal. Communication researchers, however, have found that nonverbal messages have great impact. Over a quarter century of research suggests that approximately 35 percent of social meaning comes from verbal statements, while the remaining 65 percent comes from nonverbal behavior.[9] Furthermore, when nonverbal behavior seems to contradict a verbal message, the spoken words carry less weight than the nonverbal cues.[10] While the claim that nonverbal cues carry almost twice the weight of speech might seem preposterous, consider as an example how facial, bodily, and vocal behavior could shape the meaning of a statement like "Thanks a lot for your ideas. I'll think about them." The same words could convey sincere appreciation, indifference and dismissal, or sarcasm and anger. This example (and you can think of many others) shows the critical role that nonverbal communication plays in conveying meaning.

CHARACTERISTICS OF NONVERBAL COMMUNICATION

Now that we have defined nonverbal communication and discussed its importance, we need to take a look at some of its characteristics. Nonverbal communication resembles verbal communication in some ways and is quite different in others.

Nonverbal Behavior Always Has Communicative Value You may not always *intend* to send nonverbal messages, but everything about your appearance, every movement, every facial expression, every nuance of your voice has the potential to convey meaning.[11] You can demonstrate this fact by imagining that your boss has called you on the carpet, claiming that you haven't been working hard enough. How could you not send a nonverbal message? Nodding gravely would be a response; so would blushing, avoiding or making direct eye contact, or shaking your head affirmatively or negatively. For that matter, so would rolling yourself into a ball or leaving the room. While you can shut off your linguistic channels of communication by refusing to speak or write, it is impossible to avoid behaving nonverbally.

One writer learned this fact from movie producer Sam Goldwyn while presenting his proposal for a new film. "Mr. Goldwyn," the writer implored, "I'm telling you a sensational story. I'm only asking for your opinion, and you fall asleep." Goldwyn's reply: "Isn't sleeping an opinion?"

Nonverbal Behavior Is Ambiguous Some books claim that "body language" is the key that makes it possible to read a person like a book. While an awareness of nonverbal behavior can certainly boost your understanding of others, it will never transform you into a mind reader.

Nonverbal messages may be constantly available, but they are not always easy to understand. Compared to verbal language, nonverbal behavior is highly ambiguous. Does a customer's yawn signal boredom or fatigue? Are your co-workers laughing with or at you? Is a subordinate trembling with nervousness or cold? Most nonverbal behaviors have a multitude of possible meanings, and it is a serious mistake to assume that you can decide which is true in any given case.

Nonverbal Communication Primarily Expresses Attitudes While it is relatively easy to infer general interest, liking, disagreement, amusement, and so on from another's actions, messages about ideas or concepts don't lend themselves to nonverbal channels. How, for instance, would you express the following messages nonverbally?

"Sales are running 16 percent above last year's."

"I need more change at checkstand 2."

"Management decided to cancel the sales meeting after all."

"Let's meet at two to plan the agenda for tomorrow's meeting."

It's apparent that such thoughts are best expressed in speech and writing. It's also apparent, though, that nonverbal behavior will imply how the speaker *feels* about these statements: whether the speaker is pleased that sales are up or worried that they're not as high as expected, how urgently the cashier at checkstand 2 needs change, and so on.

Much Nonverbal Behavior Is Culture-Bound   Certain types of nonverbal behavior seem to be universal. For example, there is strong agreement among members of most literate cultures about which facial expressions represent happiness, fear, surprise, sadness, anger, and disgust or contempt.[12] Many nonverbal expressions do vary from culture to culture, however. For instance, an American's "okay" hand sign has a different and obscene meaning in some other

---

Head shakes are particularly difficult to interpret. People in the United States shake their heads up and down to signify "yes." Many British, however, make the same motions just to indicate that they hear—not necessarily that they agree. To say "no," people shake their heads from side to side in the United States, jerk their heads back in a haughty manner in the Middle East, wave a hand in front of the face in the Orient, and shake a finger from side to side in Ethiopia. . . .

The pointing of a finger is a dangerous action. In North America it is a very normal gesture, but it is considered very rude in many other parts of the world—especially in areas of Asia and Africa. It is therefore much safer to merely close the hand and point with the thumb.

Other forms of communication have also caused problems. The tone of the voice, for example, can be important. Some cultures permit people to raise their voices when they are not close to others, but loudness in other cultures is often associated with anger or a loss of self-control. . . .

A lack of knowledge of such differences in verbal and nonverbal forms of communication has resulted in many a social and corporate blunder. Local people tend to be willing to overlook most of the mistakes of tourists; after all, they are just temporary visitors. Locals are much less tolerant of the errors of business people—especially those who represent firms trying to project an impression of permanent interest in the local economy. The consequences of erring, therefore, are much greater for the corporation.

David A. Ricks, *Big Business Blunders*

---

cultures. The nod that means yes in some cultures means no in others, while in still other cultures it means only that the other person understood the question.

In this age of international communication in business, it is especially important to understand that there are cultural differences in the meaning assigned to nonverbal behaviors. Consider the different rules about what distance is appropriate between speakers. One study revealed that the "proper" space between two speakers varied considerably from one culture to another. To Japanese, a comfortable space was 40.2 inches; to Americans, 35.4 inches; and to Venezuelans, 32.2 inches.[13] It's easy to see how this could lead to problems for a native of the United States doing business overseas. To a Latin American, the North American would seem too withdrawn, whereas a Japanese might see the same businessperson as too aggressive.

TYPES OF NONVERBAL COMMUNICATION

We have already mentioned several types of nonverbal messages. We will now discuss each in more detail.

Voice   Your own experience shows that the voice communicates in ways that have nothing to do with the words a speaker utters. You may recall, for instance, overhearing two people arguing in an adjoining room or apartment; even though you couldn't make out their words, their emotions and the fact that they were arguing were apparent from the sound of their voices. Similarly, you have probably overheard people talking in a language you didn't understand; yet the speakers' feelings—excitement, delight, exhaustion, boredom, grief—were conveyed by their voices.

Social scientists use the term *paralanguage* to describe a wide range of vocal characteristics, each of which helps express an attitude.

pitch (high–low)	resonance (resonant–thin)
range (spread–narrow)	tempo (rapid–slow)
articulation (forceful–relaxed)	dysfluencies (*um, er,* etc.)
rhythm (smooth–jerky)	pauses (frequency and duration)

The paralinguistic content of a message can reflect a speaker's feelings. For instance, a subordinate who begins to stammer as he says "Everything is going fine here" might sound nervous or doubtful to his manager—as if everything were *not* fine and the subordinate were afraid that would be discovered. A statement such as "I can't make the meeting Friday morning" may be heard as "I'm very sorry" or "I couldn't care less about the meeting" or even "Everything's getting out of control"—depending on how the speaker says it.

While paralanguage reflects feelings and attitudes, the *emphasis* a speaker puts on certain words can also change the meaning of a statement radically. Notice the differences in this one statement:

"*I* need this job done right now." (Others might not.)

"I *need* this job done right now." (It's important!)

"I need *this* job done right now." (Forget the other jobs.)

"I need this job done *right now.*" (Immediately!)

While a person's tone of voice, speed in talking, and so on are often significant, they are also ambiguous. A subordinate who is speaking very fast may be nervous, although possibly more so about making a presentation to a superior than about the content of the message. A manager who "sounds hostile" when he says "Thank you for your ideas" may not want to hear your ideas, but he may also be distracted and more concerned about another problem, or he may be unaware that his normal manner gives people the impression of hostility.

Appearance   Although we have been warned since childhood not to judge a book by its cover, appearance plays a tremendous role in determining how a communicator's messages will be received in business and elsewhere. As a rule, people who *look* attractive are considered to be likable and persuasive, and they generally have successful careers.[14] For example, research suggests that beginning salaries increase about $2,000 for every 1-point increase on a 5-point attractive-

---

While no dress code fits all business settings, conservative clothing is the safest approach. The attire described below will wear well in a wide range of situations and will rarely be inappropriate. Once you are familiar with a particular setting you can vary your wardrobe without risk of clashing with local fashion norms.

WOMEN

- Tailored clothing only. No frills, ruffles, straps, or plunging necklines. People won't take you seriously if you affect a "feminine" style.
- Suits and blazers in plain, neutral colors or understated plaids.
- Dresses in dark colors, worn with or without blazers.
- Scarves for color accents.
- Skirts that are pleated, straight, or dirndl, with no extreme slits.
- Basic dark pumps with medium or low heels.
- Stud earrings, gold or pearl necklaces. Avoid dangling bracelets.

MEN

- Dark or gray suits, solid, pinstripe, or shadow plaid. Navy blazer and gray trousers.
- Dress shirts in solid colors, mostly white, pale blue, or yellow.
- Variety of ties in muted colors but in contrast to the suit. Solids, stripes, or small patterns.
- Calf-length hose in dark colors to match suits.
- Black or brown one-inch belt.
- Tassel loafers, wingtips, or lace-up shoes.
- Avoid flashy cuff links, rings, or neck chains.

Business Week's Guide to Careers

The size of the office is only the beginning of a system that is as intricate as ranks in the German army. High-level employees qualify for Venetian blinds and drapes; lower-level employees have to adjust the light with shades. A water carafe and cups are assigned to employees of a certain rank and above. Employees of certain lower rankings have desks of plastic and steel, while those of higher station have desks of oak or walnut. The number of chairs in one's office is a clear sign of grade, just like the number of windows. Some of the steerage-class employees are apparently not expected to have visitors at all, because the only chair they are entitled to is the one behind their desks.

George Lee Walker, *The Chronicles of Doodah*

---

ness scale, and that more attractive men (but not more attractive women) are given higher starting salaries than their less handsome counterparts.

A number of factors contribute to how attractive a person seems. For instance, potential employers, customers, and co-workers are usually impressed by people who are trim, muscular, and in "good shape." One study, in fact, shows that people who are overweight have more trouble getting job offers.[15] Some aspects of physical appearance cannot be changed very easily. One very significant factor in appearance, though—and one over which you may have the most control—is clothing.

A nurse's white uniform or a doctor's white coat stands for these individuals' particular professions. Clothing provides a variety of clues about the wearer's occupation, socioeconomic status, attitudes, and so on. As such, clothing often plays an important role in determining such issues as whether a job applicant is hired, a sales representative makes a sale, or an employee is promoted.

Clothing is so important to business and professional success that many "wardrobe engineers" make their livings advising clients and writing books about how to "dress for success." Most of these consultants agree that the most appropriate attire for both men and women in their first job interviews and first jobs are suits—for women, a skirted suit. One consultant, Lois Fenton, recommends five basic suits for the "core wardrobe."[16] Navy blue is the first color choice, but conservative colors such as gray and tan and conservative styles are also appropriate in most offices. This advice might seem too restrictive, but research confirms the fact that dressing conservatively, especially for women, is the smartest approach. One recent study showed that favorable hiring decisions increased with the masculinity of the clothing that female job applicants wore.[17] The most negative ratings were given to a woman who was dressed in a light beige dress in a soft fabric, with a small round collar, gathered skirt, and long sleeves. The same woman received higher ratings when she wore a tailored navy-blue skirted suit and a white blouse with an angular collar.

Dressing carefully can be just as important for men as for women. George Ball, chief executive officer of Prudential-Bache Securities, describes how the clothing of another company's representatives affected an important decision:

When we met with them, two or three of their senior executives were dressed in suits with large patterns; they had almost a garish appearance. The decision was made not to finance their company. It was in part their general appearance that resulted in the "no go" decision.[18]

Stories like this confirm the saying "The right suit can't guarantee they'll see it your way, but the wrong suit could mean not seeing you at all."

The latest style and appropriate business attire are often not the same thing. Former San Francisco mayor Dianne Feinstein has this advice:

> Use your appearance to create an image of strength. That means, in essence, don't dress for the fad. A man working in a corporate world, a legal world, a political world, generally has the sense of strength that's given by the pin-striped suit, the necktie, the haircut. It is all an image that has a united appearance to it. I believe a woman must do that as well.
>
> What you wear has an impact on how people see you. If you're a faddist, very often your ideas can be regarded as part of a fad. . . . What you care about is the image of professionalism and strength that you project to the people you work with. If you go to work [dressed frivolously], your ability to develop an image that is strong and serious is hurt.[19]

Appropriate attire varies according to your profession, your company, even your rank. The conservatively cut pin-striped suit that is correct for a banker or a Wall Street broker would not be appropriate for a high-fashion business such as advertising or in many computer companies, where even highly paid engineers and executives traditionally wear blue jeans. Although the navy-blue suit is almost universally appropriate for your first job interviews, the best way to choose your working wardrobe is to observe the successful people and the people of your own rank in the field or company you are considering. Patricia McKee, an assistant manager at a Washington, D.C., brokerage, says, for example, "In the 23-to-27 age group, all the women here wear suits. The longer you work for the firm, the easier it gets to wear clothing that shows your personality . . . but the younger women who wear suits still get further ahead."[20]

The Face and Eyes   On an obvious level, a person's face communicates emotions clearly: a subordinate's confused expression indicates the need to continue with an explanation, a customer's smile and nodding signal the time to close a sale, and a colleague's frown indicates that your request for help has come at a bad time. Facial expressions, like other nonverbal signals, are ambiguous (a co-worker's frown could come from a headache rather than the timing of your request). Nonetheless, researchers have found that accurate judgments of facial expressions can be made.[21]

The eyes themselves communicate a great deal. A skilled nonverbal communicator, for example, can control an interaction by knowing when and where to look to produce the desired results. Since visual contact is an invitation to speak, a speaker who does not want to be interrupted can avoid looking directly at people until it is time to field questions or get reactions.

Eye contact may be the best indicator of how involved a person is in a situation. The advice to "always look people straight in the eye" has been partially contradicted by research: in most two-person conversations, most people seem to look at their partners somewhere between 50 and 60 percent of the time, often alternating short gazes with glances away. Still, a person who makes little or no eye contact seems to have little involvement in the situation. A job applicant who never looks at the interviewer seems to be purposely remaining detached or nervous or to be falsifying his or her credentials. A manager who doesn't make eye contact when she says "I want you to work over in Parts for a few days" may, among other things, give a salesclerk the impression that she doesn't care what *his* feelings are about being moved.

Eye contact, too, can be deceptive; some people *can* lie while looking you "right in the eye." And even barely perceptible changes in eye contact can send messages that may or may not be accurate. The following story illustrates how eye contact can be misleading—with serious repercussions.

> Discussing his corporation's financial future in front of television cameras, the chief executive officer of a *Fortune* 500 company lowered his eyes just as he began to mention projected earnings. His downcast eyes gave the impression—on television—that the executive wasn't on the level. Wall Street observers discounted the CEO's optimistic forecast, and the company's stock price dropped four points over the next few trading days. It took two years to build it up again—even though the projection had proved to be accurate.[22]

The Body   A person's body communicates messages in several ways. The first is through posture. The way you sit at your desk when you're working can express something about your attitude toward your job or how hard you're working to anyone who cares to look. A less obvious set of bodily clues comes from the small gestures and mannerisms that every communicator exhibits at one time or another. While most people pay reasonably close attention to their facial expression, they are less aware of hand, leg, and foot motions. Thus, fidgeting hands might betray nervousness, a tapping toe impatience, and clenched fists or white knuckles restrained anger.

A study on privacy in the workplace by GF Business Equipment Company describes ways in which such gestures can be used to discourage visits from co-workers. In addition to avoiding eye contact with your visitor, the company suggests that you

> shuffle papers or make notes to indicate a desire to return to work . . . keep pen or pencil poised—that communicates an aversion to engage in conversation . . . and if interrupted when dialing a call, don't hang up the receiver.[23]

Body movement and gestures can be used deliberately or inadvertently. Psychologist Albert Mehrabian suggests that our desire to be close to people we like or to avoid people we don't like often shows up in our body movements. It may be difficult to avoid a co-worker who annoys you, and because of social conventions or the rule of the job, you may not be able to spend as much time as you would like with another co-worker or a superior. But, according to Mehrabian, approach and avoidance behaviors may still be expressed in abbreviated forms. A supervisor who approves of a subordinate's remarks, for instance, may move slightly closer when they stand in the hall to talk; if they're seated, the supervisor may lean forward. Conversely, if an outside contractor whom she doesn't want to see intrudes without an appointment, the supervisor may pull back—stepping slightly away or leaning back in her chair.

Good communicators will recognize this tendency and tailor their behavior accordingly. They will notice a forward-leaning position as an indication that their remarks are being well received and will capitalize upon the point that led to this reaction. When a remark results in a pulling back, a smart communicator will uncover the damage and try to remedy it. Awareness of such subtle messages can make the difference between success and failure in a variety of business settings: interviews, presentations, group meetings, and one-to-one interactions.

Body relaxation or tension is a strong indicator of who has the power in one-to-one relationships. As a rule, the more relaxed person in a given situation has the greater status.[24] This is most obvious in job interviews and high-stake situations in which subordinates meet with their superiors—requesting a raise or describing a problem, for example. The person in control can afford to relax, while the supplicant must be watchful and on guard.

While excessive tension does little good for either the sender or receiver, total relaxation can be inappropriate for a subordinate. A job candidate who matched the interviewer's casual sprawl would probably create a poor impression. In superior-subordinate interactions, the best posture for the one-down person is probably one that is slightly more rigid than the powerholder's. Table 3-2 lists other nonverbal indicators of power and privilege.

Personal Space and Distance   The distance we put between ourselves and others also reflects feelings and attitudes, and it affects communication. Anthropologist Edward Hall has identified four distance zones used by middle-class Americans: intimate (ranging from physical contact to about 18 inches), casual-personal (18 inches to 4 feet), social-consultative (4 to 12 feet), and public (12 feet and outward).[25]

In some cases the distance zones don't apply at all—or at least the distances aren't flexible enough to reflect the attitudes of the parties. Dentists and barbers, for instance, work within intimate distance—actual physical contact; yet the relationship between dentist and patient or barber and client may be rather impersonal.

In other cases, though, the distance that people put between themselves and others is significant. For example, distance can reflect the attitude of the person who does the choosing. Research shows that a person who expects an unpleasant message or views the speaker as unfriendly takes a more distant position than does someone expecting good news or viewing the speaker as friendly.[26] An observant communicator can thus use the distance others choose with respect to him or her as a basis for hunches about their feelings. ("I get the feeling you're worried about something, Harry. Is there anything wrong?")

TABLE 3-2   Gestures of Power and Privilege (Examples of Nonverbal Behaviors)

	BETWEEN STATUS EQUALS		BETWEEN STATUS NONEQUALS		BETWEEN MEN AND WOMEN	
	Intimate	*Non-intimate*	*Used by Superior*	*Used by Subordinate*	*Used by Men*	*Used by Women*
1. Address	Familiar	Polite	Familiar	Polite	Familiar?*	Polite?*
2. Demeanor	Informal	Circumspect	Informal	Circumspect	Informal	Circumspect
3. Posture	Relaxed	Tense (less relaxed)	Relaxed	Tense	Relaxed	Tense
4. Personal space	Closeness	Distance	Closeness (option)	Distance	Closeness	Distance
5. Time	Long	Short	Long (option)	Short	Long?*	Short?*
6. Touching	Touch	Don't touch	Touch (option)	Don't touch	Touch	Don't touch
7. Eye contact	Establish	Avoid	Stare, ignore	Avert eyes, watch	Stare, ignore	Avert eyes, watch
8. Facial expression	Smile?*	Don't smile?*	Don't smile	Smile	Don't smile	Smile
9. Emotional expression	Show	Hide	Hide	Show	Hide	Show
10. Self-disclosure	Disclose	Don't disclose	Don't disclose	Disclose	Don't disclose	Disclose

* Behavior not known.

From Nancy M. Henley, *Body Politics* (Englewood Cliffs, N.J.: Prentice-Hall, 1977), p. 181. Copyright © 1977 by Simon & Schuster, Inc. Reprinted by permission of Simon & Schuster, Inc.

Besides reflecting attitudes, distance also creates feelings. In one study, subjects rated people who communicated at a greater distance as less friendly and understanding than those who positioned themselves closer.[27] (Closeness has its limits, of course. Intimate distance is rarely appropriate for business dealings.) Thus, an effective communicator will usually choose to operate at a casual-personal distance when a friendly atmosphere is the goal.

Interpersonal distance is another nonverbal indicator of power. One unspoken cultural rule is that the person with higher status generally controls the degree of approach. As Mehrabian puts it, "It is easy enough to picture an older person in this culture encouraging a younger business partner by patting him or her on the back; but it is very difficult to visualize this situation reversed; that is, with the younger person patting the older and more senior partner."[28] This principle of distance explains why subordinates rarely question the boss's right to drop in to their work area without invitation, while they are reluctant to approach their superior's office even when told "the door is always open."

When a subordinate does wind up in the office of a superior, both tension and distance show who is in charge. The less powerful person usually stands until invited to take a seat and, when given the choice, will be reluctant to sit close to the boss. Wise managers often try to minimize the inhibiting factor of this status gap by including a table or comfortable easy chairs in their offices so that they can meet with subordinates on a more equal level.

Some managers try to promote informal communication by visiting employees in the employees' own offices. David Ogilvy, head of one of the largest advertising agencies in the country, says, "Do not summon people to your office—it frightens them. Instead, go to see them in *their* offices."[29]

Time The way we use time provides a number of silent messages.[30] Leonard Berlin, senior financial analyst at Exxon, attributes his reputation as a hard worker to the fact that he routinely arrives at work half an hour early. "That's a big thing to my boss," he says. "It doesn't matter that I leave at the regular time; getting here early shows an interest. I think that if I stayed to seven every night it would make less impression."[31]

Many business advisors recommend that you be particularly scrupulous about your use of time during the first few months you are on the job:

> If . . . in that first ninety days, you're late or absent frequently, or seen as a clock watcher, you may earn yourself . . . negative scrutiny for a long time thereafter by your superiors. Rather than excusing any "infractions" of the rules, they'll be looking for slip-ups and a reason potentially to discharge you.[32]

The amount of time we spend on a task or with a problem is also a good indication of how much importance we give it. The manager who never has time to talk over a problem with an employee or who postpones performance reviews because he or she "doesn't have time" is saying something about his or her regard for subordinates—as is the manager who takes time to converse casually with employees every few weeks. The person who cuts one meeting short to attend another is making a statement about the relative importance of the two meetings.

Rules and customs about time vary widely from one culture to another. Whereas most North Americans and northern Europeans value punctuality, other cultures are much more casual about appointments and deadlines. Chris Pagliaro, an American football coach, learned this lesson the hard way when he spent a season leading Milan's team in the Italian league. His realization that time is treated differently began to dawn on him when he arrived for the first practice session, scheduled for 8:30 P.M.

> We got out there at 8:30 P.M. I'm dressed, I've got my whistle, my (American) assistant coach is there, the two American players are there.
>
> And there's no Italians. It's ten 'til nine and I don't see anybody: [not] the owner, nobody. Around 9 o'clock, a couple of them start trickling in.
>
> I had made a practice schedule—typical American coach: At 8:30 we do this, at 8:35 this, at 8:50 this. You might as well throw that one out the window. We got started around 9:20 or 9:30.[33]

The coach was smart and flexible enough to realize that he couldn't fight against a lifetime of cultural conditioning. He developed a compromise between the American need for punctuality and the casual Italian attitude about time:

By Friday, I knew it was useless. So what I did, I made a schedule and waited around. While the team ran laps, we set our watches back to 8:30. That's the only way I could do it. So we were always starting at 8:30, regardless of what time it was.

Physical Environment   So far we have discussed how personal behavior sends nonverbal messages. The physical environment in which we operate also suggests how we feel and shapes how we communicate.

Consider the way space is allocated in an organization. Power locations become apparent when we look at the amount and location of existing space given to various employees and groups. In many organizations, for instance, an employee's status may be measured by whether his or her office is next to the boss's or is in a dark corner. An office with a window or an office on the corner often indicates higher status than an inside office with no window. Sometimes lower-ranking employees who do the same job, such as processing orders, are all located in a single large room, while the supervisors have private offices.

In addition to reflecting status and power, the physical layout of an organization also shapes the ways its members interact with one another. For example, the temperature and humidity of a room can have profound effects on the success of communication. One study revealed that as temperatures and humidity increase, impressions of a speaker's attractiveness decline.[34] Understanding this fact can help you avoid scheduling presentations or meetings in hot, stuffy rooms, where the results may be doomed before a word is spoken.

Another way in which environments shape communication is proximity. The distance that separates people is perhaps the most important factor in shaping who talks with whom. Other things being equal, officemates will talk with one another more than with the people next door, and workers in the same area deal with one another more than with similarly employed people in another area. Researcher Thomas J. Allen studied workers in research facilities, medical laboratories, and business schools. He found that the frequency with which a person spoke to colleagues was a direct function of the distance between their desks.[35] In addition to the simple distance separating people, the difficulty of navigating that distance can also reduce interaction.[36] Corners that must be turned, doors that have to be wrestled open, and counters that block access keep people apart. One manager described the obstacle course that separated him from his boss's office:

I go from my office past the receptionist and down the hall to the other end of the building. I take the elevator to twelve, get off, and take another one to twenty-one. I get off and walk to the other end of the building, and pass through three doors, and I'm at his office—about a hundred feet straight above where I started![37]

Furniture arrangement also plays a big role in the way people communicate. For example, in one study of a medical office, only 10 percent of the patients were "at ease" when conversing with a doctor seated behind a desk, while the figure rose to 55 percent when the desk was removed.[38]

This sort of information can be useful on the job. You may be able to relocate your work to an area that will give you the interaction you want. Beyond this, realize that several places in your working environment will probably allow you to interact informally with desirable communication partners. Employee lounges, elevators, and dining areas are a few examples. Even rest rooms can be handy places to establish contact, though you will probably want to continue your business in a more congenial spot. If you are interested in making your bosses more aware of your work, it's important to be visible to them. On the other hand, if you would just as soon be left alone, the old axiom "Out of sight, out of mind" applies here.

If you are a manager, think about arranging your subordinates' working areas to increase communication between people you want to interact and to separate those who don't need to talk to one another. You can encourage communication between groups of workers by arranging gathering spots where congregation is easy. A good setting for informal contact needs to meet three criteria.[39] First, it ought to be centrally located so that people have to pass through it on their way to other places. Second, it should contain places to sit or rest, to be comfortable. Finally, it must be large enough so that the people gathered there won't interfere with others passing through or working nearby. Of course, if you want to discourage contact at a central spot (the copying machine, for example), simply change one or more of these conditions.

When it comes to managing interaction between members of an organization and its public, you can create the most desirable degree of accessibility by use of space and barriers. Proximity and visibility encourage contact, while distance and closure discourage it.

SUMMARY

Whatever the goal and whatever the context, business and professional communication involves both verbal and nonverbal messages. Verbal messages are most clear when they contain unequivocal and nonabstract language and a minimum of unfamiliar jargon. While clarity is usually the goal, ambiguous messages are sometimes useful ways of promoting harmony, facilitating change, and softening the blow of difficult messages.

Language can sometimes communicate and generate undesirable emotions. Biased terms seem to be objective but actually convey the speaker's attitudes. Trigger words arouse strong emotional reactions in a listener. Effective communicators avoid unintentionally biased language and trigger words. Effective speakers also understand how to communicate power by their speech when they seek to boost their influence. They do so by minimizing the use of powerless language such as hedges, hesitations, overly polite terms, tag questions, and disclaimers.

Nonverbal communication also carries a great deal of meaning, but where words normally express ideas, nonverbal behavior conveys attitudes and emotions. Nonverbal messages are always available, since it is impossible to avoid communicating non-verbally. These messages should be interpreted with caution, however, since they are usually ambiguous and are often culture-bound.

Nonverbal messages can be expressed vocally, through appearance (physical stature and clothing), and through the face, eyes, posture, gesture, distance, and time.

The physical environment in which an organization operates also has an important effect on communication, both internal and external. The location and design of a building often makes a statement to employees and the public about the organization's philosophy and power structure. In addition, the spatial arrangement of units can make interaction between them easy or difficult, and it can also indicate their relative perceived importance. The type and arrangement of space and objects within a given area also have a strong effect on communication, affecting who talks with whom, the amount of interaction, and the quality of that interaction.

ACTIVITIES

1. Describe how each of the following sentences is likely to be misunderstood (or not understood at all). Then translate each into clearer language.

    a. "Things are going pretty well."
    b. "There are just a few small problems to clear up."
    c. "I just need a little more time to finish the job."
    d. "I think I understand what you mean."

2. Identify three specialized jargon terms used in your field of work or study. Answer the following questions concerning each term:

    a. How does each term make communication more efficient?
    b. What confusion might arise from the use of such terms with certain listeners? In cases where confusion or misunderstandings might arise, suggest alternative words or phrases that could convey the meaning more clearly.

3. Describe a former co-worker twice. In your first account, use terms with positive emotional connotations. In the second description, discuss the same person, using words with negative connotations.

4. Sharpen your awareness of emotive language by playing a game Bertrand Russell called "Conjugating Irregular Verbs." For example,

    I'm cost-conscious
    You're tightfisted
    She's cheap

    I'm candid
    You're blunt
    He shoots off his mouth

    Now conjugate each of the following:

    I'm punctual
    He's too negative
    She's a dictator
    You're being naïve

5. Become more aware of your own emotional triggers by following these instructions.

    a. In each category shown, identify two words that trigger positive reactions for you and two other words that make you react negatively.

    A person's name
    A rule or policy
    A product or procedure of your organization

b. How do you react, both internally and observably, when you hear these terms? What might be the consequences of these reactions?

c. Use the same categories to identify words that trigger positive and negative reactions in a person you work with. What are the consequences of using these emotion-laden words with that person? Which of the terms should you continue to use, and which should you replace with more neutral words?

6. Develop honest but ambiguous ways to rephrase each of the following statements. Describe whether the blunt statement or the ambiguous one would be preferable.

a. You've done a sloppy job here.

b. I can't understand what you're trying to say in this letter.

c. Nobody likes your idea.

d. Would you please hurry up and get to the point?

7. Rehearse powerful and powerless ways of delivering each of the following messages:

a. Asking for a raise in pay (or a higher grade on a class assignment)

b. Describing a way to improve the effectiveness of your work unit

c. Explaining the importance of finishing a job on time to the person responsible for doing the work

d. Requesting the help of a fellow worker on a difficult job

8. Prove to yourself that nonverbal communication is constant and impossible to stop.

a. Observe the nonverbal behavior of another person you work with. What messages do you get from your observations?

b. Describe an alternative interpretation for the nonverbal behaviors you have noticed.

c. Speculate on which of your interpretations is more accurate. Are you certain you are right? How could you find out?

9. Identify two people who are successful in their careers and two other people who have not been successful. What nonverbal behaviors distinguish the successful people from their less successful counterparts?

Communicator Profile

George Thompson, President
Verbal Judo Institute
Albuquerque, New Mexico

When people think about verbal skill, they usually focus on being clear—on using language precisely. That's important, but the psychological power of language is at least as necessary. You have to choose words that don't make people feel threatened or defensive.*

"Verbal judo" is the art of using language and nonverbal communication to achieve voluntary compliance—using the mind and the mouth instead of the baton and the gun. In the last nine years, the Verbal Judo Institute has trained over 40,000 police officers to use words instead of physical force. We have also trained corporate clients from organizations like IBM and Metropolitan Life, but frankly I prefer to work with law-enforcement people. Whether you sell another machine or insurance policy isn't a life-or-death matter. Nobody is going to get hurt if sales go down. But if a police officer doesn't get the job done right, somebody could die.

I learned about the power of verbal judo when I was a rookie police officer. My partner and I answered a domestic-dispute call. We arrived at a noisy tenement apartment at 2:00 A.M. to find a couple screaming threats at one another. Instead of ordering the husband and wife around, my partner sat down on a couch and began reading the newspaper. After about two minutes, he lowered the paper and said to the husband, "Look at this, a 1950 Dodge in prime condition! I know it's late, but I want to call on this one. Got a phone?" The couple was so astonished that they stopped fighting and brought a phone. After my partner called about the car, he asked them, "Is there something I can help you with?" The husband said, "Well,

no." The wife said, "Nah." We chatted with them and left. My partner had literally civilized two people by redirecting them into the role of host.

I realized then that a police officer's most valuable tools are the mind and mouth, not the nightstick or gun. A study at Rutgers showed that law-enforcement work is 97 percent to 98 percent *verbal* interaction. We train police officers how to use rhetorical skills to prevent the need to use physical force. Since I have a Ph.D. in English and taught college rhetoric for ten years before becoming a police officer, I decided to combine my background in language arts with law enforcement and develop a systematic way to improve verbal skills. The results show that verbal judo works. For example, the Los Angeles County Sheriff's Department monitored the citizen complaints before and after we trained their officers. They found that the complaints dropped by 40 percent in the year after our training.

When people think about verbal skill, they usually focus on being clear—on using language precisely. That's important, but the *psychological* power of language is at least as necessary. You have to choose words that don't make people feel threatened or defensive. For example, an officer who says "Come here" is asking for it. "Come here" means "You're in trouble." It's often better to say, "Excuse me, I need to chat with you for a second." There are other phrases that can trigger problems. "What's your problem?" is one. "Don't you know any better?" is another. Even ordering someone to "calm down" is a bad idea. Have you ever known anybody who calmed down just because you told him to? An officer should never argue with a citizen. As soon as you start arguing, you've given up a large amount of your power. Instead, it's better to explain the consequences of cooperating and the results of not cooperating, and then convince people that it's in their interest to comply.

Along with using the right language, a police officer needs to choose a nonverbal approach that suits the situation. There may be times when crowding up to someone and sounding gruff can bully them into cooperating, but in many situations using this approach is asking for trouble. Some people are looking for a fight, and trying to intimidate them will backfire. With people like this, it's better to sound firm but pleasant. A concerned facial expression works better than a scowl, and openhanded gestures are less threatening than a closed fist or hand on the pistol. Of course, you always have to be ready for trouble, but using the right approach can prevent problems from developing.

A skilled police officer knows when to rely on coercion and when to use words. We persuade our clients to learn a lesson from the chameleon who changes appearance to fit the environment. Good police officers can also match their communication style to the situation. If you rely only on force all the time, you're asking for trouble.

4

After reading this chapter, you should understand:

- The organizational and personal benefits of listening effectively
- The reasons for poor listening
- The guidelines for listening effectively for information, responding nondefensively to criticism, evaluating messages, and responding empathically to others' problems

You should be able to:

- Identify the settings in which listening better could lead to personal and organizational gains
- Identify the reasons why you listen ineffectively and list methods of overcoming those reasons
- Use the information in this chapter to improve your accuracy at understanding others' messages
- Respond to criticism nondefensively by using the methods introduced in this chapter
- Use the information in this chapter to become a more effective critical listener
- Evaluate the effectiveness of the responding styles you use when helping others and choose more productive alternatives when necessary

LISTENING

Silence has so many different selling applications. If you stop talking and start listening, you might actually learn something, and even if you don't you'll have a chance to collect your thoughts. Silence is what keeps you from saying more than you need to—and makes the other person want to say more than he means to.

Mark McCormack, *What They Don't Teach You at Harvard Business School*

"I told them *twice* the job had to be printed on eight by ten inch paper and not eight and a half by eleven, but they still got it wrong. Now we're going to miss the deadline."

"He said he was listening, but he'd obviously made up his mind before I started. He didn't give me a minute to talk before he started interrupting. That's the last time I'll try to present a better way to do anything as long as I'm working for *him*."

"Something went wrong down the line. I warned those people to watch the temperature carefully, but they don't listen. Now a whole batch of vegetables has spoiled. What does it take to get them to understand?"

"I told that distributor months ago that we had to have the new parts by October first. Today, he told me they were back-ordered and won't be here until January. Doesn't he understand that we do sixty percent of our business in December?"

Situations like these are disturbingly common in business. They show how frequent listening failures are and how costly they can be. You may not be able to make others listen better, but you *can* boost your own ability to listen carefully to the scores of important messages you are likely to hear every business day.

As you will learn in the following pages, listening effectively is hard work. It involves far more than sitting passively and absorbing others' words. It occurs far

---

I only wish I could find an institute that teaches people how to *listen*. After all, a good manager needs to listen at least as much as he needs to talk. Too many people fail to realize that real communication goes in both directions. . . .

You have to be able to listen well if you're going to motivate the people who work for you. Right there, that's the difference between a mediocre company and a great company. The most fulfilling thing for me as a manager is to watch someone the system has labeled as just average or mediocre really come into his own, all because someone has listened to his problems and helped him solve them.

Lee Iacocca with William Novak, *Iacocca: An Autobiography*

more frequently than speaking, reading, or writing and is just as demanding and important.

THE IMPORTANCE OF LISTENING

Business experts agree that listening is a vitally important skill. Tom Peters, business consultant and co-author of *In Search of Excellence* and *A Passion for Excellence,* is sometimes called "the guru of excellence." He emphasizes that one key to business success is careful listening: "Find out what the customers really care about, and then act. Listening—that's the key."[1] Betty Harragan, a business consultant and job counselor who has written two career-strategy books, states, "Good managers have always sought, or listened to the opinions of their staff and key subordinates."[2] Business writer Kevin Murphy sums up the opinion of most business professionals when he says, "The better you listen, the luckier you will get."[3]

Why is listening so important? One major reason is time: listening is the most frequent—and, arguably, the most important—type of on-the-job communication. Studies conducted over sixty years ago indicated that adults spent an average of 29.5 percent of their waking hours listening. This is almost a third more time than they spent talking and virtually twice as much time as they spent reading.[4] A more recent study focused on listening in business settings. Personnel at all levels—including top-, middle-, and lower-level managers as well as workers with no managerial responsibilities—were asked to note the time they spent engaged in various types of communication during a typical week.[5] The results were impressive:

listening	32.7%	writing	22.6%
speaking	25.8%	reading	18.8%

Top executives spend even more time listening than other employees. A study of chief executive officers' communication showed that they spend at least 65 percent of the working day listening to someone.[6] Another piece of research revealed that effective managers almost constantly ask questions of their subordinates; in a half-hour conversation, some ask literally hundreds.[7]

Listening on the job is not only frequent, it is important as well. When 282 members of the Academy of Certified Administrative Managers were asked to list the skills most crucial for managerial ability, "active listening" was rated number one and was placed in the "supercritical" category.[8] In another survey, 170 businesspeople were asked to describe the communication skills they considered most important and that they wished had been taught in college; in each category, listening was the number-one response.[9]

Listening is vital to organizations. It can improve quality, boost productivity, and save money. Poor listening can have the opposite effect. As one consultant says:

With more than 100 million workers in this country, a simple $10 listening mistake by each of them, as a result of poor listening, would add up to a cost of a billion dollars. And most people make numerous listening mistakes every week.

Because of listening mistakes, letters have to be retyped, appointments rescheduled, shipments rerouted. Productivity is affected and profits suffer.[10]

Listening skills can play a major role in career success. A recent study of employees in the insurance industry revealed that better listeners occupied higher levels in their company and were more upwardly mobile.[11] The ability to listen well was highly related to the ability to argue persuasively, which helps explain the success of good listeners. As Chapter 15 explains in detail, the ability to persuade others depends in great part on understanding their wants and needs, and one of the best ways to learn this information is to listen.

Listening can not only help you advance in your career, it can also help you do a better job in the positions you achieve. Supervisors who were rated as "open" communicators displayed a surprising number of behaviors that indicate good listening.[12] They were likely to ask for suggestions, listen to complaints, invite personal opinions of both their superiors and subordinates. It's easy to see how these behaviors can lead to better ratings and performance.

Listening skills are also important to individuals in the organization. They can help you learn important information such as how a contract should be drawn up, how much money or how many people are available for a particular project, how management expects to make up for a bad sales year, whether a productive employee seems dissatisfied at being passed over for a promotion. The information you gather from listening can also help you present your own ideas and needs more successfully. For example, if you know management is trying to cut costs until after the first of the year, you might decide to delay proposing an expensive program or be prepared to show how the bulk of the costs won't affect the budget until then. Listening to prospective customers can help you select the best product or system you have for their individual needs.

Listening has other advantages as well. Listening carefully to subordinates' or co-workers' suggestions lets them know that they are important to you and that you value their suggestions—whether or not you follow them. Listening to prospective customers lets them know you are interested in their needs—not just in making a sale. As one consulting team says, "Showing a real interest in what prospective customers are saying is one of the simplest ways of getting them to listen to you."[13]

REASONS FOR POOR LISTENING

Despite the importance of understanding others, the quality of listening is generally poor in most organizations. Listening expert Ralph Nichols estimates that the average white-collar worker listens at about a 25 percent efficiency level.[14] This dismal figure is supported by research showing that immediately after a ten-minute presentation, a normal listener can recall only 50 percent of the information presented. After forty-eight hours, the recall level drops to 25 percent.[15]

A number of studies have revealed reasons why people listen poorly, despite the advantages of doing just the opposite.[16] Some of the most important factors include the following:

EGOCENTRISM

One common reason for listening poorly is the belief—usually mistaken—that your own ideas are more important or valuable than those of others. Besides preventing you from learning useful new information, this egocentric attitude is likely to alienate the very people with whom you need to work. Self-centered listeners are rated lower on social attractiveness than communicators who are open to others' ideas.[17] While a certain amount of self-promotion can be helpful in career advancement, advancing your own ideas at the expense of others' can cause you to slip down a rung or two as you climb the career ladder. As an old saying puts it: "Nobody ever listened themselves out of a job."

MESSAGE OVERLOAD

It is hard to listen carefully when the phone rings every few minutes, people keep dropping in to give you quick messages, a co-worker has just handed you cost estimates on a new product line, and you're trying to organize your notes for a presentation you have to make the next day. Coping with a deluge of information is like juggling—you can only keep a few things going at one time.

PREOCCUPATION

Business and personal concerns make it difficult to keep your mind on the subject at hand. Even when your current conversation is important, other unfinished business can divert your attention: the call to an angry customer, the questions your boss asked about your schedule delays, the new supplier you heard about and want to interview, the problems you anticipate getting home in time for a dinner engagement.

RAPID THOUGHT

Listeners can process information at a rate of about 500 words per minute, while most speakers talk at around 125 words per minute. This difference leaves us with a great deal of mental spare time. While it is possible to use this time to explore the speaker's ideas, we most often let our minds wander to other matters—from the unfinished business just mentioned to romantic fantasies.

PHYSICAL DISTRACTIONS

A stuffy room, noisy machinery, the cold you feel developing, or a conversation going on nearby are only a few of the distractions that can make listening difficult. Next time you decide not to listen to a speaker, use the spare thinking time to notice all the distractions in the environment.

HEARING PROBLEMS

While most listening failures are due to environmental or psychological reasons, some people do suffer from hearing deficiencies. Once these problems are recognized, they are usually easy to treat. The biggest problems come up when a hearing loss goes undetected and employees get annoyed about the boss "ignoring" them or a superior gets angry when her instructions are bungled.

FAULTY ASSUMPTIONS

One common, though mistaken, belief is that the responsibility for successful communication rests with the sender. Management expert Peter Drucker recognized this fact when he wrote: "It is the recipient who communicates. The so-called communicator, the person who emits the communication, does not communicate. He utters. Unless there is someone who hears . . . there is only noise."[18]

As Drucker suggests, even the most thoughtful, well-expressed idea is wasted if the intended receiver fails to listen. The clearest instructions won't prevent mistakes if the employee receiving them is thinking about something else, and the best of products will never be made if the client or the manager isn't paying attention to the presentation. Both the speaker *and* the listener share the burden of reaching an understanding.

A second misconception is that listening is basically a passive activity in which the receiver is a sponge, quietly absorbing the speaker's thoughts. In fact, good listening can be hard work. Sometimes you have to speak while listening—to ask questions or paraphrase the sender's ideas, making sure you have understood them. Even when you remain silent, silence should not be mistaken for passivity. Famous attorney Louis Nizer described how he would often emerge dripping with sweat from a day in court spent mostly listening. Sperry executive Del Kennedy, commenting on his company's well-known listening training program, says, "Most people don't know how exhausting listening can be."[19]

Sometimes, effective listening requires seeking out people. Barbara Fine, once a buyer at a major New York City department store and now owner of a fashionable boutique, describes the effort—and importance—of doing so:

> It is easy as the owner of a retail business to get stuck behind a desk, relying on third parties instead of customers to tell you what is and isn't selling. However devastating it may be to your ego, there is no substitute for being out on the floor and finding out how right or wrong you are in your selection of merchandise. The fashion press might report that blouses are not selling this season because the weather is too cold, but your customers may tell you it is because the designers cut the sleeves too wide and the blouses look horrible on them. That way when they are offered in the same proportions for winter, you will have the sense not to buy them.[20]

A third faulty assumption is the listener's assumption that a message contains nothing new. In many such cases, careful attention and questioning show two things: you never fully understood the speaker, or the current message has new material. The attitude "I've heard it all before" could be replaced with "I never thought about it this way before," or "He's actually come up with a *good* idea this time," or "I've heard of the theory, but we never had market research to support it before."

A fourth misconception about listening is that talking has more apparent advantages. At first glance, it seems that speakers control things while listeners are the followers. The people who do the talking are the ones who tell the department about the company's new sales and marketing policy, who entertain the new employees with stories, or who talk a prospective client into giving the agency's creative talents a chance. The ability to speak well is certainly a vital skill, but listening is also tremendously important. Writer and management professor David J. Schwartz makes this point clearly.

> In an office recently I noticed a sign which said, "To sell John Brown what John Brown buys, you've got to see things through John Brown's eyes." And the way to get John Brown's vision is to listen to what John Brown has to say.[21]

Schwartz goes on to stress the value of listening:

> In hundreds of interviews with people at all levels I've made this discovery: The bigger the person, the more apt he is to encourage *you* to talk; the smaller the person, the more apt he is to preach to you.
>
> Big people monopolize the *listening.*
> Small people monopolize the *talking.*
>
> Note this also: Top-level leaders in all walks of life spend much more time requesting advice than they do in giving it. Before a top man makes a decision, he asks, "How do you feel about it?" "What do you recommend?" "What would you do under these circumstances?" "How does this sound to you?"[22]

LACK OF TRAINING

Listening may seem like a natural ability—like breathing. "After all," you might say, "I've been listening since I was a child." We could all say the same thing about talking; but even though almost everyone does it, this doesn't mean most people do it well.

Until recently, listening wasn't viewed as a skill worth formal instruction. In 1948, only one college in the United States—Stephens College—offered a course in listening. In 1962, a survey showed that there were over fifty thousand speech courses but still only a handful devoted to listening.[23]

Since that time, matters have improved. Major organizations such as 3M, American Telephone and Telegraph, General Electric, and Dun and Bradstreet have included listening skills in their training programs. Xerox Corporation's program for improving listening has been used by over 1.5 million employees in 71,000 companies, and Sperry Corporation invested more than $4 million to advertise its message "We know how important it is to listen." In addition, Sperry has set up listening seminars for its 87,000 employees in an effort to make its advertising campaign more than a string of empty slogans.

TYPES OF LISTENING

The first step in developing your own skills as a receiver is to realize that there are several different types of listening. Sometimes you listen for information. At other times, the challenge is to understand others' critical comments. In some circumstances, you need to evaluate others' arguments critically. Finally, from time to time, you need to listen as a way of helping others solve their problems.

The following pages will offer suggestions for each type of listening. Before reading on, you may find it useful to complete the Listening-Skill Questionnaire in Table 4-1.

LISTENING FOR INFORMATION

This is the most common type of listening in most occupations. We use informational listening to understand a wide variety of messages accurately: a caller's phone number, a supervisor's instructions, a subordinate's problems, a customer's needs. The following strategies can improve your ability to understand informational messages.

Withhold Judgment   It seems obvious that you should understand another person's ideas before judging them. Despite this fact, a common mistake is to confuse informational and evaluative listening, forgetting that your original goal was to learn, not to criticize. For example, you might ask for a customer's reaction to your company's product or service, then spend your mental energy judging the answer instead of trying to understand it. ("Doesn't this guy have anything better to do than make petty complaints?" "Yeah, sure, he'd like us to deliver on a tighter schedule, but he'd scream his head off if we billed him for the overtime.") Or you might find yourself judging the ideas of a boss, co-worker, or subordinate before he or she has finished explaining them. ("Uh-oh. I hope this doesn't mean I have to spend a week in the field, trying to get market information." "These college kids come in and want to take over right away.") Listen first. Make sure you understand. *Then* evaluate.

Be Opportunistic   Sometimes a speaker's ideas are so boring or irrelevant that it's hard to stay awake, let alone pay close attention. Still, in situations like this,

---

Be interested in the topic under discussion. Bad listeners usually declare the subject dry after the first few sentences.

We ought to say to ourselves: "What's he saying that I can use? What worthwhile ideas has he? Is he reporting any workable procedures? Anything that I can cash in, or with which I can make myself happier?"

Ralph Nichols, "Listening Is a 10-Part Skill," *Nation's Business*

TABLE 4-1 Listening-Skill Questionnaire

How well do you listen on the job? How do others rate you? You can compare your answers to these questions to the way others view you by first completing the questionnaire yourself and then by having others use the same questions to rate you. Low answers (UF, AAF) can indicate problem areas, as can answers where your response differs significantly from others' ratings.

KEY: AAT   The statement is almost always true.
UT   The statement is usually true.
UF   The statement is usually false.
AAF   The statement is almost always false.

AAT	UT	UF	AAF	1. I consider all evidence carefully before coming to a conclusion.
AAT	UT	UF	AAF	2. I am sensitive to the speaker's unstated feelings as well as to what he or she says explicitly.
AAT	UT	UF	AAF	3. I take notes when listening in order to remember information or better understand a complex idea.
AAT	UT	UF	AAF	4. I concentrate on what the speaker is saying instead of dwelling on unrelated thoughts.
AAT	UT	UF	AAF	5. I listen openly when others disagree with me. I may not accept what they say, but I'm willing to consider their opinions.
AAT	UT	UF	AAF	6. I encourage others to express their ideas instead of hogging the stage myself.
AAT	UT	UF	AAF	7. I am able to extract key ideas from others' comments, even when their remarks are disorganized.
AAT	UT	UF	AAF	8. I am curious about people and ideas. Nobody could accuse me of valuing only my own ideas.
AAT	UT	UF	AAF	9. I let others speak instead of interrupting them or changing the topic of conversation to suit my agenda.
AAT	UT	UF	AAF	10. I make other speakers feel comfortable and at ease when they are talking.
AAT	UT	UF	AAF	11. I remember important ideas others have told me, even when I'm busy.
AAT	UT	UF	AAF	12. I let others know when I'm confused about what they are saying instead of pretending that I understand when I really don't.
AAT	UT	UF	AAF	13. I recognize that people change over time, and I accept new information instead of judging others only by their past beliefs and actions.
AAT	UT	UF	AAF	14. I help others find solutions to their problems by being a good listener.
AAT	UT	UF	AAF	15. I can cut through overly emotional appeals and judge the soundness of a speaker's thoughts.
AAT	UT	UF	AAF	16. I am good at knowing when to speak and when to listen.

Adapted from Judy Brownell, "Perceptions of Listening Behavior: A Management Study," SHA Research Workshop (December 1987).

you can often find reasons to listen by asking yourself how you can use the information. One trainer described this opportunistic approach:

At a convention recently I found myself in an extremely boring seminar (on listening, ironically enough). After spending the first half-hour wishing I had never signed up, I decided to take advantage of the situation. I turned my thought, "This guy isn't teaching me how to run a seminar on listening," into a question: "What is he teaching me about how *not* to run a seminar?" While providing a negative example was not the presenter's goal, I got a useful lesson.

You can use the same technique in your life. Ask yourself the question "What's a better way of explaining this?" Your answer will often clarify your understanding. Similarly, asking yourself what you *don't* understand about a topic can help you formulate questions that will improve your knowledge. Perhaps the best question to ask in boring settings is "What does this have to do with me, anyhow?" You can probably find an answer and in doing so learn some valuable information. Your ability to think more than three times faster than a speaker talks will let you ask and answer questions like these while still attending to a speaker's words.

Look for the Main and Supporting Points   "What are you getting at?" We are often tempted to ask this of a long-winded speaker, but it's also an ideal question to consider when you're listening for information. Sometimes it is appropriate to ask—politely—for the speaker's thesis: "I'm trying to pull together what you've been telling me about the problems you've been having meeting your quotas. Could you summarize for me?" "I'd like to be sure the procedure we work out meets your needs as fully as possible. Could you tell me, briefly, which of these problems are the most damaging?" Sometimes, however, it isn't appropriate to ask for the speaker's thesis outright. When you're one of five hundred employees sitting in a darkened banquet room while senior executives try to promote corporate unity by giving short descriptions of what each of their divisions has done that year, you probably shouldn't ask, "Overall, then, would you say your division is losing its market share?" You can still do your own mental job of organizing and looking for patterns in this kind of situation.

Your ability to listen for information will also improve if you can identify the reasons behind a speaker's thesis. Why is a customer dissatisfied? How many steps are there in the new procedure, and what are they? Identifying main points such as these will help you understand and remember information.

Ask Questions and Paraphrase   By now it's clear that being a listener does not necessarily mean just keeping quiet. In fact, listeners who don't respond when they have the chance to are probably not listening closely.

Questions are one of the best ways to build understanding, and paraphrasing is another valuable tool. You can *paraphrase* by periodically describing in your own words what you understand the speaker to be saying. Paraphrasing is preceded by phrases such as "Let me make sure I understand what you're saying . . . " or "In other words, you're saying. . . . " When paraphrasing, it is important *not* to become a parrot, repeating the speaker's statements word for word. Instead, understanding comes from translating the speaker's thoughts into your own language, then playing them back to ensure their accuracy. The following conversations should illustrate the difference between effective and ineffective paraphrasing:

My first boss . . . is one of the smartest people I know. He was smart enough and comfortable enough with himself to ask really elementary (some would say dumb) questions. The rest of us were scared stiff; we assumed that since we were being paid an exorbitant fee, we shouldn't ask dumb questions. But the result was we'd lose 90 percent of the strategic value of the interview because we were afraid to display our ignorance.

Mostly, it's the "dumb," elementary questions, followed up by a dozen more elementary questions, that yield the pay dirt.

Tom Peters, *Thriving on Chaos*

Print supervisor:	I'm having trouble getting the paper to run that job. That's why I'm behind schedule.
Plant manager:	I see. You can't get the paper to run the job, so you're running behind schedule.
Print supervisor:	Yeah. That's what I said.

After this exchange, the plant manager still doesn't have a clear idea of the problem—why the print supervisor can't get the paper, or what he means when he says he can't get it. Effective paraphrasing, however, could help to get to the root of the problem:

Print supervisor:	I'm having trouble getting the paper to run that job. That's why I'm running behind schedule.
Plant manager:	In other words, your paper supplier hasn't shipped the paper you need for this job.
Print supervisor:	No, they shipped it, but it's full of flaws.
Plant manager:	So the whole shipment is bad.
Print supervisor:	No, only about a third of it. But I've got to get the whole batch replaced, or the dye lots won't match—the paper won't be exactly the same color.
Plant manager:	No problem—the colors can be a little off. But I have to have at least half of that order by Tuesday; the rest can wait a couple weeks. Can you print on the good paper you have now, then do the rest when the new paper comes in?
Print supervisor:	Sure.

Questioning and paraphrasing may seem to achieve the same goal, but in fact they are different processes. Questions seek new, additional information ("How far behind are we?" "When did it begin?"), while paraphrasing reviews everything a speaker has said. This is an important difference. You know from experience that we frequently think we understand another person only to find later that we were wrong. Paraphrasing is a kind of safety check that can highlight misunderstandings. People who practice paraphrasing are astonished to find out how many times a speaker will correct or add information to a message that had seemed perfectly clear.

Take Notes   Students know they need notes to recall important information for a test. Note taking can be just as valuable in business settings. You are unlikely to remember every deadline, every comment, or even every topic in a meeting or conversation unless you jot it down. This doesn't mean that you have to scribble every word in every setting, but when the topic is important, put it in writing.

Repeat What You Heard   It isn't always possible to take notes, and repetition works well in such cases. Remember that untrained listeners remember only about half of what they hear immediately after hearing it and then only half of that after forty-eight hours. One way to minimize this loss is to go over the important parts of a message as soon as possible. For best results, restate these ideas aloud—to a co-worker, your secretary or assistant, or a friend. Some businesspeople who have access to a typing and dictation pool describe important ideas into a dictaphone and get a typed record the next day.

Which is better, taking notes or repeating ideas aloud? Notes work reasonably well when they're taken on the spot, especially for recording specific facts such as dates, figures, or people to contact. They aren't an especially efficient method of recall for ideas or plans, though. When you describe aloud the ideas you've heard, you will find yourself bringing in details that don't come up or seem alive when you try to construct an outline on paper.

LISTENING TO CRITICISM

Perhaps the most difficult listening challenge occurs when you are faced with criticism. Think about your own experience: it is hard enough to stay non-defensive when the criticism is valid; when the attack is unjustified, however, maintaining your composure can seem almost impossible.

When faced with criticism, the two most common listening responses are "fight" and "flight." Fighters react by counterattacking. "It's not my fault," they might protest. Another fighting response is to blame others: "I'm not the only one who's at fault here. I could have done better if I had gotten more support." Even if discretion or fear keeps you from blurting out a defensive response, you might mentally dispute your critic. Whether a fighting response is overt or internal, this sort of defensiveness can prevent you from hearing what might be at least partially legitimate criticism.

"Flight" is a second reaction to criticism. Most businesspeople are too mature to run away physically from a critic, but there are other ways of evading negative remarks. Sometimes you *can* physically avoid critics—steering clear of their offices or not returning their phone calls, for example. Even when you can't escape unpleasant remarks, you can mentally disengage by refusing to listen thoughtfully to the criticism.

Since neither fighting nor fleeing is likely to satisfy your critics or help you understand legitimate criticism, you need alternatives that allow you to listen nondefensively without losing face. Fortunately, two such alternatives exist.

Seek More Information   Asking your critic to explain the problem gives you a constructive option to fighting or fleeing. By asking your critic for more information, you are showing that you take the criticism seriously but, at the same time, you aren't accepting blame for the problem.

There are several ways to seek more information. You can *ask for examples or clarification:* "You've said I'm not presenting a good attitude to customers. Can you describe exactly what I'm doing?" Even if the critic isn't willing or able to offer specifics, you can *guess about details of the criticism:* "Was it the way I handled Mr. Tyson when the bank sent back his check for insufficient funds?" A third way to seek information is to *paraphrase the critic:* "When you say I have a bad attitude toward customers, it sounds like you think I'm not giving them the service they deserve." You can also *ask what the critics wants:* "How could I behave in a better way around customers?"

Agree with the Criticism   An obvious but often overlooked way of responding nondefensively is to agree with the criticism. Although this approach might seem like a form of self-punishment, it can be extremely effective. There are two ways to agree with a critic. First, you can *agree with the facts.* Sometimes you are confronted with facts that can't be disputed. In these cases, your best approach is probably to face up to the truth: "You're right. I *have* been late three times this week." Notice that agreeing with the facts doesn't mean that you are accepting responsibility for every imaginable fault. In the case of being late to work, you might go on to point out that your lateness is a fluke in an otherwise spotless work record; but arguing with indisputable information isn't likely to satisfy your critic, and it will probably make you look bad.

Sometimes you can't honestly agree with the criticism. For example, a customer might unjustly accuse you of not caring about good service. After asking for more information to find out the basis of the criticism (a shipment didn't arrive on time, for example), you can *agree with the critic's perception.* With this approach, you acknowledge how the other person might view you as being at fault: "I can understand why it might seem that I don't care about your needs. After all, you did tell me that you absolutely had to have that shipment by last Friday, and I told you that it would be there. I'd be mad too if I were you."

Notice that agreeing with the perception doesn't require you to *accept* your critic's evaluation as accurate, although you might indeed find that it does have some merit. What you are doing is acknowledging the other person's right to view the issue in a way that may differ from yours. To see the value of this approach, consider how offensive the alternative would be. To say or imply "Your view of the issue is completely wrong and mine is right" isn't likely to satisfy the other person—nor is it a reasonable position in most cases.

CRITICAL LISTENING

When faced with a speaker who is trying to persuade you, the proper attitude is one of evaluation. What are the speaker's motives? How accurate are the speaker's facts? Predictions? Do you need what the speaker is trying to "sell"?

The most obvious type of persuasion involves selling in the literal sense. But selling goes on in many other contexts as well. When you try to persuade your boss to adopt an idea, you are selling. When subordinates make requests of you, they are selling.

The following pointers can help you to listen effectively as an evaluator.

Seek Information Before Evaluating   As obvious as this might seem, it is tempting to begin judging an idea before you know enough. A consultant on business information systems recently described this behavior. "A lot of small businesses are buying computers these days," he said. "Even though they pay me good money to help them decide on the best product, many of them seem to have their minds made up before we begin. Some want IBM, some Apples, and so on. They get their opinions in the oddest ways—from advertising or because a friend uses one for an entirely different purpose. People like this aren't really interested in the facts. They have their minds made up in advance."

Consider the Speaker's Motives   An argument carries more weight when the speaker doesn't have a personal stake in the outcome of your decision. The statement "The Xerox 6100 is the most reliable machine on the market" is easier to accept from *Consumer Reports* magazine than from a Xerox sales representative, for example.

Similarly, reports from customers that they are having no problems getting replacement parts are probably more credible than the same report from the manager of the order fulfillment department—who may feel that any problem could threaten his job. This does not mean you should disregard every statement from an interested party, only that you should look closely at the evidence for the statement.

Examine the Speaker's Supporting Data   As an evaluative listener, you need to ask yourself several questions about the evidence a speaker gives you to support her or his statements. First, does it exist at all? What evidence does the order fulfillment manager give that the current computer system is causing problems or that a new one will be better? Does a sales representative back up the claim that a product will pay for itself in less than a year?

Once you have identified the evidence, you need to make sure it is valid. The success of the flexible-hours program instituted in the New York office doesn't mean that the same program will work as well in the factory in West Virginia, where a certain number of people have to be operating the machinery at any given time. The two or three employees unhappy with the new office furniture might be the exceptions rather than representative of the majority, while the one or two satisfied customers you hear about could be the only happy ones. Carefully researched statistics that look at more than a few isolated cases are a much stronger form of proof than a few random examples. The following questions can help you to examine the overall validity of supporting material.

Is the evidence given true?

Are enough cases cited?

Are the cited cases representative of the whole being considered?

Are any comparisons of persons or events given relevant to the case at hand?

Are there any exceptions to the points the speaker is making?

Do these exceptions need to be considered?

4. **Consider the Speaker's Credentials**   A statement that has value when made by a qualified speaker might not be worth considering when uttered by someone else. Your attorney's legal advice on whether a client has grounds for a lawsuit, for instance, is probably better than your tax accountant's, a co-worker's, or your brother-in-law's ideas on the subject. Competence is not universal: a person can be an expert in one area and less qualified in others. Your comptroller could be a whiz at finding ways to cut costs, for example, but be totally ignorant of the market demands that determine what you need to spend to sell your product.

5. **Examine Emotional Appeals**   Sometimes emotional reactions are a valid basis for action. The sympathy we feel for underprivileged children is a good reason for donating money to their welfare. The desire to cut down on your own fatigue may be a good reason to hire an assistant.

In some cases, though, emotional appeals can obscure important logical considerations that might dissuade you from accepting a proposal. We can see this by thinking about fund raisers who seek money for underprivileged children. Your sympathy might not justify allowing a fund raiser to wander around your building soliciting funds from employees: your employees could resent being asked to give money to *your* favorite cause rather than one of theirs, especially if they have just been asked to donate to another cause. The particular agency asking for your donation might not be the best vehicle for helping underprivileged children: it may have excessive overhead so that much of your contribution never reaches any children, or other organizations might serve needier people.

EMPATHIC LISTENING

We listen informationally and critically for our own benefit. Empathic listening is different: the primary goal is to help the speaker in some way. Sometimes the help is personal, as when a friend asks advice about career planning or how to manage a conflict with a co-worker. At other times, the help meets organizational goals, as when a subordinate asks you for advice about a technical problem or a sales representative asks you how to persuade a particular customer.

Most empathic, helping responses fall into five categories. The most common is *advising:* "Here's what I think," "You ought to . . .," "If I were in your position. . . ." Sometimes advice is appropriate, especially when someone asks you for help with a problem on which you have particular expertise. In other cases, though, this kind of help is not helpful. For instance, your career advice to a new employee might be wrong if you're not aware of the person's background and skills or if you're not sure how promotions are made in her department.

In other cases, the advice might be right for you but wrong for the other person. For example, you may find that the best way to react to a supervisor's bad moods is to kid him out of it, but a co-worker may only make the same supervisor angrier if he tries humor. If your advice doesn't prove useful, the other person may blame you for his or her failure. Finally, people who ask for advice often don't really want it. Instead, they are looking for someone to confirm a decision they have already reached.

Another helping style involves *analyzing* the speaker's problem: "The real problem seems to be . . .," "Here's what I see going on." Analysis is especially helpful when you have more experience or insight than the speaker. For instance, a product manager might be able to help analyze a situation that a new sales representative reports: "A lot of Fieldweather's customers have been dealing with that company since 1935, when Fieldweather was the only company in the business. Since none of your prospect's objections to our product seem very substantial, I bet that's what you're running into here."

Analysis is not a productive response when you are unsure of your analysis or when your goal is to show off your brilliance at the expense of confusing the help-seeker. Analysis is also inappropriate when the person is looking for a sympathetic friend, not a calculating machine or a psychiatrist. A co-worker who has just heard that she's been passed over for a promotion would probably rather hear "Oh, I'm sorry—I know you wanted that job," rather than "You know why that happened? It's your attitude."

A third kind of helping response involves *questioning* the speaker: "Exactly how much money is missing?" "When did you start getting complaints about orders being filled incorrectly?" "Why does it bother you that Bob has taken over that end of operations?" The right questions can help you analyze a problem and offer good advice and help the other person recognize important facts that were previously buried. In other cases, though, questions can do more harm than good. Irrelevant questions ("Couldn't we have installed an automatic verifying system and avoided this problem?") can leave the person more confused than ever. Some questions are also disguised forms of advice or subtle traps. "Have you ever considered offering more money to get experienced keypunchers?" "Why haven't you told me about this?"

Helping also takes the form of *supporting,* either as reassurance or comfort: "I know you'll make the best decision." "We're all behind you." Such support can sometimes provide a morale boost, giving someone added strength to face a tough situation. At other times, it is not helpful at all. For instance, telling someone who is filled with self-doubt that no problem exists can have a bad impact even when your intentions are good. The person might interpret your remark to mean any competent person could handle the problem easily. Discouraging the help-seeker from facing a problem ("Don't worry, things will work themselves out") might just prolong or compound it.

Another response style is *paraphrasing.* Just as in informational settings, empathic paraphrasing involves restating the speaker's message in your own language. Here, however, the restatement should include both the speaker's thoughts and the speaker's feelings, whether or not they were explicitly stated: "It sounds like you're confused [feeling]. You can't decide whether to take the risk of a new job or stick with the safe one [thoughts]." "You sound angry at Jess [feeling], but you're afraid to confront him [thought]. Is that it?"

Paraphrasing responses like these can be a useful way to help someone explore a problem. They take you off the hook of giving advice, since help-seekers can often make the best decisions for themselves once they have considered all the alternatives. Even when no perfect answer to the problem exists, paraphrasing can let the troubled person blow off steam and feel understood. But this style of listening is usually not appropriate for information-seeking questions ("I can't figure out how to amortize this loan"), and it rarely works when you are itching to give advice. But when you have the time and the problem is a complex personal one, it can be a useful way of responding.

The following suggestions can improve your helpfulness as an empathic listener.

Use a Variety of Response Styles, As Appropriate   It is usually a mistake to rely heavily on one style of responding. From the full repertoire of response styles just described, choose the one that is most appropriate.

Talk Less, and Listen More   Gathering information is just as much a prerequisite to helping as it is to evaluating. Once you learn to say less, you will be surprised to find that simply being there and listening is often more helpful than any other response.

Avoid Being Judgmental   You may sometimes be tempted to judge the behavior of an advice-seeker. "If you kept your records up to date, you would have noticed that your shipments were going out late." If your goal is to be truly helpful, this sort of evaluation is probably out of place. Most people receive all the judgments they need. Far more rare is a sympathetic listener who will let them express thoughts and feelings without fear of criticism.

Sometimes it is impossible to approve of others' behavior. Being non-judgmental does not mean that you have given such approval; it just means that you haven't evaluated the behavior one way or another. You can help co-workers or subordinates to solve a problem, for instance, without telling them it's their own fault it happened. They probably know that already anyway.

Listen for Feelings As Well As Ideas   Often, the feeling is the most important part of a speaker's problem. Despite this fact, most people don't express—or even recognize—their emotions. Ask yourself what emotions might be contained in these statements:

> "That's the third time he canceled an appointment on me—who does he think he is?"

> "Whenever a deadline comes, I get excuses instead of results—this can't go on much longer."

> "One minute she says we have to spend money to make money, and the next minute she talks about cutting costs—I can't figure out what she really wants."

In each example there are at least two or three possible emotions:

anger, hurt, and self-doubt

anger, frustration, and worry

anger, confusion

Paraphrasing the emotion you sense can give the speaker a chance to agree with or contradict your interpretation: "Yeah, I guess it did hurt my feelings," or "I'm more worried than mad." In either case, this sort of response can help the other person to clarify how he or she is feeling and to deal with those emotions.

SUMMARY

For most workers, listening is the most frequent type of communication on the job, occupying more time than speaking, writing, or reading. Effective listening is important for several reasons. First, it aids the organization in carrying out its mission. In addition, effective listening helps individuals to advance in their careers. It provides information that helps them to learn about important happenings in the organization, as well as assisting them in doing their own jobs well. Listening also helps build strong personal relationships.

Despite these advantages, most workers are poor listeners for a variety of reasons, including message overload, preoccupation, wasting mental spare time, physical distractions, hearing problems, faulty assumptions about the listening process, and lack of training.

Listening falls into three categories. The first involves information seeking. Success in this area comes from avoiding premature judgments, being opportunistic, listening for the speaker's main and supporting ideas, asking questions and paraphrasing, taking notes, and repeating what has been heard soon after hearing it.

The second type of listening involves understanding and reacting to criticism from others without becoming unnecessarily defensive. Since arguing with or avoiding critics is rarely constructive, two alternative approaches can be useful. The first involves seeking more information from the critic: asking for examples or clarification, guessing about the criticism, paraphrasing the critical statement, and asking what the critic wants. Another useful response is to agree with the critic either by accepting the truth or by acknowledging the critic's perception, even though it may differ from yours.

A third type of listening occurs when the goal is to evaluate the quality of a message. Skill in this area comes from seeking adequate information before forming judgments, considering the speaker's motives, examining the speaker's supporting data, considering the speaker's credentials, and examining emotional appeals dispassionately.

Empathic listening involves responding in a way that helps others resolve their problems. Most people rely excessively on one or two of the following styles of empathic listening: advising, analyzing, questioning, supporting, and paraphrasing. Listeners can increase their helpfulness by using a variety of styles instead of just one or two, talking less and listening more, avoiding judgmental responses, and listening for the speaker's feelings as well as for thoughts.

ACTIVITIES

1. Recall three on-the-job incidents in which you had difficulty listening effectively. For each incident, describe which of the following factors interfered with your listening effectiveness:

   message overload
   preoccupation
   using mental spare time to think of something else
   physical distractions
   hearing problems
   faulty assumptions
       clear communication is the speaker's responsibility
       listening is a passive activity
       the speaker has nothing new to say
       talking has more advantages
   your lack of training in listening

2. Practice your skill at questioning and paraphrasing by trying the following activity:

   a. Choose a person who will talk about one of the following topics:
       how to perform a task
       how to advance in your career
       how to defend a co-worker whose behavior you disapprove of
   b. In each conversation, make it your task to *understand* the speaker. The measure of your understanding should be your ability to restate the speaker's position in your own words to his or her satisfaction.

3. After completing the conversations in Activity 2, answer the following questions:

   a. Was paraphrasing difficult? Why?
   b. Did you learn any useful information in the conversations? Would you have gained as much by responding in your more usual manner?
   c. How could you use paraphrasing and valid questioning to help in your everyday work?

4. Practice your ability to respond nondefensively to criticism by joining with a partner and rehearsing the kinds of critical messages you are likely to receive on the job.

a. Designate one of the two as A and the other as B.

b. A begins by describing the kinds of critical messages he or she is likely to receive and who expresses them.

c. B then takes the role of the critic and delivers the critical message. A uses the skills described on page 103 to respond nondefensively.

d. After the role-playing session, A and B discuss how the nondefensive listening skills could be used in a real-life situation.

e. A and B change roles and repeat the procedure.

5. Recall three recent instances in which you listened evaluatively. For each example, answer these questions:

a. Was this an appropriate occasion for evaluating, or should your real goal have been information gathering?

b. If evaluation was appropriate, did you have enough information to pass judgment?

6. Practice your empathic listening skills by trying the following experiment:

a. Imagine that a co-worker approaches you with one or more of the following messages:

"The boss keeps telling me crude sexual jokes. I think it's a come-on, and I don't know what to do."

"I never have enough time to do my work. Every time I solve one problem, another one comes up. And the phone never stops ringing. I'm going crazy!"

"This job looks like a dead end to me. I'd like to quit, but it's a tight job market. I don't know what to do."

b. Decide how you would respond to such comments. Identify your response as advice, analysis, questioning, support, or active listening. Which of these styles do you most commonly use when others seek your help?

c. Continuing with whatever situation you have chosen, write out responses for each of the styles you did not originally use.

d. Now decide which of the five responses would be most helpful.

e. How could you become a more effective empathic listener by broadening your range of response styles?

Communicator Profile

John Post, Marketing Manager
Fidelity USA
Boston, Massachusetts.

My advice . . . is to prepare to face a lot of criticism on the job. . . . Much . . . will be less fair and more rude than anything you've received during your education.

Fidelity USA manages finances for clients who live and work all over the United States. More than 200 telephone representatives answer calls from investors twenty-four hours a day, every day of the week. Since this amounts to over half a million calls a year, we must listen well and respond accurately to our callers, whether prospective clients or current customers. We manage most of our customers' assets in one package: investments, checking, savings, mutual-fund investments, and even bill payments. Tact and accuracy are very important.

The phone skills of our representatives are so important, in fact, that we provide financial bonuses for effective performance. Our customer representatives receive constant training. In weekly sessions, we role-play typical phone calls and suggest how to handle them. We also record each representative's phone conversations and review them to learn which situations were handled well and which could have been handled better.

We believe service is the most important ingredient of our product. If our employees aren't responsive to the customers' needs, all the technology and performance in the world won't build our business. Listening to customers goes beyond merely hearing what they've said. We also have to evaluate what's *not* being said. Is this call part of a trend we should recognize? Is a problem caused by something that isn't immediately apparent? Our representatives are trained to watch for these questions. Fidelity representatives must also respond in a way that shows our customers we *care* about their welfare, which means being respectful and empathizing with them. Our goal is to have callers hang up feeling that they've been treated fairly and with concern.

Investing more time and effort listening to our customers will help us spend less time and money solving problems. A few years ago, a number of customers complained about our monthly statement, saying the format was confusing. We listened to those criticisms and redesigned our statements. Since then, the number of callers who are confused by the information we send them has dropped almost to zero. This makes customers happier and also increases our profits since we spend less time responding to problems.

My advice to college students about listening is to prepare to face a *lot* of criticism on the job, both from people within your organization and from the public. Much of that criticism will be less fair and more rude than anything you've received during your education. Don't resent or tune out these attacks. If you listen to them carefully, you'll be amazed by the benefits. Your critics will respect you more, and you will learn a tremendous amount of helpful information—about yourself, your job, and human nature.

CHAPTER 5

After reading this chapter, you should understand:

- The importance of personal communication skills in a career
- The differences between confirming and disconfirming messages
- The seven types of disconfirming messages
- Six elements of confirming, supportive messages
- The inevitability of on-the-job conflict and the need to manage it constructively
- The characteristics of avoiding, accommodating, competing, collaborating, and compromising conflict styles
- The characteristics and typical consequences of bargaining, lose-lose, and win-win negotiating styles

You should be able to:

- Identify the confirming and disconfirming behaviors (both yours and those of others) that create the communication climate in a specific setting
- Describe the specific responses you could use to communicate in a more confirming way in a specific setting
- Identify your conflict style and describe its consequences
- Raise a delicate issue assertively, using the guidelines in this chapter
- Describe the appropriate negotiating approach to use in a given situation
- Demonstrate your ability to use the win-win negotiating style within an appropriate context

PROBLEM SOLVING, CONFLICT MANAGEMENT, AND NEGOTIATION

What does it take to succeed in your career? Talent, good ideas, a good education, technical expertise, skills, hard work, motivation, initiative—all of these are important. Because all jobs also require you to get things done through other people—co-workers, customers, management, people in other departments in the company—career success also depends on your ability to communicate effectively. That ability, often called "people skills," is the ability to work *with other people*, solve problems, negotiate differences, and handle conflicts so that you can do your job effectively.

A recent survey of 1,000 personnel directors in the United States revealed just how important communication skills are in a career.[1] When asked to describe the "ideal management profile," the number-one characteristic was "ability to work well with others one-on-one." The personnel managers understood clearly that communication is at the heart of people skills: all three of the top characteristics that were identified as necessary for successful job performance were communication skills. Chrysler chairman Lee Iacocca summed up the importance of maintaining good interpersonal working relationships when he said:

> There's one phrase I hate to see on any executive's evaluation, no matter how talented he may be, and that's the line: "He has trouble getting along with other people." To me that's the kiss of death.[2]

Many businesspeople at many levels are greatly concerned about their relationships with other people on the job. Andrew Grove, president of Intel Corporation, discovered the extent of that concern when he began writing a weekly question-and-answer newspaper column on management:

> I couldn't overlook the fact that the overwhelming majority of writers asked for help with interpersonal relationships at work. People wanted ideas on how to deal with the boss who never gives feedback, with the employee who doesn't care about her work, with the customer who propositions them, with coworkers who steal or who crack their gum loudly. In other words, people wanted ideas on how to *manage* better at their workplace, manage as in "the boss manages his employees," and also manage as in "make do" or "get along."[3]

In this chapter, we focus on how to develop and improve the personal communication skills that are so important for individuals and organizations. We describe the ingredients that foster a positive communication climate within a firm. We describe how to manage the inevitable conflicts that arise whenever people work together so that the results are positive. Finally, we offer guidelines for handling important negotiations skillfully.

COMMUNICATION CLIMATE

Social scientists use the term *communication climate* to describe the quality of personal relationships in an organization. Do people feel respected? Do they trust one another? Do they believe that they are appreciated? The weather metaphor

Treat people as adults. Treat them as partners; treat them with dignity; treat them with respect. Treat *them*—not capital spending and automation—as the primary source of productivity gains. These are fundamental lessons from the excellent companies research. In other words, if you want productivity and the financial reward that goes with it, you must treat your workers as your most important asset.

Thomas J. Peters and Robert H. Waterman, Jr., *In Search of Excellence*

suggested by the term *climate* is apt. Your own experience shows that the mood of a workplace can be described as sunny and calm, cold and stormy, or in similar terms. After surveying members of successful organizations, researchers Carl Larson and Frank LaFusto identified four communication characteristics that create a positive climate:

- *Honesty*—communication that is complete and truthful; no lies, no exaggerations
- *Openness*—willingness to share information and receptivity to the ideas of others
- *Consistency*—predictable behavior; the confidence that members of an organization can be depended on
- *Respect*—treating others with dignity and consideration[4]

As these qualities suggest, the climate of an organization comes not so much from the specific tasks that members perform as from the feelings they have about those tasks and each other. For example, a secretary's resentment at being sent for coffee has less to do with the job itself than what the errand says about her boss's perception of her role. If the boss fetched his own coffee on occasion, the communication climate would be improved; if he asked her opinion on business matters within her experience, she would also feel less like a servant.

A positive climate can exist under the worst working conditions: in a cramped, poorly furnished, understaffed office; during the graveyard shift of an urban newspaper; or even in a road gang cleaning up trash by the highway. Conversely, the most comfortable, prestigious settings can be polluted by a hostile climate. Table 5-1 provides a tool for diagnosing the communication climate of a working group.

DISCONFIRMING COMMUNICATION

While communication climates are created by a variety of messages, their common ingredient is validation: positive climates result when people believe they are valued, and negative climates occur when they don't believe they are appreciated. Scholars have labeled messages that express feelings of value as *confirming* and those that fail to express valuing—or those that explicitly show a lack of valuing—as *disconfirming*.[5]

TABLE 5-1 Managerial Communication Climate Questionnaire

KEY: AAT   The statement is almost always true.
         UT   The statement is usually true.
         UF   The statement is usually false.
         AAF   The statement is almost always false.

To indicate your response, draw a circle around *one* of the four symbols preceding each item.*

AAT   UT   UF   AAF   1. It's easy to find out what's going on; there are few secrets around here.

AAT   UT   UF   AAF   2. People feel free to say what's on their minds when they're talking to their bosses.

AAT   UT   UF   AAF   3. You can count on the truth and accuracy of what company management says about such matters as profits and losses, long-range plans, and impending changes of policy.

AAT   UT   UF   AAF   4. Other managers at my level in the company are people with whom I can easily and frankly discuss mutual problems.

AAT   UT   UF   AAF   5. My superiors keep me informed on what's expected of me—of what I must do to get ahead.

AAT   UT   UF   AAF   6. Managers encourage subordinates to come up with new ideas, and they protect them when they stick their necks out by making suggestions.

AAT   UT   UF   AAF   7. Company statements are noted for their clarity and freedom from bureaucratic prose.

AAT   UT   UF   AAF   8. Management treats everyone with respect—as mature adults rather than as children.

AAT   UT   UF   AAF   9. Management is candid in disclosing bad news; the rule is, "We tell it like it is."

AAT   UT   UF   AAF   10. Performance appraisals are conducted in such a way that the subordinate knows where he or she stands and participates in setting his or her own goals for continued progress.

AAT   UT   UF   AAF   11. The underlying assumption in the company is that just about everybody has good ideas, and that these ideas should contribute to all major decision making.

AAT   UT   UF   AAF   12. When you send messages to higher management, you get a prompt and honest response.

AAT   UT   UF   AAF   13. When you see a crisis building up, it's easy to alert higher management about it.

AAT   UT   UF   AAF   14. Generally speaking, I receive all the information I need to perform my job effectively.

AAT   UT   UF   AAF   15. People representing different departments and different specialties have ample opportunity to consult with each other.

AAT   UT   UF   AAF   16. This company plays down status differences between superiors and subordinates.

AAT   UT   UF   AAF   17. Managers at all levels are encouraged to be their own bosses—hence, to take risks.

AAT   UT   UF   AAF   18. In this company, we stress that managers should act more as counselors and helpers than as order givers and watchmen.

AAT   UT   UF   AAF   19. Although I am treated with consideration at all times, I am "stretched" to achieve high performance goals.

TABLE 5-1 *(Continued)*

AAT	UT	UF	AAF	
AAT	UT	UF	AAF	20. The general spirit around here is: "We're all in this boat together, and we sink or swim together" (rather than: "The way to get ahead is to outmaneuver your rivals").
AAT	UT	UF	AAF	21. I find it relatively easy to get feedback from my subordinates about their problems, feelings, and accomplishments.
AAT	UT	UF	AAF	22. I find it relatively easy to get feedback from my superiors when I send messages asking for information, answers to questions, and so on.
AAT	UT	UF	AAF	23. Our publications, for both managers and employees, are known for candor, for completeness, and for providing "gutsy" information.
AAT	UT	UF	AAF	24. Higher management is willing to listen to criticism; it approaches new ideas with an open mind, even when these ideas imply criticism.
AAT	UT	UF	AAF	25. The company provides a systematic and safe means for anyone to raise questions or criticisms; and questions are answered promptly, fully, and accurately by appropriate line managers.
AAT	UT	UF	AAF	26. When someone offers an idea or makes a proposal in decision-making conferences, my approach is: "Let's see why this might be a good idea" (rather than: "What's wrong with it?").
AAT	UT	UF	AAF	27. In this company, people feel that managers are sincerely interested in their welfare and progress.
AAT	UT	UF	AAF	28. If I am making a major proposal to higher management, I know that I'll get a fair hearing; I'll be subjected to searching questions, but I can talk back without fear of the consequences.
AAT	UT	UF	AAF	29. When one of my own subordinates is making a major proposal, I give him or her a fair hearing; I subject the proposal to searching questions, but I encourage the subordinate to talk back without fear of the consequences.
AAT	UT	UF	AAF	30. When important news about the company is announced, both managers and employees hear it first before it's released to the general public.

*Potential problems can be identified by false answers (UF, AAF).

From *The Corporate Manager's Guide to Better Communication* by W. Charles Redding. Copyright © 1984 by Scott, Foresman and Company. Reprinted by permission.

Disconfirming messages fall into several categories. Taken together, they form a list that reads like a prescription for poor relationships.

Impervious Responses   These do not acknowledge the other person's attempt to communicate. Failing to return a phone call, answer a customer's letter of complaint, or respond to an employee's description of a problem are examples of impervious responses.

Interrupting Responses   These most often occur when one person is so eager to make a point that he or she won't let the other finish a sentence:

> *A:* "I'm trying to get a second bid because . . . "
> *B:* "If those orders don't go out *today*, we won't be able to get Skyler to do the job."

The implied message of an interruption is "I'm not interested in what you have to say."

Irrelevant Responses   These are unrelated to what the other person has just said.

> *A:* I need to talk to you about why you turned down my request to attend the workshop in Los Angeles next month.
> *B:* I'm glad you came by. Have you seen last month's sales figures?

Tangential Responses   Such responses acknowledge the message but then brush it off and steer the conversation in another direction. A tangential response in the last example might be "That meeting is about increasing sales effectiveness, isn't it? That reminds me—I'd like you to get a complete printout of last month's sales."

Impersonal Responses   These are superficial reactions. Instead of treating the other person's feelings or ideas on a personal level, impersonal responses provide only a cliché or overly intellectual comment. For example, a worker might respond to a friend's failure to win a promotion by saying, "Well, we all have to pay our dues."

Ambiguous Responses   These are obscure or hard to understand. An aspiring young employee says to her manager, "I have some ideas about the Allison account that I'd like to share with you." The manager replies ambiguously, "Sure, we'll have to do that sometime."

Incongruous Responses   These contain two messages that seem to contradict each other. Often a verbal message conveys one response, while the nonverbal behavior says something different. A clenched jaw contradicts the statement "I'm not angry." The manager's wandering gaze contradicts his statement "I want to hear about your ideas."

CONFIRMING COMMUNICATION

Confirming messages make others feel better about themselves and you. Psychologist Jack Gibb described six types of supportive statements that are likely to promote a confirming climate.[6] Gibb's supportive categories provide a list of ways to promote positive, confirming relationships.

Use Descriptive "I" Language   Many communicators unnecessarily attack the other person when delivering a message:

> "The report is too sloppy. You'll have to retype it."

> "This is the third time this month that you've been late for work. You'll have to be more punctual."

"That was a dumb promise to make. We can never have the job done by the end of the month."

Attacking, evaluative statements like these are often called "you" language because they point a verbal finger of accusation at the receiver: "You're lazy," "You're wrong." By contrast, *descriptive* speech is termed "I" language since it focuses on the speaker instead of judging the other person. Notice how each of the above statements has been rephrased in descriptive "I" language:

"I'm afraid the boss will get angry at both of us if we turn in a report with this many errors. We'll get a better reaction if you retype it."

"Since you've been coming in late, I've had to make a lot of excuses when people call asking for you. I'm uncomfortable with that, and that's why I hope you'll start showing up on time."

"I'm worried about the promise you made. I don't see how we can get the job done by the end of the month."

Statements like these show that it's possible to be nonjudgmental and still say what you want without landing any verbal punches. In fact, descriptive statements like the ones you just read are *more* complete than are typical everyday complaints since they express both the speaker's feelings and the reason for bringing up the matter—things most evaluative remarks don't do.

Focus on Solving Problems, Not Controlling Others   Control is forcing someone to do something he or she doesn't agree with or understand. If you're up against a tight deadline, for example, it's easy to say, "Look, I don't have time to explain—just do it my way." Because control shows a lack of regard for the other person's need, interests, or opinions, however, it can cause problems in the relationship even if it gets you what you want now.

In contrast, *problem-oriented* communication aims at solving both persons' needs. The goal isn't to solve a problem "my way" or "your way," but rather to develop a solution that meets everyone's needs. Frederick W. Smith, founder and chairman of Federal Express, claims, "A supervisor or manager must understand that he is there to help the workers do their jobs and to understand how they feel. He must not have the attitude that he can force his ways on them just because he is the boss."

Sometimes it is important that a job be done "your way." A company system, for example, might demand that the financial analysis of a new project follow a certain format so that management can read the figures and understand them easily, and so that the share of overhead allocated to each new product line is accounted for. If that's the case, you can still take a problem-solving approach by explaining why the analysis must be done that way. Many tasks, however, permit more flexibility. One consultant advises that you discuss such tasks in detail:

Rather than telling [the person] flatly what to do and how to do it, describe the results you want. Let him explain how he will get them. If he proposes procedures you cannot approve, explain your objections and ask him to work out an alternative.[7]

You will learn more about how to achieve problem-oriented solutions when we discuss win-win negotiating strategies later in this chapter.

Be Honest; Don't Manipulate   Once people discover that they have been manipulated, a defensive reaction is almost guaranteed. For example, if workers are surveyed on their preferences for the layout of new offices and then discover that the plan was completed without tabulating their responses, they will resent being "set up as suckers"—a label nobody likes to accept.

By contrast, *spontaneity* or simple honesty is less likely to generate defensiveness. Telling your subordinates outright that the new office plan was designed by an executive planning committee may not make them ecstatic, but they won't feel that they've been used to justify a closed decision. Even though others might sometimes dislike what you have to say, your reputation for candor will earn you the respect of subordinates, co-workers, and management.

What about the times when honesty can get you into trouble? Honesty doesn't require you to volunteer information that others don't request. You may know that the design committee for the new office layout was told to put as many people in as little space as possible to allow room for an executive dining room, but you also might wisely choose not to pass that information on to your own employees. Nor does honesty require you to be blunt or cruel. As you saw in the section on descriptive language, you can choose nonattacking ways of expressing your feelings and beliefs. Finally, you can usually combine a criticism with an honest compliment, thus being both honest and positive. You might respond to a colleague's question "What do you think of my idea?" by sharing something you like about the thought as well as your reservations.

Show Concern for Others   As you have already seen, indifference—lack of acknowledgment or concern for others—is a strong disconfirming message.

The opposite of this sort of neutrality is sincere *empathy* or concern for the position or feelings of another. A simple apology for making you wait can do wonders. The salesperson who approaches you as you enter the store to find out if you're looking for something particular and lets you know he's available can make your shopping trip a good experience. The secretary who takes the time to find the right person to answer your questions can leave you feeling grateful and worthwhile, encouraging you to do business with that company again. The manager who seems genuinely concerned with your problem and tries to relieve you of other tasks while you solve it might even make you feel willing to work late to solve it faster.

Demonstrate an Attitude of Equality   People who act superior imply that others are inferior, which is clearly a disconfirming message. Nobody likes to feel less valuable than another person, and an air of superiority communicates these sorts of messages.

But aren't some people in fact superior to others? And isn't it dishonest to pretend otherwise? Not really, for the kind of superiority that arouses defensiveness isn't based as much on intelligence, talent, or skill as on dignity and respect. Talent doesn't justify arrogance. You have probably encountered sales representatives and clerks who acted as though their product knowledge made them superior to their customers, physicians who couldn't be bothered to explain test results to you, employers who felt their subordinates were stupid, and others who acted as if you belonged to a race of beings less deserving of respect than theirs. This sort of superior attitude causes defensiveness. Al Neuharth, founder of *USA Today,* has earned a reputation as a tough, abrasive boss. His superior, evaluative comments like the following one suggest why: "When I criticize a female or when I criticize a grossly overweight person or anybody else, it's because, damn it, I think they ought to do better, just as I do."[8]

This sort of superior attitude can enrage others. A steelworker described his reaction in one such instance:

> This one foreman I've got, he's a kid. He's a college graduate. He thinks he's better than everybody else. He was chewing me out and I was saying, "Yeah, yeah, yeah." He said, "What do you mean, yeah, yeah, yeah. Yes, *sir.*" I told him, "Who the hell are you, Hitler?[9]

In contrast, an attitude of *equality* communicates respect for the other person. The plant manager who listens carefully to an experienced line worker's diagnosis of a problem, an executive who has lunch with each of his junior managers from time to time, an administrative assistant who greets the telephone operators and mail-room staff by name are all showing respect. Coming from a talented or high-status individual, the implied message of equality is "I may have more responsibility or a higher rank than you, but you deserve a polite response and your work deserves my respect and appreciation."

Listen with an Open Mind Whether the people you're dealing with are in your department or another, subordinates or customers, they probably have knowledge that you don't. As career specialist Shirley Sloan Fader points out, "Because they're the ones tackling the hands-on jobs, subordinates often know parts of your job better than you do. Give people the opportunity to respond to your plans and come up with ideas. You may learn about potential problems and necessary improvements."

Consider how you would feel if you had carefully researched a proposal to avoid raising the price on a product line, only to be told, "I see no evidence that we should keep the price down." Suppose, instead, that your supervisor had said, "I have strong reasons for raising the price, but maybe you'll change my mind" or had at least listened carefully to your idea and promised to give it some thought. Even if your supervisor eventually decides against your proposal, you will probably feel that your ideas are heard and respected—provided that the supervisor gives you good reasons for rejecting your plan.

CONSTRUCTIVE CONFLICT MANAGEMENT

Conflict is part of any job. Consider these examples:

> A new computer system has been installed, and you're having trouble getting orders shipped to customers. You've called the people in the computer division, but all they can tell you is that "it takes time to work out the bugs." Meanwhile, the sales force is complaining to you.

> You're running over budget on a project, and your manager tells you to cut costs now. You know that if you don't spend the money now, though, the project won't work right when it's finished.

> There are five people at your level in your department, and you're supposed to divide work evenly. Lately, though, one of the other people has been lagging, which means more work for everyone else.

> You share an office with a heavy smoker, and cigarette smoke makes you feel ill. When you ask him to smoke somewhere else, he says, "But I need to smoke when I'm thinking."

Conflict comes in many forms. Even the most competent, intelligent, ethical people will differ from time to time. Sometimes conflict involves work-related issues: scheduling, funds, work assignments, and so on. In other cases, it focuses on personal issues: sexual harassment, the amount of socializing appropriate during working hours, or whether a shared assistant is doing his or her work efficiently. The dispute may be loud and argumentative, calm and rational, or so indirect that it is never mentioned outright.

Conflict may be equated with the common cold—unavoidable, unpleasant, and counterproductive. To most people, the fewer conflicts the better. The problem isn't with conflict itself, however, but rather with *the way in which conflict is handled.* With the right approach, conflict can produce good results. The Chinese language represents this fact well; in Chinese, the figure that represents crisis is made up of two characters: danger and opportunity. A poorly handled organizational conflict certainly can be dangerous; relationships suffer and productivity declines. On the other hand, a skillfully handled conflict can result in several benefits.[10] It can function as a safety valve, letting people ventilate frustrations that are blocking their effective functioning. It can lead to solving troublesome problems. James Baldwin said it best: "Nothing can be changed until it is faced." Problems seldom go away just because they are ignored; they usually grow worse. Facing them can promote group loyalty and cohesiveness. People who overcome conflicts successfully often feel that together they have made progress toward their mutual goals. Such experiences often draw people closer.

APPROACHES TO CONFLICT

When faced with a conflict, you have several choices about how to respond (see Figure 5-1). Each of these approaches has different results.[11]

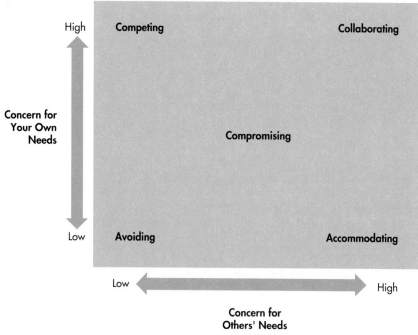

Figure 5-1   A two-dimensional model of conflict styles. (Adapted from Kenneth W. Thomas, "Introduction" to *California Management Review* 21(2).)

Avoiding   One way to deal with conflict is to avoid it whenever possible and withdraw when confronted. Sometimes avoidance is physical: refusing to take phone calls, staying barricaded in the office, and so on. In other cases, however, avoidance can be psychological: denying that a problem exists or that it is serious, repressing emotional reactions, and so on. In the workplace, a communicator who avoids conflicts might accept constant schedule delays or poor-quality work from a supplier to avoid a confrontation or cover up for a co-worker's frequent absences even if it means doing the other person's work. As these examples suggest, avoidance may have the short-term benefit of preventing a confrontation, but there are usually long-term costs, especially in ongoing relationships.

Despite its drawbacks, avoidance is sometimes a wise choice. Table 5-2 lists some circumstances in which keeping quiet may be the most appropriate course of action. For example, when standing up for your rights would be hopeless, silence might be the best policy. You might simply tolerate a superior's unreasonable demands while you look for a new job or steer clear of an angry co-worker who is out to get you. In many cases, however, avoidance has unacceptable costs: you lose self-respect, you become frustrated, and the problem may only get worse.

Accommodating   Whereas avoiders stay away from conflicts, accommodators give in as a way of maintaining harmony. In many cases, accommodating is hard

TABLE 5-2   Factors Governing Choice of a Conflict Style

USE AVOIDING
1. When an issue is genuinely trivial, or when more important issues are pressing
2. When you have no chance of winning
3. When the potential for disruption outweighs the benefits of resolution
4. To let others cool down and regain perspective
5. When the long-term costs of winning may outweigh short-term gains
6. When others can resolve the conflict more effectively

USE ACCOMMODATING
1. When you find you are wrong
2. When the issue is important to the other party and not important to you
3. To build social credits for later issues
4. To minimize loss when you are outmatched and losing
5. When harmony and stability are more important than the subject at hand
6. To allow others to learn by making their own mistakes

USE COMPETING
1. When quick, decisive action is vital (e.g., emergencies)
2. On important issues where unpopular actions need implementing (e.g., cost-cutting, enforcing unpopular rules)
3. When others will take advantage of your noncompetitive behavior

USE COLLABORATING
1. To find solutions when both parties' concerns are too important to be compromised
2. When a long-term relationship between the parties is important
3. To gain commitment of all parties by building consensus
4. When the other party is willing to take a collaborative approach

USE COMPROMISING
1. When goals are important but not worth the effort or potential disruption of more assertive modes
2. When opponents with equal power are committed to mutually exclusive goals
3. To achieve temporary settlements of complex issues
4. To arrive at expedient solutions under time pressure
5. As a backup, when collaboration is unsuccessful

Adapted from Kenneth W. Thomas, "Toward Multi-dimensional Values in Teaching: The Example of Conflict Behavior," *Academy of Management Review 2*, no. 3 (1977): 487.

to defend. It can be equivalent to appeasement, sacrificing one's principles, and putting harmony above dealing with important issues. Nonetheless, as Table 5-2 shows, accommodating does have merit in some circumstances. If you are clearly wrong, then giving up your original position can be a sign of strength, not weakness. If harmony is more important than the issue at hand—especially if the issue is a minor one—then accommodating is probably justified. For example, if you don't care strongly whether the new stationery is printed on cream or gray paper and fighting for one color might be a big concern for others, then giving in is probably smart. Finally, you might accommodate if making the other person happy is important to your welfare. You might, for example, put up with an abusive customer to make an important sale.

Competing   A competitive approach to conflicts is based on the assumption that the only way for one party to reach its goals is to overcome the other. This bargaining approach is common in many negotiations, as you will see later in this chapter. Sometimes a power-based approach to conflict is based on simply disregarding the other person's concerns. Unsympathetic management might turn a deaf ear to the request of employees to make provisions for on-site exercise facilities, implying—or even stating outright—that the physical condition of employees is not the concern of the employer and that providing easy access to exercise would require a cash outlay and reduce time spent on the job.

In many cases, a competitive attitude is unnecessary. As the section of this chapter on win-win negotiating shows, it often *is* possible for both sides in a conflict to reach their goals (see pages 131–138). For instance, an employer might find that the cost of providing on-site exercise equipment is more than offset by reduced absenteeism and greater appeal when recruiting new employees. Furthermore, a competitive orientation can generate ill will that is both costly and unpleasant. In our physical-fitness example, workers whose needs are ignored are likely to resent their employer and act in ways that ultimately wind up costing the company a great deal.

Despite its drawbacks, competition isn't always a bad approach. In some cases, an issue isn't important enough to spend the time working it out. In other instances, there isn't time to collaborate on solutions. Finally, if others are determined to gain advantage at your expense, you might be forced to compete out of self-defense.

Collaborating   Rather than taking a competitive approach, collaborative communicators are committed to working together to resolve conflicts. Collaboration is based on the assumption that it is possible to meet one's own needs and those of the other person. This approach is reflected in Rabbi Hillel's statement "If I am not for myself, who will be? If I am only for myself, what am I?"

Whereas avoiding and accommodating are based on the assumption that conflict should be avoided, and competing is based on the belief that conflict is a struggle, collaboration assumes that conflict is a natural part of life and that working with the other person will produce the best possible solution. The benefits of collaboration are clear: not only can the issue at hand be resolved, but the relationship between the parties is improved.

Despite its advantages, collaborative communication isn't a panacea. It takes time to work with others, and a mutually satisfactory outcome isn't always possible. Furthermore, collaboration requires the cooperation of everyone involved. If the other party isn't disposed to work with you , then you may be setting yourself up for exploitation by communicating openly and offering to work cooperatively.

Compromising   Compromising contains elements of both collaboration and power strategies. On the one hand, this approach is cooperative, recognizing that the agreement of both parties is necessary to resolve a conflict. On the other hand, compromise is based on each party pursuing his or her self-interest to get the best possible deal.

Compromise is a middle-range approach. It is more assertive than avoiding and accommodating, yet less aggressive than competing. It is cooperative, yet less so than collaboration. While it does not give any of the parties in a dispute everything he or she seeks, it provides an outcome that, by definition, everyone involved can live with. As Table 5-2 shows, compromise may not be the perfect approach, but under many circumstances it is the best one.

HANDLING CONFLICTS ASSERTIVELY

When you accommodate another's demand or avoid a conflict, few communication skills are necessary. But if you decide to address an issue directly—either to collaborate, compete, or seek a compromise—the way you present yourself can make a big difference. An aggressive approach is likely to antagonize the other person. But an assertive style of communicating allows you to present your own concerns in a way that shows respect for the other person. Showing this sort of respect isn't only right as a matter of principle, it also is likely to improve the communication climate and thus make it easier to produce the outcome you are seeking. You stand the best chance of getting across your message in the most effective way when you follow some simple guidelines.

The first thing to remember when raising a delicate issue is to *stop and think* before approaching the other party. Flying off the handle may be the easiest way to react and feel satisfied in the short run, but the defensive, hostile reaction you get is likely to create more problems than it solves. Before you say anything, do three things:

Identify the Goal You Are Seeking   What do you want to happen after you have spoken up? Do you want to change the other person's mind or explain your position, or are you simply interested in blowing off steam? The approach you take will differ according to your goal.

Choose the Best Time to Speak Up   Timing may not be everything, but it is among the most important factors in getting (or not getting) results. Raising a delicate issue when the other person is tired, grumpy, or distracted by other business will lower the odds of getting the results you are seeking.

Rehearse the Statement   Think over what you want to say and how you can best say it. Preparing your thoughts in advance will help make your point quickly and clearly, and prevent you from blurting out an angry statement you'll regret later. When planning your remarks, be sure to think about how you can use "I" language instead of delivering defense-arousing "you" messages. Rehearsing your approach doesn't mean you should memorize your remarks word for word; this approach will sound canned and insincere. Think about your general ideas and perhaps a few key phrases you'll use to make your ideas clear.

When the time comes actually to deliver your delicate message, follow these guidelines:

Pinpoint the Specific Behavior You Want to Discuss   Describe the delicate issue in neutral terms without using the kind of emotive language you read about in Chapter 4. The best descriptions are *specific* and *objective*. They avoid accusations or mind reading about the other person's motives, both of which provoke defensiveness even when they are correct.

WRONG	RIGHT
"You're wasting time on the job."	"The last three status reports have been a week or more late."
"You're being too critical of my work."	"The last few times we've met, you've complained about my work."
"You've been gossiping about me lately."	"Yesterday I couldn't help overhearing you tell Terry you thought I was padding my expense account."

Explain Your Reaction to the Behavior   Your explanation should include both your *interpretation* of the behavior—what you thought it meant—and your *feelings* about the action. It is vital to identify both the interpretation and feelings as yours. It is here that the difference between assertive "I" language and attacking "you" language is clearest:

WRONG	RIGHT
"You're not trying as hard as you could."	"I'm disappointed because it seems to me the reports ought to be ready on time."
"You've gotten awfully critical lately."	"It seems to me you've been awfully critical lately, and I'm confused. I don't know why you've changed so much."
"Why don't you trust me?"	"It sounds as if you think I'm ripping the company off, and that upsets me."

Notice the provisional nature of these statements. They say "here's how it looks to me" instead of claiming that a personal perception is absolute fact. Besides minimizing defensiveness, such tentative statements are more accurate. Your interpretation might be mistaken, and a provisional description leaves the door open for a correction without any loss of face.

Make a Request   The third part of an assertive statement asks for some action from your listener. The best requests are specific and are limited to one or two changes at a time. They also ask for responses that are within the ability of the other person to give:

WRONG	RIGHT
"Try to be more punctual from now on."	"I'd like your promise that the reports will be ready on time from now on."
"Why have you been so hard on me lately?"	"I want to know whether you think my work has not been satisfactory lately."
"Quit talking about me behind my back."	"If you have any complaints about how I handle my expense accounts, let's talk about it privately."

Describe the Consequences   The consequence statement should discuss the payoffs (both for you and the other person) of reaching accord. These payoffs can be tangible (money, time) and intangible (psychological comfort, friendship).

WRONG	RIGHT
"You'd better speed up before it's too late!"	"If the reports are on time, neither of us will have to hassle with this anymore."
(No consequence statement.)	"Once I understand how you feel, I can do a better job. I want the new product line to succeed as much as you do!"
"If you don't stop your gossiping, you'll be sorry!"	"Both of us have better things to do than feel bad about each other. I know we can work out any problems."

NEGOTIATING SKILLS

Even the most skillful requests and the most positive communication climates don't guarantee a positive response. Whenever two parties do not initially agree about an issue, they have three choices:

They can accept the status quo:

"I've tried to talk with him, but it doesn't work. There's nothing more I can do."

"We can't agree on a price, so the deal's off."

The more powerful side can try to impose a solution:

"I'm the manager. I'll decide how the job will be done."

"Either you give me the transfer, or I'll file a grievance with the union."

The parties can reach an agreement by negotiating:

"Let's figure out a schedule we can both live with."

"We'd both like to make the deal. Let's see if we can work out some terms."

Negotiation occurs when two or more parties—either individuals or groups—discuss specific proposals in order to find a mutually acceptable agreement. Negotiation is a common way of settling conflicts in business. Individuals use negotiation to reach agreement on everything from the price of a used car to who will handle an unpleasant job. Managers and workers use it to reach agreements on such issues as how much responsibility a worker should take or what she needs to do to be promoted. As one consultant explains, "Negotiations are seldom formal, sit-around-the-table affairs. In fact, almost any form of business problem or disagreement—from a threatened union walkout to 'Who's going to pay this $500 expense?'—is resolved by some form of negotiation."[12]

There is nothing magic about negotiation. When poorly handled, it can leave a problem still unsolved and perhaps worse than before. ("I tried to work things out with him, but he just tried to railroad me. I'm going to the union this time.") When negotiation is handled skillfully, though, it can improve the position of one or even both parties. In the remainder of this chapter, we outline four negotiating styles, showing methods that you can use to resolve your own problems.

NEGOTIATION STYLES AND OUTCOMES

Negotiations can be approached in four ways. Each of these approaches produces a different outcome.

Bargaining Orientation   This is the approach taken by competitive communicators. Bargaining is based on the assumption that only one side can reach its goals and that any victory by that party will be matched by the other's loss.

Despite the fact that it produces losers as well as winners, a bargaining orientation can sometimes be the best approach to negotiating. If the other party is determined to take advantage of you and cannot be convinced that collaboration is possible, then you probably need to adopt a competitive stance out of self-defense. You also may need to bargain if your interests truly conflict and collaborating or compromising is not a satisfactory option. For example, in a one-time commercial transaction (the sale of a car, for instance), your concern for helping the other party may take a back seat to getting the best possible deal for yourself—without violating your ethical principles, of course.

When bargaining, information about the other party is perhaps the most powerful asset you can possess. For example, imagine how much stronger your position would be when negotiating a salary with a potential employer if you knew the answers to such key questions as:

What is the financial condition of the company?

How much is management paying people in equivalent positions?

Who else are they considering for the position?

What salary would these people be willing to pay?

How much does management want you?

Likewise, when dickering over the price of an item, your knowledge of the buyer and the marketplace would give you an advantage:

How much does the buyer want or need the item you are selling?

Are there alternative sources available? Is the buyer aware of them?

How much is the buyer prepared to pay?

Before and during a negotiating session, you should do everything possible to collect such information. You can gather intelligence through personal observations and contacts with people who are familiar with your opponent. Reading about your negotiating partner's situation, his or her business, and the industry at large is also a valuable way to gather information. Finally, you can ask your opponent for information: "How much do other department heads earn in salary and bonuses?" "What would it take to get your signature on the contract?" Of course, there is no guarantee that the answers you get will always be honest. In a salary negotiation, the employer would probably refuse to answer rather than lie, but in sales negotiations, bluffing can be part of the game: "I couldn't possibly pay more than $17.50 per unit," when in reality the buyer would go as high as $20.00.

While a bargaining approach to negotiations is sometimes obvious and appropriate, there are also cases when it is less apparent and destructive. For example, working groups often set themselves up for bargaining outcomes by following the principle of majority rule. If 51 percent of the group votes for a proposal, then 49 percent are losers—hardly a prescription for future harmony. Whenever the parties approach a problem by taking positions—that is, by stating specific outcomes they are seeking—they are forcing negotiations toward a bargaining outcome. For example, if an employee who wants to spend more time with his child approaches his boss with a specific request such as asking for a seven-hour day, the stage is set for a bargaining outcome. If the boss doesn't like the proposal, someone will be disappointed. Either the employee will get the time he needs with his child while the boss will have a staff shortage, or the boss will prevail and the employee will have to settle for the current schedule or quit.

Lose-Lose Orientation   Nobody seeks a lose-lose outcome. Nonetheless, there are too many times when both parties leave a negotiation unsatisfied. Lose-lose outcomes occur most frequently when each party tries to win at the other's expense. Like armies that take mortal losses while trying to defeat their enemies, disputants who go for a bargaining victory often find that they have hurt themselves as much as their opponents. Consider our example of the working parent who insists on a seven-hour workday. By forcing the issue, he may wind up having his request denied and then quitting or being fired as a result of his nonnegotiable demand. In this case, everyone suffers: the employer loses a talented worker and the employee's career and bank balance suffer. Lose-lose outcomes occur on larger issues as well: unreasonable union demands can drive employers into bankruptcy, and employers can destroy their workers' effectiveness by taking advantage of them. Mutual destruction can also arise from personal disputes; both parties in a feud may ruin their own careers, finding themselves characterized as "unable to get along with others" or as "poor team players."

Compromise   Sometimes it seems better to compromise than to fight battles in a bargaining manner and risk a lose-lose outcome. There certainly are cases in which compromise is the best obtainable outcome—usually when disputed resources are limited or scarce. If two managers each need a full-time secretary but budget restrictions make this impossible, they may have to compromise by sharing one secretary.

While compromises may be necessary, by definition the outcome is that both parties lose at least some of what they were seeking. Buyers, for instance, may pay more than they can afford, while sellers receive less than they need. Sometimes a series of compromises can leave neither getting what he or she really wants. For example, if a supplier and a purchasing officer start out from a "horse trading" perspective, the purchasing officer might end up with more supplies than the company needs at a higher total expenditure than his business can afford, while the supplier might be getting a lower price than her firm would like. In the case of the employee who wants extra time with his child, a compromise wouldn't be of much help to either party. There might still be times when the employee couldn't be with his child, and the boss would still be short of help. Compromises clearly aren't the best kind of outcome.

Win-Win Orientation   This collaborative approach to negotiation assumes that solutions can be reached that satisfy the needs of all parties. As Table 5-3 shows, a win-win approach differs significantly from the preceding negotiating styles. Most important, it looks beyond the conflicting *means* of both parties (my way versus your way) and focuses on satisfying the *ends* each is seeking.

The key to finding win-win solutions is to take the kind of problem-solving, noncontrolling approach described earlier in this chapter. Instead of viewing your negotiating partner as an adversary who needs to be defeated (a bargaining attitude), the key is to seek ways to satisfy both your needs and those of the other party. Win-win outcomes are possible in the many cases when the parties' needs aren't incompatible—just different. Consider again the case of the employee

TABLE 5-3   *Characteristics of Negotiating Styles*

BARGAINING	COMPROMISE	WIN-WIN
Controlling orientation exists (us versus them).	Problem orientation exists (us versus the problem).	
One party's gains are viewed as other party's losses.	Mutual gain is viewed as attainable.	
Argument over positions leads to polarization.	Seeking various approaches increases chances for agreement.	
Each side sees issue only from its own point of view.	Parties understand each other's point of view.	
Short-term approach focuses only on immediate problems.	Long-term approach seeks good relationship.	
Only task issues are usually considered.	Both task and relationship issues are considered.	

seeking a reduced workday. The employee needs care for his child before and after school. The boss needs to have a certain amount of work done. While these needs appear to conflict, they are not necessarily mutually exclusive. Sometimes the parties' needs are not only compatible but *identical*. In our example, both parties want the employee to continue on the job, and both want to maintain a happy relationship.

When the goals of the negotiating parties are compatible or similar, a win-win solution in which everyone is satisfied becomes possible. In this case, a number of win-win solutions are possible, for example:

- The employee could do some work at home during nonbusiness hours.
- The employee could share his full-time position with another worker, giving the boss the coverage the boss needs and the employee the free time. If the employee needs additional income, he could take part-time work that could be done at home at his convenience.
- The boss could help the employee locate a source of child care, possibly providing additional work time for the employee to earn the funds necessary to pay for it.

This list of solutions wouldn't work for everyone. The specific solutions that will work for a problem differ in each case. As you will soon read, the parties actually involved in a dispute should develop a list of possible solutions, and this list will differ according to the situation. The important point is that parties working together *can* find no-lose solutions to their problems.

Research shows that a win-win approach is superior to other problem-solving styles. In one study, researchers compared the problem-solving styles used in six organizations. They found that the two highest-performing ones used a win-win approach to a greater degree than the less effective organizations, while the lowest-performing organizations used that style less than the others.[13]

In another survey, seventy-four managers described how they and their immediate superiors dealt with conflicts. Five methods of conflict resolution were identified: withdrawal (which we have labeled as avoidance), smoothing, com-

---

Win-Win Negotiating in Action

Creative thinking and a collaborative attitude can transform potential lose-lose situations into win-win outcomes. Consider these examples.

Shorter Working Hours. As part of their job, teachers at a preschool were expected to keep school equipment clean and organized. Since there was never enough time during the school day to do this job, the director asked the teachers to come in over weekends. Even though they were paid for their time, the teachers resented giving up part of a Saturday or Sunday. A brainstorming session between the teachers and director produced a solution that satisfied everyone's needs: substitutes were hired to cover for the teachers during regular school hours while the teachers sorted and cleaned equipment. This approach had several benefits. Not only were the teachers' weekends left free, but they got a welcome break from child care during the regular week. Furthermore, the director was happy because paying the substitutes cost less than having the teachers work overtime.

Increasing Employee Compensation. The employees of a contractor wanted a raise. The owner agreed that they deserved one, but he opened his books to the workers to show that he was not financially able to provide the increase that they deserved. After considering alternatives together, the boss and employees came up with a plan that pleased everyone. Workers were allowed to use company vehicles during nonworking hours, saving them the expense of purchasing an extra car or truck. The owner made his vacation home in a popular mountain resort available for employees at a bargain rental rate. Finally, the boss negotiated arrangements with local merchants for his employees to buy home furnishings and appliances at favorable prices. Taken together, these benefits amounted to a solid increase in the employees' buying power—provided at little cost to the boss.

---

promise, forcing, and confrontation (or win-win style).[14] Each manager's conflict style was then compared with his or her effectiveness. The style that correlated most highly with supervisory effectiveness was confrontation (win-win). By contrast, compromise, forcing (bargaining), and withdrawal all had negative correlations with constructive outcomes. In other words, research shows that a win-win approach has the best chance of achieving good results.

The win-win approach is most successful when it follows five steps:

Identify the Needs of Both Parties   The key here is to avoid taking polar positions (arguing over means) and instead to identify the *ends* or goals of both parties. In their excellent book *Getting to Yes,* Roger Fisher and William Ury suggest two questions that can help to identify needs.[15] First, *ask why.* Put yourself in the other person's shoes, and ask yourself why the issue is so important to the other person. Once you have identified his or her needs, try to find answers that satisfy the other party. Second, *ask why not.* Try to discover what makes the other party unwilling to meet your request. Then try to find an answer that eliminates this objection.

It is important to identify personal, relational needs as well as task-related ones.[16] Common personal needs include the desire to be understood by the other party, to be treated with respect, and to have one's needs acknowledged as important. Unless these are recognized, you are unlikely to gain the cooperation of the other party.

The case of Roseanne, a senior manager, and Kurt, her assistant, shows how win-win problem solving begins with the identification of task and relational needs.

Kurt learned that his department was about to launch a particularly ambitious project and asked Roseanne if he could be in charge of it.

> "I'm sorry," she said, "but that's a major project. I need someone with more experience, especially in public relations, to handle that job. I've asked Greta to handle it."

> "I guess I understand," Kurt said doubtfully. "But I'd really like to take on more responsibility. This is the second time a big job went to somebody else, and I'm starting to wonder whether I'll get a shot at proving myself."

> "Well," Roseanne said, "I don't blame you for wanting to know where you stand. Your work has been good, though you still need some experience before you take on jobs like the one Greta will tackle. Let's try to figure out a way that you can have the responsibility and recognition you want and I can feel confident that the job is the right size."

Brainstorm a List of Possible Solutions   In this step, the goal is to work *with* the other party to develop a large number of solutions that might satisfy everyone's needs. Recall the problem-oriented approach introduced earlier in this chapter: instead of working against one another (How can *I* defeat *you*?), the parties work together against the problem (How can *we* beat the *problem*?).

The key to success here is to avoid evaluating any possible solutions for the time being. Nothing deflates creativity and increases defensiveness as much as evaluation. You can judge the quality of each idea later; but for now, the key is quantity. Perhaps one person's unworkable idea will spark a productive suggestion.

Kurt and Roseanne worked together to brainstorm several possible ways to meet their goals.

> "You could put me in charge of a major project—one not quite as big as this one," Kurt said, "and I could just check everything with you along the way."

> "Or," Roseanne said, "I might be able to team you up with someone who has experience in areas where you're weak, and you could run the project together."

> "What if I took on a less important project," Kurt proposed, "one that called for me to figure out problems in these areas?"

"Or I could get you to assist Greta on this project, so you could get some experience under her supervision and see how the aspects all fit together."

"Maybe you could assign me to handle the public relations on someone else's project, so I could concentrate on doing it right."

Evaluate the Alternative Solutions   Now is the time to decide which solutions are most promising. During this stage, it is still critical to work for an answer that meets the important needs of all the parties. Cooperation will only come if everyone feels satisfied with the solution.

Kurt and Roseanne's evaluation covered all the possibilities they had previously developed.

"All of these are possibilities," Roseanne said. "Let's see which of them will best suit us both. I could put you in charge of a major project, I guess, but you would need a lot of support, and I'm afraid I don't have enough time to give it to you."

Kurt agreed. "Plus it would drive us both crazy if I had to check every detail with you. But I don't really want to team up with someone, either. The whole idea is for me to get some experience where I need it, and a person who has that experience will just handle those concerns—which gets me nowhere."

"On the other hand," Roseanne said, "I don't want to just put you on your own. How would you feel about handling the public relations on Greta's project? She could use some extra help, and having that help would give her time to train you. It would also help you get a sense of the whole project— not just part of it."

Implement the Solution   Once the best plan is chosen, make sure everyone understands it, then give it a try. Kurt agreed to the idea of handling Greta's public relations.

"Just one thing," he insisted. "I want Greta to know that my job is to be responsible for that part of the project—not just to be her assistant."

"Sounds fair to me," Roseanne replied. "I'll talk to Greta and make sure she's agreeable. I do think she has a lot of good advice to offer, though. You'd be foolish not to consider her opinions. And, of course, both she and I will have to support your decisions. But I'll be sure both of us give you the freedom to come up with your own plan—and the responsibility that goes with the freedom."

Follow Up on the Solution   Even the most appealing plans may need revision when put into action. After a reasonable amount of time, plan to meet with the other parties and discuss how the solution is working out. If necessary, return to step 1, and identify the needs that are still unmet; then repeat the problem-solving procedure.

Roseanne, Kurt, and Greta met several weeks after developing their plan to check its progress.

> "I'm feeling pretty good about the arrangement," Kurt began. "I appreciate the chance to be responsible for one part of such a big project. Just one thing, Greta. When we agree on the way I'll do a job, I feel uncomfortable when you keep checking on how I'm doing. It makes me wonder whether you think I'll mess it up."

> "Not at all, Kurt," Greta replied. "I thought you'd want to know that I'm available for support. Of course, I do want to keep posted, but I don't have any intention of being a snoop. What do you suggest?"

> "How about letting me come to you," Kurt suggested. "I promise to keep you on top of things, and I do appreciate your advice. I'd just like to have a little more operating room."

> "Sounds like a good arrangement," Roseanne said. "Let's give it a try and get together next week at this time to see how it works."

Since a win-win approach is so obviously superior to the other negotiating methods, it is hard to imagine why a person would reject it. Despite this, some people do seem unwilling to cooperate. Most such rejections come from the other person's inability to imagine how both parties could succeed. When you suspect this is the case, a selling job is in order. Begin by paraphrasing your understanding of the other's ends: "It sounds to me that what you need is . . . " Once you have clarified these ends, point out the possibility of achieving the other person's goals and your own and sharing the beneficial consequences of such a win-win outcome. For instance, if Kurt had refused to accept Roseanne's decision to assign the project to Greta, the negotiation between them might have gone this way:

> "I just can't accept your saying that the job is too big for me," Kurt said. "I've been here over a year now, and I'm starting to wonder if I'll ever have a chance to show what I can do. I *know* I can handle this one."

> "It sounds like you need to know you have a future with us, Kurt, and that you want a chance to prove yourself," said Roseanne. "I'm with you on both counts. I'm just not comfortable turning you loose on this job, but let's see if we can work out some other arrangement that will give you the responsibility and visibility you're after."

There are also cases in which an unwillingness to cooperate comes from malice. The other person may have a personal goal that involves trying to punish you by denying what you seek. For example, if Roseanne disliked Kurt and wanted to force him out of the company by refusing to let him grow in his job, her success would depend on his disappointment. In such instances, it is often difficult to get the other person to admit to such an ignoble goal. You can, however, increase the chances of identifying and sidetracking progress toward that goal by using the assertive message format described earlier in this chapter: "When you refuse even to discuss my ideas about how we could both get what we want [description], I get the idea that it's important to you that I wind up unhappy, which leaves me confused and worried [explanation]. I'd like to know if you are mad at me and, if you are, why [request]." You can then go on to outline the positive consequences of cooperating for both of you ("I'd be more valuable to you if I could get more experience") and perhaps the negative consequences of failing to reach agreement ("I hope we can settle this between us before management starts asking what's going on"). Success here depends on persuading the other person that he or she will be better off (in terms of money, time, self-respect, friendships, stress) with a solution that satisfies you both than with one that fails to meet either of your needs.

WHICH NEGOTIATING STYLE TO USE

The fundamental decision that negotiators face is whether to adopt a win-win approach or to use bargaining tactics. The other two options are rarely first choices: no rational person would seek a lose-lose outcome, and compromises are usually a second choice when it is impossible to win everything one wants.

Win-win and bargaining negotiating styles are fundamentally incompatible: the behaviors that enable one style to work make the other one impossible. The differences between these approaches fall into four categories.

Cooperation Versus Competition   Parties in bargaining negotiations view one another as opponents. They assume that one side's gain is the other's loss. On the other hand, win-win negotiators cooperate. They believe that it is possible for both sides to get what they want. The decision about whether the other party is an ally or an opponent can be a self-fulfilling prophecy. If you treat someone like an enemy, the person is likely to behave that way. Cooperating with a negotiating partner, however, increases the odds of getting cooperation in return. Nonetheless, there are some times when it is unrealistic to expect cooperation—when the other side will lose in proportion to your gains, for example.

Power Versus Trust   Power is the name of the game in a bargaining contest. Parties fear—often justifiably—that the other side will take advantage of any weaknesses they show. In a win-win situation, however, parties do not take advantage of each other. Power is replaced by trust.

Distorted Versus Open Communication   Although it is impossible to justify telling deliberate lies, negotiators who bargain may withhold information, exaggerate, and bluff. You might, for example, flinch and complain about a price that you really would be willing to pay in order to get a further concession, and you

---

A little bit of dishonesty can create a lot of distrust. If one statement of mine in a hundred is false, you may choose not to rely on me at all. Unless you can develop a theory of when I am honest and when I am not, your discovery of a small dishonesty will cast doubt over everything I say and do.

Roger Fisher and Scott Brown, *Getting Together*

---

could act cool toward an offer that really excites you in the hope that your adversary will sweeten it. In a win-win situation, however, honesty is the best policy. Both parties place all their cards on the table, trusting that their openness won't be exploited.

Self-Centered Versus Mutual Concern　In bargaining, each party focuses on its own goal. Parties give ground only when forced to. By contrast, parties who use a win-win approach listen openly to each other and come to understand each other's position. Furthermore, they try to help each other achieve satisfaction.

SUMMARY

"People skills" are an essential ingredient for success in any career. These skills create a positive communication climate in which people feel valued. The key to building a positive climate is confirming communication, which conveys respect for the other person, even during a conflict. Confirming messages are phrased in descriptive "I" language. They focus on solving problems, not imposing solutions. They are honest, show concern for the other party, demonstrate an attitude of equality, and reflect the communicator's open-mindedness. Disconfirming responses exhibit the opposite traits: some ignore or interrupt other communicators; others are irrelevant, tangential, impersonal, ambiguous, or incongruous.

On-the-job conflicts are inevitable. The goal should not be to avoid them, but to handle them constructively. There are five ways to handle conflict: by avoiding, accommodating, competing, collaborating, or compromising. Each of these approaches has both advantages and drawbacks, so situational factors will usually govern which one to use at a given time.

Negotiations occur when two or more parties discuss specific proposals to find a mutually acceptable agreement. Negotiations can result in four types of outcomes: bargaining, lose-lose, compromise, and win-win. The approach that parties take during negotiations often determines which of these outcomes will result. The chapter outlined when to use bargaining and win-win negotiating methods. Win-win outcomes arise when parties identify their needs clearly, brainstorm, and evaluate a variety of possible solutions before choosing the best one and following up on the solution after implementing it.

ACTIVITIES

1. Describe the communication climate where you work. Identify the confirming and disconfirming behaviors that contribute to this climate.

2. If you asked a co-worker to describe your confirming and disconfirming behaviors,

   a. What kinds of behaviors would be identified? In what situations do they occur?
   b. What are the results of these behaviors for you and the other people involved?

   Describe specifically how you could behave in a more confirming manner.

3. Recall your behavior in three recent conflicts. These conflicts needn't have been "fights"; they can consist of any situation in which you and another party were faced with apparently incompatible goals.

   a. Describe your conflict style in each situation. Was it avoiding, accommodating, competing, collaborating, or compromising?
   b. What were the consequences of this style? Describe both the immediate and long-term results.
   c. How might you have changed your style to produce more constructive results?

4. Describe an avoiding, accommodating, competing, collaborating, and compromising response to each of the following situations:

   a. At 4:30 P.M. a boss asks her secretary to work late in order to retype a twenty-five-page report due the next morning. The secretary has an important date that evening.
   b. A worker finds the smoke from a colleague's cigarettes offensive.

   c. The assistant manager of a bookstore is faced with a customer demanding a refund for a book he claims was a gift. The book has several crumpled pages and a torn cover.
   d. A supervisor is faced by an irate employee complaining about another worker's "unfair" promotion to a position the employee had sought.

5. Recall a conflict from your own experience that resulted in a lose-lose outcome. Did the parties approach the issue with a bargaining orientation? If not, how did such an outcome result?

6. Identify the compatible and identical needs in each of these conflicts:

   a. A landlord-tenant dispute over who should pay for an obviously necessary painting job
   b. A disagreement between two co-workers over who should deliver a proposal to an important client
   c. A disagreement between a sales manager and the sales representatives over the quota necessary to earn bonuses
   d. A disagreement between a marketing manager and a product development manager about the kind of advertising that should be used for a new product

7. Decide which negotiating style is most appropriate in each of the following situations. Supply details as necessary to explain your choice.

   a. Your boss wants you to work during a time you have planned for an out-of-town vacation.
   b. You are not satisfied with the quality of a recent shipment of metal fasteners, which you use in assembling a product.

c. You want to rent office space for your small business at a rate that is 5 to 10 percent less than the advertised price.

d. You need an extra week to complete a long, complex assignment.

Communicator Profile

Dianne Corso
Senior Negotiator
State of Alaska

I think the classical definition of rhetoric—"a good person speaking well"—captures the idea. You have to be "good"—that is, ethical, honest, true to your word—or all the negotiation skills under the sun aren't going to be worth anything.

My job is never boring! I am responsible for labor negotiations with all unionized state employees in Alaska: 10,000 to 12,000 employees. Also, I supervise grievance arbitration and other dispute resolution procedures. During a typical day, I might deal with everything from an individual employee's performance problem—alcohol abuse is typical—to a budget cut in which hundreds of employees are going to get laid off.

When contracts are negotiated, I go to the bargaining table. Typically, it takes four or five months to hammer out an agreement, but some negotiations can take considerably longer. One we just finished, which involved 8,500 employees, took eighteen months to complete. Since the downturn in oil prices starting in 1986, we have been in exceptional times. State employees didn't have a raise in five years, and the threat of a layoff is always present, so feelings run high in my work.

I've come to believe that the ability to communicate is absolutely crucial. In ten years, on both the union and management sides of the table, the only people I've ever fired were people who couldn't communicate. When I hire someone, I look for good oral and written communication skills. The practices and procedures of labor relations can be learned on the job.

Sometimes compromises are the best outcome you can achieve in a negotiation. Economics may make it impossible for both sides to win everything they want. For example, there has to be a compromise if the union is asking for a 10 percent raise but there's no money to give. Even in cases like this, a win-win outcome is possible if one or both of the parties redefine what it means to "win." For instance, if employees are willing to trade a demand for more pay to get greater job security or more flexible working hours, everyone can be satisfied with the results.

Most working relationships are long-term—people have to work together after the immediate issue is resolved. That means people have to feel like they're in an overall win-win cooperative mode, even if they lose specific disputes once in a while. That's why, in my work, we try to resolve as much as possible before a formal grievance or a strike. Informal conflict resolutions are less expensive, and they keep the climate as positive as possible.

The most important qualities in conflict resolution and communication in general are sensitivity and flexibility. I may talk in one-syllable words on one phone call and then pick up the phone the next time and use my best Ph.D. terminology. You have to be versatile. I may walk in one door and say "If you do that again, you're fired" and then go into arbitration the next day and use "hearsay objections" and other legal terminology.

Another essential part of communication

is to treat your audience or adversary with respect. There are few, if any, long-term benefits to an aggressive or indirect approach. You can beat the other guy into submission, but, if you do, you will have to deal with direct consequences eventually, when the next contract comes up for negotiation. No matter how much you disagree, whatever your objective, you must try to respect the other side.

I used to teach communication myself, and I think the classical definition of rhetoric— "a good person speaking well"—captures the idea. You have to be "good"—that is, ethical, honest, true to your word—or all the negotia- tions and techniques under the sun aren't going to be worth anything.

When there is integrity and respect and the communication goes well, when you can go forward in a friendly, businesslike manner after the conflict is resolved, that's a real win-win. I strive for that in my work. The way I measure my success is that some of the most active people on the other side of the bargaining table have stayed in touch and even called me up and sent me some get-well cards when I was sick. That human element is most important to me, when we can remain friends and not adversaries.

6

After reading this chapter, you should understand:

- How interviewing differs from other types of conversation
- The steps necessary in planning and conducting an interview
- The characteristics, advantages, and disadvantages of highly scheduled, moderately scheduled, and unscheduled interview structures
- The characteristics of various types of questions: open and closed, fact and opinion, primary and secondary, direct and indirect, hypothetical, leading, and loaded
- The responsibilities of interviewer and respondent in an interview

You should be able to:

- Develop specific objectives for an upcoming interview
- Analyze the other party in an upcoming interview and develop an appropriate interview strategy based on your analysis
- For an upcoming interview, choose a structure, question sequence, and specific questions that will best achieve your objectives
- As interviewer, follow the guidelines for behavior during the opening, body, and closing of a real-life or simulated interview
- Participate in an interview in an ethical, responsible manner

PRINCIPLES OF INTERVIEWING

Sharon, a marketing manager for a building-supplies manufacturer, is preparing for a trade convention. Although her firm produces more than a thousand products, she can show only a few at the convention. She calls the convention coordinator and asks questions that will help her plan the exhibit: Are the builders who attend the convention mostly concerned with large public buildings, mostly with private homes, or a combination of both? How large will her exhibit space be? Will electrical outlets be available, and can they handle large power demands?

Daniel, the publicity coordinator for a health workers' organization, is starting a newsletter. Several members have volunteered to help—more than he needs, at least at the beginning. He asks each one to come into his office and explains the idea of the newsletter and the help he will need to design, write, edit, and produce the newsletter. He asks them whether they have ever done anything in any of these areas and how much time they will be able to contribute. Eventually, he chooses three people to handle major tasks and asks the others to help out as needed.

The release date on a new product has been delayed four times in five months, and Carol, the department head, is worried that the new line will not be ready for Christmas. She asks Marian, who is in charge of coordinating the schedule, to explain the problems and any ideas she has for making up lost time.

Susan has worked in the accounting department for three months when Lloyd, her supervisor, calls her into his office. "Is there a problem?" she asks nervously. "No, no," Lloyd replies. "I wanted to let you know we've been pleased with your performance and to find out how you feel about your work in the last three months. I'd also like to know more about how you see yourself in the company in the future."

Each of these conversations is an interview, *a two-party conversation in which at least one person has a specific, serious purpose.* This definition makes it clear that interviewing is a special kind of conversation, differing from other types in several ways. Most important, interviewing is always *purposeful.* Unlike more spontaneous conversations, an interview includes at least one participant who has a serious, predetermined reason for being there. Interviews are also more *structured* than most conversations. As you will soon learn, every good interview has several distinct phases and always involves some sort of question-and-answer format. Interviews also have an element of *control* not present in more casual interaction. The interviewer's job is to keep the conversation moving toward a predetermined goal. Interviews are also *bipolar,* always involving just two parties. While there may be several interviewers (as sometimes occurs in employment situations) or multiple respondents (as in a "Meet the Press" journalistic format), there are always two parties: interviewer and respondent. A final difference between interviewing and other conversation involves the *amount of speaking* by each party. While the speakers in most informal conversations speak equally, experts suggest that participation in most interviews (with the possible exception of sales and information-giving types) ought to be distributed in roughly a 70 to 30 percent ratio, with the interviewee doing most of the talking.[1]

Some people in business spend much of their time in interviews. For example, salespeople spend a great deal of time in sales interviews to assess a customer's needs. Health-care professionals, including nurses, doctors, dental hygienists, and emergency-room receptionists, interview patients to learn about their problems. Most managerial jobs also require some interviews. Many consultants recommend that managers practice "management by walking around" and regularly interview their subordinates about progress, problems, and concerns. For example, Ed Gresham, president of ERA Realty, often spends six hours a day talking with managers about their work.[2] In fact, communication authorities claim that interviews are the most common form of planned communication.[3]

There are many kinds of interviews, each of which requires some special skills. Many common principles, however, apply to planning and conducting most interviews.

PLANNING THE INTERVIEW

A successful interview begins before the parties face each other. Whether you are the interviewer or the respondent, background work can mean the difference between success and disappointment.

DEFINE THE GOAL

Sometimes the purpose of an interview isn't as obvious as it seems at first. For instance, if you are a hotel manager and have received several complaints about the surly manner of a desk clerk, you would certainly speak to the employee. What would your purpose be?

An obvious answer would be to change the clerk's behavior, but this goal isn't precise enough. Will you reprimand the clerk, insisting on a change in behavior? Will you act as a counselor, trying to correct the problem by understanding the causes of the employee's rudeness? Or will you take the role of an explainer, teaching the clerk some new customer-relations skills? While the general goal of each approach is identical (changing the clerk's behavior), the precise goal influences your approach.

The same principle operates in other types of interviews. In a selling situation, is the goal to get a single order or to build a long-term relationship? Is your goal in a grievance interview to ask for specific changes or simply to have your past concerns acknowledged?

In any interview, you should make your goal as clear as possible, as in the following examples:

Vague: Improve clerk's behavior
Better: Teach clerk how to handle registration problems
Best: Teach clerk what to tell guests when rooms are not ready

Vague: Turn prospect into a customer
Better: Show customer features and benefits of my product
  Best: Identify prospect's needs and show how my product can satisfy them, resulting in trial order

The interviewee should also have a clear purpose. Notice, for example, the interviewee's purposes in the following grievance and employment interviews:

Vague: Complain about unfair supervisor
Better: Protest unfair scheduling of assignments
  Best: Have supervisor develop fair method of scheduling future assignments

Vague: Get job offer
Better: Get job offer by demonstrating my competence
  Best: Get job offer by describing my work experience, referring to my favorable references, and describing my ideas for the position

IDENTIFY AND ANALYZE THE OTHER PARTY

Whether you are the interviewer or the interviewee, your interviews will be more useful and successful if you select the right person to talk to whenever you have a choice. If you are looking for information, the person you select to interview may greatly influence the quality of the information you get. For example, if you want to know more about the safety procedures in a manufacturing area, the plant manager or foreman can tell you more about them than, say, publicity staff—who

---

Identifying the appropriate interviewee, the person who makes purchasing decisions, is vital in sales. Mark H. McCormack, owner of a sports promotion agency, describes the situation:

> One of the biggest problems we have had as a sales organization is figuring out who within another company will be making a decision on what. Very often in our business we don't know if it's the advertising department, the marketing department, or someone in PR or corporate communications. It may very well turn out to be the chairman and CEO of a multibillion-dollar corporation if the subject is of personal interest to him.
>
> In certain companies, particularly multinational, multisegmented operations, it is almost impossible to figure out the decision-making process, or to find any sort of central authority. . . . In most companies, however, the decision-making process is not only there somewhere, it is discernible—as are the names of the decision makers. To find them, it is mostly a matter of doing your homework and asking the right questions.

Mark H. McCormack, *What They Don't Teach You at Harvard Business School*

probably get their information from the plant manager anyway. Identifying the decision maker can be vital for many interviews. For example, if you want to find out how you can coordinate your efforts with another department's, it may be useful to talk to the person who coordinates that department before you talk to anyone in your own department.

The Other's Concept of Self   The self-image of the other party can have a strong effect on what goes on in an interview. Imagine yourself as interviewee, and consider the self-image of the interviewer.

For example, if your boss is interviewing you about a project that isn't going well, consider whether she sees herself as a colleague who might be able to help you, an authority whose advice you should take, or an employee who will be in trouble if she has to defend a failure to her own superiors. Likewise, if you are the interviewer, the interviewee's self-concept should influence how you approach the session. A subordinate who feels personally responsible for a failure will need to be treated differently from one who feels that the failure was not his or her fault.

Knowledge Level   Your questions and answers should be tailored to the information the other person has. A sales representative who bombarded a prospective client with overly technical information would probably be making a mistake, as would a supervisor who sought managerial advice from an employee who has no experience in leading others.

Your Image   Who you are isn't as important as who the other party *thinks* you are. In an employment interview, a knowledgeable applicant who *appears* uninformed is in trouble. In the same way, an employee may want to discuss constructively a problem with the boss, but if the boss thinks the subordinate only wants to complain, the employee's chances for success are limited.

Attitude   Even if the other party has a favorable image of you, his or her feelings about the topic might require careful planning on your part. One interior designer learned this fact the hard way. She was interviewing the partner of a nationally recognized architectural firm about various areas of professional specialization. While discussing the merits of publicly versus privately funded jobs, she asked about requirements for handicapped access. The architect launched into a half-hour tirade about the irrationality of "dumb bureaucratic rules," leaving no time for the designer to cover several important areas.

You may find three sources of information particularly useful. First, you can listen to *what people say.* Co-workers, friends, and even the media can be sources for learning about the other person. "I'm going to ask for a raise," you might tell a friend with whom you work. "How do you think I should bring it up?" If you interview an executive about career opportunities, knowing your subject's career history or education might help you build rapport and ask useful questions.

If you have known the other person before the interview, *what that person has said* can be a good source of information. If you are asking for a raise, you may have once heard your boss comment favorably about an employee who "really had facts and figures to back up what he said." This information could give you an important clue about how to present your arguments.

Finally, you can discover a great deal about the person you will interview by *observation*. If you have seen the other party dress casually, use informal language, or joke around, you might behave differently than if you had observed more straight-laced behavior. Does he or she seem to encourage drop-in visits or prefer prearranged appointments?

Even if you are meeting the person for the first time, you can still learn something from observation. One sales authority recommends:

> Be observant. Many times there are clues all around the office that will give you ideas that may assist you in talking the prospect's language and, thus, making the sale. Look for trophies, pictures, books, decor, awards, and plaques. It's a safe bet that the prospect is very proud of anything that is on display in the office.[4]

PREPARE A LIST OF TOPICS

Sometimes the topics an interview should cover will become clear as soon as you've listed your objectives. An insurance-claims investigator, for example, usually covers a standard agenda when collecting data on an accident: road conditions, positions of the vehicles, nature and extent of injuries, and so on. In other cases, however, some background research is necessary before you can be sure an agenda is complete. An office manager who is considering the purchase of a new computer might need to do some reading and talk with her staff before she can know what questions to ask the sales representatives who will be calling on her. She will probably want to learn about the following topics:

Objective: To purchase an affordable word processing system that will be easy to learn and use

List of Topics

Attitudes of the staff toward computers
Funds available to allocate for computer use
The general price range of the product
Whether computer companies have fixed or negotiable prices

Interviewees, too, should have goals and agendas. A job-seeker approaching an employment interview might have a program like this:

Objective: To have the interviewer view me as a bright, ambitious, articulate person who knows about and can serve the company's needs

List of Topics

Discuss my short-term and long-term career goals
Answer all questions completely and in an organized way
Share my knowledge of the company's products and financial condition

CHOOSE THE BEST INTERVIEW STRUCTURE

There are several types of interview structures. Each calls for different levels of planning and produces different results.

A *highly scheduled* interview consists of a standardized list of questions. In its most extreme form, it even specifies their precise wording and the order in which they are asked. Highly scheduled interviews are most common in market research, opinion polls, and attitude surveys. Most of the questions allow only a limited range of answers: "How many televisions do you own?" "Which of the following words best describes your evaluation of the company?" The answers to closed questions such as these are easy to tabulate, which makes them convenient for surveying large numbers of respondents. Because of their detailed structure, highly scheduled interviews call for less skill by the questioner.

Highly scheduled interviews have drawbacks, however, that make them unsuitable for most situations. The range of topics is limited by a predetermined list of questions, and there is no chance for the interviewer to follow up intriguing or unclear answers that might arise during the conversation.

The *nonscheduled* interview stands in contrast to its highly scheduled counterpart. It usually consists of a topical agenda without specific questions. Many managers make a point of regularly "dropping in" on their employees. The conversation may be generally directed at finding out how the employees are doing with their work, whether they are satisfied with their jobs, whether they have any problems—personal or work-related—that the manager should know about, but there are no specific questions planned. Such nonscheduled interviews allow considerable flexibility about the amount of time and nature of the questioning in the various content areas. They permit the conversation to flow in whatever direction seems most productive.

Nonscheduled interviewing looks easy when it's done with skill, but it's actually very difficult. It's easy to lose track of time or to focus too much on one topic and neglect others. When you're worried about what to ask next, you may forget to listen closely to the interviewee's answer and miss clues to ask for more information.

The *moderately scheduled* interview combines features of the other types. The interviewer prepares a list of topics to be covered, anticipates their probable order, and lists several major questions and possible follow-up probes. These make up a flexible plan, which the interviewer can use or adapt as circumstances warrant. The planned questions ensure coverage of important areas, while allowing for examination of important but unforeseen topics.

CONSIDER POSSIBLE QUESTIONS

After clarifying your purpose, setting an agenda, and deciding on a format, you are ready to think about specific questions. As you might expect, the type and quality of questions are the biggest factor in determining the success or failure of an interview.

The proper questions to ask might seem to be obvious once an agenda is finished, but this is not always the case. An interviewer should consider several types of questions when planning an interview.

Open Versus Closed Questions   Closed questions restrict the interviewee's response. Some ask the respondent to choose from a range of answers: "Which of the three shifts would you prefer to work on?" "Do you think Mary, Dave, or Leonard would be best for the job?" "Would you rather stay in this department or have a transfer?" Other closed questions ask for specific data: "How long have you worked here?" "When do you think the order will be ready?"

Open questions invite a broader, more detailed range of responses. "What makes you interested in working for this company?" "Start at the beginning, and tell me about the problem." "What would you do if you were in my position?"

As an interviewee, you may sometimes want to turn a closed question into an open one so that you can share more information:

> *Question:* Do you have any experience as a manager?
> *Answer:* Not on the job, but I've studied management in several college courses, and I'm looking forward to developing the skills I learned there. I'm especially excited about using the situational leadership approach I learned in my business communication course. I understand you've sent several of your people to workshops on the subject.

As Table 6-1 shows, both open and closed questions have their advantages.

Factual Versus Opinion Questions   Some questions investigate matters of fact: "Have you taken any courses in accounting?" "Are you willing to relocate if we have an opening in another city?" "Can we apply lease payments to the purchase price, if we decide to buy?" Others ask for the respondent's opinion: "Which vendor do you think gives the best service?" "Do you think Al is being sincere?" "Is the investment worth it?"

Whether you approach a topic seeking facts or opinions can greatly influ-

TABLE 6-1   Use of Open and Closed Questions

WHEN TO USE OPEN QUESTIONS	WHEN TO USE CLOSED QUESTIONS
1. To relax the interviewee (if the question is easy to answer and nonthreatening)	1. To maintain control over the conversation
2. To discover the interviewee's opinions	2. When specific information is needed and you are not interested in the interviewee's feelings or opinions
3. To evaluate the interviewee's communication skills	3. When time is short
4. To explore the interviewee's possession of information	4. When the interviewer is not highly skilled
5. To discover the interviewee's feelings or values	5. When a high degree of standardization between interviews is important

Adapted from Gerald L. Wilson and H. Lloyd Goodall, Jr., *Interviewing in Context* (New York: McGraw-Hill, 1991), pp. 75–80.

ence the results. A manager trying to resolve a dispute between two employees could approach each one subjectively, asking, "What's the source of this problem?" This is a broad opinion-seeking question that invites disagreement between the disputants. A more factual question would be: "Tell me when you first noticed the problem, and describe what happened."

This doesn't mean that it is always better to ask factual questions. Opinions are often precisely what you are seeking. A client seeking financial advice from an investment counselor would be making a mistake by asking "How have energy stocks done in the past?" when the real question is "How do you expect they'll do in the future?" Your decision about whether to seek facts or opinions has to be based on your reason for asking the question.

Primary and Secondary Questions   Primary questions introduce new topics or areas within topics: "How did you hear about our company?" "Do you have any questions for me?" "How often do you use the transit system?" Secondary questions aim at gathering additional information about a topic that has already been introduced: "Tell me more about it." "What do you mean by 'commitment'?" "Does that price include shipping costs?"

Secondary questions are useful in several circumstances:[5]

- When a previous answer is *incomplete:* "What did Marilyn say then?"
- When a previous answer is *superficial or vague:* "What do you mean, you *think* the figures are right?"
- When a previous answer is *irrelevant:* "I understand that the job interests you. Can you tell me about your training in the field?"
- When a previous answer seems *inaccurate:* "You said everyone supports the idea. What about Herb?"

Direct and Indirect Questions   The best way to get information is usually to ask for it directly: "What area of our business interests you most?" "I hear you've been unhappy with our service. What's the problem?"

Sometimes, however, a straightforward approach won't work. One such case is when the respondent isn't *able* to answer a direct question accurately. This inability may come from a lack of information, as when a supervisor's question "Do you understand?" gets a "Yes" from employees who mistakenly believe that they do. A respondent may not be *willing* to give a direct answer that would be risky or embarrassing. A boss who asks a subordinate "Are you satisfied with my leadership?" isn't likely to get a straight answer if the employee thinks the boss is incompetent or unfair.

DIRECT QUESTION	INDIRECT QUESTION
"Do you understand?"	"Suppose you had to explain this policy to other people in the department. What would you say?"

DIRECT QUESTION	INDIRECT QUESTION
"Are you satisfied with my leadership?"	"If you were manager of this department, what changes would you make?"

Sometimes even the most skillful indirect questions won't generate a good response. But there is another indirect way of judging a response—the interviewee's nonverbal behavior. Facial expressions, postures, gestures, eye contact, and other nonverbal behaviors offer clues about another person's emotional state. Here is a description of how one attorney uses nonverbal behaviors when selecting members of a jury:

> To gauge nonverbal clues, Fahringer may ask the potential juror, "Mr. Jones, I'm going to ask you to do me a favor. Will you look at my client, Billy Williams, right now, and tell me whether you can think of him as being innocent." At that instant, Fahringer concentrates on the juror's face. "If he has difficulty looking at my client, or, when he glances at him, drops his eyes, rejecting him, he has told me all that I need to know."[6]

The same technique can work in the business world. For example, a manager who thinks an employee may be afraid to admit problems with a project can watch how the employee reacts nonverbally to a question such as "Is everything still on schedule for the September fifteenth opening?"

Hypothetical Questions   These questions seek the respondent's answer to a what-if question. They can be a useful way of indirectly getting a respondent to describe beliefs or attitudes: "If we were to take a poll about the morale level around here, what do you think the results would be?"

Hypothetical questions are also a useful way of learning how people would respond in certain situations. A bank manager might test candidates for promotion by asking, "Suppose you became assistant operations manager, and you had to talk to one of the tellers about her manner toward customers. What would you do if she accused you of acting bossy and forgetting your friends since your promotion?" Again, there is no guarantee hypothetical answers will reflect a person's real behavior, but their specificity and realism can give strong clues.

Leading Questions   Leading questions force or tempt the respondent to answer in one way. They frequently suggest the answer the interviewer expects: "How committed are you to our company's philosophy of customer service?" "You aren't really serious about asking for a raise now, are you?" Leading questions may have their place in persuasive interviews when the goal is to sell a product, but they are rarely appropriate in other types of interviews.

Some questions are only mildly leading: "I came across this idea yesterday in the *Wall Street Journal*. It looks interesting. What do you think of it?" In other cases, questions are highly leading. Using emotionally charged words and name calling, they indicate the only acceptable answer: "You haven't fallen for those worn-out arguments, have you?" Other highly loaded questions rely on a bandwagon effect for pressure: "Do you agree with everyone else that it's best to put this incident behind us and forget the whole thing?"

ORGANIZE QUESTIONS EFFECTIVELY

Besides planning individual questions, the interviewer needs to consider the arrangement of groups of questions. There are three basic types of arrangements.

Funnel Sequence   A funnel sequence begins with a broad, open question and proceeds to seek increasingly specific information, as the following example illustrates:

> *Manager:*   (in a problem-solving interview) We've lost several good workers in the past year, and we'd hate to lose any more. What do you think is going on?
>
> *Employee:*   Well, a couple of people mentioned pay, but I don't think that's the biggest problem.
>
> *Manager:*   What do you think it is?
>
> *Employee:*   I think it comes down to being bored—not challenged or appreciated.
>
> *Manager:*   What kinds of challenges? What kinds of appreciation?
>
> *Employee:*   Well, I know that Smith and Jones both talked about having some good ideas about how to do the job better, but they complained that nobody seemed interested in listening.
>
> *Manager:*   If you were the manager, how would you listen better?

A funnel sequence is useful when the interviewer is not sure what information she or he is seeking. In the example above, the manager knew that good people were leaving the company, but he didn't know why. His open questions let the employee offer some suggestions. Funnel sequences work best when the respondent knows the topic well or when the interviewer wants to encourage the expression of feelings. They also avoid predisposing the respondent to give a certain type of answer. Imagine, for example, how the conversation might have differed if the manager had started by asking, "Do you think we're paying our people well enough?"

Inverted Funnel Sequence   An inverted funnel begins with closed questions and gradually broadens the range of possible answers.

> *Colleague A:*   I'd like to get your ideas about how I should approach the boss. Do you think I ought to send her a memo about my idea or talk to her about it first?

Colleague B: If I were in that position, I'd mention it briefly and then send her a memo. Then you could go over it together after she's read the memo.

Colleague A: How much detail do you think I ought to go into in the memo?

Colleague B: I'd keep it to a page or two at the most. She's busy, and she gets impatient sometimes.

Colleague A: Here's a rough draft. What do you think of it?

An inverted funnel sequence works well when the subject might be reluctant to offer information at first. The early closed questions are relatively easy to answer, and the answers they provide can lead to more revealing open questions later.

Tunnel Sequence   A tunnel sequence consists of a series of questions that are similar in depth. They are usually primary in nature, requiring little follow-up. An interviewer surveying consumer attitudes might use a tunnel sequence by asking the following:

"What, if any, magazines do you subscribe to?"

"Which ones do you read thoroughly on a regular basis?"

"Have you stopped subscribing to any magazines within the past year?"

"Can you tell me the names of any other magazines you would enjoy reading regularly?"

ARRANGE THE SETTING

A manager at a major publishing company regularly interviews subordinates over lunch at a restaurant where company employees frequently eat together. "The advantage of meeting here," the manager says, "is we're both relaxed. They can talk about their work without feeling as though they've been called on the carpet to defend themselves. They're also more inclined to ask for help with a problem than if we were in the office, and I can ask for improvements and make suggestions without making it seem like a formal reprimand. We also have time to talk without people dropping in or the phone ringing. Of course, if I'm not happy with the person, or if I'm about to fire them, I certainly wouldn't do it over lunch. If that happened, or if they had a serious, confidential problem to discuss, I'd take them in my office, close the door, and have my secretary hold all calls."

The physical setting in which an interview occurs can have a great deal of influence on the results. With some planning of time and place, you can avoid the frustrations of trying to discuss a confidential matter with a co-worker within earshot of people who would love to overhear your conversation or of trying to stop your boss in the hall to ask for a raise when she's on her way to a meeting and the easiest way to get free of you is to say no.

Time   When you plan an interview, give careful thought to how much time you will need to accomplish your purpose, and let the other person know how much time you expect to take. If you ask a co-worker in another department to spend half an hour with you to answer some questions about a mutual project, he can schedule his time so you won't have to cut the session short or try to cram an important discussion into fifteen minutes.

Other things to consider are the time of day and what the people involved have to do before and after the interview. For example, if you know your boss has an important meeting this afternoon, you can reasonably assume she will be too preoccupied or too busy to talk to you right beforehand and perhaps immediately afterward. You may also want to avoid scheduling an important interview right before lunch so that neither person will be more anxious to eat than to accomplish the goal of the interview.

Place   The right place is just as important as the right time. The first consideration here is to arrange a setting that is free of distractions. The request "Hold all my calls" is a good sign that you will have the attention of your interviewing partner. Sometimes it's best to choose a spot away from the normal habitat of either person. Not only does this lessen the chance of interruptions, but people often speak more freely and think more creatively when they are in a neutral space, away from familiar settings that trigger habitual ways of responding.

The physical arrangement of the setting can also influence the interview. Generally, the person sitting behind a desk—whether interviewee or respondent—gains power and formality. On the other hand, a seating arrangement in which the parties face each other across a table or sit with no barrier between them promotes equality and informality. Distance, too, affects the relationship between interviewer and respondent. Other things being equal, two people seated forty inches apart will have more immediacy in their conversation than will the same people discussing the same subject at a distance of six or seven feet.

Isn't it usually desirable to create a casual atmosphere in an interview? As with other variables, the choice of closeness or distance depends on your goal. A medical interviewer who wants to seek personal information without embarrassing the respondent or a supervisor who wants to assert his authority during a reprimand session might choose to increase distance and sit behind a desk. On the other hand, a sales representative who wants to gain the trust of a customer would probably avoid the barrier of a desk.

CONDUCTING THE INTERVIEW

After careful planning, the interview itself takes place. An interview consists of three stages: an opening (or introduction), a body, and a closing. We will now examine each one in detail.

OPENING

A good introduction can shape the entire interview. Research suggests that people form lasting impressions of one another in the first few minutes of a conversation.[7] Dave Deaver, a national management recruiter, describes the importance of first impressions in a job interview this way: "The first minute is all-important in an interview. Fifty percent of the decision is made within that first 30 to 60 seconds. About 25 percent of the evaluation is made during the first 15 minutes. It's very difficult to recover the last 25 percent if you've blown the first couple of minutes."[8] These initial impressions shape how a listener regards everything that follows.

A good introduction ought to contain two parts: a greeting and an orientation. The opening is also a time for motivating the interviewee to cooperate and giving a sense of what will follow.

Greeting and Building Rapport   The interviewer should begin with a self-introduction (if necessary) or a greeting, and follow with a few minutes of informal conversation. This small talk sets the emotional tone of the interview—formal or informal, nervous or relaxed, candid or guarded.

The most logical openers involve common ground. A mutual friend or acquaintance is a good example: "How's Mary's new job working out?" "Did you hear that Charlie's wife had a little boy?" Shared interests are also a good starting point: "How was your skiing trip?" "I understand you just bought a new house. We're thinking about moving ourselves. Were you happy with your real-estate agent?" A third type of common ground involves job-related topics, though usually unrelated to the subject of the interview itself. An employee whose goal is to discuss a problem with a co-worker might begin the talk with his boss by asking, "How's the new parking plan we proposed last month working out?" In other cases, noteworthy current events can provide a good starting place: "Did you hear about the fire last night?" "I just read that the prime rate went up again."

The interviewee's skill at building rapport can also make the difference between success and failure during these critical few minutes. Author Anthony Medley describes one such incident:

> As a student I once entered an interview room at the end of a warm spring day, and the interviewer was standing with his back to me staring out the window. It was obvious that he was bored to tears. He had had twenty-five interviews with students who were carbon copies of one another, and he had a few more to go of the same monotonous questions and answers.
>
> I had just heard some news on the radio, so before he could start into his routine of questions, I asked, "Did you hear that Khrushchev was overthrown?"
>
> His eyes lit up, and we spent several minutes talking of Russia, which we had both visited. Suddenly his routine was broken, and right off the bat we had something in common.[9]

Orientation   In this stage of the opening, the interviewer gives the respondent a brief overview of what is to follow. This orientation helps put the interviewee at ease by removing a natural apprehension of the unknown. At the same time, it helps establish and strengthen the interviewer's control since it is the interviewer who is clearly setting the agenda. In the orientation, be sure to do the following things:

Explain the Reason for the Interview   A description of the interview's purpose can both put the interviewee at ease and motivate him or her to respond. If your boss called you in for a "chat" about "how things are going," curiosity would probably be your mildest response. Are you headed for a promotion? Are you being softened up for a layoff? Did somebody complain about you? Sharing the reason for an interview can relieve these concerns: "As you know, we're thinking about opening a branch office soon, and we're trying to plan our staffing. I'd like to find out how you feel about your working situation now and what you want so we can consider your needs when we make the changes."

Explain What Information Is Needed and How It Will Be Used   A respondent who knows what the interviewer wants will have a greater likelihood of supplying it. In our example, the boss might be seeking two kinds of information. In one case, a statement of needed information might be "I'm not interested in having you name names of people you like or dislike. I want to know what parts of the business interest you and what you'd consider to be an ideal job." A quite different request for information might be "I'd like to hear your feelings about the people you work with. Who would you like to work with in the future, and who do you have trouble with?"

A description of how the information will be used is also important. In our current example, the boss might explain, "I won't be able to tell you today exactly what changes we'll be making, but I promise you we'll do the best we can to give you what you want." In many situations, it's important to define the confidentiality of the information you are seeking: "I promise you that this talk will be off the record. Nobody else will hear what you tell me."

Mention the Approximate Length of the Interview   An interviewee who knows how long the session will last will feel more comfortable and give better answers.

Motivation   In some situations, such as a job interview, both people feel the interview is important to them personally. Sometimes, however, you need to give interviewees a reason that will make them feel the interview is worthwhile for them. In some cases, you can simply point out the payoffs: "If we can figure out a better way to handle these orders, it will save us both time." "We'd like to know what you'd like in the new office building so we can try to make everyone as comfortable as possible." If the interview won't directly benefit the other person, you might appeal to his or her ego or desire to help other people: "I'd like to try out a new promotional item, and you know more about them than anyone." "Although you're leaving the company, perhaps you can tell us something that will make it a better place for other people to work."

BODY

It is here that the questions and answers are exchanged. While a smooth interview might look spontaneous to an outsider, you have already learned the importance of preparation.

It's unlikely that an interview will ever follow your exact expectations, and it would be a mistake to force it to do so. As an interviewer, you will think of important questions—both primary and secondary—during the session. As a respondent, you will probably be surprised by some of the things the interviewer asks. The best way to proceed is to prepare for the general areas you expect to be covered and do your best when unexpected issues come up.

Responsibilities of the Interviewer   The interviewer performs several tasks during the question-and-answer phase of the discussion.

Control and Focus the Conversation   If an interview is a "conversation with a purpose," it is the interviewer's job to make sure that the discussion focuses on achieving the purpose and doesn't drift away from the agenda. A response can be so interesting that it pulls the discussion off track: "I see you traveled in Europe after college. Did you make it to Barcelona?" Such discussion about backgrounds might be appropriate for the rapport-building part of the opening, but it can get out of control and use up time that would better be spent achieving the interview's purpose.

A second loss of control occurs when the interviewer spends too much time in one legitimate area of discussion, thereby slighting another. Difficult as it may be, an interviewer needs to allot rough blocks of time to each agenda item and then to follow these guidelines during the interview.

Listen Actively   Some interviewers—especially novices—become so caught up in budgeting time and planning upcoming questions that they fail to hear what the respondent is saying.

Salespeople don't just pitch products to customers. In order to be effective, they need to find out what the customer needs or wants. Art Parrish, president of Parrish Power Products, explains this process:

> This is how a potential supplier begins to determine your needs. This process can be called many things, but it amounts to communication.
>
> To determine your needs, the salesman must ask some questions, some subtle, some not so subtle. He is looking for information that will uncover a need as well as potential pitfalls. Is there a need for technical support from the supplier? Are there delivery problems? Are there features about this product that will reduce your inventory? Is price an obstacle?

Art Parrish, "A Little Understanding Goes a Long Way"

Use Secondary Questions to Probe for Important Information   Sometimes an answer may be incomplete. At other times, it may be evasive or vague. Since it is impossible to know in advance when probes will be needed, the interviewer should be ready to use them as the occasion dictates.

An interviewer sometimes needs to *repeat* a question before getting a satisfactory answer.

Interviewer: Your résumé shows you attended Arizona State for four years. I'm not clear about whether you earned a degree.

Respondent: I completed all the required courses in my major field of study, as well as several electives.

Interviewer: I see. Did you earn a degree?

When a primary question doesn't deliver enough information, the interviewer needs to seek *elaboration.*

Interviewer: When we made this appointment, you said Bob has been insulting you. I'd like to hear about that.

Respondent: He treats me like a child. I've been here almost as long as he has and I know what I'm doing!

Interviewer: Exactly what does he do? Can you give me a few examples?

Sometimes an answer will be complete but unclear. This requires a request for *clarification.*

Respondent: The certificate pays 11 percent interest.

Interviewer: Is that rate simple or compounded?

A *paraphrasing* probe restates the answer in different words. It invites the respondent to clarify and elaborate upon a previous answer.

Interviewer: You've been with us for a year now and already have been promoted once. How do you feel about the direction your career is taking?

Respondent: I'm satisfied for now.

Interviewer: So far, so good. Is that how you feel?

Respondent: Not exactly. I was happy to get the promotion, of course. But I don't see many chances for advancement from here.

Often *silence* is the best probe. A pause of up to ten seconds (which feels like an eternity) lets the respondent know more information is expected. Depending on the interviewer's accompanying nonverbal messages, silence can indicate interest or dissatisfaction with the previous answer. *Prods* ("Uh-huh," "Hmmmm," "Go on," "Tell me more," and so on) accomplish the same purpose.

Respondent: I can't figure out where we can cut costs.

Interviewer: Uh-huh.

Respondent: We've already cut our travel and entertainment budget 5 percent.

Interviewer: I know.

Respondent: Some of our people probably still abuse it, but they'd be offended if we cut back more. They think of expense accounts as a fringe benefit.

Interviewer: (silence)

Respondent: Of course, if we could give them something in return for a cut, we might still be able to cut total costs. Maybe have the sales meeting at a resort—make it something of a vacation.

The Interviewee's Role   The interviewee can do several things to help make the interview a success.

Give Clear, Detailed Answers   A piece of obvious advice interviewees often ignore is *to answer the question the interviewer has asked.* An off-the-track answer suggests the respondent hasn't understood the question, is a poor listener, or might even be evading the question. Put yourself in the interviewer's position, and think about what kind of information you would like to know. Then supply it.

Correct Any Misunderstandings   Being human, interviewers sometimes misinterpret comments. Most interviews are important enough for the respondent to be sure the message given has been received accurately. Since you can't ask the interviewer "Were you listening carefully?" two strategies can help get your message across. The first involves *restating* your message. This can be done orally, both in the body and conclusion phases of the interview.

Interviewer: So, everything will be at the exhibit booth when we get to the convention, and all we have to do is set up the exhibit.

Interviewee: Not quite. The brochures won't be ready in time to ship to the convention, so you'll have to carry them with you on the plane.

In addition, it is sometimes wise to summarize important ideas in a memo that can be delivered before, during, or after the session.

Cover Your Own Agenda   Interviewees often have their own goals. In a selection interview, the employer's goal is to pick the best candidate, while the applicant's aim is to prove that his or her qualifications make him or her the best. This may involve redefining the concept of *best.* For instance, a relatively inexperienced candidate might have the goal of showing the employer that experience isn't as important as education, enthusiasm, or social skills.

CLOSING

An interview shouldn't end with the last answer to the last question. As with most other types of communication, certain functions need to be performed to bring the interview to a satisfactory conclusion.

Review and Clarify the Results of the Interview   Either party can take responsibility for this step, though in different ways. The person with the greater power (usually the interviewer) is most likely to do so declaratively. For example, in an interview exploring a grievance between employees, a manager might say, "It sounds like you're saying that both of you could have handled it better." When the party with less power (usually the interviewee) does the reviewing and clarifying, the summary often takes the form of a question. A sales representative might close by saying, "So the product sounds good to you, but before you make your final decision you'd like to talk to a few of our clients to see how it has worked out for them. Is that right?"

Establish Future Actions   When the relationship between interviewer and respondent is a continuing one, it is important to clarify how the matter under discussion will be handled. A sales representative might close by saying "I'll put a list of our customers in the mail to you tomorrow. Then why don't I give you a call next week to see what you're thinking?" A manager might clarify the future by saying "I'd like you to try out the arrangement we discussed today. Then let's all get together in a few weeks to see how things are going. How does the first of next month sound?"

Conclude with Pleasantries   A sociable conclusion needn't be phony. You can express appreciation or concern, or mention future interaction:

"Your ideas were terrific. I know I can use them."

"I appreciate the time you've given me today."

"Good luck with the project."

"Let me know if I can help."

"I'll see you Thursday."

THE ETHICS OF INTERVIEWING

The exchange of information that goes on between interviewer and interviewee should be guided by some basic ethical guidelines and responsibilities.[10] In addition to the moral reasons for following these guidelines, there is often a pragmatic basis for behaving ethically. Since the interview is likely to be part of an ongoing relationship, behaving responsibly and honorably will serve you well in future interactions. Conversely, the costs of developing a poor reputation are usually greater than the benefits of gaining a temporary advantage by behaving un-ethically or irresponsibly.

OBLIGATIONS OF THE INTERVIEWER

A conscientious business communicator will follow several guidelines when conducting an interview.

Only Make Promises You Are Willing and Able to Keep   Don't make offers or claims that may later prove impossible to honor. For example, an employer should not encourage a job applicant about the chances of receiving an offer until she is sure an offer will be forthcoming. To make this sort of promise and then be overruled later by the boss or to find out that the budget doesn't permit hiring at this time would be both dishonest and unfair. Likewise, a candidate should not indicate a willingness to start work immediately if she cannot begin work until she has sold her home and moved to the town where her new job is located. Despite the temptations, avoid making any commitments that sound good but are not firm.

Keep Confidences   Interviewers should not reveal confidential information to interviewees, nor should they disclose any private information gained during a session to people who have no legitimate reason to know it. For example, a supervisor who learns about an employee's personal problems should only reveal them with the employee's permission. Likewise, employees who learn confidential information in the course of their jobs—income levels, company plans, and so on—are obliged to make sure that that information stays private.

Allow the Interviewee to Make Free Responses   An interview that coerces the subject into giving unwilling answers is a charade of an honest conversation. For example, a supervisor conducting a performance appraisal asks a subordinate "Who do you think is responsible for the problems in your area?" should be willing to accept whatever answer is given and not automatically expect the employee to accept the blame. Trying to *persuade* an interviewee is a normal part of doing business, but coercing one is not ethical.

Treat Every Interviewee with Respect   With rare exceptions, the interviewer's job is to help the interviewee do well. This means making sure that the interviewee feels comfortable and understands the nature of the session. It also means the interviewer must design questions that are clear and help the interviewee answer them as well as possible.

OBLIGATIONS OF THE INTERVIEWEE

The interviewee is also obliged to behave in an ethical and responsible way during a session. Several guidelines apply here.

Don't Misrepresent the Facts or Your Position Whether the setting is an employment interview, a performance review session, or an information-gathering survey, it can be tempting to tell interviewers what they want to hear. The temptation is especially great if your welfare is at stake. But besides being unethical, misrepresenting the facts is likely to catch up with you sooner or later and harm you more than telling the truth in the first place would have.

Don't Waste the Interviewer's Time If the choice exists, be sure you are qualified for the interview. For example, it would be a mistake to apply for a job you have little chance of landing or to volunteer for a customer survey if you aren't a member of the population being studied. If preparation for the interview is necessary, be sure to do your homework. Once the interview has begun, be sure to stick to the subject in order to use the time most wisely.

SAMPLE INTERVIEW PLAN

The following plan shows the kind of work that should go on before an interviewer and interviewee sit down to or even schedule a meeting. Every important interview requires the kind of planning exhibited here in order to achieve its goals. As you read this account, notice that it follows the advice outlined in this chapter.

[*Analysis and Research*] I know that I'll never build the kind of financial security I am seeking by relying only on the income I earn from my job. Investing successfully will be the path to financial success. I also know that I'm very unsophisticated when it comes to investing, so I want to get myself a financial advisor who can teach me about the world of finance and who can help me set up and follow a plan.

Picking a financial advisor is like choosing a doctor. Skill is important, but it's not the only thing that matters. I need to find someone who has a personal style that I'm comfortable with and whose philosophy matches mine. I also need to find someone who is willing to devote time to me even though I don't have a great deal of money to invest . . . yet!

I've compiled a list of possible advisors from friends, newspaper articles, and listings in the phone directory. I will call several of the people on this list to set up appointments for interviews.

[*Goal*] Based on my needs, the goal for my interviews will be "to identify a financial planner with expertise in the field, whose investment philosophy matches mine, and who has a personal style that I am comfortable with."

[*Interview Strategy*]   I definitely want to conduct these interviews in the offices of each financial planner. Seeing where and how they do business will probably give me a good idea of my comfort level before asking any questions. For instance, seeing a shabby or disorganized office would cause me to doubt the competence of an advisor. On the other hand, a very plush office might make me wonder if I was being charged too much just to support a lavish lifestyle.

I'll also be interested to see how much time each person gives me for the interview. If the person is rushed when trying to get a new client, this could mean I won't get the time or attention I need once my money is in the planner's hands.

It will be interesting to see how much each person lets me explain my concerns and how much they control the conversation. I'm no financial expert, but I don't like the attitude "I'm the expert, so don't waste time asking too many questions." Since I *would* like someone who is willing to explain investing to me in a way that I can understand, I'll be looking for a good teacher.

[*Topics and Questions*]   As my goal suggests, I want to explore three topics. The following list shows the questions I'm planning to ask in each topic area as well as follow-up questions I can anticipate asking. I'm sure there will be a need for other secondary questions, but I can't predict all of them. I'll have to think of them on the spot.

TOPIC A: EXPERTISE IN INVESTMENTS AND FINANCIAL PLANNING

This series of questions follows an inverted funnel sequence, beginning with a closed question and following with increasingly open ones.

1. What credentials do you have that qualify you as a financial planner? How important are credentials? If they aren't important, what is the best measure of a financial planner's qualifications?

Again, the questioner uses an inverted funnel sequence to move from a narrow to a broader focus.

2. Do you have any areas of specialization? How and why did you specialize in this area?

These indirect questions are a way of finding out whether the advisor's performance has been satisfactory.

3. How many clients have you served in the last five years? What is the length of relationship with your clients? How many have you retained, and how many are no longer with you?

The average portfolio size is one measure of the advisor's expertise.

4. What's the average amount of money you have managed for your clients?

Answers to these closed questions will provide references for follow-up interviews.

5. May I see a list of your past and current clients and call some of them for referen-ces?

The first question is a broad, open one. The second, closed question will produce a specific answer that can be compared with those of other potential advisors.

6. How would you describe your track record in terms of investment advice? Specifically, what has been the ratio of successful to unsuccessful advice?

TOPIC B: INVESTMENT PHILOSOPHY

This broad, open question gives the advisor a chance to describe his or her approach.

1. How would you describe your investment philosophy?

A hypothetical question that provides specific information about how a client-advisor relationship might operate.

2. If I became your client, what would be the steps you would recommend to start and maintain a financial program?

This inverted funnel sequence of questions moves from specific to broad topics in a logical order.

3. What kind of products do you like to deal in? Which specific ones might you recommend for me? Why?

This two-question sequence again follows an inverted funnel sequence. The most important information for the client is contained in the second question.

4. I've read that some financial advisors make their income from commissions earned when their clients buy and sell investments. Other advisors charge a fee for their time. What approach do you take? Can you explain how this approach is in my interest as well as yours?

Although this sounds like a closed question, it is likely to generate a long answer.

5. How much would I expect to pay for your advice?

TOPIC C: PERSONAL STYLE

This indirect question really asks, "Would we work well together?"

1. What kind of clients do you like to work with? What kinds don't you work well with?

The first question here is really an indirect way of discovering how much attention the advisor has paid to the potential client.

2. Have you looked over the papers I sent you about my financial condition? What did you think of them?

This clever hypothetical question has a better chance of generating a useful answer than the more direct "What can *you* tell me about the kind of service I can expect?"

3. If I were to call one of your clients at random, what would he or she tell me about the type of service and frequency of communication I can expect with you?

A straightforward, open question.

4. If we were to develop a relationship, what would you expect of me?

This hypothetical question anticipates an important issue.

5. Suppose I were to disagree with your advice. What would you say and do?

SUMMARY

Interviewing is a face-to-face conversation in which at least one party has a specific, serious purpose. As such, it is perhaps the most common form of planned communication. Interviewing differs from other types of conversation in its purposeful nature, its degree of structure, its imbalance of control and speaking by one party, and its bipolarity.

A good deal of planning should occur before an important interview begins. The first step involves defining the objective as clearly as possible. At the same time, each party should analyze the other, tailoring the interview to the other's self-concept, knowledge level, image of the interview partner, and attitude toward the topic. The best ways to obtain this information are through what others say, what the person in question says, and what you observe.

Having defined the objectives, both interviewer and respondent should prepare agendas, listing the areas they want to cover during the meeting. The interviewer should also decide whether a highly scheduled, moderately scheduled, or nonscheduled structure is most desirable. It is also important to plan important primary and secondary questions in advance of the interview. When forming questions, considerations include desired depth, open versus closed nature, direct or indirect approach, whether fact or opinion is sought, and whether hypothetical or actual inquiries will be most productive. Leading and loaded questions ought to be avoided. It is also important to decide whether questions ought to be organized in funnel, inverted funnel, tunnel, or mixed sequences. Finally, the interviewer and interviewee ought to choose a setting that promotes the best possible outcome.

The interview itself consists of three parts. The opening establishes rapport, orients the respondent, and offers motivation for contributing. During the body, the interviewer should keep the conversation focused, listen actively, and probe for additional information when necessary. The respondent should give clear and detailed answers, correct any misunderstandings, and cover his or her own agenda. The closing ought to review and clarify what has occurred, establish what actions will occur in the future, and conclude with pleasantries.

Besides practical considerations, participants in an interview are obliged to behave in an ethical manner. Interviewers should treat every interviewee with respect, keep confidences, only make promises they are prepared to honor, and avoid coercing the respondent. Interviewees should prepare for the session to avoid wasting the interviewer's time and should represent both facts and their positions honestly.

ACTIVITIES

1. Identify the problem with the following leading questions, and rephrase each question so that it is more effective.

   a. (In a problem-solving interview) If everyone is willing to work one Saturday morning per month, we can catch up on our backlog by the end of the quarter. How does that sound to you?
   b. (In a selection interview) You don't mind traveling once or twice a month, do you?
   c. (In a survey interview) We think the best features of our product are its price and durability. What do you think?
   d. (In a performance-appraisal interview) Are you still bothered by not getting that promotion?
   e. (In a problem-solving interview) We're really optimistic about the new job-sharing plan. What do you think?

2. Identify each of the following questions as open or closed. Rephrase each closed question to make it an open one.

   a. Is our product something you can use?
   b. How did the problem begin?
   c. Do you understand how the machine works?
   d. Whose fault do you think it was?
   e. How would you describe the situation?

3. For each of the following situations, describe whether an open or closed question would be more appropriate, explaining your choice. If you think more than one question is necessary to discover the essential information, list each one.

   a. You want to find out whether your boss would support your request to attend a convention in a distant city.
   b. A manager wants to know whether a project will exceed its projected budget.
   c. An insurance sales representative wants to determine whether a customer has adequate coverage.
   d. An employer wants to find out why an applicant has held four jobs in five years.

4. For each of the following situations:

   a. Write one factual and one opinion question.
   b. Decide which of these questions is most appropriate for the situation.
   c. Write two secondary questions as follow-ups for the primary question you have chosen:

   You want to know if you are justified in asking your boss for a raise, and you decide to question a co-worker.

   A supervisor wants to discover whether an employee's request for a one-month personal leave of absence to visit a sick parent is essential.

   You are planning to buy an electronic typewriter or a portable computer. You want to decide whether the computer is worth the extra five hundred it will cost.

5. Create indirect questions that could elicit the following information:

   a. How hard a worker are you? (selection)
   b. Do you agree with my evaluation? (appraisal)
   c. Does the product have any drawbacks? (sales)
   d. Are you telling me the real reason you're leaving? (exit)
   e. Do you really believe my idea is a good one, or are you just going along? (problem solving)

6. Arrange to take part in an interview that has some real utility for you. You may choose to interview a co-worker, superior, or subordinate to learn more about some aspect of your work. You could look into the possible purchase of some product you are sincerely interested in. You might seek an appraisal of your performance from an instructor, supervisor, or colleague. You may want to pursue a grievance. Using the principles discussed in this chapter, describe and evaluate the interview.

Communicator Profile

Larry Kaufmann, President
Analytics Inc.
Mt. Prospect, Illinois

One of the interviewing skills I teach my employees is to imagine a mental ladder leaning against a wall. You must design each new question to step up to the next rung, supported by the question on the previous rung.

Analytics is a marketing research firm that analyzes the pros and cons of proposed new products and recommends improvements in ones that already exist. Our clients include McDonald's, Johnson's Wax, and Young and Rubicam Advertising. We devise research strategies to determine what the public wants or doesn't want. Often, we conduct focus groups in which we pay selected people to discuss various issues, the goal being to figure out what will sell and what won't. We've conducted over 2,000 such groups over the past twenty years on topics ranging from environmental awareness to VCRs.

Interviewing is central to what we do. First, we sit down with our clients and determine what information or data they need. Then, we devise our strategy for accurately gathering those data. This often involves more interviewing, but this time of the general public. Next, we propose the plan to the clients and carefully respond to their reaction. Then, we conduct the research and present the findings to the client in a closing interview.

Obviously, quality of interviews is crucial. The computer industry's maxim "Garbage in yields garbage out"—GIGO—is quite apt for us. A great deal depends on the native ability of your interviewer. You have to be intelligent. You must be conscientious, reporting exactly what you hear and being painstaking in getting it correct. Finally, you can't be "nervous in the service," as I call it. You have to be confident, likable, and have a sense of humor. A lilt in the voice helps, too.

We handled an interesting project in the late sixties that illustrates the importance of the interview. Two electronic companies came to us with an interest in producing a new machine which would record not only voice but also the moving image. We devised a strategy and ended up conducting and recording hundreds of phone interviews. I wanted every gasp, cussword, pregnant pause, or whatever, on those tapes. We determined there was a market for such a device, but people wanted the ability to tape things when they weren't there—in other words, the concept we all know today as the VCR. Those phone interviews helped us decide that there was a market for what turned out to be one of the great innovations of our time and allowed the makers to discover one of the most vital features that consumers wanted in this product.

One of the interviewing skills I teach my employees is to imagine a mental ladder leaning against a wall. You must design each new question to step up to the next rung, supported by the question on the previous rung. For example, suppose I asked you what kind of car you prefer—one from Detroit or one from Japan. You say, one from Japan. Then I ask why, and you say you've had good luck with cars from Japan. Since "good luck" is not something I can tell a client to build into his car, I then say, what do you mean by "good luck"? Your answer might be "Well, I've almost never had to get them repaired." This helps me zero in on what I'm trying to learn.

The open-ended "what else" question is the worst mental door-closer there is. It's better to structure the questions based on previous leads, as I said above. A well-thought-out, more specific question lets you crawl around in someone's head and provides dependability. If someone gives a vague answer to a question, it's good to go back to something they've said earlier and ask them to clarify or explain it further. The probe question "Why?" is a useful open-ended question *if* you've based it on a series of detailed questions leading up to it. It all comes back to the right interview question at the right time.

7

After reading this chapter, you should understand:

■ The various types of interviews and their specific applications

■ The steps necessary in planning an information-gathering interview

■ The shortcomings of traditional job-seeking methods and the value of conducting background research and cultivating a personal network of contacts as an alternative

■ The steps necessary in conducting an effective selection interview

■ The functions of performance appraisal interviews

■ The three steps in a performance appraisal interview

■ The advantages and disadvantages of the three appraisal interviewing styles

■ The characteristics of effective praise and criticism in performance appraisal

You should be able to:

■ Identify the types of interviews you participate in now and those you will encounter most often in the future

■ Collect background information, write objectives and questions, and conduct an information-gathering interview

■ Conduct "three R" interviews to develop a personal network of contacts that will help you achieve your career goals

■ Identify and prepare answers for questions you would be likely to face in a selection interview, then present yourself in a manner that is most likely to lead to a job offer

■ Identify the criteria for effective performance in a job you are familiar with and state these criteria in the form of behavioral objectives

■ Identify the most effective style of performance appraisal for a given employee

■ Present feedback to a subordinate or colleague in a manner that follows the guidelines in this chapter

■ Respond constructively to an appraisal of your performance

TYPES OF INTERVIEWS

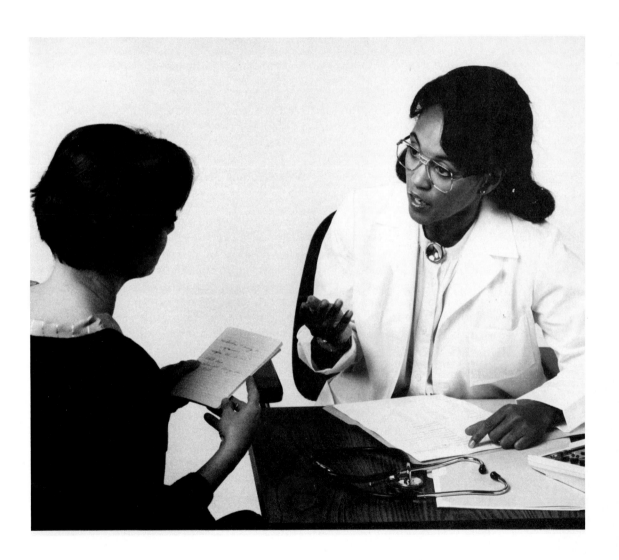

The range of interviews you are likely to encounter in the course of your work can be surprisingly broad.

Your company is trying to decide whether to convert to a new voice mail system for handling telephone messages. You sit down with the sales representative from one firm to see what her company's system can offer.

Your boss calls you in for a meeting to rate your performance over the last few months.

One of your best customers is angry with the job your company has done. In an effort to get to the bottom of the problem, you invite him to meet with you.

You are interested in a new job. After making some inquiries, you are invited to meet with the potential employer to discuss your future with that company.

All of these situations call for some sort of interview. Different jobs call for different kinds of interviews. Three kinds of interviews, however, are required for almost any job or career: information-gathering interviews, selection interviews (usually called job interviews), and performance appraisal interviews. In this chapter, we will focus on the particular skills required for each of these three special types of interview.

THE INFORMATION-GATHERING INTERVIEW

Interviewers seek information for a variety of purposes. *Survey* interviews gather information from a number of people. They are used to provide information from which to draw conclusions, make interpretations, and determine future action. Manufacturers and advertisers use them to assess market needs and learn consumer reactions to new products. Employers use them to gather employees' ideas about how space should be allotted in a new location or how much a new benefits program might be needed. *Diagnostic* interviews allow health-care professionals, attorneys, counselors, and other business and professional workers to gather information that helps them to respond to the needs of their clientele. *Research* interviews provide information upon which to base future decisions. An entrepreneur who is thinking about opening a chain of restaurants might interview others with related experience when developing the concept and question people familiar with the target area to collect ideas about locations and clientele. On a more personal level, an employee thinking about a career change might interview several people who work in the field she is considering to seek advice about how to proceed. *Investigative* interviews gather information to determine the causes of an event, usually a problem. Finally, *exit* interviews help to determine why an employee is leaving an organization. Since research is the most common type of information-gathering interview for most businesspeople, we will examine it in depth.

COLLECT BACKGROUND INFORMATION

In many cases, preinterview research is well worth the effort. Suppose, for instance, that you are interested in proposing a job-sharing plan—a system in which two people would share the responsibilities and salary of one full-time job. You decide you need to interview several people in your company before presenting your idea formally. Before conducting these interviews, however, you need to research the answers to some basic questions: How common is job sharing? In what industries does it occur? What forms does it take? Has it been tried by any firms in your field? What have the results of such arrangements been? Until you know at least the rough answers to these questions, you won't be ready to bring up the idea in your company.

Besides conducting traditional library research, you can get answers to questions like these by interviewing knowledgeable people. In this sense, talking about a single information-gathering interview is really an oversimplification, for you will usually conduct several during various stages of a task. You might, indeed, collect some fundamental background during your first round of interviews. Perhaps you know someone who worked for a company that already has a job-sharing policy. An acquaintance might have mentioned a recent newspaper article on the subject, and you can get the reference that will help you locate it. During this phase, your questions will be necessarily vague, similar to the request you might make of a reference librarian: "I'm looking for information about job sharing. How do you think I ought to go about it?"

Once you have collected the necessary background information, you can use this knowledge to plan an intelligent approach to your second round of interviews—perhaps with people suggested by your earlier research or with the key decision makers who are your ultimate target.

DEFINE INTERVIEW GOALS AND QUESTIONS

Defining the specific goal of your interview is always a key step. Your goal ought to be as specific as possible and worded in a way that will tell you whether you have the answers you were seeking. Here are examples of how you might define a goal for an information-gathering interview.

VAGUE	SPECIFIC
I want to learn about tax-free municipal bonds.	Will tax-free municipal bonds give me liquidity, appreciation, safety, and tax shelter better than my present investments?
What happened at the accident yesterday?	What caused the accident, and could it have been prevented?
Should I buy a database management system?	Will a database management system be affordable, easy to use? Will it improve my efficiency enough to justify the purchase?

Once you have identified your purpose, you must develop questions that will help you achieve it. For example:

Purpose: To learn what steps I need to take to have a job-sharing arrangement approved by management.

Questions

Whom should I approach first?

Who will be the key decision maker on this issue?

Should I present my formal proposal first, or should I start by mentioning the subject informally?

What objections might management have to the proposal?

Is anyone else in the company (nonmanagement personnel) likely to oppose or support the idea?

What arguments (such as precedent, cost savings, employee morale) will most impress management?

What influential people might support this idea?

As you develop your questions, use the guidelines in Chapter 6. Make sure you gather both facts and opinions—and recognize which is which. Be prepared to follow up your primary questions with secondary queries as necessary.

CHOOSE THE RIGHT INTERVIEWEE

The ideal respondent within an organization will be part of an informal communication network and may have no official relationship with you on the organizational chart. It might be naïve to talk with your boss about the job-sharing proposal until you have consulted other sources who could suggest how to broach the subject: perhaps a politically astute co-worker, someone who has experience making proposals to management, or even the boss's secretary, if you are friends, will be helpful.

After you have established the purpose and the appropriate person to interview, follow the guidelines in Chapter 6 to plan and conduct the interview.

THE SELECTION INTERVIEW

The few minutes spent facing a potential employer can be the most important interview of a lifetime. Consider the stakes. Most workers spend the greatest part of their adult lives on the job—roughly 2,000 hours per year or upward of 80,000 hours during a career. The financial difference between a well-paid position and an unrewarding one can also be staggering. Even without considering the effects of inflation, a gap of only $200 per month can amount to almost $100,000 over the course of a career. Finally, the emotional results of having the right job are considerable. A frustrating job not only makes for unhappiness at work; these dissatisfactions have a way of leaking into nonworking hours as well.

How important is an interview in getting the right job? The Bureau of National Affairs, a private research firm that serves both government and industry, conducted a survey to answer this question. It polled 196 personnel executives, seeking the factors that were most important in hiring applicants. The results showed that the employment interview is the single most important factor in landing a job.[1] Further research revealed that the most important factor during these critically decisive interviews was communication skills. Employers identified the ability to communicate effectively as more important in shaping a hiring decision than grade-point average, work experience, extracurricular activities, appearance, and preference for job location.[2]

The best candidate does not necessarily get the job. In most situations, *the person who knows the most about getting hired usually gets the desired position.* "Chemistry is the paramount factor in hiring," states Wilhelmus B. Bryan III, executive vice-president of William H. Clark Associates, a New York recruiting firm.[3] While job-getting skills are no guarantee of qualifications once the actual work begins, they are necessary to get hired in the first place.

PRE-INTERVIEW STEPS

Scanning the newspaper for openings and then filing an application with the company's personnel department is one way of looking for a job but often not the most effective. Many employers never advertise jobs, and one study reveals that between 75 and 85 percent of employers in typical American cities did not hire *any* employees through want ads during an entire year.[4]

Even when a company does advertise, the odds are against an applicant who replies with an application and résumé. Since most job announcements attract many more applicants than an employer needs, the job of the personnel department becomes *elimination,* not selection. The goal is to reduce the pool of job-seekers to a manageable number by rejecting as many applicants as possible. Given this process of elimination, any shortcoming becomes welcome grounds for rejecting the application and the applicant. Many consultants, therefore, suggest identifying and contacting the person who has the power to hire you *before* an opening exists. The process has several steps.

Conduct Background Research   The first step is to explore the types of work and specific organizations that sound appealing to you. This involves doing library research, reading magazines and newspaper articles, taking classes, and simply fantasizing about jobs you might find interesting. The result of your research should be a list of organizations and names of people who can tell you more about your chosen field.

Develop a Personal Network   The old phrase "It isn't what you know, it's who you know" is certainly true when it comes to getting a job. The results of one

TABLE 7-1   Success Rates of Sources for Job Opportunities

Professional associates, former colleagues, friends	75%
Fellow students	60%
People holding a similar job	50%
Professional association placement services	40%
Former teachers	30%
Newspaper or magazine advertisements	25%
Relatives	25%
University placement offices	10%
Social acquaintances	10%
Writing corporate officers	5%
Leads from former employers	5%
Mass mailings to employers	5%
State placement offices	2%
Professional placement agencies	1%

Adapted from C. J. Stewart and W. B. Cash, Jr., *Interviewing: Principles and Practices,* 4th ed. (Dubuque, Iowa: Wm. C. Brown, 1985), p. 213.

survey, pictured in Table 7-1, shows the important role of personal contacts in looking for new jobs.

The nature and value of personal networks were demonstrated when researcher Mark Granovetter surveyed over 280 residents of a Boston suburb who had taken a new job within the past year. While only 17 percent of the people surveyed found their jobs through close friends or relatives, the majority learned about their new positions from people who were only distant associates—old college friends, former colleagues, parents of a child's playmate, and so on.[5] Weak ties are often more useful than close acquaintances in finding jobs because your close associates rarely know more than you do about career opportunities. Distant acquaintances, however, are connected to other, less familiar communication networks, networks that often contain valuable information about new jobs.[6]

If you cannot find the information you need from anyone you know, you may have to go looking for people. Candace Sneberger, vice-president of a major travel agency in Philadelphia, applied for a job as an airline attendant when she was finishing college "with the hope of progressing into management." "I didn't know how to go about this," she says, "and so late at night, when I thought someone would have time to talk with me, I'd call the toll-free airlines reservations number and ask for help." Soon after, she had interviews and job offers from two major airlines and accepted a job with American.[7] One career specialist advises, "If you cannot locate a contact in the company you're hoping to work for, call and ask for the number of the person in charge of the department in which you would like a job."[8]

The key to finding the wealth of unadvertised positions is to cultivate a network of contacts who can let you know about job opportunities and pass along your name to potential employers. You can build this network by conducting a series of what is most easily remembered as "three R" interviews. These interviews get their name from their three goals:

To conduct research that helps you learn more about the field and specific organizations that interest you.

To be remembered by making contacts who will recall you at an appropriate time and either offer you a position or suggest you to a potential employer.

To gain referrals to other people whom you might contact for help in your job search. As Figure 7-1 shows, the referrals from an initial three-R interview can easily lead to meetings with six more useful contacts, all of whom might mention you to *their* friends and associates.

You might wonder why the kind of important person you would like to see in a three-R interview would be willing to meet with you. There are actually several reasons. First, if you have made contact through a referral, your subject will probably see you in deference to your mutual acquaintance. If you can gain a referral, you are most likely to get a friendly reception. Interviewees might also be willing to see you for ego gratification. It is flattering to have someone say "I respect your accomplishments and ideas" and difficult for even a busy person to say no to a request that accompanies such a comment. A third reason is simple altruism. Most successful people realize they received help somewhere along the line, and many will be willing to do for you what others did for them. Finally, you may get an interview because the person recognizes you as ambitious, someone who might have something to offer his or her organization.

Whenever you approach a three-R interviewee, you ought to accompany your oral communication with some important written correspondence. It's

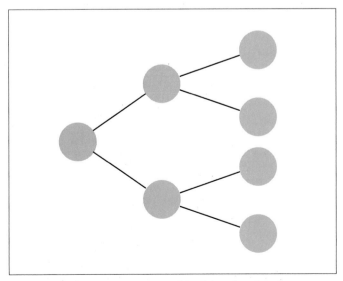

Figure 7-1   A personal network can grow quickly through referrals.

usually wise to make your first contact in a letter. A telephone call runs the risk of not getting through; and even if you do reach the interviewee, your call may come at a bad time. Your first letter, like the one in Figure 7-2, should introduce you, explain your reason for the interview (stressing that you are *not* seeking employment), state your availability for a meeting, and promise a follow-up telephone call. A second letter should precede the interview and confirm its date, place, and time. Finally, a post-interview letter should express thanks for the interviewee's time and mention how helpful the information was. Besides demonstrating common courtesy, these letters become a tangible reminder of you and provide a record of your name and address that will be useful if the interviewee wants to contact you in the future. Of course, all correspondence should be typed neatly: your letters are a reflection on you.

Contact Potential Employers   At some point, your research and networking will uncover one or more job leads. You might read a newspaper story about the need of a local employer for people with interests or training like yours. Perhaps a three-R interview subject will say, "I know someone over at _____ who is looking for a person like you." You might learn through a friendly contact that a desirable firm is about to expand its operations. In such a case, it is time to approach the person who has the power to hire you and explore how you can help meet the company's needs.

In such cases, it is better to avoid the personnel department, if you can. A division manager in a CBS-owned company explained that "personnel departments aren't equipped to hire a technical person like an engineer or computer programmer, or judge how good an inexperienced person might be at sales. They can only see whether you've been to college and count how many words a minute you can type." A leading career advisor has another reason: "The personnel department will rate your qualifications only for the job it has been asked to fill. If your credentials don't match the job description closely, personnel probably won't send you on for other interviews."[9] The mechanical nature of this screening function is illustrated by reports that computers are beginning to take over the first stages of the application screening process.[10] A software program called Computer Employment Applications serves as the job candidate's first evaluator.

Apart from visiting it [the personnel department] briefly . . . you will probably still find it (generally speaking) wise to avoid that department. I know too many stories about people who have been turned down by a particular company's personnel department, who then went back to square one, found out who, in that very same company, had the power to hire for the position they wanted, went to that woman or man, and got hired—ten floors up from the personnel department that had just rejected them.

Richard Bolles, *What Color Is Your Parachute: A Practical Manual for Job-Hunters and Career-Changers*

1165 East Marion St.
Columbia, S.C. 29209
803-555-1213

February 21, 1992

Mr. Tony DiAngelo
DiAngelo Design Team
P.O. Box 1173
Columbia, S.C. 29201

Dear Mr. DiAngelo:

Like many others in the Columbia area, I have enjoyed your imaginative "Take me to the . . . " (Zoo, Museum, etc.) campaign for the Metropolitan Transit District. Sonia Henry at the Metropolitan District tells me you've won an Advertising Roundtable award for the series—congratulations!

As a marketing major at the University of South Carolina, I am interested in learning more about the skills it takes to create the kind of effective advertising you produce. Ms. Henry thought you might be willing to meet briefly with me to suggest how I might best prepare myself for a successful career in marketing.

I would be grateful to meet with you for a half hour or so at your convenience. Early mornings, lunchtime, and late afternoons are best for me, although other times are also possible. It would be my pleasure to be your host if a breakfast or lunch meeting is most convenient for you.

Please rest assured this is not a job-seeking interview. Your advice about how to proceed with my career is the best payoff I can imagine.

I'll be phoning your office within the next few days to arrange a meeting time. In the meantime, congratulations again on the MTD award.

Sincerely,

Paula Cohen

Figure 7-2 Letter requesting a three-R interview.

The process is a private encounter between applicant and machine, with no interviewer present. The candidate reads questions on the computer screen and types answers into the computer, which then prints out a profile of the applicant as compared to job criteria. It is obvious that programs like this are likely to reject applicants whose experience does not precisely fit the job description even if the applicants might be capable of doing an excellent job in the new position.

This sort of screening—whether it's done by computers or the personnel staff—explains why many successful businesspeople recommend contacting the person or people who can employ you directly. When Sharon Borklund, now national sales manager for Rodale Sport Publications, first decided she wanted to go into sales, she got an industry directory to identify opportunities and began calling people directly. "Sure I was scared, but I made direct contacts instead of sending my résumé," she says. Bonnie Freeman, now a meeting planner and public-affairs worker in an aerospace company, recommends the same procedure. She began her job search by conducting thirty-five information-gathering interviews to assess her skills and career possibilities, then "networked like crazy and approached employers directly."[11] If you can show that you can help the organization, you will almost certainly be met with interest. In addition, your willingness to seek out the company will set you apart from the herd of ordinary job-seekers and label you as someone with that prized quality—initiative.

CONDUCTING THE INTERVIEW

If your fate in the selection process was determined by a skilled, objective interviewer, the need for strategic communication might not be essential. Research, however, shows that the rating you are likely to receive from an interviewer can be influenced by a variety of factors as varied as the time of day, the sex of the interviewer and interviewee, whether the candidates before you did well or poorly, and the employer's mood.[12] Since the interview is not a scientific measure of your skills, it is especially important to do everything possible to make the best impression. Interviewing expert Anthony Medley describes one memorable example that illustrates the importance of first impressions:

> A candidate I once interviewed for a secretarial position could type 90 words per minute and take shorthand at 120 words per minute. She was attractive, presentable, and had good references. But after showing up ten minutes late, she called me "Mr. Melody" throughout the interview.
>
> The two things I remembered about her were that she had kept me waiting and constantly mispronounced my name. I finally offered the position to someone whose typing and shorthand skills were not nearly so good.[13]

Dress Appropriately The information from employers summarized in Table 7-2 confirms the common belief that first impressions are lasting ones.[14] Once an interviewer forms a general impression of you—whether positive or negative— that image will influence his or her perceptions of everything you say in the

TABLE 7-2 *Most Frequent Interviewer Complaints About Interviewees*

1. Poor personality, manners, lack of poise, confidence, arrogant, egotistical, conceited
2. Poor appearance, lack of neatness, careless dress
3. Lack of enthusiasm, shows little interest, no evidence of initiative, lack of drive
4. Lack of goals and objectives, lack of ambition, poorly motivated, does not know interests, uncertain, indecisive, poor planning
5. Inability to express self well, poor oral expression, poor habits of speech
6. Unrealistic salary demands, overemphasis on money, more interested in salary than opportunity, unrealistic concerning promotion to top jobs
7. Lack of maturity, no leadership potential
8. Lack of extracurricular activities, inadequate reasons for not participating in activities
9. Failure to get information about our company, lack of preparation for the interview, inability to ask intelligent questions
10. Lack of interest in security and benefits, "what can you do for me" attitude
11. Objects to travel, unwilling to relocate

Victor R. Lindquest, *The Northwestern Endicott Report 1988,* The Placement Center, Northwestern University, Evanston, Ill.

remainder of the conversation. For this reason, it is essential to present a professional image.

Looking good when you meet a potential employer is vitally important. In one survey, recruiters ranked clothing as the leading factor in shaping their initial impressions of applicants (ahead of physical attractiveness and résumé). Furthermore, 79 percent of the recruiters stated that their initial impressions influenced the rest of the interview.[15] While the best attire to wear will depend on the job you are seeking, it is at always safest to dress on the conservative side, if you have any doubts.

Know the Organization and the Job Your background research will pay dividends during the employment interview. One criterion most interviewers use in rating applicants is "knowledge of the position," and a lack of information in this area can be damaging. One example illustrates the advantages that come from knowing even a small amount about a position.

When I first took a job as a young attorney for Litton Industries, I was interviewing for the position as an assistant division counsel for their Guidance Control Systems Division. That name alone was enough to boggle my mind. A scientist I was not. After a little research, I found that they made something called an inertial navigation system. That was worse than the name of the division. What was an inertial navigation system?

Finally I went to a fraternity brother who had majored in engineering and asked him if he knew what it was all about. He explained to me that inertial navigation was a method of navigating whereby the system allows you, if you know your starting point, to measure speed and distance and therefore know where you are at all times. He also explained the components of the system.

Career Strategies, a newsletter for the upwardly mobile, says many employers are looking for team players more than talented loners. "Talking about what you did alone is the kiss of death," the publication states flatly. Rather than stating individual accomplishments in a résumé, it's better to feature phrases such as "led the group that . . . " or "with two subordinates, executed a successful plan which . . . "

Every job with management responsibilities calls for the ability to work with people, and even the most talented person won't be productive without a team orientation.

American Business

When I went into my interview with the division counsel, I astounded him by my ability to talk the jargon of inertial navigation. . . .

He later told me that I was the first person he had interviewed for the job to whom he did not have to explain inertial navigation. Since he didn't understand it any better than I did, his being relieved of this obligation was a big plus in my favor. Also he said that he knew that it was not an easy task for me to find someone who could explain the subject and to understand it well enough to have the confidence to discuss it. My initiative and interest in going to this extent to prepare for the interview had impressed him.[16]

Respond to the Employer's Needs   While you may need a job to repay a college loan or finance your new Porsche, these concerns won't impress a potential employer. Companies hire employees to satisfy *their* needs, not yours. Although employers will rarely say so outright, the basic question that is *always* being asked in an employment interview is: "Are you a person who can help this organization?" Your approach in an interview, then, should be to show your potential employer how your skills match the company's concerns. Background research will pay off here, too: if you have spent time learning about what the employer needs, you will be in a good position to show how you can satisfy company needs and concerns.

Prepare for Important Questions   Most employment interviewers ask questions in five areas:

Educational background. Does the candidate possess adequate training for a successful career? Do the candidate's grades and other activities predict success in this organization?

Work experience. Do any previous jobs prepare the candidate for this position? What does the candidate's employment history suggest about his or her work habits and ability to work well with others?

Career goals. Does the candidate have clear goals? Are they compatible with a career in this organization?

Personal traits. Do the actions and attitudes of the candidate predict good work habits and good interpersonal skills?

Knowledge of organization and job. Does the candidate know the job and organization well enough to be certain that he or she will feel happy in it?

While the specifics of each job are different, many questions will be the same for any position. Table 7-3 lists the most common questions asked by interviewers. In addition, knowledge of the company and job should suggest other specific questions to you.

It is important to realize that some questions are indirect, seeking information that goes beyond their literal and obvious intent. For example, the question "Where do you see yourself five years from now?" most likely asks, "How ambitious are you? Do you have clear, realistic goals? Do your goals fit in our organization?"

Be Honest   Whatever else an employer may be seeking, honesty is a mandatory job requirement. If an interviewer finds out that you have misrepresented yourself by lying or exaggerating about even one answer, then everything else you say will be suspect. Emphasize your strengths and downplay your weaknesses, but always be honest.

Emphasize the Positive   Although you should always be honest, it is also wise to phrase your answers in a way that casts you in the most positive light. Consider the difference between positive and negative responses to these questions:

Interviewer: "I notice you've held several jobs, but you haven't had any experience in the field you've applied for."

Negative answer: "Uh, that's right. I only decided that I wanted to go into this field last year. I wish I had known that earlier."

Positive answer: "That's right. I've worked in a number of fields, and I've been successful in learning each one quickly. I'd like to think that this kind of adaptability will help me learn this job and to grow with it as technology changes the way the company does business."

Notice how the second answer converted a potential negative into a positive answer. If you anticipate questions that have the ability to harm you, you can compose honest answers that present you in a favorable manner.

Another important rule is to avoid criticizing others in an employment interview. Consider the difference between these answers:

Interviewer: "From your transcript, I notice that you graduated with a 2.3 grade-point average. Isn't that a little low?"

TABLE 7-3   Commonly Asked Questions in Employment Interviews

EDUCATIONAL BACKGROUND

Why did you choose your major field of study?
How do you feel about your education?
How has your education prepared you for a career?
Why did you choose your college or university?
Describe your greatest success (biggest problem) in college.
What subjects in school did you like best (least)?
What was your most rewarding college experience?
How did you finance your education?

WORK EXPERIENCE

Tell me about your past jobs. (What did you do in each?)
Which of your past jobs did you enjoy most? Why?
Why did you leave your past jobs?
Describe your greatest accomplishments in your past jobs.
What were your biggest failures? What did you learn from them?
How have your past jobs prepared you for this position?
What were the good and bad features of your last job?
This job requires initiative and hard work. What in your experience demonstrates these
   qualities?
Have you supervised people in the past? In what capacities? How did you do?
How do you think your present boss (subordinates, co-workers) would describe you?
How do you feel about the way your present (past) companies were managed?

CAREER GOALS

Why are you interested in this position?
Where do you see yourself in five years? Ten years?
What is your eventual career goal?
Why did you choose the career you are now pursuing?
What are your financial goals?
How would you describe the ideal job?
How would you define success?
What things are most important to you in a career?

SELF-ASSESSMENT

In your own words, how would you describe yourself?
How have you grown in the last _____ years?
What are your greatest strengths? Your greatest weaknesses?
What things give you the greatest satisfaction?
How do you feel about your career up to this point?
What is the biggest mistake you have made in your career?
Do you prefer working alone or with others?
How do you work under pressure?
What are the most important features of your personality?
Are you a leader? (a creative person? a problem solver?) Give examples.

KNOWLEDGE OF THE JOB

Why are you interested in this particular job? Our company?
What can you contribute to this job? Our company?

TABLE 7-3 *(Continued)*

KNOWLEDGE OF THE JOB *(continued)*

Why should we hire you? What qualifies you for this position?
What do you think about _____ (job-related topic)?
What part of this job do you think would be most difficult?

OTHER TOPICS

Do you have any geographical preferences? Why?
Would you be willing to travel? To relocate?
Do you have any questions for me?

> *Negative answer:* "Sure, but it wasn't my fault. I had some terrible teachers during my first two years of college. We had to memorize a lot of useless information that didn't have anything to do with the real world. Besides, professors give you high grades if they like you. If you don't play their game, they grade you down."

> *Positive answer:* "My low-grade point average came mostly from very bad freshman and sophomore years. I wasn't serious about school then, but you can see that my later grades are much higher. I've grown a lot in the past few years, and I'd like to think that I can use what I've learned in this job."

Back Up Your Answers with Evidence Making claims without evidence can sound self-serving. But if you offer evidence to support your answers, the objective facts will confirm your strengths.

> *Interviewer:* "What strengths would you bring to this job?"

> *Weak answer:* "I'm a self-starter who can work without close supervision."

> *Stronger answer:* "I'm a self-starter who can work without close supervision. In my last job, I spent roughly two weeks of every month on the road. I was responsible for organizing my own schedule, calling on customers, keeping records, and sending in reports to the home office. In my most recent performance review, my manager wrote that I handled responsibility well without needing close supervision. I have a copy of the evaluation form here, if you'd like to see it."

Keep Your Answers Brief It is easy to rattle on in an interview out of enthusiasm, a desire to show off your knowledge, or nervousness, but in most cases long answers are not a good idea. The interviewer probably has a lot of ground to cover, and long-winded answers won't help. A good rule of thumb is to keep your responses under two minutes. An interviewer who wants additional information can always ask for it.

Find Common Ground While nobody likes a bootlicker, research does indicate that candidates who agree with an interviewer are seen as being more competent than other applicants, and they wind up receiving offers for higher-paying jobs.[17] Whenever possible, try to find common ground with the interviewer: past experiences, shared beliefs, common goals, and so on.

Have Your Own Questions Answered   Any good employer will recognize that you have your own concerns about the job. After you have answered the interviewer's questions, you should be prepared to ask a few of your own. Realize that your questions make indirect statements about you just as your answers to the interviewer's inquiries did. Be sure your questions aren't all greedy ones that focus on salary, vacation time, benefits, and so on. Some good questions include:

> What changes do you see occurring for the company in the next five or ten years?

> What career paths do people like me wind up following?

> What, in your opinion, are the most important qualities that people need to succeed in your company?

> How much choice do employees have in choosing a geographic location?

> I was interested in your remark about the company's new product line. Can you tell me more about it?

POST-INTERVIEW FOLLOW-UP

Without exception, every employment interview should be followed immediately by a letter to the person who interviewed you. This follow-up letter serves several purposes. First, it demonstrates common courtesy. Second, it reminds the employer of you. Third, a letter gives you a chance to remind the interviewer of important information about you that came up in the interview and to provide facts you may have omitted then. Fourth, a letter can correct any misunderstandings that may have occurred during the interview. Fifth, the letter can tactfully remind the interviewer of promises made, such as a second interview or a response by a certain date.

INTERVIEWING AND THE LAW

Many laws govern what questions are and are not legal in employment interviews, but the general principle that underlies them all is simple: questions may not be asked for the purpose of discriminating on the basis of race, color, religion,

---

A signal that the interview is drawing to a close comes when you are asked whether you have any questions. Ask questions, and by doing so, highlight your strengths and show your enthusiasm. . . .

   Don't discuss salary, vacation, or benefits. It is not that the questions are invalid, just that the timing is wrong. Bringing up such topics before you have a job offer is asking what the company can do for you—instead, you should be saying what you can do for the company.

Martin Yate, *Knock 'Em Dead: With Great Answers to Tough Interview Questions*

Even if you don't accomplish your immediate goal in an interview, planning and preparation can pay off later. One manager provides this example from her own experience:

> [One person] put in a bid for a promotion, backed up with her résumé, references and work samples, and although I didn't promote her (I wanted to bring in fresh blood), I was impressed with her energy and excellent training. Several years later I recommended her for a similar high-level position at another company, and she's still there.

Jane Ciabattari, "When It's Your Turn to Be Boss"

sex, disabilities, national origin, or age. Employers may still ask about these areas, but the U.S. government's Equal Employment Opportunity Commission (EEOC) permits only questions that investigate a "bona fide occupational qualification" (BFOQ in bureaucratic jargon) for a particular job. This means any question asked should be job-related. The Supreme Court has said that "the touchstone is business necessity."[18] Table 7-4 lists questions that are generally not considered as BFOQs as well as those that are legitimate.

There are several ways to answer an unlawful question:[19]

1. *Acceptance without comment:* Answer the question, even though you know it is probably unlawful: "I'm forty-seven."

2. *Acceptance with comment:* Point out that the question is probably unlawful but answer it anyway: "I don't think the law allows you to ask my age, but I'm forty-seven."

3. *Confrontation:* Meet the interviewer head-on by asking about the question's appropriateness. "Why did you ask me that?" "Does my age have anything to do with whether I will be hired?"

4. *Rationalization:* Ignore a direct response to the question and point out your qualifications for the position. "My age has nothing to do with my ability to perform the job as described. As you have presented it to me, I have the education, experience, track record, attitude, and desire to excel in this position."

5. *Challenge:* Make the interviewer tell you why this question is a BFOQ. "Please explain to me why age is a criterion for this job."

6. *Redirection:* Refer to an antecedent (something that has come before) to shift the focus of the interview away from your age toward the requirements of the position itself. "What you've said so far suggests that age is not as important for this position as is willingness to travel. Can you tell me more about the travel requirement?"

TABLE 7-4 Questions Interviewers Can and Cannot Legally Ask

Federal law restricts employer interviewer questions and other practices to areas clearly related to job requirements. The following are some questions and practices that are generally considered legitimate and others that are not.

SUBJECT	UNACCEPTABLE	ACCEPTABLE
NAME	Maiden name	Name "Have you ever used another name?" *or* "Is any additional information relative to change of name, use of an assumed name, or nickname necessary to enable a check on your work and education record? If yes, please explain."
RESIDENCE	"Do you own or rent your home?"	Place of residence
AGE	Age Birth date Dates of attendance or completion of elementary or high school Questions that tend to identify applicants over age 40	Statement that hire is subject to verification that applicant meets legal age requirements "If hired, can you show proof of age?" "Are you over eighteen years of age?" "If under eighteen, can you, after employment, submit a work permit?"
BIRTHPLACE, CITIZENSHIP	Birthplace of applicant, applicant's parents, spouse, or other relatives "Are you a U.S. citizen?" *or* citizenship of applicant, applicant's parents, spouse, or other relatives Requirements that applicant produce naturalization, first papers, or alien card *prior to employment*	"Can you, after employment, submit verification of your legal right to work in the United States?" *or* statement that such proof may be required after employment
NATIONAL ORIGIN	Questions as to nationality, lineage, ancestry, national origin, descent, or parentage of applicant, applicant's parents, or spouse "What is your mother tongue?" *or* language commonly used by applicant How applicant acquired ability to read, write, or speak a foreign language	Languages applicant reads, speaks, or writes, if use of a language other than English is relevant to the job for which applicant is applying
SEX, MARITAL STATUS, FAMILY	Questions that indicate applicant's sex Questions that indicate applicant's marital status Number and/or ages of children or dependents Provisions for child care Questions regarding pregnancy, child bearing, or birth control Name or address of relative, spouse, or children of adult applicant "With whom do you reside?" *or* "Do you live with your parents?"	Name and address of parent or guardian, if applicant is a minor Statement of company policy regarding work assignment of employees who are related

TABLE 7-4 *(Continued)*

SUBJECT	UNACCEPTABLE	ACCEPTABLE
RACE, COLOR	Questions as to applicant's race or color Questions regarding applicant's complexion or color of skin, eyes, hair	Statement that photograph may be required after employment
PHYSICAL DESCRIPTION, PHOTOGRAPH	Questions as to applicant's height and weight Require applicant to affix a photograph to application Request applicant, at his or her option, to submit a photograph Require a photograph after interview but before employment	
PHYSICAL CONDITION, HANDICAP	Questions regarding applicant's general medical condition, state of health, or illnesses Questions regarding receipt of workers' compensation "Do you have any physical disabilities or handicaps?"	Statement by employer that offer may be made contingent on applicant passing a job-related physical examination "Do you have any physical condition or handicap that may limit your ability to perform the job applied for? If yes, what can be done to accommodate your limitation?"
RELIGION	Questions regarding applicant's religion Religious days observed *or* "Does your religion prevent you from working weekends or holidays?"	Statement by employer of regular days, hours, or shifts to be worked
ARREST, CRIMINAL RECORD	Arrest record *or* "Have you ever been arrested?"	"Have you ever been convicted of a felony?" Such a question must be accompanied by a statement that a conviction will not necessarily disqualify an applicant from employment
MILITARY SERVICE	General questions regarding military service such as dates and type of discharge Questions regarding service in a foreign military	Questions regarding relevant skills acquired during applicant's U.S. military service
ORGANIZATIONS, ACTIVITIES	"List all organizations, clubs, societies, and lodges to which you belong."	"Please list job-related organizations, clubs, professional societies, or other associations to which you belong—you may omit those that indicate your race, religious creed, color, national origin, ancestry, sex, or age."
REFERENCES	Questions of applicant's former employers or acquaintances that elicit information specifying the applicant's race, color, religious creed, national origin, ancestry, physical handicap, medical condition, marital status, age, or sex	"By whom were you referred for a position here?" Names of persons willing to provide professional and/or character references for applicant

7. *Refusal:* Say that you will not provide the information requested. "I'm not going to answer that question now, but if I'm hired, I'll be happy to tell you."

8. *Withdrawal:* Physically remove yourself from the interview. End the interview immediately and leave.

Choosing the best response style depends on several factors.[20] First, it is important to consider the probable intent of the interviewer. The question may, indeed, be aimed at collecting information that will allow the employer to discriminate, but it may just as well be a naïve inquiry with no harm intended. Most interviewers are unsophisticated at their job. In fact, fewer than 60 percent of the recruiters polled in one survey had received any formal training in interviewing.[21] An illegal question may be the result of ignorance rather than malice. The interviewer who discusses family, nationality, or religion may simply be trying to make conversation.

A second factor when considering how to respond to an illegal question is your desire for the job at hand. You may be more willing to challenge the interviewer when a position isn't critical to your future. On the other hand, if your career rides on succeeding in a particular interview, you may be willing to swallow your objections. A third factor to consider is your feeling of comfort with the interviewer. For example, a female candidate with school-age children might welcome the chance to discuss child-care issues with an interviewer who has identified herself as a single mother who faces the same challenges. A fourth item to consider is your own personal style. If you are comfortable asserting yourself, you may be willing to address an illegal question head-on. If you are less comfortable speaking up, especially to authority figures, you may prefer to respond more evasively.

If you choose to take an aggressive approach to illegal questioning, you have the right to file a charge with the EEOC and your state Fair Employment Practices Commission within 180 days of the interview. In practice, the EEOC will withhold its investigation until the state commission has completed its inquiry. Federal and state agencies have a backlog of cases, however, so it may take years to complete an investigation. A quicker but potentially more expensive course is to sue the employer. Realize, however, that a suit is not likely to make you an attractive candidate to other employers who hear of your action. Blacklists may be unfair, but they are often a fact of business life.

SAMPLE SELECTION INTERVIEW

The following transcript is based on a real interview. As you read it, pay attention to both the interviewer's questions and the applicant's responses. In both cases, notice the strengths and the areas needing improvement. What parts of this interview would you like to incorporate in your style? What parts would you handle differently?

Interviewer:	Monica Hansen? I'm Chris Van Dyke. Welcome.
Applicant:	It's good to meet you.
Interviewer:	Did you have any trouble finding us?
Applicant:	The directions were perfect. And thanks for the parking pass.
Interviewer:	Oh, yes. That's a necessity. The garage costs twelve dollars per day if you don't have one. We'll have about a half hour this morning to talk about the personnel administrator's position you've applied for. I'd like to learn about you. And, of course, I want to answer any questions you have about us.
Applicant:	Great. I'm looking forward to it.
Interviewer:	Good. Let's begin by having you tell me about your most recent position. Your résumé says you were at ITC in Springfield, is that right?
Applicant:	That's right. My official job title was personnel assistant, but that really doesn't describe the work I did very well. I recruited nonexempt employees, processed the payroll, oriented new employees, and maintained the files.
Interviewer:	Were you involved with insurance?
Applicant:	Yes. I processed workers' compensation claims and maintained the insurance reports for our health-care plans.
Interviewer:	And you said you were involved in hiring?
Applicant:	Yes. I was responsible for recruiting and interviewing all the clerical and secretarial people.
Interviewer:	How did that go?
Applicant:	It was tough in Springfield. There's actually a shortage of talented secretarial people there. It's an expensive town to live in, and there aren't a lot of people who can afford living there on a secretary's salary. It's not like Atlanta, where there's plenty of good secretarial help.
Interviewer:	What did you learn about hiring from your experiences at ITC?
Applicant:	I learned to look further than the résumé. Some people seem great on paper, but you find there's something wrong when you hire them. Other people don't have much experience on paper, but they have a lot of potential.
Interviewer:	How did you get beyond paper screening?
Applicant:	Well, if someone looked at all promising, I would phone their former employers and talk to the people they actually worked for.

Interviewer: What would you do if this was their first job?

Applicant: I found that almost everyone had done some kind of work—part time or vacation. And I could check up on that. Or I would even ask for the names of a few teachers and phone them up, if the person was just graduating.

Interviewer: Didn't that take a lot of time?

Applicant: Yes, it did. But it was worth it in the long run, since we got much better employees that way. We almost never had to dismiss someone whom we'd done a phone check on.

Interviewer: You were promoted after a year. Why?

Applicant: I was lucky to be in the right place. The company was growing, and we were very busy. I tried to take advantage of the situation by offering to do more and by taking classes at night.

Interviewer: What classes did you take?

Applicant: I took an applied human relations class last spring. And before that, a couple of computer classes: one in Lotus 1-2-3 and one in desktop publishing. Our department was thinking about starting an employee newsletter, and I wanted to see if we could produce it in-house.

Interviewer: It sounds like you've done very well at ITC. Why do you want to leave?

Applicant: In some ways I *don't* want to leave. The people are great . . . most of them . . . and I've enjoyed the work. But I'm looking for more challenges, and there isn't much chance for me to take on more responsibility there.

Interviewer: Why not?

Applicant: Well, my boss, the personnel director, is very happy in her job and has no plans to leave. She's young, and there's very little chance I'll be able to advance.

Interviewer: I see. Well, that is a problem. And what kind of responsibilities are you looking for?

Applicant: I'd say the biggest one is the chance to help make policy. In my past jobs, I've been carrying out policies that other people—management—have made. That's been fine, but I'd like to be involved in setting some policies myself.

Interviewer: What kinds of policies?

Applicant: Oh, there are several. Designing benefits packages. Coming up with a performance review system that people will take seriously. Teaching our supervisors how to interview and hire more systematically.

Interviewer: I see. Well, the position you've applied for certainly does have those sorts of responsibilities. Let me ask you another question. What do you enjoy most about personnel work?

Applicant: Well, I really enjoy the chance to work so much with people. Of course, there's a lot of paperwork, too, but I especially like the chance to work with people.

Interviewer: When you say "people," what kinds of work are you thinking of?

Applicant: I guess the common denominator is making people happy. Lots of employees got involved with the personnel department—once they've been hired, that is—because they have problems. Maybe it's an insurance claim or a problem with their performance review. It makes me feel good to see them leave feeling satisfied, or at least feeling better after they've come in so upset.

Interviewer: Are you always able to help them?

Applicant: No, of course not. Sometimes a person will want the impossible, and sometimes there just won't be any answer.

Interviewer: Can you give examples of these times?

Applicant: Well, one example of an impossible request comes up a lot with health insurance. At ITC we could choose from two plans. With one plan you could use any doctor you wanted. You had to make a copayment with that one. With the other plan, you had to choose a doctor from a list of "preferred providers," but there was no copayment. If an employee chose the preferred-provider plan and later decided he or she wanted to use a doctor that wasn't on the list, we just couldn't do anything about it.

Interviewer: We've had that problem here, too. How did you handle it?

Applicant: Being sympathetic helped a little. Even if I couldn't give them what they wanted, at least saying I was sorry might have made it seem less like a total rejection. I also pointed out that they *could* switch plans during the open enrollment period, which comes every year. I've also suggested to my boss that we do a better job of informing people about the restrictions of the preferred-provider plan before they sign up and maybe even getting them to sign a statement that says they understand them. I think that would reduce the surprises that come up later.

Interviewer: That's a good idea. Monica, what qualities do you think are important for a personnel officer?

Applicant: Knowing the job is definitely important, but I'd say getting along with people might be even more important.

Interviewer: And how would you describe your ability to get along?

Applicant: Sometimes I think I deserve an Academy Award for acting the opposite of the way I feel.

Interviewer: Really? Tell me about it.

Applicant: Every so often someone will come in with an attitude problem, and I try to calm them down by acting more pleasant than I feel. For example, we've had people who think they're entitled to take six months off for a workers' compensation claim, when the doctor has said they're ready to come back after a few weeks. They come in and yell at us, and it's tough to be pleasant at times like those. But I don't think there's any point in being blunt or rude. It just makes them more angry.

Interviewer: I see what you mean. Let's shift gears, Monica. If you were to pick a boss, what are the important traits that he or she should have?

Applicant: Let me see . . . certainly lots of follow-up—letting people know where they stand. The ability to give criticism constructively and to compliment good work. Giving people a task and then leaving them alone, without nagging.

Interviewer: But still being there to help if it's needed, right?

Applicant: Sure. But also giving me the space to finish a job without staying *too* close.

Interviewer: Anything else?

Applicant: Being available for help, as you said. Being consistent. And being willing to train employees in new jobs, letting them grow. And considering the personal goals of employees.

Interviewer: In personnel work, there's a need for confidentiality. What does that mean to you?

Applicant: That's an important area. You see lots of personal information, and it's easy to make offhand remarks that could upset someone.

Interviewer: What kinds of things do you have to be careful about?

Applicant: Oh, even something as simple as a person's birthday. Most people wouldn't care, but some people might be offended if their birthdays got out. I've learned to be constantly on guard, to watch what I say. I'm a private person anyway, so that helps.

Interviewer: Monica, I've been asking you a lot of questions. Let me ask just one more, then it can be your turn. What are the factors that motivate you?

Applicant: Well, I like to be busy. If things aren't busy, I still work, but I like to be stimulated. I seem to get more work done when I'm busy than when there's plenty of time. It's crazy, but true. I'm also motivated by the chance to grow and take on as much responsibility as I can handle.

Interviewer: Monica, what questions do you have for me? What can I tell you about the job or the company?

Applicant: What kind of growth do you see for the company?

Interviewer: Well, we have 155 employees now. As I think you know, we're five years old, and we started with five employees. Our sales were up 14 percent last year, and it looks like we'll be expanding more.

Applicant: How many employees do you think will be added?

Interviewer: Well, we hired twenty new people last year, and we expect to hire almost the same number this year.

Applicant: And what's the turnover like?

Interviewer: That's a good question for a personnel person to ask! We've been growing so much, and people have been able to move into more responsible jobs, so they've been satisfied for the most part. Our turnover has been pretty low— about 15 percent annually.

Applicant: Will the person you hire be involved in making policy?

Interviewer: Yes, definitely. We're still trying to catch up with ourselves after growing so fast. A big project for this year is to put together an employee handbook. Too many of our policies are verbal now, and that's not good. Developing that handbook would mean working directly with the president of the company, and that definitely involves developing policy.

Applicant: Of course, I'm interested in learning about the benefits and salary . . .

Interviewer: Of course. Here's a copy of our benefits summary for you to study. We can talk about salary later. Right now I'd like you to meet a couple more of our managers. After you've spoken with them, we can get back together to discuss salary and other matters.

We will definitely be making our decision within the next ten days, so I promise you you'll have an answer before the first of next month.

It's been a real pleasure talking to you, Monica. You certainly express yourself well. I'll talk with you again soon.

Applicant: Thanks. I've enjoyed the talk, too. I'll look forward to hearing from you.

THE PERFORMANCE APPRAISAL INTERVIEW

A working group is like an athletic team: even the best players need the guidance of a coach to help them do their individual best and work with other members. Managers are the coaches in most organizations, and the performance appraisal interview is one way they help their team members.

DEFINITION AND IMPORTANCE

Performance appraisal interviews are scheduled regularly between superior and subordinate to discuss the quality of the subordinate's performance.[22] More specifically, these interviews have several functions, including

- *Letting the employee know where he or she stands.* This kind of feedback includes praising good work, communicating areas that need improvement, and conveying to the employee his or her prospects.
- *Developing employee skills.* The review can be a chance for the employee to learn new skills. Among their other roles, managers and supervisors should be teachers. The performance appraisal interview can be a chance to show an employee how to do a better job.
- *Improving employment relationship.* Performance reviews should improve superior-subordinate relationships and give employees a sense of participation in the job. Ideally, employees should leave the interview feeling better about themselves and the organization.
- *Helping management learn the employee's point of view.* Performance appraisal should include upward communication as well as downward. It provides a chance for subordinates to explain their perspective to managers.
- *Counseling the employee.* An appraisal interview provides the chance for managers to learn about personal problems that may be affecting an employee's personal performance and to offer advice and support.
- *Setting goals for the future.* One result of every performance appraisal interview should be a clear idea of how both the superior and subordinate will behave in the future.

Despite the potential threat of being evaluated, performance appraisals can be welcomed by employees. One of the greatest hungers that workers have is to know where they stand with management. Researchers have found that receiving "personal feedback" correlates highly with job satisfaction,[23] and appraisal interviews offer a periodic session dedicated to providing just that feedback. Despite this fact, 40 percent of all employees report that they don't receive a regular performance review.[24]

Just because employees want feedback doesn't mean that they are always satisfied with the performance appraisals they do receive. Sometimes performance reviews can be contaminated by organizational politics, generating resentment and undermining morale.[25] Intentionally or not, many unskilled managers turn appraisal sessions into criticisms of past shortcomings that do little besides arouse resentment and defensiveness in employees. The interviewing skills outlined in this section can help make sure that a performance review meets the needs of both management and employees.

Performance review should be an ongoing process, not something that only happens at infrequent intervals during a scheduled interview.[26] The functions of performance appraisal listed on page 196 can and should be performed constantly in the kind of process pictured in Figure 7-3. This doesn't mean that formal interviews are useless, for they provide a chance to focus on how well the ongoing job of judging and improving performance is proceeding. The value of a formal review is captured by Chrysler chairman Lee Iacocca, who describes how the procedure works in his company:

> Every three months, each manager sits down with his immediate superior to review the manager's past accomplishments and to chart his goals for the next term. Once there is agreement on these goals, the manager puts them in writing and the supervisor signs off on it. As I'd learned from McNamara, the discipline of writing something down is the first step toward making it happen. In conversation, you can get away with all kinds of vagueness and nonsense, often without even realizing it. But there's something about putting your thoughts on paper that forces you to get down to specifics. That way, it's harder to deceive yourself—or anybody else.[27]

STYLES OF APPRAISAL INTERVIEWING

In his near-classic book, Norman R. F. Maier identifies three styles of appraisal interviewing: "tell and sell," "tell and listen/listen and tell," and "problem solving."[28]

Tell and Sell Telling and selling can range from a friendly persuasive style to an authoritarian approach. In any case, the manager who tells and sells believes that his or her evaluation is correct and aims at passing along this assessment to the subordinate.

This style has its drawbacks. First, it can be unfair and unproductive if the manager's evaluation is incorrect. If, for instance, a worker's lack of productivity is due to outside factors and not a lack of effort, as the supervisor suggests, then the evaluation will be unfair and any increase will be in the employee's resentment and defensiveness, not in productivity.

Despite its drawbacks, tell-and-sell interviewing can work well in certain situations: (1) with inexperienced employees who are unable to evaluate themselves; (2) with employees who have much lower status than their bosses and, as a result, are willing to accept the superior's judgments; (3) with employees who are very loyal to the organization or who identify strongly with the manager; and (4) with employees who are not willing to evaluate themselves and who appreciate direction.

Figure 7-3 The performance appraisal process.

Tell and Listen/Listen and Tell   This approach adds a new element to the interview—namely, the manager's willingness to hear the employee's point of view. After describing his or her assessment, the boss lets the subordinate react to the assessment. During the final part of a tell-and-listen interview the manager again takes control, identifying future goals for the employee.

Despite its increased two-way communication, a pure tell-and-listen approach is still basically persuasive. The manager's motive for listening is to let the employee have a say, but there is no guarantee that the subordinate's comments will change the boss's ideas.

A more employee-oriented variation of this style is the *listen-and-tell* approach. Here the boss lets the subordinate begin the session by describing his or her beliefs, after which the manager has a turn. This structure has three advantages: First, it makes the subordinate's contribution more than just a defensive reaction to the interviewer's evaluation. Second, it lets the manager adjust the evaluation, if the employee's remarks so warrant. Finally, it gives the manager an idea of how well the employee knows his or her own strengths and weaknesses.

Listen-and-tell interviews work best when the interviewer is sincerely interested in the employee's point of view. If the listening phase is just a device to let employees think that they are important, the defensive results will be worse than with a straightforward tell-and-tell session. The listen-and-tell approach is most successful with employees who fit at least one of the following categories: feeling misunderstood by management, having a high need for participation, or having the ability to understand their jobs and their own behavior.

Problem Solving   A problem-solving interview involves the employee to a greater degree than the previous two approaches. In it, the manager and employee work together to define areas of concern and to develop appropriate solutions. Thus, the problem-solving manager becomes less of a judge and more of a helper.

Problem-solving interviews are built on the idea of mutual interest and win-win problem solving described in Chapter 5. Both boss and employee realize that their best interests are served by having the employee succeed, and they have the attitude that approaches are possible that leave both parties satisfied. While the interviewer still retains the power that comes with a managerial position, boss and employee cooperate so that neither orders nor threats are necessary.

STEPS IN THE APPRAISAL PROCESS

Whatever approach is taken, an appraisal session should begin with an opening. After an initial exchange of pleasantries—usually brief—the manager should provide a rationale for the interview, an outline of what information will be covered and how it will be used, and a preview of the interview's probable length. After the preliminaries, the body of an appraisal interview should go on to cover three areas: a review of the criteria established in past meetings, a discussion of the employee's performance, and a setting of goals for the future.

Review Progress   The first step in the body of any appraisal interview should be to identify the criteria by which the employee is being evaluated. Ideally, these

Some bosses and employees complain that performance reviews are a nuisance. Management guru Robert Townsend agrees—to a point. "Printed forms for performance appraisal and MBOs are used by incompetent bosses in badly managed companies," he claims. Loews Corporation executive Alan Momeyer agrees. He states that an obsession with developing the perfect evaluation form is misguided.

Despite these criticisms, authorities on communication agree that most managers and supervisors need to give employees *more* feedback, not less. "Day-to-day coaching is the most overlooked step of the performance process," says *One Minute Manager* co-author Kenneth Blanchard. Townsend agrees: "Real managers manage by frequent eyeball contact," he insists, quoting one good boss's description of the process: "Half our meetings are held in the hall, the other half in the washroom."

Perhaps these management experts have a point. If bosses spent more time giving employees informal feedback and setting goals on a day-to-day basis, there might be less need for quarterly or seminannual formal meetings. But one way or the other, performance review is one of the most important responsibilities a manager has.

Robert Townsend, *Further Up the Organization;* Alan Momeyer, *Training;* and Kenneth Blanchard, "Rating Managers on Performance Reviews," *Today's Office*

---

criteria will already be clear to both the manager and employee, but it is wise to restate them. A manager might say:

> Bill, as I'm sure you remember, we decided at our last meeting to focus on several targets. We agreed that if you could reach them, you'd be doing your present job very well and you'd be setting yourself up for an assistant sales manager's position. Here's the list of targets we developed last time (shows employee list). So these are the areas we need to look at today.

Discuss Successes, Problems, and Needs   After the criteria have been defined, the discussion can focus on how well the employee has satisfied them. The nature of the discussion will depend on the style of interview that has been chosen. In a problem-solving format, there will be a give-and-take discussion between superior and subordinate. In a tell-and-sell interview, the evaluation will be dominated by a one-way, top-down style. A tell-and-listen (or listen-and-tell) meeting will combine elements of persuasion and problem solving.

Whatever the interview style, discussion will be easiest when the goals are measurable: Are sales up 15 percent? Have jobs been completed on time? If the employee has explanations for why targets were not reached, it is the manager's job to consider these fairly. Some goals are subjective, so the evaluation of their performance will be a matter of judgment as well. Even seemingly vague goals like "being more patient with customers" can be at least partially clarified by turning them into simple behavioral descriptions such as "letting customers talk without interrupting them."

When evaluating past performance, it is important to maintain a balance among the points under consideration. Without meaning to let it happen, a manager and employee can become involved in discussing (or debating) a relatively unimportant point at length, throwing the overall look at the employee's performance out of perspective. A skillful interviewer will only focus on the most important criteria, usually dealing with no more than three areas that need work. Even the most demanding manager will realize upon reflection that changing old habits is difficult and that it is unrealistic to expect dramatic improvement in too many areas within a short time.

Set Goals Once the employee and manager have discussed past successes, problems, and needs, the task becomes defining goals for the future. The goals should meet several criteria.

- They should focus on the most important aspects of the job. The tried-and-true 80:20 rule applies here: changing 20 percent of a worker's behavior will usually solve 80 percent of the problems.
- The goals should be described as specifically as possible so that both manager and employee will know what actions constitute the target.
- A time period should be stated for each target. People often work best when faced with a deadline, and setting dates lets both parties know when the results are due.
- The targets ought to provide some challenge to the worker, requiring effort yet being attainable. A manageable challenge will produce the greatest growth and leave workers and managers feeling pleased with the changes that occur.

The Written Record The appraisal process commonly has a written dimension in addition to the interview itself. Before the meeting, the manager often completes an evaluation form listing characteristics or behaviors important to the job. Ideally, the information on this form is taken from the goals set at the previous interview. In some organizations, the subordinate also fills out a self-rating form covering similar areas. In most companies, a performance review is summarized and documented with a written evaluation. In most cases, the manager completes a final report that summarizes the results of the session. The employee usually has the option of adding his or her own response to the manager's report. This document then becomes part of the employee's records and is used as a basis for future evaluations, as well as providing information for decisions about promotions. (See Table 7-5.)

GIVING FEEDBACK

Even when an appraisal is conducted with the best of intentions, its evaluative nature raises the odds of a defensive response. Feedback will be best received when it meets several criteria. Observing these guidelines can boost the chances of keeping the interview's tone constructive.

TABLE 7-5   Checklist for Performance Appraisal Interviewing

Interview covers key areas
  ___ Orients employee
  ___ Establishes positive climate
  ___ Reviews past achievement of goals
  ___ Identifies successes, problems, and needs in employee's area of responsibility
  ___ Establishes new goals with employee
Feedback delivered constructively
  ___ Information is accurate
  ___ Feedback appropriate to critic's role
  ___ Balance of praise and constructive criticism
Praise delivered effectively
  ___ Praise is sincere
  ___ Specific behaviors identified
  ___ Emphasis on progress, not perfection
  ___ Praise communication by deeds as well as by words
Criticism expressed constructively
  ___ Criticism limited to key areas
  ___ Criticism delivered in face-saving manner
  ___ Criticism accompanied by offer to help
  ___ Benefits of cooperating emphasized
Interview accomplishes all necessary functions
  ___ Lets employee know where he or she stands
  ___ Develops employee skills
  ___ Improves communication climate, boosts morale
  ___ Helps management understand employee's point of view
  ___ Counsels employee as appropriate
  ___ Sets goals for future

- *Feedback should be accurate.* Perhaps the worst mistake an evaluator can make is to get the facts wrong. Before you judge an employee, be sure you have an accurate picture of his or her performance and all the factors that affected it. A tell-and-listen approach can help the manager understand an employee's performance more fully.

- *The feedback should be relevant to the job.* For example, it may be legitimate to comment on an employee's appearance in a job that involves contact with the public, but it is probably out of line to be critical about the way he or she handles personal matters after business hours.

The best chances of success occur when the review offers a balance of praise and constructive suggestions for improvement. The following guidelines offer specific advice about how to handle both areas.

Delivering Praise   The old saying "You can catch more flies with honey than with vinegar" is especially true in performance appraisal. Both everyday experience and research have demonstrated the power of positive reinforcement. One study revealed that the commitment level of employees dropped when their behavior was only identified as "satisfactory."[29] A manager who uses praise in appraisal interviews should keep the following points in mind:

- *Be sincere.* Phony compliments are worse than no praise at all. Besides stirring resentment—"Do you think I'm a fool?"—false reinforcement can cast doubt on other praise that is genuine.
- *Be specific.* The most useful praise defines the desirable behavior clearly. Instead of offering the vague comment "You've worked hard," a more specific comment is better: "Thanks to you, we didn't miss a single day's business during the switch to the new computer system."
- *Praise progress, not perfection.* Being perfect is usually impossible. It is far better to acknowledge an employee's development by noting progress since the last evaluation: "Your production increased by over 25 percent since our last evaluation. If you keep up this kind of improvement, by next year you'll be as good as anybody in the company."
- *Praise by deed as well as by words.* One of the best ways to show that an employee's behavior is praiseworthy is to show increased appreciation. Although a raise in pay is one measure of appreciation, there are other measures. Giving more responsibility is a token of respect for talent and hard work. Asking the employee's opinion is another way of showing how valuable he or she is.

Delivering Constructive Criticism   Sooner or later, even the most outstanding employee will need to hear criticism about his or her work. Delivering negative information is one of the biggest challenges a manager or supervisor can face. Handling critical situations well isn't just the boss's responsibility; the subordinate needs to behave responsibly too. The guidelines for coping nondefensively with criticism outlined on pages 102–103 should be helpful when it is your turn to receive critical messages. If the supervisor is able to deliver negative feedback skillfully, difficult messages will be easier to understand and accept. The following guidelines will make this sort of communication most successful:

- *Limit criticism to key areas.* Choose the most important areas that need improvement instead of overwhelming the employee with a shopping list of complaints. Change in one, two, or even three areas may be possible, but more than a few complaints can be discouraging and impossible to remedy.
- *Criticize in a face-saving manner.* Every effort should be made to spare the employee unnecessary embarrassment. At the very least, this means delivering the critical remarks in private. Embarrassment can also be minimized by avoiding evaluative language (e.g., "lazy," "sloppy") and using more neutral terms. Focusing on the behavior, not the person, is a key to successful criticism.

■ *Accompany criticism with an offer to help.* Evaluators shouldn't just describe what is wrong: it is far more constructive to find ways to help remedy deficient behavior. The responsibility for changing may ultimately rest with the employee, but the manager will get best results by supporting improvements in any possible way.

■ *Show the benefits of cooperating.* Emphasizing the value of improvement can cast criticisms in a positive light. Saying "If this problem continues, we may be forced to demote you" is discouraging and threatening. The same information will probably produce better results if phrased differently: "If we can clear up this problem, your position here will be secure. We could even start to talk about promoting you to a more responsible position."

While following these guidelines won't guarantee a successful performance review, it can increase the chances that the meeting will be genuinely constructive and serve the interests of both the superior and the subordinate.

SUMMARY

Chapter 7 focused on three important types of interviews: information gathering, selection, and performance appraisal. The most common type of information-gathering interview aims at conducting research. The research interviewer should begin by collecting background information on the subject and the interviewee. This information is used to define the general goals of the interview and identify the specific questions that should be asked. Equally important is identifying whom to interview to get the desired information.

Selection interviews are critically important for even the most qualified job applicant, for the person who receives a job offer is often the one who knows the most about how to get hired. Since many positions are never advertised, a job-seeker should begin the selection process long before an official job interview. The first step involves building a network of personal contacts by conducting a series of "three R" interviews to research potentially interesting fields, to be remembered by the interviewee, and to gain referrals for other helpful contacts. When these three-R interviews or other sources lead to a job interview itself, candidates should constantly focus on showing how they can help the organization reach its goals. Effective behavior for the interviewee includes looking good, being honest, answering questions briefly, and finding common ground with the interviewer. Every employment interview should be followed by a letter of thanks from the applicant to the interviewer.

Federal and state laws restrict interviewers from asking questions that are not related to the bona fide occupational qualifications of a job. In this chapter, we listed both acceptable and unacceptable questions and practices and suggested strategies for responding to illegal questions.

Performance appraisal interviews give superiors and their subordinates a structured way to look at the quality of the subordinate's performance. When conducted skillfully, these sessions are welcomed by most employees as a chance to learn how they are viewed by management.

Three styles can be used in performance appraisal interviews: tell and sell, tell and listen/listen and tell, and problem solving. The best style varies from one type of employee to another. Whatever the approach, all appraisal interviews should begin with a definition of the criteria used to evaluate the employee. Next, the employee's performance should be evaluated according to these criteria. Finally, manager and employee should set goals for the next evaluation period.

The nature of feedback and the way it is delivered can have a major impact on the outcome of a performance appraisal interview. Praise is valuable when it is sincere and specific, and when it focuses on progress instead of perfection. Praise can be delivered demonstratively as well as verbally. Constructive criticism is limited to key topics, given in a face-saving manner, and accompanied by an offer of help. Employees will accept criticism best when they recognize the benefits of following the advice contained in their evaluation.

ACTIVITIES

1. Choose the three types of interviews most common in your experience. For each of these types, identify a specific interview you have taken part in in the past or will encounter in the future.

   a. Describe the stakes in the situations you have identified. Is money involved? Self-esteem? The future of a career?

   b. For the past interviews, describe how satisfied you were with your behavior. For future interviews, predict how satisfied you expect to be with your behavior, given your present level of interviewing skill.

2. Select a person in your chosen career who plays a role in hiring new employees. Conduct an information-gathering interview to discover the following:

   a. What methods are used to identify job candidates?

   b. What format is used to interview applicants?

   c. What formal and informal criteria are used to hire applicants?

   d. What personal qualities impress your subject, both positively and negatively?

3. Identify at least two people you could interview and one or more specific objectives for each of the following information-gathering interviews:

   a. Learning more about a potential employer. (Name a specific organization.)

   b. Deciding whether to enroll in a specific class. (You choose which one.)

   c. Deciding whether to purchase a personal computer (or a piece of software, if you already own a computer).

   d. Exploring the career opportunities in a city of your choice.

   e. The best savings or investment vehicle for you at this time.

4. Choose one of the subjects from the preceding questions, and conduct a three-R interview to explore it.

a. Identify a promising interviewee.

b. Write a letter requesting an interview.

c. Follow up your letter with a phone call to arrange a date.

d. Develop a list of questions that will achieve your stated purpose. Be sure that these questions follow the guidelines in Chapter 6.

e. Conduct the interview, and report your results.

f. Write a thank-you letter to your subject.

5. Identify a specific organization you would like to work for.

a. Identify the person—by title and name, if possible—who has the power to hire you.

b. Using research and the results of three-R interviews, analyze the requirements for the position you would like to hold.

c. Develop a list of questions a potential boss might ask in a selection interview.

d. Prepare answers to these questions.

For even more practice, role-play an actual interview, with a companion filling the role of your potential employer.

6. Imagine that a supervisor or instructor is preparing an evaluation of your performance. The areas to be covered are

a. Quality of work

b. Productivity

c. Communication skill

d. Attitude

Based on your actual behavior on the job, translate these terms into

a. Behavioral descriptions of your performance during the last month

b. Behavioral objectives for the coming month

7. Feedback isn't only given by superiors to their subordinates; from time to time, it becomes necessary to deliver it to a fellow worker. Use the guidelines on pages 200–203 to offer both praise and constructive criticism to a fellow worker or classmate.

Communicator Profile

Giles Bateman, Executive Vice-President
Price Company
San Diego, California

In an interview, I am annoyed when a candidate is unfamiliar with our company. After all, people interested in working with us should display enough initiative to find out what they might be getting into.

In just fourteen years, Price Company has grown from nothing to a wholesale/retail merchandising business with annual sales of over $5.9 billion. I directly hire my managers and also speak to approximately 300 people who report to me through them. And I give my opinion on executive candidates in other parts of the company.

I never hire anyone on the basis of a written application and résumé. I'm most confident about hiring people I have known personally on either a business or social basis. How people operate when coaching a youth soccer team or on a PTA committee reveals a lot about their personal style, which is at least as important as any technical knowledge they have. Incidentally, I am almost always willing to meet an organized, articulate person who is looking for ways to grow in his or her career.

If I don't know a candidate personally, the next best step is to hire someone who comes recommended by an acquaintance I trust. In fact, I met the man who hired me through a friend's referral. I hope the job offer came because of my own merits, but I wouldn't have had such a good chance to explain my strengths without the personal contact.

I am not impressed by unsolicited letters and résumés. We turn down almost all applications that come this way. I am also put off by résumés longer than one page and by those with vague descriptions of previous jobs.

In an interview, I am annoyed when a candidate is unfamiliar with our company. After all, people interested in working with us should display enough initiative to find out what they might be getting into. I am unimpressed with people whose major concern is their starting salary. Income is certainly important, but only after you have considered the more fundamental questions: Is this a job that will take advantage of my strengths? Will it let me live the kind of life I want? Where can it lead? Will it be fun?

I am impressed by candidates who have succeeded in some area of their life. These accomplishments needn't be in a career. Being a marathon runner, a youth worker, or a church board member reflects dedication and skills that can apply to a job. I'm most impressed by successes that involve working with other people. I value good organization highly and am impressed by someone who can present a complex idea clearly and simply. I also look for people who are positive and who don't fuss or complain about the problems that are bound to come with any job.

Finally, I am impressed with people who know what they want in their lives. Many new graduates don't seem to have the faintest idea what a particular job really involves. Some uncertainty is natural, of course: it's not realistic to have the rest of your life planned in detail. But it is possible to explore fields and organizations that sound interesting. Find out if they involve the kind of work that appeals to you and matches your strengths. See if they fit with the lifestyle that you are seeking.

Answer these questions by talking to people who understand your concerns and can introduce you to still more contacts. Use what you have learned to decide what kind of work suits you best, then do everything you can to find that job. Along with one's family, a career is the most important part of life. Planning it carefully is worth whatever effort is necessary.

PART III

WORKING IN GROUPS

After reading this chapter, you should understand:

■ The characteristics that distinguish a true group and the advantages of groups in problem solving

■ The steps used for systematic problem solving and the stages of development that groups are likely to encounter as they follow these steps

■ The variety of ways groups can make decisions and the conditions under which each method is best used

■ The contributions that designated leaders and group members can make in influencing group effectiveness

■ The range of methods that can improve both task- and maintenance-related communications in groups

You should be able to:

■ Use the reflective-thinking method to arrive at a high-quality decision in a group

■ Choose the decision-making method that best suits a given situation

■ Choose, as a designated leader, the style that most effectively enables a group to achieve its goals

■ Identify and use the kinds of power available to you to influence the operation of a group

■ Describe the process through which a leader emerges in a zero-history group

■ Identify the group goal and the probable individual goals of members, and suggest ways both can be achieved

■ Promote the development of desirable norms in a new group and understand how to operate effectively with established norms in an existing group

■ Identify the functional roles that must be filled at any point in a group's life and fill those roles as necessary

■ Suggest ways to increase the cohesiveness of a working group

■ Encourage creative, effective solutions from all members of a group

COMMUNICATING
IN GROUPS

Working in groups is a vital part of almost every job. Regardless of the business, you can expect to coordinate tasks and schedules with others, share information, solve problems, generate and make decisions. In all but the smallest companies, employees work on project teams, task forces, production crews, and committees—all groups of one sort or another.

In his book *Tales of a New America,* Robert Reich describes the role groups play in an increasingly technological age:

> Rarely do even Big Ideas emerge any longer from the solitary labors of genius. Modern science and technology is too complicated for one brain. It requires groups of astronomers, physicists, and computer programmers to discover new dimensions of the universe: teams of microbiologists, oncologists, and chemists to unravel the mysteries of cancer. With ever more frequency, Nobel prizes are awarded to collections of people. Scientific papers are authored by small platoons of researchers.[1]

Groups are not just important in scientific endeavors; in more familiar fields, working as a team is as common and as important. A national survey of architects and landscape architects revealed that over 75 percent of these professionals reported that they "always" or "often" worked in teams.[2] Even in giant corporations with thousands of employees, small groups of people are often responsible for vital decision making and problem solving. Business consultants Thomas J. Peters and Robert H. Waterman, Jr., discovered that many successful companies rely on "skunk works," which they described as "eight or ten zealots off in a corner."[3] At one $5-billion company, Peters and Waterman discovered that three of the five most recent new product ideas came from one skunk works, located in a dingy second-story loft six miles from the corporate headquarters. A senior executive at Digital Equipment Company endorsed the importance of small creative groups: "When we've got a big problem here, we grab ten senior guys and stick them in a room for a week. They come up with an answer *and* implement it."[4] Andrew S. Grove, president of Intel Corporation, flatly states that group decision making is so important that companies that use it "will prosper, and those that don't, won't."[5]

That groups *can* be effective doesn't guarantee that they always *will* succeed. Some groups are monumental time-wasters, and others produce poor results. But when a group is well conceived and managed, it has several advantages over the same number of individuals working alone. One of these advantages is *productivity.* Research shows that the old saying "Two heads are better than one" can be true: well-managed groups produce more solutions than individuals working alone, and the solutions are likely to be better.[6]

Along with greater productivity, the *accuracy* of an effective group's work is higher than that of individuals.[7] Consider the task of creating a new product. A group of people from sales, marketing, design, engineering, and manufacturing is likely to consider all the important angles, while one or two people without this breadth of perspective would probably miss some important ideas.

Groups don't only produce better products, they also generate more *enthusiasm* from the members who created them. People are usually more committed to a decision if they have had a part in making it. Recognizing this principle, many American companies create participatory management programs and quality circles that involve employees in important decisions. For example, William Deardon, chief executive officer of Hershey Foods Corporation, established a corporate planning committee to make the major plans and decisions for the company. "I figured that if we worked it out together," he explained, "the members of the group would feel that it was their plan and our plan—not my plan—and they'd work harder to implement it."[8]

Effective group communication requires special skills. The communication concepts and principles we have discussed in the preceding chapters also apply to communication in groups. To work effectively in the groups you will encounter in your own career, however, you will also need some special skills.

CHARACTERISTICS OF GROUPS

The word *group* is often used to refer to any assembly of people—the commuters on the morning train, the sightseers gathering for a walking tour of the downtown area, the rock band at a local nightspot. When we talk about the importance of groups on the job, the label *team* is more accurate. We will use the two words interchangeably in this chapter. For our purposes, the working definition of a group or team is "a small, interdependent collection of people with a common identity who interact with one another, usually face to face over time, in order to reach a goal." Using this definition, we can single out several significant characteristics of work-centered groups that, in turn, can guide you in developing your group communication skills.

SIZE

Most experts say that a twosome is not a group since the partners do not interact in the same way that three or more people do. For instance, two people working together can resolve disputes only by persuading one another, giving in, or compromising. In groups, however, members can form alliances and outvote or pressure the minority.[9]

Less agreement exists about when a collection of people becomes too large to be considered a group; at some point, a group can more properly be called an *organization*.[10] The difference isn't just a matter of labels. Members of organizations have formally specified roles and titles. Organizations are more hierarchical, with clearly defined lines of authority. Members are replaceable, and the welfare of the group becomes more important than the satisfaction of individuals. For reasons like these, adding members to a group does not always translate into better results. Research on a number of companies has found that ten-person teams often produce better results at a quicker rate and with higher profits than do groups of several hundred.[11] As groups become larger, members have fewer chances to participate. A few talkative members are likely to dominate the group. Quieter members lose their identity and become less committed to the team.[12]

Most communication experts suggest that the optimal size for small decision-making groups is either five or seven members.[13] The odd number of participants eliminates the risk of tie votes. Teams with fewer than five members lack the resources to come up with good ideas and to carry them out, while larger groups suffer from the problems of anonymity, domination, and lack of commitment.

INTERACTION

A collection of people working at their desks is merely coacting until the individuals begin to exchange information with one another. In fact, such lack of interaction could even be a problem. A project manager and a marketing manager who don't communicate enough, for example, might find that they are duplicating each other's efforts, with both conducting market research. A project could lag because the financial officer doesn't realize that the production department is waiting for final cost estimates before starting up. A quality-control department could be completely ineffective if its members don't share an understanding of company standards and one person rejects samples that another approves.

INTERDEPENDENCE

Group members don't only interact; they depend on one another. A roomful of telephone salespeople who are working on commission have little effect on one another, and thus they can hardly be called a team. By contrast, consider the workers in a restaurant. If the kitchen crew fails to prepare orders promptly or correctly, the servers' tips will decline. If the employees who clear tables don't do their jobs quickly and thoroughly, the servers will hear complaints from their customers. If the waiters fail to take orders accurately, the cooks will have to fix

---

One manager let employees know how valuable they are with the following memo:

You Arx a Kxy Pxrson

Xvxn though my typxwritxr is an old modxl, it works vxry wxll—xxcxpt for onx kxy. You would think that with all thx othxr kxys functioning propxrly, onx kxy not working would hardly bx noticxd; but just onx kxy out of whack sxxms to ruin thx wholx xffort.

You may say to yoursxlf—Wxll I'm only onx pxrson. No onx will noticx if I don't do my bxst. But it doxs makx a diffxrxncx bxcausx to bx xffxctivx an organization nxxds activx participation by xvxry onx to thx bxst of his or hxr ability.

So thx nxxt timx you think you arx not important, rxmxmbxr my old typx-writxr. You arx a kxy pxrson.

---

some meals twice. In a restaurant, as in any real team, the employees are part of an interdependent system.

DURATION

A group that interacts over a period of time develops particular characteristics. For example, a group will tend to develop *norms,* "shared standards of appropriate behavior," that members are expected to meet. Typical norms include how promptly meetings begin, what contribution each member is expected to make to certain routine tasks, what kind of humor is appropriate, and so on.

GOAL-DIRECTEDNESS

Many informal gatherings of people may develop the characteristics we have just described. For example, a group of secretaries who meet regularly for lunch, the project managers who go bowling together on Thursday nights, the noontime runners in a department, a therapy group, a group of friends, or even a family are all, in a sense, groups. In our study of business and professional communication, however, we are principally concerned with *decision-making* and *problem-solving* groups—people who are meeting to accomplish a common task.

PROBLEM-SOLVING COMMUNICATION

In the past decades, researchers have developed several methods for helping groups solve problems and make decisions effectively. By taking advantage of these methods, groups can come up with the highest-quality work possible.

SYSTEMATIC PROBLEM SOLVING

The range of problems that groups face on the job is almost endless. How can we cut expenses? Increase market share? Reduce customer complaints? Offer a better employee-benefits program? Research shows that groups have the best chance of developing high-quality solutions to problems like these when they follow a systematic method for solving problems.[14] The best-known problem-solving approach is the *reflective-thinking sequence,* developed over eighty years ago by John Dewey and used in many forms since then.[15] In its most useful form, the reflective-thinking sequence is a seven-step process.

1. Define the Problem   A group that doesn't understand the problem will have trouble finding a solution. Sometimes the problem facing a group is clear. It doesn't take much deliberation to understand what's necessary when the boss tells you to work out a vacation schedule for the next six months. On the other hand, some problems need rewording because they are too narrow as originally presented.

How Effective Is Your Team?

What makes some teams effective and others failures? Communication researchers Carl Larson and Frank LaFusto spent nearly three years interviewing members of over seventy-five groups that were clearly winners. The groups came from a wide range of enterprises including a Mount Everest expedition, a cardiac surgery team, the presidential commission that studied the space shuttle *Challenger* accident, the group that developed the IBM personal computer, and two championship football teams. Although the groups pursued widely different goals, they all shared eight important characteristics.

You can understand both why your team functions as it does and how to improve its effectiveness by analyzing how well your group fits the profile of these winning teams. For each factor, rate your group as follows:

5   The group fits this description perfectly.
4   The group usually resembles the characteristics in this area.
3   The group occasionally fits the characteristics described in this area.
2   The group rarely matches this description.
1   The group does not fit this description at all.

The number of points scored by your team will probably confirm what you already know about your group's effectiveness. The instrument is more useful as a tool to diagnose how ineffective groups can improve their functioning. Characteristics with low scores suggest areas that need to be changed.

____ 1. *Clear and inspiring team goals*
Members of a winning team know why the group exists, and they believe that the purpose is important and worthwhile. Ineffective teams have either lost sight of their purpose or they do not believe that the goal is truly important.

____ 2. *A results-driven structure*
Winning teams are organized in a way that allows them to get the job done in the most efficient manner. Members know what is expected of them. They do whatever is necessary to accomplish the task. Poor teams either are not organized at all, or they are structured in an inefficient manner.

____ 3. *Competent team members*
Members of winning teams have the skill necessary to accomplish their goals. Less effective groups lack people possessing one or more key skills.

____ 4. *Unified commitment*
People in successful groups share a commitment to the job and to one another. They put the group's goals above their personal interests. While this commitment might seem like a sacrifice to others, for members of winning teams, the personal rewards are worth the effort. Members of unsuccessful teams are lukewarm or indifferent about getting the job done.

____ 5. *Collaborative climate*
Another word for collaboration is "teamwork." Successful groups trust and support one another. Members of unsuccessful groups look out for themselves before they consider teammates.

____ 6. *Standards of excellence*
In winning teams, doing outstanding work is an important norm. Each member is

expected to do his or her personal best. In less successful groups, getting by with the minimum amount of effort is the standard.

___ 7. *External support and recognition*

Successful teams need an appreciative audience who recognizes their effort and provides the resources necessary to get the job done. The audience may be a boss, or it may be the public the group is created to serve. In any case, without recognition and support, the group is likely to become handicapped and demoralized.

___ 8. *Principled leadership*

Winning teams usually have leaders who can create a vision of the group's purpose. They are able to create the changes that are necessary to get the job done. Finally, they have the ability to unleash the talent of group members. Unsuccessful teams either lack leaders, or those leaders do not possess one or more key skills.

The research described in this section was originally reported in Carl Larson and Frank LaFusto, *Team Work: What Must Go Right/What Can Go Wrong*

TOO BROAD	BETTER
"How can we reduce employee turnover?"	"How can we reduce turnover among new employees?" (This suggests where to look for the nature of the problem and solutions.)
"How can we boost morale of the office staff?"	"How can we solve the secretaries' complaints about too much work?"

The best problem statements are phrased as probative questions, ones that encourage exploratory thinking:

POOR	BETTER
"Should we phone people to request United Way donations?"	"What's the best way to boost United Way donations?"
"Should we increase our advertising budget?"	"What's the best way to publicize our product?"
"Should we prohibit business flights of less than three hundred miles?"	"How can we cut our travel expenses?"

By avoiding questions with either-or answers, the group is most likely to consider a large number of possible solutions instead of arguing over one or two options.

2. Analyze the Problem   At this stage, the group tries to discover the causes and extent of the problem, probably by doing some research between meetings. Questions that are usually appropriate in this stage include: "How bad is that problem?" "Why does it need to be resolved?" "What are its causes?" It can be just as useful to focus on the positive aspects of the situation during this phase in order to consider how they can be strengthened. Questions in this area include: "What forces are on our side?" "How do they help us?" "How can we strengthen them?"

A group analyzing the question "How can we solve the secretaries' complaints about too much work?" might find that the problem is especially bad for certain secretaries. It might discover that the problem is worst when the secretaries have to type long reports at the last minute. It might learn that the major complaint doesn't involve hard work as much as it does resentment at seeing other typists apparently having a lighter load. Positive research findings might be that the secretaries understand the importance of their role, that they view being chosen to do important jobs as a sign of respect for the quality of their work, and that they don't mind occasional periods of scrambling to meet a deadline.

3. Establish Criteria for a Solution Rather than rushing to solve the problem, it's best to spend some time identifying the characteristics of a good solution. Who would it have to satisfy? What are the cost constraints? What schedule needs to be met? Sometimes criteria like these are imposed from outside the group. Other requirements come from the members themselves. Regardless of the source of these requirements, the group needs to make them clear before considering possible solutions. Without defining the criteria of a satisfactory solution, the group may waste time arguing over proposals that have no chance of being accepted.

The office group dealing with the problem of unhappy secretaries might define three criteria for a solution to its problem:

No hiring of new employees (company policy).

Fair distribution of work among staff (from the unhappy secretaries).

On-time completion of last-minute jobs (from the managers assigning tasks).

4. Consider Possible Solutions to the Problem This is the time for using the brainstorming technique described on pages 242–243. A major hazard of group problem solving is that it may get bogged down in arguing over the merits of one or two proposals without considering all the other solutions that might exist. Besides limiting the quality of the solution, such squabbling also leads to personal battles between members.

The most valuable feature of brainstorming is the emphasis on generating many ideas before judging any of them. This sort of criticism-free atmosphere encourages people to volunteer solutions that, in turn, lead to other ideas.

A brainstorming list for the overworked typists might include the following:

■ Instead of having one typist reporting to two or three people, everybody should have his or her own secretary.

■ A typist would only report to two or three people who were in a single line of command; the senior person would decide whose project has priority.

- ■ To cut down on the number of jobs that have to be done over, set up a company style book that shows how letters are to be set up, contract clauses phrased, and so on.
- ■ Typists would help each other out—someone with too much work to do could ask someone else to take over a project.
- ■ Establish a typing pool—instead of assigning a typist to a specific person or group, turn over all typing tasks to a group leader who will distribute them. Since the typists work as a group, they can train new typists themselves.

5. Decide on a Solution   Once the group has considered all possible solutions to a problem, it can go back and find the best answer to the problem. This is done by comparing each idea to the list of criteria developed earlier by the group. In addition to measuring the solution against its own criteria, the group should judge any potential solutions by asking three questions. First, will the proposal bring about all the desired changes? If it solves only part of the problem, it isn't adequate without some changes. Second, can the solution be implemented by the group? If the idea is good but is beyond the power of this group to achieve, it needs to be modified or discarded. Finally, does the idea have any serious disadvantages? A plan that solves one set of problems while generating another probably isn't worth adopting.

In the case of the overworked typists, the first solution is rejected since it doesn't meet the criterion of not adding staff. The second has possibilities, but it is rejected after discussion; among other problems, most higher-level managers already have their own secretaries working overtime, and using more executive time to organize and establish priorities on secretarial work doesn't seem practicable. The third solution seems to have possibilities, but it doesn't solve most aspects of the problem. The fourth seems good. The fifth is even better since it will systematize distribution of work and the group leader can be a head typist. The committee agrees to recommend the fifth solution as essential and the third as an additional step to solve some problems.

6. Implement the Solution   Inventing a solution isn't enough. The group also has to put the plan into action. This probably involves several steps. First, it's necessary to identify the specific tasks that must be accomplished. Second, the group must identify the resources necessary to make the plan work. Third, individual responsibilities must be defined: Who will do what, and when? Finally, the group should plan for emergencies. What will happen if someone is sick? If the project runs over budget? If a job takes longer than expected? Anticipating problems early is far better than being caught by surprise.

In reorganizing the typing pool, the committee needs to appoint someone to oversee the change. It needs to consider how much time it will take to switch to the new system, and what delays are likely to occur with the changeover. A team leader must be chosen to delegate jobs once the typing pool is created. The group must decide how to respond if some supervisors still act as if particular secretaries "belong" to them.

7. Follow Up on the Solution   Even the best ideas don't always work out perfectly in practice. For this reason, the group should check up on the implementation of the solution to see if any adjustments are needed. In the case of the secretarial pool, for example, it might be necessary to remind some managers that their former secretaries no longer "belong" just to them.

STAGES IN GROUP PROBLEM SOLVING

The systematic problem-solving approach described above is certainly sensible, but the feelings of the individual members can make it difficult for them to follow this kind of rational approach faithfully. As groups tackle the everyday problems of business, their discussions are likely to move through several phases characterized by different types of communication. Aubrey Fisher identified four of these stages: orientation, conflict, emergence, and reinforcement.[16]

The first stage in a group's development is *orientation*. This is a time of testing the waters. Members may not know one another very well and so are cautious about making statements that might offend. For this reason, during the orientation stage team members aren't likely to take strong positions even on issues they regard as important. It is easy to mistake the lack of conflict during this phase as harmony and assume that the task will proceed smoothly. Peace and quiet, however, are often a sign of caution, not agreement. Despite the tentative nature of communication, the orientation stage is important since the norms that can govern the group's communication throughout its life are often formed here.

After the team members understand the problem and have a feel for one another, the group typically moves to the *conflict* stage. This is the time when members take a strong stand on the issue and defend their positions against others. Disagreement is likely to be greatest during this phase, as are bruised egos. The norms of politeness that were formed during orientation may weaken as members debate with one another, and there is a real risk that personal feelings will interfere with the kind of rational decision making described on pages 213–218. Sometimes the members keep arguing about one solution or another without ever resolving the issue satisfactorily. In other cases, conflicts take on a more personal tone as members find fault with one another's behavior. Conflicts may be openly discussed, or they can be conducted more subtly under a thin cover of politeness. In either case, struggle is the main theme.

Some groups never escape from the conflict stage. Their interaction—at least about the problem at hand—may end when time pressures force a solution that almost no one finds satisfactory. The boss may impose a decision from above, or a majority might overrule the minority. Time may even run out without any decision being made. Not all groups suffer from such unhappy outcomes, however. Productive teams manage to work through the conflict phase and move on to the next stage of development.

The *emergence* phase of problem solving occurs when the members end their disagreement and solve the problem. The final decision can be unanimous, leaving everyone satisfied. In other cases, though, members may compromise or settle for a proposal they didn't originally prefer. In any case, the key to emergence is acceptance of a decision that members willingly (if reluctantly) can support. Communication during the emergence phase is less polarized. Members back off from their previously held firm positions. Comments like "I can live with that" and "Let's give it a try" are common here. Even if some people have doubts about the decision, there is a greater likelihood that they will keep their concerns to themselves. Harmony is the theme.

The fourth phase of discussion is *reinforcement.* Groups that reach this point not only accept the decision, but actively endorse it. Members who found arguments against the decision during the conflict stage now present evidence to support it. In school, the reinforcement stage is apparent when students presenting a group project defend it against any complaints the instructor might have. On the job, the same principle applies: if the boss finds fault with a team's proposals, the tendency is to band together to support them.

In real life, groups don't necessarily follow this four-step process neatly. In an ongoing team, the patterns of communication in the past can influence present and future communication.[17] Teams with a high degree of conflict might have trouble reaching emergence, for example, whereas a group that is highly cohesive might experience little disagreement.

Sometimes a group can become stuck in one phase, never progressing to the ones that follow. Members might never get beyond the superficial, polite interaction of orientation. If they do, they might become mired down in conflict. Ongoing groups might move through some or all of the stages each time they tackle a new problem, as pictured in Figure 8-1. In fact, a group that deals with

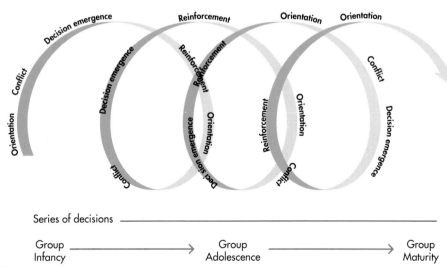

Figure 8-1 Cyclical stages in an ongoing problem-solving group. (From John K. Brilhart and Gloria J. Galanes, *Effective Group Discussion,* 6th ed. Dubuque, Iowa: W. C. Brown, 1989, p. 167.)

several issues at one time might be in different stages for each problem.

Knowing that a group to which you belong is likely to pass through these stages can be reassuring. Your urge to get down to business and quit wasting time during the orientation phase might be tempered if you realize that the cautious communication is probably temporary. Likewise, you might be less distressed about conflict if you know that the possibility of emergence may be just around the corner.

DECISION-MAKING METHODS

Disagreement may be a healthy, normal part of solving problems on the job, but sooner or later it becomes necessary to make a decision as a group. Whether the issue is who will work over the weekend, how to split the year-end bonus money among members, or what approach to advertising is best, there usually has to be one answer to a problem. There are a number of ways to make business decisions like these.

Consensus Consensus is a collective group decision that every member is willing to support. The purest form of consensus is a unanimous choice: the belief of every member that the decision reached is the best possible one. An entire employee search committee might, for instance, agree that a particular candidate is perfect for a job. This state of unanimity isn't always possible, however, and it isn't necessary for consensus. In the case of the new employee, the committee members might agree on a candidate that is the second choice of some members since the people who will actually be working with her are her most enthusiastic supporters.

Consensus has both advantages and drawbacks. While it has the broadest base of support from members, reaching consensus takes time. It requires a spirit of cooperation among group members, a willingness to experience temporary disagreements, a commitment to listen carefully to other ideas, and a win-win attitude. While consensual decisions are often superior to other types, the cost in time and frustration isn't always worth the effort, especially for relatively minor issues. Furthermore, there are times when it simply isn't possible to reach consensus.

Majority Vote Whereas consensus requires the agreement of the entire group, deciding by a majority vote needs only the support of a plurality of the members. Thus, majority voting decisions are much quicker and easier to reach. A ten-person staff choosing a decorating scheme for the new office might talk almost endlessly before reaching consensus, but with a majority vote, the decision would require the agreement of only six members. While majority vote works well on relatively minor issues, it is usually not the best approach for more important decisions (at least not in small groups) since it can leave a substantial minority unsatisfied and resentful about being railroaded into accepting a plan they don't support.

Minority Decision   In business, a few members often make decisions affecting the entire group. The executive committee of a corporation often acts on behalf of the board of directors, who, in turn, represent the shareholders. Minority decisions are also made in less exalted circumstances. A steering group responsible for planning the company picnic might delegate tasks like publicity, entertainment, and food to smaller collections of members. As long as the minority has the confidence of the larger group, this method works well for many decisions. While it doesn't take advantage of the entire group's creative thinking, the talents of the subgroup are often perfectly adequate for a task.

Expert Opinion   When a single person has the knowledge or skill to make a decision, the group may be best served by relying on this expert. As one observation puts it, "If you want a track team to win the high jump, you find one person who can jump seven feet, not seven people who can jump one foot." Some group members are experts because of specialized training: a structural engineer working with a design team on a new building, a senior airline mechanic who decides whether a flight can depart safely, or a systems analyst involved in the development of a new data control system. Other people gain their expertise by experience: the purchasing agent who knows how to get the best deals, or a labor negotiator seasoned by years of contract deliberations.

Despite the obvious advantages, following an expert's suggestions isn't always as wise an approach as it might seem. First, it isn't always easy to tell who the expert is. Length of experience isn't necessarily a guarantee since the business world abounds with old fools. Even when a member clearly is the expert, the other members must *recognize* this fact before they will willingly give their support. Unfortunately, some people who are regarded as experts don't deserve the title, while some geniuses may be ignored.

Authority Rule After Discussion   Most business groups have a clear authority structure. A chairman or manager may be responsible to a superior for the group's actions, or one member may actually be the top boss. In settings like this, the designated leader often makes the final decision. This doesn't mean that these leaders must be autocratic: they often listen to the ideas and suggestions of members before making the decisions themselves. The owner of a family business might invite employees to help choose a new company logo, while selecting the final design after hearing their opinions. A store manager might consult with employees about scheduling work hours, while reserving the final decisions to herself. The input from group members can help an authority to make higher-quality decisions than would otherwise be possible. One major risk of inviting suggestions from subordinates, however, is the disappointment that might follow when these suggestions aren't accepted.

Authority Rule Without Discussion   Business leaders often make decisions without consulting the groups that will be affected. What will the sales quotas be for the next season? Which candidate will be promoted? Who gets a raise? Only naïve employees believe that businesses are democracies in which the employees have an inalienable right to govern their own affairs. Nonetheless, wise managers realize that they can't afford to abuse their power to make unilateral decisions without losing the respect and loyalty of their subordinates. When a manager has the necessary knowledge, when time is of the essence, or when subordinates can't easily agree on a course of action, the best course may be for a quick decision by the person in charge. Much of the time, however, the other methods of decision making described in this section may produce better results.

Choice of a Decision-Making Method   Each decision-making method has its advantages and disadvantages. The choice of which one to use depends on several factors.

What Type of Decision Is Being Made?   If the decision can best be made by one or more experts or if it needs to be made by the authorities in charge, then involving other group members isn't appropriate. If, however, the task at hand calls for creativity or requires a large amount of information from many sources, then input from the entire group can make a big difference.

How Important Is the Decision?   Trivial decisions don't require the involvement of the entire group. It's a waste of time and money to bring everyone together to make decisions that can easily be made by one or two people.

How Much Time Is Available?   If time is short, it simply may not be possible to consult everyone in the group. This is especially true if the members are not all available—if some are away from the office or out of town, for example. Even if everyone is available, the time-consuming deliberations that come with a group discussion may be a luxury you can't afford.

What Are the Personal Relationships Among Members?   Even important decisions might best be made without convening the whole group, if members are on bad terms. If talking things out will improve matters, then a meeting may be worth the emotional wear and tear that it will generate. But if a face-to-face discussion will just make matters worse, then the decision might best be made in some other way.

> Many hands make light work.

> If you want to win the broad jump, get one person who can jump seven feet, not seven people who can jump one foot.

These conflicting proverbs reflect two sides of groups. On the one hand, a well-functioning group can be an effective way of doing business. On the other, a poorly run group can be a time-waster of the first magnitude.

In the last chapter, we discussed some methods of generating ideas, making decisions, and solving problems in groups. But to make these methods work most effectively, members need the additional skills described in this chapter.

APPROACHES TO LEADERSHIP

There is probably no topic more important in business than leadership. The number of books, articles, and seminars on the subject seems almost endless. The concern with leadership makes sense: without a sense of purpose and direction, a group can resemble a rudderless ship—potentially powerful but drifting aimlessly, out of control.

The following pages outline some key approaches to leadership. They show that leadership can take many forms. Sometimes it rests in one person, who directs the functioning of everyone else on the team. In other cases, however, leadership is less centralized and less noticeable. Whatever the approach, communication plays a key role in influencing how groups operate and the results these groups produce.

DESIGNATED LEADERSHIP

When most people think of leadership, they visualize a single person with an official title—what social scientists call a *designated leader*. The leader's title varies from one setting to another: boss, chairperson, coach, teacher, and so on. Designated leaders may be appointed by some higher authority (a single boss, hiring committee, board of directors), or they may earn their title because they have started up a business themselves.

The difference between effective and ineffective leaders can be dramatic: a losing team gets a new coach and, with the same players, begins winning against the same opponents; a demoralized division gets a new sales manager, and orders increase; a production crew gets a new supervisor, and workers who once spent their time complaining find new enjoyment and productivity. Whatever the nature of the organization, we count on the person "in charge" to make the enterprise work. As one writer put it, "People expect leaders to bring change about, to get things done, to make things happen, to inspire, to motivate."[18]

What qualities make leaders effective? Sometimes that question is difficult to answer. Many effective leaders seem to perform their role effortlessly, and people seem to follow them naturally; others seem to rule by sheer force. Scholars and researchers have studied leadership from many perspectives. Following are some leadership approaches.

Trait Approach   One of the earliest beliefs was that all leaders possessed common traits that led to their effectiveness. The earliest research sought to identify these traits, and by the mid-1930s scores of studies pursued this goal. Their conclusions were contradictory. Certain traits did seem common to most leaders, including physical attractiveness, sociability, desire for leadership, originality, and intelligence.[19] Despite these similarities, the research also showed that these traits were not *predictive* of leadership. In other words, a person possessing these characteristics would not necessarily become a leader. Another research approach was necessary.

Style Approach Beginning in the 1940s, researchers began to explore managerial style to see if it determined a leader's effectiveness. Some leaders are *authoritarian,* using legitimate, coercive, and reward power at their disposal to control members. Others are more *democratic,* inviting members to help make decisions. A third leadership style is *laissez-faire:* the nominal leader gives up the power of that position and transforms the group into a leaderless collection of equals.

Early research seemed to suggest that the democratic style produced the best results,[20] but later experiments showed that matters weren't so simple. For instance, groups with autocratic leaders were more productive in stressful situations, while democratically led groups did better when the conditions were nonstressful.[21]

One of the best-known stylistic approaches is the *Leadership Grid®* by Robert

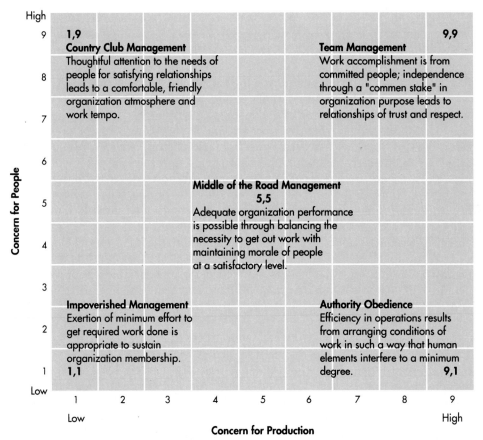

Figure 8-2   The Leadership Grid®. (Figure from *Leadership Dilemmas—Grid Solutions,* by Robert R. Blake and Anne Adams McCanse. Houston: Gulf Publishing Company, p. 29. Copyright © 1991, by Scientific Methods, Inc. Reproduced by permission of the owners.)

Blake and Jane Mouton (see Figure 8-2),[22] which shows that good leadership depends on skillful management of the task and social functions described on pages 235-238. The horizontal axis of the grid measures a manager's concern for task or production—getting the job done. Blake and Mouton's grid counteracts the tendency in some naïve managers to assume that if they focus solely on the task, good results will follow. Blake and Mouton argue that the most effective leader is one who adopts a 9.9 style, showing high concern for both product *and* people.

Contingency Approaches   Unlike the style approach, contingency theories argue that the "best" leadership style is flexible—it changes from one situation to the next. For instance, a manager who successfully guides a project team developing an advertising campaign might flop as a trainer or personnel officer. Psychologist Fred Fiedler conducted extensive research in an attempt to discover when a task-oriented approach works best and when a relationship-oriented style is most effective.[23] He found that a decision about whether to emphasize task or relationship issues in a situation depends on three factors: (1) *leader-member relations,* including the attractiveness of the manager and the loyalty of the followers; (2) *task structure,* involving the degree of simplicity or complexity of the job; and (3) *the leader's power,* including job title and the ability to coerce and reward.

Generally, Fiedler's research suggests that a task-oriented approach works best when circumstances are extremely favorable (good leader-member relations, highly structured tasks) or extremely unfavorable (poor leader-member relations, unstructured task, weak leader power). In moderately favorable or unfavorable circumstances, a relationship-oriented approach works best. While these findings are useful, it is important not to overstate them. In most cases, good leadership requires a mixture of relationship and task concerns. The question is not which dimension to *choose,* but which one to *emphasize.*

A more sophisticated model of situational leadership is the *life-cycle* approach developed by Paul Hersey and Kenneth Blanchard.[24] As Figure 8-3 shows, the life-cycle theory suggests that a leader's concern for task and relationships ought to vary, depending on the maturity of the subordinate or subordinates. As Hersey and Blanchard use it, the term *maturity* has little to do with chronological age. Instead, maturity involves three factors: the employee's level of motivation, the employee's willingness to take responsibility, and the amount of knowledge and experience the employee has in a given situation.[25] A young, ambitious, well-trained recruit might be more mature than a bored, complacent worker who is ready for retirement. It is also important to note that a worker might have a low maturity rating in one situation and a high rating in another.

According to the life-cycle theory, an extremely immature subordinate needs a style of leadership that is highly directive and task-related, with little concern for social issues. As the group member becomes more competent and motivated, the manager ought to offer rewards in terms of social reinforcement. As the subordinate becomes able to perform the task without the guidance of the boss, the manager ought to withdraw the task-related supervision even more, while encouraging the employee's new ability. Finally, when the worker's ability

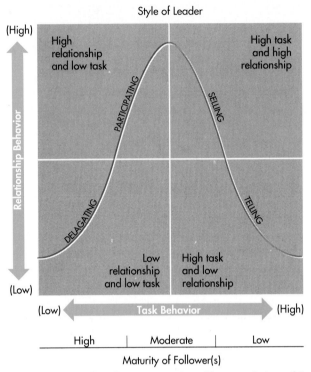

Style of Leader

Figure 8-3 Life-cycle leadership theory. (Reprinted by permission of Paul Hersey, Center for Leadership Studies. All rights reserved.)

to handle a task is superior, the boss can withdraw socioemotional support in this area, knowing that the worker is functioning at the highest level and that any reinforcements are now primarily internal.

Although withdrawal of social support for mature employees might seem like a kind of punishment, Hersey and Blanchard would say it is not for two reasons. The first is because reducing the frequency of social reinforcement doesn't mean eliminating it altogether. Thus, an appreciative boss might signal pleasure by an occasional comment and punctuate that satisfaction with a yearly bonus. The second reason that social reinforcement isn't as scarce as it might seem is because employees function at different maturity levels in different areas of their jobs. Thus, while a new systems analyst might be receiving little immediate social reinforcement from the boss for his work on one project, he would probably be getting a great deal of attention in other areas where he is less mature.

SHARED LEADERSHIP: A BALANCE OF POWER

Not all groups have a single leader who shapes the group's performance. In fact, something would probably be wrong with a group that depended on its desig-

Many American companies are discovering what may be *the* productivity break-through of the 1990s. Call the still-controversial innovation a self-managed team, a cross-functional team, or, to coin a phrase, a superteam. . . .

What makes superteams so controversial is that they ultimately force managers to do what they had only imagined in their most Boschian nightmares: give up control. Because if superteams are working right, *mirabile dictu*, they manage themselves. No boss required.

Brian Dumaine, "Who Needs a Boss?" *Fortune*

nated head to make every decision. It is more useful to think of leadership as a property that can be shared among members.

Some organizations—including major corporations—take shared leadership so seriously that they have formed teams that operate without a designated leader.[26] For example, at one General Mills cereal plant, teams schedule, operate, and maintain machinery so effectively that the plant runs with no managers present during night shifts. The company reports that productivity at plants that rely on self-managed teams is as much as 40 percent higher than at traditional factories. Teams at 3M were so creative that they tripled the number of new products in their division. A group of Federal Express clerks spotted and solved a billing problem, saving the company $2.1 million in just one year. This sort of success is gaining recognition in corporate circles. A survey of 476 Fortune 1000 companies showed that, while less than 10 percent of the work force is currently organized into self-managed teams, half the companies questioned reported that they will be relying significantly more on them in years ahead.[27]

Self-managed teams work best for relatively complex jobs that require a variety of perspectives. For example, a group that is developing a new product can profit from the perspectives of representatives from every part of the business: engineers know what it takes to make the item work, financial types understand costs and budgets, salespeople can represent the customers' needs, and marketing experts know how to promote the product. By contrast, self-management has less value for simple, repetitive tasks like assembly-line work.

One key to understanding the value of shared leadership is to recognize that every member of a group has power to shape events. When a member uses that power in a way that helps the group achieve its goal, then leadership has occurred.[28] Power comes in several forms; and even in a traditional group with a designated leader, all members of a team can possess some types.[29]

Legitimate Power   This is the ability to influence that comes from the position one holds. We often do things for the boss precisely because he or she holds that title. While legitimate power usually belongs to nominal leaders, lesser positions sometimes possess it, often depending on circumstances. The chief executive of a multinational corporation, for instance, must wait for a key set of figures until the accounting staff has compiled them.

Coercive Power   This is the power to punish, and we often follow another's bidding because failure to do so would lead to unpleasant consequences. Nominal leaders do have coercive power: they can assign unpleasant tasks, deny pay raises, and even fire us. Other members have coercive power, too, though it is usually subtle. A committee member or officemate who acts as a blocker when things don't go his way is coercing others to take his views into account, implying, "If you don't follow at least some of my suggestions, I'll punish the group by continuing to object to your ideas and refusing to cooperate with you."

Reward Power   The ability to reward is the flip side of coercive power. Nominal leaders control the most obvious rewards: pay raises, improved working conditions, and the ability to promote. But, again, other members can give their own rewards. These come in the form of social payoffs, such as increased goodwill and task-related benefits like voluntary assistance on a job.

Expert Power   This power comes from the group's recognition of a member's expertise in a certain area. Nominal leaders aren't always the experts in a group. In a manufacturing firm, for example, a relatively low-ranking engineer could influence management to alter a project by using her knowledge to declare that a new product wouldn't work. Problems can arise either when management doesn't recognize a knowledgeable member as an expert or when unqualified people are granted expert status.

Referent Power   Referent power refers to the influence members hold due to the way others in the group feel about them: their respect, attraction, or liking. It is here that the greatest difference between nominal leaders and true influence occurs. An unpopular boss might have to resort to his or her job title and the power to coerce and reward that come with it to gain compliance, while a popular person without a leadership title can get others to cooperate without threatening or promising.

Information Power   Some members influence a group due to the information they possess. This information is different from the kind of knowledge that we defined as expert power. Whereas an expert possesses some form of talent based on training or education, an information-rich group member has access to otherwise obscure knowledge that is valuable to others in the group. A new employee who was hired away from a competitor, for example, is likely to play a key role in the decisions of how his new company will compete against the old one. Likewise, a member who is well connected to the organizational grapevine can exert a major influence on how the group operates: "Don't bring that up now. Smith is going through a divorce and he's saying no to everything." "I just heard there's plenty of money in the travel and entertainment budget. Maybe this is the time to propose that reception for the out-of-town distributors we've been thinking about."

Connection Power   In the "real world" of business, a member's influence can often come from the connections he or she has with influential or important people inside or outside the organization. The classic example of connection power is the son or daughter of the boss. While the official word from the top may be "Treat my kid just like any other employee," this is easier said than done. Not all connection power is harmful. If one member sees a potential customer socially, he is in a good position to help the business. If another one knows a government official, she can get off-the-record advice about how to handle a government regulation.

If we recognize the influence that comes with connection power, the old saying "It isn't what you know that counts, it's who you know" seems true. If we look at all types of power described in this section, we can see that a more accurate statement is "What counts is *whom* you know (connection power), *what* you know (information and expert power), who *respects* you (reward and coercive power), and who you *are* (legitimate power)." This range of power sources makes it clear that the power to influence a group is truly shared among members, all of whom have the ability to affect how well a group works together and the quality of the product it turns out.

LEADERSHIP EMERGENCE

Sometimes leaders are appointed by higher-ups, but in many cases they emerge from a group. *Emergent leaders* may be chosen by the members of a group either officially or informally. An athletic team may elect a captain. The owners' association of a condominium chooses a head. Union members pick a team to represent them in contract negotiations with management. Volunteers organizing a fund-raising drive for the local school or church nominate a chairperson.

Emergent leaders don't always have official titles. A group of disgruntled employees might urge one person to approach the boss and ask for a change, for example. A team of students assigned to develop a class project might agree that one person is best suited to take the lead in organizing and presenting their work. Sometimes emergent leaders are officially recognized, but in other cases their role is never acknowledged overtly. In fact, there are often cases where the designated leader may be the titular head, while an emergent leader really runs the show. Fans of late-night movies recall how the young, inexperienced lieutenant learns to defer to the grizzled, wise sergeant. This pattern often repeats itself in everyday working situations, when new managers or supervisors recognize the greater knowledge of old-timers who are subordinates on the organizational chart. In cases like these, the new manager is smart to defer to the unofficial, emergent leader—at least until he or she gains some experienced and wisdom.

Communication researcher Ernest Bormann has studied how emergent leaders gain influence, especially in newly formed groups.[30] According to

Bormann, a group selects a leader by the *method of residues*—a process of elimination in which potential candidates are gradually rejected for one reason or another until only one remains. This process of elimination occurs in two phases. In the first, members who are clearly unsuitable are rejected. The surest path to rejection is being quiet: untalkative members were never chosen as leaders in the groups Bormann studied. Failing to participate verbally in a group's work leaves the impression of indifference and lack of commitment. Another ticket to early rejection is dogmatism: members who express their opinions in strong, unqualified terms are usually perceived as being too extreme and inflexible to take a leading role. A third cause of elimination as leader is a lack of skill or intelligence: competence is obviously a necessary condition for successful leadership, and members who lack this quality are rejected early.

Quietness, dogmatism, and incompetence are almost always grounds for disqualification. Beyond these factors, a communication style that members find irritating or disturbing is likely to knock a member out of consideration as a leader. A variety of behaviors fall into this category, depending on the composition of the group. In one case being too serious might be grounds for rejection, while in a different situation a joker would earn disapproval. Using inappropriate language could be a disqualifier. In a group with biased members, gender or ethnicity might be grounds for rejection.

After clearly unsuitable members have been eliminated, roughly half of the group's members may still be candidates for leadership. This can be a tense time since the jockeying for a role of influence may pit the remaining candidates against one another. In some groups, the contenders for leader acquire what Bormann calls lieutenants, who support their advancement. If only one candidate has a lieutenant, his or her chances of becoming leader are strong. If two or more contenders have supporters, the process of leader emergence can drag out or even reach a stalemate.

One way to stand out among competitors for leadership is to provide a solution in a time of crisis. How can the group meet a deadline? Gain the sale? Get the necessary equipment? Members who find answers to problems like these are likely to rise to a position of authority.

If you are interested in seeking a leadership position—and you almost certainly will be at one time or another—Bormann's research suggests several steps to take.[31]

- *Participate early and often.* Talking won't guarantee that you will be recognized as a leader, but failing to speak up will almost certainly knock you out of the running.
- *Demonstrate your competence.* Make sure your comments identify you as someone who can help the group succeed. Demonstrate your expert, connection, and information power.
- *Don't push too hard.* It's fine to be assertive, but don't try to overpower other members. Even if you are right, your dogmatism is likely to alienate other members.

EFFECTIVE COMMUNICATION IN GROUPS

Whether you are a leader or a follower, you can communicate in ways that help a group work effectively and make the experience satisfying. For the group to function well, each member, including the leader, must take into account the issues and problems that may arise whenever people try to communicate.

USE TIME EFFECTIVELY

Even productive groups take considerable time to do the job. Just organizing meetings can require phone calls or a series of memos that must be written, typed, distributed, and read. Meetings take time—not only for discussing the problem at hand, but also for waiting for members to arrive, tangential discussions, and so on.

Sometimes groups take too long to act. Chrysler president Lee Iacocca describes this problem:

> I like to go duck hunting, where constant movement and change are facts of life. You can aim at a duck and get it in your sights, but the duck is always moving. *In order to hit the duck, you have to move your gun.* But a committee faced with a major decision can't always move as quickly as the events it's trying to respond to. By the time the committee is ready to shoot, the duck has flown away.[32]

Iacocca's criticism of slow-moving groups is true in some cases, especially where a lack of speed is the norm. But groups aren't necessarily cumbersome: with enough commitment to moving quickly, a collection of people can arrive at decisions with surprising speed. You can test this principle for yourself. Imagine that you are on a team with your fellow workers and that your boss has promised to give the team 10 percent of any savings it can make for the company by improving corporate productivity. The only catch is that the team must propose all solutions in the next half hour, its recommendations being endorsed unanimously by the group. Would your team be able to develop a list of suggestions?

RECOGNIZE BOTH GROUP AND PERSONAL GOALS

Every business and professional group operates to achieve some specific goal: selling a product, providing a service, getting a job done, and so on. In addition to a group's goals, members usually also have their own *individual* goals. Sometimes an individual's goal in a group is identical (or nearly identical) to the shared goal of the group. For example, a retailer might join the community Christmas fund-raising campaign out of a sincere desire to help the needy. In most cases, however, people also have more personal motives for joining a group. The retailer, for instance, might realize that working on the fund-raising campaign will improve both his visibility and his image in the community—and ultimately lead to more business. Notice the relationship between some common group and individual goals.

GROUP GOAL	INDIVIDUAL GOAL
Athletic team wants to win league championship.	Athlete wants to be star for social rewards.
Sales department wants to meet annual sales target.	Sales representative wants to earn bonus and receive promotions.
Retailer wants to expand hours to attract new business.	Employees want to avoid working nights and weekends.
Company wants employee to attend seminar in Minneapolis.	Employee wants to visit family in Minneapolis.

Personal goals aren't necessarily harmful to a group or an organization if they are compatible with the group's objectives. In fact, under these circumstances they can actually help the group to achieve its goals. For instance, sales representatives who want to increase their commissions will try to sell more of the company's products. Similarly, an otherwise reluctant employee might volunteer to attend a January seminar in Minneapolis to see her family during the visit.

Only when an individual's goals conflict with the organization's or group's goals do problems occur. If Lou and Marian hate each other, their arguments could keep the group from getting much done in meetings. If Bill is afraid of losing his job because of a mistake that has been made, he may concentrate on trying to avoid being blamed rather than on solving the problem. If Nancy needs to make more money, she may take an extra job at night and be too tired to be as productive as she had been.

When members have goals that conflict with the group's mission, the results can sometimes be catastrophic. During the summer of 1987, Delta Airlines suffered a string of safety-related problems that endangered the lives of many people. The incidents were so serious that the Federal Aviation Administration conducted an extensive investigation. The team's conclusions demonstrated the dangers that can arise when members of a group put their personal concerns ahead of the task: "There is no evidence that Delta's crews are (on the whole) either unprofessional or purposefully negligent. Rather, it was observed that crew members are acting as individuals rather than as members of a smoothly functioning team."[33]

The range of personal goals that can interfere with group effectiveness is surprisingly broad. One or more team members might be concerned with finishing the job quickly and getting away to take care of personal business. Others might be more concerned with being liked or appearing smart than with doing the job as quickly or effectively as possible. Someone else might want to impress the boss. All these goals, as well as dozens of others, can sidetrack or derail a group from doing its job.

Sometimes we announce our personal goals. For example, an employee might let his supervisor know he expects a raise and a promotion if he does well at his current job. In other cases, though, stating a personal goal outright could be embarrassing or counterproductive. A committee member wouldn't confess, "I volunteered to serve on this committee so I could find new people to date." An employee would never say openly, "I'm planning to learn everything I can here and then quit the firm and open my own business." Personal goals that are not made public are called *hidden agendas.* Hidden agendas are not necessarily harmful. The dating goals of a member needn't interfere with group functions. Similarly, many other personal motives are not threatening or even relevant to a group's business. Some hidden agendas are even beneficial. For instance, an up-and-coming young worker's desire to communicate competence to the boss by volunteering for difficult jobs might well help the group.

Other hidden agendas, however, are harmful. Two feuding members who use meetings to disparage each other can only harm the group, and the person collecting ideas to go into business himself will most likely hurt the organization when he takes its ideas elsewhere.

You can boost the effectiveness of groups by following these guidelines.

Try to Satisfy Personal Goals   Groups will be happiest and most efficient when the members are reaching their personal goals. You can boost the effectiveness of your group by doing everything possible to help members satisfy those goals. If the people in your group are looking for fun and companionship, consider ways to tackle the job at hand that also give them what they want. On the other hand, if they are in a hurry due to busy schedules, concentrate on keeping meetings to a minimum. If some members like recognition, stroke their egos by offering compliments whenever you can sincerely do so. The extra effort that you spend catering to individual needs of members will pay dividends in terms of the energy and loyalty that the group gains from happy members.

Be Cautious About Handling Hidden Agendas   There is no single best way to deal with harmful hidden agendas. Sometimes the best course is to bring the goal out into the open. For example, a manager might speak to feuding subordinates one at a time, let them know she recognizes their problem, and work with them to solve it directly and constructively (probably using the conflict management skills described in Chapter 5). If an employee has personal problems that make him less productive and less reliable than he normally would be, the manager might discuss the effects on the group with him and possibly recommend counseling. When you do decide to bring a hidden personal goal into the open, it's almost always better to confront the member privately. The embarrassment of being unveiled publicly is usually so great that the person becomes defensive and denies that the hidden goal exists.

At other times, it is best to treat a hidden personal goal indirectly. For example, if a member's excessive talking in meetings seems to be a bid for recognition, the best approach might be to make a point of praising his valid contributions more frequently. If two feuding subordinates continue to have trouble working together, the manager can assign them to different projects or transfer one or both of them to different groups.

PROMOTE DESIRABLE NORMS

Norms are agreements about what behavior is appropriate in a group. Some norms—laws, rules, and regulations—are *explicit*. Most organizations have official, explicit rules about everything from safety procedures to expense accounts.

In addition to these official rules, there is an equally strong set of *implicit* or unstated norms. Some of these norms govern the way tasks are handled, while others shape the social interaction of the group. As Table 8-1 shows, the norms in some groups are constructive, while other groups have equally powerful rules that damage their effectiveness.

While some norms are clearly helpful or harmful to a group's functioning, others are idiosyncratic. In some groups, it is customary to discuss one's personal life, use profanity occasionally, smoke; in other groups, such behavior is taboo. The same goes for other norms such as style of dress, how much socializing is done away from the job, or what kinds of jokes are acceptable.

Whatever a group's norms may be, members who violate them create a crisis for the rest of the team, who respond in a series of escalating steps.[34] Consider, for example, a worker who violates the norm of not following up on her obligations between group meetings. Her teammates might react with increasing pressure.

- *Delaying action.* Members talk among themselves but do not approach the deviant, hoping that she will change without pressure.
- *Hinting about the violation.* Members tease the violator about being a "flake" or about being lazy, hoping that the message behind the humor will cause her to do her share of work.
- *Discussing the problem openly.* Members confront the nonconformist, explaining their concerns about her behavior.
- *Ridiculing and deriding the violator.* Persuasion shifts to demands for a change in behavior; the group's pressure tactics may well trigger a defensive response in the nonconforming member.
- *Rejecting or isolating the deviant.* If all other measures fail, the team member who doesn't conform to group norms is asked to leave the group. If she cannot be expelled, other members can effectively excommunicate her by not inviting her to meetings and by disregarding any attempts at communicating she might make.

TABLE 8-1   Typical Constructive (and Destructive) Norms for a Working Group

- Handle (ignore) business for co-workers who are away from their desks.
- Be willing (refuse) to admit your mistakes.
- Occasional time off from work for personal reasons is (isn't) O.K., as long as the absence won't harm the company.
- Do (don't) be willing to work overtime without complaining when big, important deadlines approach.
- Say so (keep quiet) if you disagree. Don't (do) hint or go behind others' backs.

There are two ways in which an understanding of norms can help you to function more effectively in a group.

Create Desirable Norms Early   Norms are established early in a group; and once they exist, they are difficult to change. This means that when you participate in a group that is just being established, you should do whatever you can to create norms that you think will be desirable. For example, if you expect members of a committee to be punctual at meetings, it's important to begin each session at the appointed time. If you want others to be candid about their feelings, it's important to be frank yourself and encourage honesty in others at the outset.

Comply with Established Norms Whenever Possible   In an established group, you have the best chance of reaching your goals if you handle the task and social relationships in the group's customary manner. If your co-workers are in the habit of exchanging good-natured insults, you shouldn't be offended when you are the target—and you will be accepted as one of them if you dish out a few yourself. In a group in which the norm is never to criticize another member's idea directly, a blunt approach probably won't get you very far. When you are entering an established group, it's wise to learn the norms by personal observation and by asking knowledgeable members before plunging in.

It may not always be possible to follow established norms. If a group is in the habit of cracking racist jokes, doing shabby work, or stealing company property, for example, you probably would be unwilling to go along just to be accepted. This sort of conflict between personal values and group norms can lead to a major crisis in values. If the potential for conflict is great enough and the issue is sufficiently important, you may decide to do whatever you can to join a different, more compatible group.

DEAL WITH BOTH TASK AND SOCIAL NEEDS

Most groups operate on two levels. At the *task* level, communication focuses on the job at hand: working out a duty roster, coming up with an idea for a new package design, exploring possible solutions to high staff turnover, deciding how to market a new product, and so on. The *social* or *relational* level involves the personal relationships among the members. To understand the importance of the relational level of communication in groups, consider this discussion among several project members who are deciding how to approach their boss with a request for an increase in next year's budget.

Tom, the most senior member of the group, suggests a direct approach. "Let's just go in and ask for what we need," he argues. "He's probably waiting for us to tell him. If he doesn't go for it, we can figure out another approach."

Cheryl disagrees. "I think we ought to float the subject casually at first, and see whether he's considered it at all. He might realize that our costs are going up a lot. If he doesn't and he doesn't seem receptive to a budget increase, we should put together some kind of written report with the facts and figures that show why we need more money. If we ask at the start and he says no, it'll be harder to get him to change his mind." Valerie agrees with Cheryl, setting the stage for a relational problem.

While the three colleagues will probably go on discussing the *task*—their request for a budget increase—there is also a *relational* conflict that involves each member's unexpressed concerns. As in most relational conflicts, these concerns fall into three categories: inclusion, control, and affection.[35]

Tom is concerned with *inclusion,* the degree to which a member is considered part of the group: "Whenever a question comes up around here," he thinks, "it's always the women against the men."

Cheryl is concerned with *control,* which focuses on the power members have to influence the group's ideas or actions: "I hope Tom doesn't take it upon himself to barge into the boss's office and demand the increase on behalf of all three of us," she worries. "It would be just like him to try to pull seniority."

Meanwhile, Valerie has an *affection* concern; her behavior is influenced by the desire to be liked by her colleagues: "Cheryl is right," she thinks, "but I don't want either of them to get mad at me."

As a result of these unstated relational concerns, Tom insists on his plan even though he has a nagging suspicion that Cheryl's is better or at least carries less risk; Cheryl gets angry; and Valerie struggles, unsuccessfully, to reconcile the others' points of view.

Such conflicts can have long-term effects on the group, even after the three members have settled their immediate task dilemma. Tom, feeling that his need for inclusion has been denied, may retaliate by withdrawing from Cheryl and Valerie: he may continue to work with them when assigned but with less exchange of information and fewer offers to help. When Cheryl needs some help, for instance, Tom might feel less inclined to give it. Similarly, if Cheryl is eventually promoted so that Valerie then reports to her, Cheryl may feel that Valerie has withheld support—affection or control—in the past, and Valerie may find that she has a little more trouble being promoted. Neither Tom's nor Cheryl's retribution would be direct or even necessarily deliberate, but the group's interaction has nonetheless been affected.

This brief example shows the importance of understanding the relational dimension of any group. Members who discuss only the task and are blind to the relational issues of inclusion, control, or affection that influence the interaction are often baffled by the seemingly mysterious behavior of others. Yet relational concerns are usually present in groups, and the members need to respond to them if the group is to be successful. We discussed ways of dealing with relational concerns in Chapter 5 and will cover more later in this chapter and also in Chapter 9 when we focus on meetings.

Researchers have identified a number of task and social functions that must be performed if a group is to run smoothly and effectively. Table 8-2 lists these *functional roles,* as well as noting some dysfunctional behaviors that reduce the effectiveness of a group. Table 8-2 is a valuable diagnostic tool. When a group isn't operating effectively, you must determine which functions are lacking. For

TABLE 8-2 Functional Roles of Group Members

TASK FUNCTIONS

1. **Information-giver** Offers facts, evidence, personal experience, and other knowledge relevant to group task.
2. **Information-seeker** Asks other members for task-related information.
3. **Opinion-giver** States personal opinions, attitudes, and beliefs.
4. **Opinion-seeker** Solicits opinions, attitudes, and beliefs of other members.
5. **Starter** Initiates task-related behavior (for example, "We'd better get going on this").
6. **Direction-giver** Provides instructions regarding how to perform task at hand.
7. **Summarizer** Reviews what has been said, identifying common themes or progress.
8. **Diagnoser** Offers observations about task-related behavior of group (for example, "We seem to be spending all of our time discussing the problem without proposing any solutions").
9. **Energizer** Encourages members to work vigorously on task.
10. **Gatekeeper** Regulates participation of members.
11. **Reality-tester** Checks feasibility of group ideas against real-world contingencies.

MAINTENANCE FUNCTIONS

1. **Participation-encourager** Encourages reticent members to speak, letting them know that their contribution will be valued.
2. **Harmonizer** Resolves interpersonal conflicts between members.
3. **Tension-reliever** Uses humor or other devices to release anxiety and frustration of members.
4. **Evaluator of emotional climate** Offers observations about socioemotional relationships between members (for example, "I think we're all feeling a little defensive now" or "It sounds like you think nobody trusts you, Bill").
5. **Praise giver** Reinforces accomplishments and contributions of group members.
6. **Empathic listener** Listens without evaluation to personal concerns of members.

DYSFUNCTIONAL ROLES

1. **Blocker** Prevents progress by constantly raising objections.
2. **Attacker** Aggressively questions the competence or motives of others.
3. **Recognition-seeker** Repeatedly and unnecessarily calls attention to self by relating irrelevant experiences, boasting, and seeking sympathy.
4. **Playboy** Engages in joking behavior in excess of tension-relieving needs, distracting members.
5. **Withdrawer** Refuses to take stand on social or task issues; covers up feelings, does not respond to others' comments.

Adapted from Kenneth D. Benne and Paul Sheats, "Functional Roles of Group Members," *Journal of Social Issues* 4 (1948): 41–49.

instance, you might discover that several people are acting as opinion-givers but that no one is serving as an opinion-seeker—like a series of radio stations broadcasting but no one receiving. Or you might note that the group has several good ideas but that no one is summarizing and coordinating them. Or perhaps the group lacks a crucial piece of information, but no one realizes this fact.

In other cases, your diagnosis of a troubled group might show that all the necessary task functions are being filled but that the social needs of members aren't being met. Perhaps members need to have their good ideas supported ("That's a terrific idea, Neil!"). Maybe personal conflicts need to be acknowledged and resolved ("I know I sound defensive about this. I've worked on this idea for a month and I hate to see it dismissed in five minutes"). When social needs like these go unfilled, even the best knowledge and talent often aren't enough to guarantee a group's smooth functioning.

Once you have identified the missing functions, you can fill them. Supplying these missing roles often transforms a stalled, frustrated group into a productive team. Other members probably won't recognize what you're doing, but they will realize that you somehow know how to say the "right thing" at the right time.

PROMOTE AN OPTIMAL LEVEL OF COHESIVENESS

Cohesiveness can be defined as the degree to which members feel themselves part of a group and want to remain with that group. You can think of cohesiveness as a magnetic force that attracts members to one another, giving them a collective identity. As you might suspect, highly cohesive groups have happier members than less closely knit groups. Workers who belong to cohesive groups are likely to have higher rates of job satisfaction and lower rates of tension, absenteeism, and turnover than those who belong to less cohesive groups.[36]

Not all cohesive work groups are productive—at least not in terms of the organization's goals. In strikes and slowdowns, for example, highly cohesive workers can actually shut down operations. (Of course, the workers' cohesiveness in such cases may help them to accomplish other group goals such as higher pay or safer working conditions.) In less dramatic cases, cohesiveness in observing antiorganization norms ("Don't work too hard," "Go ahead and report our lunch as a business expense—we always do that," "If you need some art supplies for your kids, just take them from the supply closet") can leave group members feeling good about each other but harm the interests of the organization. A manager, therefore, should try to develop group cohesiveness that focuses on norms and goals desirable to the organization.

Cohesiveness develops when certain conditions exist in a group. Once you understand these conditions, you can apply them to groups on or off the job. You can also use them to analyze why a group's cohesiveness is high or low and choose ways to reach and maintain a desirable level of cohesiveness. Here are eight conditions that lead to cohesiveness.[37]

Certainly [unified commitment] is "team spirit." It is a sense of loyalty and dedication to the team. It is an unrestrained sense of excitement and enthusiasm about the team. It is a willingness to do anything that has to be done to help the team succeed. It is an intense identification with a group of people. It is a loss of self. "Unified commitment" is very difficult to understand unless you've experienced it. And even if you have experienced it, it is difficult to put into words.

Carl E. Larson and Frank M. J. LaFusto, *Team Work: What Must Go Right/What Can Go Wrong*

Emphasize Shared or Compatible Goals Group members draw closer together when they have a similar aim or when their goals can be mutually satisfied. For instance, the members of a construction crew might have little cohesiveness when their pay is based on individual efforts, but if the entire crew receives a bonus for completing stages of the building ahead of schedule, the members are likely to work together better.

Strive for Progress Toward These Goals When a group makes progress toward its target, members are drawn together; when progress stops, cohesiveness decreases. Members of the construction crew just mentioned will feel good about each other when they reach their target dates or can reasonably expect to do so. But if they consistently fall short, they are likely to get discouraged and feel less attraction to the group; when talking to their families or friends, there will be less talk about "us" and more about "me."

Promote Shared Norms or Values Although successful groups tolerate or even thrive on some differences in members' expressed attitudes and behaviors, wide variations in what members consider appropriate behavior reduces cohesiveness. For example, a person who insists on wearing conservative clothes in a business where everyone else dresses casually probably won't fit in with the rest of the group.

Minimize Feelings of Threat Among Members In a cohesive group, members usually feel secure about their status, dignity, and material and social well-being. When conflict arises over these issues, however, the results can be destructive. If all of the junior executives in a division are competing for the same senior position—especially if senior positions rarely open—the cohesiveness of the group is likely to suffer, at least until the job is filled. If a manager or supervisor seems more interested in assigning blame than in solving problems and helping the group to accomplish its goals, the threat of blame will interfere with the group's cohesiveness.

Create Interdependence Among Members Groups become more cohesive when members need one another to satisfy group goals. When a job can be done by one person alone, the need for unity decreases. An office team in which each member performs a different aspect or stage of a process will be less cohesive than one in which members rely on one another.

Encourage Competition from Outside the Group When members perceive an external threat to their existence or dignity, they draw closer together. Almost everyone knows of a family whose members seem to fight constantly among themselves until an outsider criticizes one of them. The internal bickering stops for the moment, and the group unites against the common enemy. An uncohesive work group could draw together in a similar way when another group competes with it for such things as use of limited company resources or desirable space in a new office building. Many wise managers deliberately set up situations of competition between groups to get tasks accomplished more quickly or to generate more sales dollars.

Enhance Mutual Perceived Attractiveness and Friendship   This factor is somewhat circular, since friendship and mutual attraction often result from other factors of group cohesiveness. Yet some groups become cohesive precisely because members like one another.

Create Shared Group Experiences   When members have been through an experience together, especially an unusual or trying one, they draw closer together. This is why soldiers who have gone through combat together often feel close for years afterward. Work groups that have accomplished difficult tasks are also likely to be more cohesive. Some organizations also provide social events such as annual "retreats" for their executives, which might include workshops to discuss particular aspects or problems of members' jobs, sports events, and parties. Annual sales meetings are often partially intended to increase group cohesiveness since these meetings are not the most cost-efficient way to distribute sales information.

ENCOURAGE BALANCED PARTICIPATION

Some group members seem to take over the discussion. If they don't have anything relevant to add, they will still say things like "Did you see the article in *Time* magazine about that?" "This is a terrible place to have a meeting. Why couldn't we use the new conference center?" "You remember when we had that problem at Hobart and Jones? Of course, their whole system was different. I remember once this sales rep called me. . . ."

Excessive talkers can get a group off track in tangential discussions about the article in *Time* or arguments about how they might have handled the situation at Hobart and Jones even though there may be no reason to expect the same problems at their own company.

Alfred P. Sloan, the man who revitalized General Motors in the 1920s when it was close to bankruptcy, appreciated the value of dialogue versus monologue. At a meeting of one of his top committees, everyone agreed to his proposal under consideration. "Gentlemen," observed Sloan, "I take it we are all in complete agreement on the decision here." Everyone around the conference table nodded. "Then," he continued, "I propose we postpone further discussion on this matter until our next meeting, to give ourselves time to develop disagreement and perhaps gain some understanding of what the decision is all about."

Executive Speechwriter

A few dominant members may also lead the group to a bad decision. Committees often adopt the decisions supported by their most talkative members,[38] although there is no guarantee that the biggest talkers have the best ideas. One method for giving every member's ideas an equal chance to be considered is the *nominal group technique* (NGT).[39] (The method's name comes from the fact that, for much of this process, the participants are a group in name only since they are working independently.) The NGT method consists of five phases:

1. Each member writes down his or her ideas on paper, which is then collected by a discussion leader. This method ensures that good ideas from quiet members will have a chance for consideration.

2. All ideas are listed for every member to see. Members can introduce their own ideas, or suggestions can be collected by the leader and posted without authorship attached. By keeping the authorship of ideas private at this point, consideration is less likely to be based on personal factors such as authority or popularity.

3. Members discuss ideas to understand them better, but criticism is prohibited. The goal here is to clarify the possibilities, not to evaluate them.

4. Each member privately rank-orders the ideas from most to least promising. Individual ranking again prevents domination by a few talkative or influential members.

5. Items that receive the greatest number of votes are discussed critically and thoroughly by the group. At this point, a decision can be made, using whichever method described on pages 220–222 is most appropriate.

The NGT method is too elaborate for relatively unimportant matters but works well for important issues. Besides reducing the tendency for more talkative members to dominate the discussion, the anonymity of the process lessens the potential for harmful conflicts.

AVOID EXCESSIVE CONFORMITY

Bad group decisions can also come about through too much agreement among members. Irving Janis calls this phenomenon *groupthink*, an unwillingness, for the sake of harmony, to examine ideas critically.[40] Janis describes several characteristics of groups that succumb to groupthink.

- **The Illusion That the Group Is Invulnerable**   "We can afford to raise the price on our deluxe-model kitchen appliances because they're so much better than anything else on the market. Even if our competitors could develop comparable models, we'd still outdo them on style."
- **Rationalizing or Discounting Negative Information**   "I know the market research says people will buy other brands if our prices go up any

more, but you know how unreliable market research is about things like that."

- ■ **Ignoring Ethical or Moral Consequences of the Group's Decision** "The waste we're dumping in the river may kill a few fish, but look, this company provides jobs and a living for all the people who live in this town."
- ■ **Stereotyped Views of Other Groups** "The labor unions are just trying to stir up trouble. All those guys want is to sit around all day and get twice the money they're worth."
- ■ **Group Pressure to Conform** "Come on, none of the rest of us is interested in direct-mail marketing. Why don't you forget that stuff?"
- ■ **Self-Censorship** "Every time I push for an innovative ad campaign, everybody fights it. I might as well drop it."
- ■ **Illusion of Unanimity** "Any executive in a major corporation has to be opposed to labor unions."
- ■ **"Mindguards" Against Threatening Information** "They're talking about running the machines around the clock to meet the schedule. I'd better not bring up what the supervisor said about how her staff feels about working more overtime."

A second type of harmful conformity has been labeled *groupshift:* the likelihood of a group to take positions that are more extreme than the members would choose on their own.[41] Groupshift can work in two directions. When members are conservative, their collective decisions are likely to be more cautious than their individual positions. More commonly, groups are prone to taking positions that are riskier than the choices members would have taken had they been acting separately. Thus, groupshift results either in taking risks that aren't justified and suffering the costs or avoiding necessary steps that the team needs to take to survive and prosper.

Paradoxically, cohesive teams are most prone to groupthink and groupshift. When members like and respect one another, the tendency to agree is great. The best way to guard against this sort of collective blindness—especially in very cohesive groups—is to seek the opinions of outsiders who may see things differently. In addition, leaders who are highly influential should avoid stating their opinions early in the discussion.[42]

ENCOURAGE CREATIVITY

One advantage of broadly based participation in groups is the greater chance for creativity. As more members bring their different perspectives to a task, the chances of coming up with a winning solution increase.

Of course, the quantity of people involved doesn't guarantee the quality of their contributions. One way to boost the creativity of the group is through *brainstorming*—an approach that encourages free thinking and minimizes conformity. The term was coined by advertising executive Alex Osborn, who noticed that groups were most creative when they let their imaginations run free.[43] He also realized that creativity was stifled when members began criticizing either their own ideas or those of others. Out of these observations came a series of steps that, with variations, are now used widely.

Conduct a Warm-Up Session   During this phase the group is reminded of brainstorming's cardinal rules:

> All evaluation and criticism of ideas is forbidden during the early phases of the process.
>
> Wild and crazy ideas are encouraged.
>
> Quantity—not quality—of ideas is the goal.
>
> New combinations of ideas are sought.

Once members understand these rules, they practice them with some nonsense issue, such as uses for a paper clip (high-tech tie clip, lightning rod for an anthill) or a brick (heat and use as a foot warmer in bed, freeze and use as a beer cooler on picnics). This sort of wild thinking loosens the group up to approach the real problem creatively.

Generate Possible Solutions   Now the group applies the brainstorming rules, as described above, to the task at hand. During this stage, a recorder lists all the ideas generated by the group on a chalkboard or flip chart that everyone can see. The leader encourages "hitchhiking" on previous ideas, so that one suggestion leads to variations. The leader should also keep the level of enthusism high to spur more contributions.

Eliminate Duplicate Ideas   After the brainstorming session is completed, duplicate suggestions are eliminated. No evaluation of ideas is made at this stage; the group simply clarifies and simplifies the list of ideas it has developed.

Evaluate Ideas   Once the group has generated all the ideas it can think of, it can begin to decide which are worth considering seriously. Unless only one or two ideas stand out as winners, it's usually best to prune the unworkable ones in several passes. Begin by scratching the clearly unworkable ideas, leaving any that have even some merit. After discussing the remainder, the group can pick the top two or three ideas for serious consideration and then decide which one is best.

SUMMARY

When used effectively, small groups are superior to individuals working alone: small groups are more productive, their results can be more accurate, and members will support decisions more enthusiastically.

A variety of communication concepts

can improve the effectiveness of working teams. The reflective-thinking sequence is a means of effective problem solving that produces high-quality results. Recognizing that working groups often go through predictable stages of orientation, conflict, emergence, and reinforcement can help members tolerate the inevitable frustrations of group problem solving. Carefully choosing the method of making a decision can use time effectively and generate an outcome that members are most likely to support.

Research has demonstrated that the best approach to leading a group varies according to the circumstances, and this chapter outlined the conditions under which a variety of styles can be used. Designated leaders aren't the only people who influence group functioning, however: several types of power are available to members, and the way this power is exercised can affect the group's functioning. In groups without a designated leader, a predictable process occurs in which a single leader often emerges.

The chapter made several suggestions about how groups can operate more successfully. These included using time effectively, recognizing and trying to fulfill both personal and group goals, promoting desirable norms, fulfilling both task and social needs of members, promoting an optimal level of cohesiveness, balancing the participation of members, avoiding excessive conformity, and boosting creativity.

ACTIVITIES

1. Along with three to six of your classmates, use the guidelines for problem solving in this chapter to develop a money-making product or service that could be marketed by students in your class.

2. With three to six of your classmates, decide which method of decision making would be most effective for your group in each of the following situations:

   a. Choosing the safest course of action if you were lost in a dangerous area near your city or town
   b. Deciding whether and how to approach your instructor to propose a change in the grading system of your course
   c. Identifying local merchants who might be willing to sponsor student interns
   d. Designing the most effective campaign for your school to recruit minority students

   e. Duplicating for distribution to your instructor and classmates the solutions to this exercise that your group developed
   f. Hiring an instructor for your department
   g. Choosing the name for a new brand of breakfast cereal
   h. Selecting a new electronic typewriter
   i. Deciding which of three employees gets the desirable vacant office
   j. Planning the weekend work schedule for the upcoming month
   k. Deciding whether the employees should affiliate with a labor union

3. Analyze the types of power that exist in your class or some other working group. Which members use each type of power? Who exerts the most influence? What kinds of power do you possess?

4. With four to six classmates, develop a table of contents for a new book entitled

Fifty Things to Do When There's Nothing to Do in (name of your town). Use the guidelines in this chapter to ensure that the ideas in the book are creative and interesting.

5. Use the skills you learned in Chapters 6 and 7 to interview one member of a work-related group. Identify the following:

   a. What is the level of the group's cohesiveness? Is this level desirable, too high, or too low?
   b. Which of the factors on pages 238–240 contribute to the level of cohesiveness in this group?

   Based on your findings, develop a report outlining specific steps that might be taken to improve the degree of cohesiveness in this group.

6. Although it may be larger than most of the groups discussed in this chapter, your class is a good model of the principles described here. Answer the following questions about your class:

   a. What are the stated goals of the class?
   b. What are your individual goals? Which of these goals are compatible with the group's goals, and which are not compatible? Are any of your individual goals hidden agendas?
   c. What are your instructor's individual goals? Were these goals stated? If not, how did you deduce them? How compatible are these goals with the official goals of the class?
   d. How do the individual goals of other class members affect the functioning of your group?

7. What task, social, and procedural norms would be most desirable for each of the following groups? How could you promote development of these norms as the group's leader? As a member?

   a. A student fund-raising committee to develop scholarships for your major department
   b. The employees at a new fast-food restaurant
   c. A group of new bank tellers
   d. A company softball team

8. Which of the functional roles in Table 8-2 do you generally fill in groups you belong to? Do you fill the same role in most groups at most times, or do you switch roles as circumstances require? How could you improve the functioning of one group you belong to by changing your role-related behavior?

Communicator Profile

John C. Huie, Executive Director
North Carolina Outward Bound School
Morganton, North Carolina

To really build an effective team, you need a healthy amount of appreciation. I see a great lack of appreciation in most businesses today. People want to work hard, but they need positive feedback. I try to have a yellow sticky note of thanks on every paycheck that goes out of this office.

I orchestrate a large group of maverick, idealistic leaders whose goals are to help people—individuals and teams—grow and learn through challenging experiences. These are usually wilderness adventures that appear very different from what people are used to. Our courses include rock climbing, backpacking, white-water rafting, high ropes courses, and group problem-solving initiatives. We use the wilderness setting for its simplicity, its beauty, and its newness. Removal from the security of the routine is a critical part of making the experience valuable because learning is more dramatic in an unfamiliar environment. Activities are designed to demand teamwork, problem solving, and perseverance. Teams never number more than twelve, and the group lives and works together twenty-four hours a day, rain or shine.

We want people to draw out of themselves qualities they didn't know they had. We make them take a fresh look at themselves, their teammates, and their objectives. Activities are specially targeted to management teams and designed to improve team relations and develop trust among co-workers. Canoeing through the Everglades, for example, builds teamwork and places a premium on planning, perseverance, and effective management of differences. White-water rafting necessitates tight communication under fire. In the words of one BellSouth employee, "When you're out of doors and covered with grime, it's hard to be a pompous ass."

Our team-building efforts may be unusual, but they do seem to work. Arthur J. Levitt, former chairman of the American Stock Exchange, has said that Outward Bound was successful in establishing communication between people who might otherwise just pass in the night. David O. Beim, vice-president of the Bankers Trust Company, says his "troops" returned with a strong feeling of camaraderie which will be key to their effectiveness. Murray Friedman, director of Corporate Auditing at Coca-Cola, says, "By going beyond what I thought my limits were, I learned that I could do the same at my work. This has been a long-lasting and powerful personal growth factor for me."

To really build an effective team, you need a healthy amount of appreciation. I see a great lack of appreciation in most businesses today. People want to work hard, but they need positive feedback. I try to have a yellow sticky note of thanks on every paycheck that goes out of this office.

One effective way for a team to approach problem solving is to temporarily try *not* to solve the problem. By that, I mean you need to get a group to move off center sometimes, become playful, build trust, then move back onto the problem. Yesterday, for example, we had a staff meeting that went on for three hours over the issue of a one-day or two-day orientation program. What needed to happen was a digression. When someone finally interrupted with a humorous story that distracted us for a while, we were able to return and resolve the issue.

Finally, it is extremely important to acknowledge and celebrate group efforts. We had a potluck last night, for example, to say goodbye to two fine leaders who are moving on. Spouses and children were there, and we presented each of them with a large collage of pictures of their years here. Then we had some very casual entertainment—my six-year-old boy played "Many Rats in the Rice Bag" on his flute. It was very low-key, but it was heartfelt. This is what makes a group effective—a genuine feeling of belonging.

After reading this chapter, you should understand:

- The types of meetings that commonly occur in business and professional settings
- The factors to consider when deciding whether to hold a problem-solving meeting
- The steps involved in planning a meeting
- The communication skills involved in conducting a problem-solving meeting

You should be able to:

- Decide whether a problem can best be solved in a meeting or by some other form of communication
- Construct an agenda for a problem-solving meeting
- Determine the appropriate time, length, location, and membership of a specified problem-solving meeting
- Open a meeting effectively
- Encourage the participation of quiet group members during a meeting
- Keep a wandering discussion on target
- Respond to negative comments in a way that encourages a positive reaction
- Conclude a meeting effectively
- Take the necessary follow-up steps to ensure the successful outcome of a meeting

EFFECTIVE MEETINGS

As they do every week, the agents of a real-estate firm meet to discuss the latest trends in the market and to share information that will help them increase their sales.

The tenants in an apartment building gather to discuss the need for better maintenance and security.

A group of employees meet with top management to discuss a list of important issues, including the need for child care, a potential series of layoffs, and health benefits.

The owner of a small business meets over lunch with the director of a local advertising agency, who outlines how her firm can increase the client's market share.

As these examples suggest, meetings are a fact of life when it comes to doing business. In one study of fifteen corporations, researchers gave pocket recorders to a wide range of key workers—from sales representatives to vice-presidents—and asked these workers to list what they were doing every twenty minutes on the job. An analysis of almost 90,000 working days showed that an impressive 46 percent of the time was spent in meetings of one sort or another.[1] Research shows that this figure is representative. According to one survey, over 90 percent of organizations hold regular meetings.[2] The number of times people meet as they do business is staggering: approximately 20 million business meetings take place each day in the United States, and businesspeople spend an average of half their time attending them.[3] If you include the time spent planning and following up on face-to-face interaction, the figure is even higher.

Just because meetings are common doesn't mean that they are always productive. A survey by one marketing research company showed that executives consider one-third of the gatherings they attend to be unnecessary.[4] Inefficient use of meeting time led one skeptic to pen this poem:

> Let's fingertap together
> In a dedicated way,
> And postpone all decisions
> Until another day.
>
> Let's orchestrate and dialogue
> In words that we adore,
> The words that we've all mumbled
> A million times before.
>
> Let's shuffle all our paper,
> And fuzzify our minds;
> Let's wrap our brains in cobwebs,
> And love red tape that binds.
>
> Let's regulate the people
> With rules, reports, and forms;
> Inspire true innovation
> As long as it conforms.

Let's optimize the status quo,
And sit right where we are,
For if we keep our profile low,
We'll get no battle scar.

Let's cut our red tape lengthwise,
Pronunciate our words,
And build great stacks of paper
The stuff that undergirds.

Yes, let's fingertap together
In a dedicated way,
And postpone all decisions
Until another day.[5]

Since meetings are so common and so prone to inefficiency, it's important to take a closer look at them. By the time you have finished reading this chapter, you should understand some methods for planning and participating in meetings that will produce efficient, satisfying results.

Group and *meeting* are not identical terms. A team of assembly-line workers or of firefighters fits our description of a group, but these people spend very little time in meetings. The members of some groups work in separate offices, separate buildings, or separate cities; they communicate with one another about their group efforts, but only occasionally do they meet all at once, face to face, to discuss shared concerns. In this chapter, we will focus specifically on how groups operate in meetings—that is, on those occasions when their members gather to discuss common concerns.

TYPES OF MEETINGS

People meet for many reasons. Some gather for personal growth or emotional support, in counseling or therapy groups. Still others meet to learn in classes, seminars, or workshops. In most business and professional settings, though, meetings fall into three categories: information sharing, problem solving, and ritual activities.

INFORMATION SHARING

In many organizations, people meet regularly to exchange information. Police officers and nurses, for example, begin every shift with a meeting in which the people going off duty brief their replacements on what has been happening recently. A medical research team experimenting with a new drug may meet regularly to compare notes on their results. In many office groups, the Monday-morning meeting is an important tool for informing group members about new developments, emerging trends, and the coming week's tasks. Perkin Elmer Corporation, a producer of scientific measuring instruments and precision optical equipment, is a typical example. The firm schedules a weekly meeting of all corporate and top executives to keep them up to date on the activities of the more than twenty divisions the company has around the world. Similar meetings occur at all levels in smaller businesses. The agents in a real-estate firm might meet for updates on new properties and interest-rate changes. A sales staff might gather to discuss new promotions.

PROBLEM SOLVING OR DECISION MAKING

In other meetings, a group may decide to take some action or make a change in existing policies or procedures. "Which supplier should we contract?" "Should we introduce a new product line?" "Should we delay production so we can work out a design flaw in our new typewriter?" "Where can we cut costs if sales don't improve this year?" "How can we best schedule vacations?" All these are questions that might be discussed in problem-solving meetings. Because problem-solving and decision-making meetings are the most challenging type of group activity, the bulk of this chapter discusses how to conduct them effectively.

RITUAL ACTIVITIES

In still other meetings, the social function is far more important than any specific task. In one firm, Friday afternoon "progress review sessions" are a regular fixture. Their apparently serious title is really an insider's tongue-in-cheek joke: the meetings take place in a local bar and to an outsider look like little more than a T.G.I.F. party. Despite the setting and apparently unbusinesslike activity, however, these meetings serve several important purposes.[6] First, they reaffirm the members' commitment to one another and to the company. Choosing to socialize with one another instead of rushing home is a sign of belonging and caring. Second, the sessions provide a chance to swap useful ideas and stories that might not be appropriate in the office. Who's in trouble? What does the boss really want? As you read in Chapter 2, this sort of informal communication can be invaluable, and the meetings provide a good setting for it. Finally, ritual meetings can be a kind of perk that confers status on the members. "Progress review committee" members charge expenses to the company and leave work early to attend. Thus, being invited to join the sessions is a sign of having arrived in the company.

Some meetings serve more than one function. In fact, the functions we've been describing are often dependent on one another. A production team deciding on what suppliers to use will share information about the quality of materials and service from past jobs. In a meeting in which a project team works out a plan to produce a new line of office furniture, a sales manager might discuss market demands in terms of functionality, appearance, and costs; a designer might suggest some ways that those needs might be met; a production manager could present information on various materials and their costs; and an engineer might provide some technical information about the strength of materials and the

Harold Geneen, former chief executive officer of ITT, described the importance of meetings in his organization. Even though few companies are as large as ITT, most businesspeople will agree that meetings are just as important in their organizations.

Our normal general manager's meetings ran from ten in the morning to ten at night. In Europe, they often went on past midnight because we could spend only a limited number of days there. Our budget and business plan meetings almost always ran on past midnight. We did not watch the clock. We worked on and on until the task at hand was completed.

Now, if you add up the days and weeks spent in those meetings, you will find that we spent three weeks in February and March on our preliminary, rough business plans and budgets for the coming year, and then twelve weeks at the end of the year reviewing and agreeing on those plans. That's fifteen weeks. One General Manager's Meeting in Brussels and one in New York, a week each, ten months of the year, and you had another twenty weeks. That's thirty-five weeks of time. Add four weeks for vacation and holiday time. and you have thirty-nine weeks. That left a scant thirteen weeks of "other" time in which to run the company. How did we do it? We did it in overtime at night and on weekends and whenever we could, for it was truly at our meetings, and the face-to-face meetings down the line in our subsidiaries, that we ran ITT.

Harold Geneen, *Managing*

capacity of the manufacturing division to work with those materials. Drawing on the knowledge and skills of all the members, the group would try to work out a general plan that would take into account all of the factors involved.

Whatever your career or profession, chances are you will be expected to participate in and even lead meetings. Your skills in planning, conducting, and concluding the meeting may be vital to your job success.

PLANNING A PROBLEM-SOLVING MEETING

Successful meetings are just like interviews, presentations, letters, and memos: they must be planned.

WHEN TO HOLD A MEETING

The most fundamental planning question is whether to hold a meeting at all. Some business can be conducted just as well—or even better—in writing, by phone, in a series of smaller face-to-face conversations, or by one person without any consultation at all (see Table 9-1). One expert advises, "If you can get the job done without holding a meeting, then calling one is a waste of time."[7]

Aside from questions of time, a meeting should be called (or a committee appointed) only when the answers to the following questions are yes.

TABLE 9-1   Appropriate Tasks for Groups and Individuals

TASK CHARACTERISTICS	ASSIGNMENT
One correct answer (for example, solution to a mathematical problem)	Most capable person
Collection of information (for example, gathering sales or production data)	Individuals working separately, coordinated by one person
Open-ended task (for example, developing grievance procedures, planning sales campaign)	Problem-solving group

Adapted from Albert C. Kowitz and Thomas J. Knutson, *Decision Making in Small Groups: The Search for Alternatives* (Boston: Allyn & Bacon, 1980), p. 133. By permission.

Is the Job Beyond the Capacity of One Person?   A job might be too much for one person to handle for two reasons. First, it might call for more *information* than any single person possesses. For example, the job of improving health conditions in a food-processing plant would probably require the medical background of a physician or other health professional, the firsthand experience of employees familiar with the work, and a manager who knows the resources available for developing and implementing the program.

A job might also take more *time* than one person has available. For instance, even if one employee were capable of writing and publishing an employee handbook, it's unlikely that that person would be able to handle the task and have much time for other duties.

Are Individuals' Tasks Interdependent?   Each member at a committee meeting should have a different role. If each member's share of the task can be completed without input from other members, it's better to have the members co-acting under the supervision of a manager.

Consider the job of preparing the employee handbook that we just mentioned. If each person is responsible for a separate section, there is little need for them to meet frequently to discuss the task. With this arrangement, meetings would be little more than "show and tell" sessions. A more efficient plan might be for the group to meet at the outset to devise an outline and a set of guidelines about style, length, and so on and then for a manager or group leader to see that each person completes his or her own section according to those guidelines.

There are times when people who do the same job can profit by sharing ideas in a group. The handbook team, for example, might get new ideas about how the book could be made better from talking to one another. Similarly, sales representatives, industrial designers, physicians, or attorneys who work independently might profit by exchanging experiences and ideas. This is part of the purpose of professional conventions. Also, many companies schedule quarterly or annual meetings of people who do similar but independent work. While this may seem to contradict the requirement for interdependence of members' tasks, there is no real conflict. A group of people who do the same kind of work can often improve their individual performance through meetings by performing some of the complementary *functional roles.* For example, one colleague might serve as "real-ity-tester." ("Writing individual notes to each potential customer in your territory sounds like a good idea, but do you really have time to do that?") Another might take the job of being "information-giver." ("You know, there's a printer just out-side of Boston who can do large jobs like that just as well as your regular printer, but he's cheaper. Call me, and I'll give you the name and address.") Others serve as diagnosers. ("Have you checked the feed mechanism? Sometimes a problem there can throw the whole machine out of whack.") Some can just serve as empathic listeners. ("Yeah, I know. It's tough to get people who can do that kind of work right.")

Is There More Than One Decision or Solution?   Questions that have only one right answer aren't well suited to discussion in meetings. Whether the sales force made its quota last year or whether the budget will accommodate paying overtime to meet a schedule, for instance, are questions answered by checking the figures, not by getting the regional sales managers or the department members to reach an agreement.

Tasks that don't have fixed outcomes, however, are appropriate for commit-tee discussion. Consider the job facing the members of an advertising agency who are planning a campaign for a client. There is no obvious best way to sell products or ideas such as yearly physical examinations, office equipment, or clothing. Tasks such as these call for the kind of creativity that a talented, well-chosen group can generate.

Not all meetings are ineffective—but many are. When asked what can go wrong in meetings, a group of managers and professionals gave 1,305 examples. Sixteen of them accounted for 90 percent of all the problems:

- No goals or agenda
- No pre-meeting orientation
- Starting late
- Poor or inadequate preparation
- Getting off the subject
- Too long
- Disorganized
- Inconclusive
- Ineffective leadership

- Irrelevant information discussed
- Time wasted
- Interruptions
- Ineffective at making decisions
- Rambling, redundant, digressive discus-sions
- Individuals dominate discussions
- No published results or follow-up action

Roger K. Mosvick and Robert B. Nelson, *We've Got to Start Meeting Like This*

Are Misunderstandings or Reservations Likely?   It's easy to see how meetings can be useful when the goal is to generate ideas or solve problems. But meetings are often necessary when confusing or controversial information is being communicated. Suppose, for instance, that changing federal rules and company policy require employees to document their use of company cars in far more detail than was ever required. It's easy to imagine how this sort of change would be met with grumbling and resistance. In this sort of situation, simply issuing a memo outlining the new rules might not gain the kind of compliance that is necessary. Only by talking out their complaints and hearing why the new policy is being instituted will employees see a need to go along with the new procedure. If just one or two members of a group are likely to be confused or disagree with an idea, it might be possible to clear up their problems in a smaller meeting without involving the entire group. Often, however, a meeting is the best way to gain the greater degree of understanding or cooperation.

SETTING AN AGENDA

A meeting without an agenda is like a ship at sea without a destination or compass: no one aboard knows where it is or where it's headed. A good agenda contains several kinds of information, all illustrated in Figure 9-1.

Time, Length, and Location   To avoid problems, all three of these details need to be present on an agenda. Without the *starting time*, you can expect to hear such comments as "I thought you said ten, not nine," or "We always started at three before." Unless you announce the *length*, expect some members to leave early, pleading, "I have another meeting" or "I didn't realize we'd run this long—I've got a doctor's appointment." Failure to note the *location* results in members stumbling in late after waiting in the "usual place," wondering why no one showed up.

Who Will Attend   The overall size of the group is important: when attendance grows beyond seven members, the likelihood of some members falling silent increases. If the agenda includes one or more problem-solving items, it's best to keep the size small so that everyone can participate in discussions. If the meeting is primarily informational, a larger group may be acceptable.

Be sure to identify on the agenda the people who will be attending. By listing who will attend, you alert all members whom to expect in the meeting. If you have overlooked someone who ought to attend, a member who received the agenda can tell you. It is frustrating and a waste of time to call a meeting and then discover that the person with key information isn't there.

Background Information   Sometimes participants will need background information to give them new details or to remind them of things they may have forgotten. Background information can also provide a description of the meeting's significance.

AGENDA

Date: March 19, 1992

To: Joy McMasters, Fred Brady, Kevin Jessup, Monica Flores, Dave Cohn

From: Ted Gross

Subject: Planning meeting for new Louisville office.

Time/Place: Tuesday, April 12, from 9:30 to 11:00 A.M. in the third-floor conference room.

Background: We are still on target for an August 10 opening date for the Louisville office. Completing the tasks below will keep us on schedule—vital if we're to be ready for the fall season.

We will discuss the following items:

1. Office Equipment

    Please come with a list of business machines and other equipment you think will be needed for the office. At the meeting we'll refine this list to standardize our purchases as much as possible. Let's try to start out with compatible equipment!

2. Office Decoration

    Ellen Tibbits of the Louisville Design Group will present a preliminary design for our reaction. She will come up with a final plan based on our suggestions.

3. Promotion

    Kevin wants to prepare a series of press releases for distribution to Louisville media a month or so before the office opens. Please come with suggestions of items that should be mentioned in these releases.

Figure 9-1 Typical agenda format.

Items and Goals   Even with the skimpiest of agendas, most people have at least a vague idea of why they are meeting. Vague ideas, however, often lead to vague meetings. A clear list of topics and goals like the ones in Figure 9-1 will result in better-informed members and more productive, satisfying meetings.

The best goals are *result-oriented*, *specific*, and *realistic*. Notice the difference between goals that do and don't meet these criteria:

POORLY WORDED

"Let's talk about how we can solve the sales problems in the northwestern region."

"We're going to talk about the new income-savings plan."

"Joe Fishman will tell you about his trip to the new supplier's plant."

BETTER

"We will come up with a list of specific ways our product can be shown to be useful in the special climate conditions of the Northwest."

"We will explain the advantages and disadvantages of our two income-savings plans so that employees can decide which best suits their needs."

"Joe will explain the facilities of our new supplier and how we can use them to cut costs."

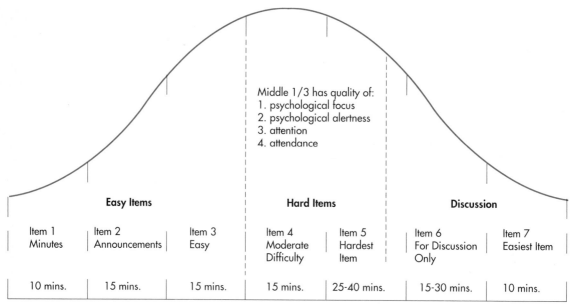

Figure 9-2   A bell-shaped agenda structure. (From John E. Tropman, "The Agenda," in *Effective Meetings, Improving Group Decision-Making*, p. 68. Copyright © 1980 by Sage Publications, Inc.)

Goals like these are useful in at least two ways. First, they help to identify those who ought to attend the meeting. Second, specific goals also help the people who do attend to prepare for the meeting, and they help to keep the discussion on track once it begins.

Pre-Meeting Work   The best meetings occur when people have done all the necessary advance work. The agenda is a good place to tell members how to prepare for the meeting by reading information, developing reports, preparing or duplicating documents, or locating facts or figures. If all members need to prepare in the same way (for example, by reading an article), adding that fact to the agenda is advised. If certain members have specific jobs to do, the meeting organizer can jot these tasks on their individual copies: "Sarah—be sure to bring last year's sales figures"; "Wes—be sure that there are enough copies of the annual report for everyone."

The order of agenda items is important. Some experts suggest that the difficulty of items form a bell-shaped curve, with items arranged in order of ascending and descending difficulty (see Figure 9-2). The meeting ought to begin with relatively simple business: minutes, announcements, and the easiest decisions. Once members have hit their stride and a good climate has developed, the group can move on to the most difficult items. These should ideally occupy the middle third of the session. Then the final third of the meeting can focus on easier items to allow a period of decompression and goodwill. (Table 9-2 is a checklist for planning a meeting.)

CONDUCTING THE MEETING

To the uninitiated observer, a well-run meeting seems almost effortless. Time is used efficiently, the tone is constructive, and the quality of ideas is good. Despite their apparent simplicity, results like this usually don't just happen: they grow

TABLE 9-2   Checklist for Planning a Meeting

- Is membership well chosen?
  - Is the size of group appropriate?
  - Are the necessary knowledge and skills represented?
- Have unproductive members been excluded (if practical)?
- Is enough time allotted for tasks at hand?
- Is meeting time convenient for most members?
- Is the location adequate?
  - Is the size appropriate?
  - Are the facilities appropriate?
  - Is there freedom from distractions?
- Is a complete agenda circulated?
  - Is it distributed far enough in advance of meeting?
  - Does it include particulars (meeting date, time, length, location, attendees)?
  - Does it contain background information as necessary?
  - Does it list goals for each item supplied?

from some important communication skills. (Table 9-3 is a checklist for conducting a meeting.)

BEGINNING THE MEETING

Effective openings get the meeting off to a good start. First, they give everyone a clear picture of what is to be accomplished. Second, they define how the group will try to reach its goal. Finally, they set the stage for good teamwork and, thus, good results.

The first few remarks by the person who called the meeting can set the stage for a constructive session. They should cover the following points:[8]

Identify the Goals of the Meeting   This is the same information listed in the agenda, but mentioning it here will remind everyone of the meeting's goals and help to focus the discussion. For example,

> "We're faced with a serious problem. Inventory losses have almost doubled in the last year, from 5 to 9 percent. We need to decide what's causing these losses and come up with some ideas about how to reduce them."

Provide Necessary Background Information   Background information gives everyone the same picture of the subject being discussed. It prevents

TABLE 9-3 Checklist for Conducting a Meeting

- Opening the Meeting
  - Have goals for the meeting been identified?
  - Has necessary background information been reviewed?
  - Are expectations for members' contributions clear?
  - Has the sequence of events for the meeting been previewed?
  - Have time constraints been identified?
- Encouraging Balanced Participation
  - Have leaders and members used questions to draw out quiet members?
  - Are off-track comments redirected with references to the agenda and relevancy challenges?
  - Do leader and members suggest moving on when an agenda item has been dealt with adequately?
- Maintaining Positive Tone
  - Are questioning and paraphrasing used as nondefensive responses to hostile remarks?
  - Are dubious comments enhanced as much as possible?
- Solving Problems Creatively
  - Is the problem defined clearly (versus too narrowly or broadly)?
  - Are the causes and effects of the problem analyzed?
  - Are clear criteria for resolving the problem established?
  - Are possible solutions brainstormed without being evaluated?
  - Is a decision made based on the previously established criteria?
  - Are methods of implementing the solution developed?

misunderstandings and helps members to understand the nature of the information the group will consider.

> "By 'inventory losses,' we mean materials that are missing or damaged after we receive them. These losses might occur in the main warehouse, en route to the stores, or within the stores themselves."

Show How the Group Can Help   Outline the contributions that members can make during this meeting. Some of these contributions will come from specific people:

> "Tom's going to compare our losses with industry figures, so we can get an idea of how much of the problem is an unavoidable cost of doing business. Chris will talk about his experiences with the problem at Sterling, where he worked until last year. That firm had some good ideas we may be able to use."

Other contributions can be made by everyone present. This is the place to define specifically how each member can help make the meeting a success.

> "We're counting on everybody here to suggest areas where we can cut losses. Once we've come up with ideas, I'll ask each of you to work out a schedule for putting the ideas to work in your department."

Preview the Meeting   If you have not already done so, outline how the meeting will run.

> "We'll begin by hearing the reports from Tom and Chris. Then we'll all work together to brainstorm a list of ways to cut losses. The goal here will be to get as many ideas as possible. Once we've come up with a list, we can decide which ideas to use and how to make them work."

Identify Time Constraints   Clarifying how much time is available helps to prevent time wasting. Sometimes it's only necessary to remind the group how much time can be spent in the meeting as a whole ("We can develop this list between now and eleven o'clock if we keep on track"). In other cases, it can be useful to preview the available time for each agenda item:

> "Tom and Chris have promised to keep their remarks brief, so by ten o'clock we should be ready to start brainstorming. If we get our list put together by ten-thirty, we'll still have a half hour to talk about which ideas to try and how to put them into action."

Following these guidelines will get your meeting off to a good start. Even if you are not in charge of the meeting, you can still make sure that the opening is

---

Some meetings should be long and leisurely. Some should be mercifully brief. A good way to handle the latter is to hold the meeting with everybody standing up. The meetees won't believe you at first. Then they get very uncomfortable and can hardly wait to get the meeting over with. If you have more than one comfortable chair for office visitors, move to a smaller office.

Robert Townsend, *Further Up the Organization*

---

a good one by asking questions that will get the leader to share the kind of information just listed:

"How much time do you expect we'll need?"

"How far do you expect we'll get today?"

"What can we do to help solve the problem?" . . . and so on.

CONDUCTING BUSINESS

No meeting will be successful without committed, talented participants. But even the best attendees do not guarantee success. Someone—either the leader or a responsible member—has to be sure that all important business is covered in a way that takes advantage of the talents of everyone present. A number of approaches are available that use meeting time effectively (see Table 9-3).

Encouraging Participation   You have already read about the dangers that result from domination of the group by a few members. How can a chairperson encourage comments from normally quiet people? Lawrence Loban, writing in *Supervision* magazine, suggests that the answer lies in using questions to draw members out.[9] He describes four types of question.

Overhead Question   An overhead question is directed toward the group as a whole, and anyone is free to answer.

"Sales have flattened out in the western region. Can anybody suggest what's going on?"

"We need to find some way of rewarding our top producers. I'd like to hear your ideas."

As long as overhead questions draw a response from all members, it's wise to continue using them. When a few people begin to dominate, however, it's time to switch to one of the following types.

Direct Question   A direct question is aimed at a particular individual, who is addressed by name.

"How would that suggestion work for you, Kim?"

"Greg, how's the new plan working in your department?"

Direct questions are a useful way to draw out quiet members, but they must be used skillfully. Never start a discussion with a direct question. This creates a "schoolroom atmosphere" and suggests the rule "Don't speak until you're called on"—hardly a desirable norm in most meetings. It's also important to give respondents a way out of potentially embarrassing questions. For example, a chairman might ask, "Tony, can you give us the figures for your department now, or will you need to check them and get back to us?"

Reverse Question   A reverse question occurs when a member asks the leader a question, and the leader refers the question back to the person who originally phrased it.

"Suppose the decision were up to you, Gary. What would you do?"

"That's a good question, Laurie. Do you think it's a practical idea?"

Reverse questions work well when the leader senses that a member really wants to make a statement but is unwilling to do so directly. It's important to use reverse questions with care: the member could be asking for information, in which case a direct answer or one of the following responses is appropriate.

Relay Question   In a relay question, the leader refers a question asked by one member to the entire group.

"Cynthia has just raised a good question. Who can respond to it?"

"Can anyone offer a suggestion for Les?"

Relay questions are especially useful when the leader wants to avoid disclosing his or her opinion for fear of inhibiting or influencing the group. Relays should usually be rephrased as overhead questions directed at the entire group. This avoids the suggestion that one member is smarter than the others. Of course, if a particular person does have special expertise, it is appropriate to direct the inquiry to him or her.

"Didn't you have a problem like that once with a distributor, Britt? How did you work things out?"

Whatever their form, Loban suggests that questions ought to meet each of the following five requirements. First, they should be *open-ended*. In Chapter 6, you learned that open questions are those that require more than a simple yes or no answer. A look at the examples just presented shows how open-ended questions encourage discussion. Questions should be *brief*. Most questions can be asked in a single sentence. Longer statements can confuse members so much that they won't know what you're asking for, much less how to reply. Besides being brief, questions should also be *worded simply*. This is usually good advice for any message. But simplicity is a relative term: some groups are comfortable using jargon that would baffle outsiders. The rule here is to make sure that everyone understands what you are asking.

For the sake of clarity, your questions should also *cover only a single point*. Some double-barreled questions aren't obvious: "We're here to discuss ways of reducing late arrivals at work. Let's get started by hearing any suggestions you have about how to reduce the parking problem." A close look will show that these remarks really ask two questions. First, "Does the parking situation contribute to lateness?" If the answer is affirmative, then—but only then—is it time to ask the second question: "How do we solve the problem?" The final guideline for asking discussion-generating questions is to be sure that they relate directly to the topic under consideration. Every question should help the group to move toward the goal stated on the agenda and in the leader's introduction.

Keeping Discussions on Track   Sometimes the problem isn't too little discussion, but too much. Groups often waste time, conducting leisurely discussions when time is short. Even when time is plentiful, members often talk on and on without moving any closer to accomplishing a goal. In other cases, someone may bring up a topic that is unrelated to the task at hand. When problems like these occur, the leader or some other member needs to get the discussion back on track by using one of the following techniques.

Remind the Group of Time Pressures   When the group is handling an urgent topic in a leisurely manner, you can remind everyone about the importance of moving quickly. But when doing so, it is important to acknowledge the value of the comments being made:

> "Radio ads sound good, but for now we'd better stick to the newspaper program. John wanted copy from us by noon, and we'll never make it if we don't get going."

Summarize and Redirect the Discussion   When members ramble on about a topic after the job is done, you can get the discussion moving again by tactfully summarizing what has been accomplished and mentioning the next task:

> "It seems as if we've come up with a good list of the factors that might be contributing to absenteeism. Can anybody think of more causes? If not, maybe we should move on and try to think of as many solutions as we can."

Use Relevancy Challenges   When a discussion wanders away from the business at hand, summarizing won't help. Sometimes the unrelated ideas are good ones that just don't apply to the group's immediate job. In other cases, they are not only irrelevant, but worthless. In either situation, you can get the group back on track by questioning the idea's relevancy. In a relevancy challenge, the questioner asks a member to explain how an apparently off-the-track idea relates to the group's task.[10] Typical relevancy challenges sound like this:

> "I'm confused, Tom. How will leasing new equipment instead of buying it help us to boost productivity?"

> "Fran asked us to figure which word-processing package to buy. Does the graphics package you mentioned have something to do with the word-processing decision?"

At this point the member who made the original remark can either explain its relevance or acknowledge that it wasn't germane. In either case, the advantage of this sort of challenge is that it isn't personal. It focuses on the *remark* and not on the *person* and thus reduces the chance of a defensive response. Of course, your question about the relevancy of a remark has to be sincere. If your tone of voice, facial expression, and other nonverbal clues suggest that the question is really a put-down ("What does *that* have to do with anything?"), you can expect a hostile reaction.

Promise to Deal with Good Ideas Later Another way to keep the goodwill of a member who has brought up an irrelevant idea is to suggest a way of dealing with it at the appropriate time:

> "That equipment-leasing idea sounds promising. Let's bring it up to Jeff after the meeting and see what he thinks of it."

> "A graphics package seems important to you, Lee. Why don't you look into what's available and we can decide whether the change would be worth the cost."

As with relevancy challenges, your suggestion about dealing with an idea later has to be sincere if the other person is going to accept it. One way to show your sincerity is to mention exactly when you would like to discuss the matter. This might be a specific time (after lunch), or it might be when certain conditions are met ("after you've worked up the costs"). Another way to show your sincerity is to inquire about the idea after the meeting: "How's the research going on the graphics package?"

Keeping a Positive Tone Almost everyone would agree that "getting along with people" is a vital ingredient in a successful career. In meetings, getting along can be especially tough when others don't cooperate with your efforts to keep the meeting on track—or, even worse, attack your ideas. The following suggestions can help you handle these irritating situations in a way that gets the job done and keeps potential enemies as allies.

Ask Questions and Paraphrase to Clarify Understanding Criticizing an idea—even an apparently stupid one—can result in a defensive reaction that will waste time and generate ill will. It's also important to remember that even a seemingly idiotic remark can have some merit. Given these facts, it's often wise to handle apparently bad ideas by asking for some clarification. And the most obvious way to clarify an idea is to ask questions:

"Why do you think we ought to let Marcia go?"

"Who would cover the store if you went skiing next week?"

"What makes you think we shouldn't have a Christmas party this year?"

You can also paraphrase to get more information about an apparently hostile or foolish remark:

"It sounds as if you're saying Marcia's doing a bad job."

"So you think we could cover the store if you went skiing?"

"Sounds as if you think a Christmas party would be a waste of money."

This sort of paraphrasing accomplishes two things. First, it provides a way to double-check your understanding. If your replay of the speaker's ideas isn't accurate, he or she can correct you: "I don't think Marcia's doing a bad job. I just don't think we need so many people up front." Second, even if your understanding is accurate, paraphrasing is an invitation for the other person to explain the idea in more detail: "If we could find somebody to work a double shift while I was skiing, I'd be willing to do the same thing for them later."

Enhance the Value of Members' Comments It's obvious that you should acknowledge the value of good ideas by praising or thanking the people who contribute them. Surprisingly, you can use the same method with apparently bad ideas. Even the most worthless comments often have some merit. You can take advantage of these merits by using a three-part response:[11]

Acknowledge the merits of the idea.

Explain any concerns you have.

Improve the usefulness of the idea by building on it or asking others for suggestions.

Notice how this sort of response can enhance the value of apparently worthless comments:

"I'm glad you're so concerned about the parking problem, Craig [acknowledges merit of comment]. But wouldn't requiring people to carpool generate a lot of resentment [balancing concern]? How could we encourage people to carpool voluntarily [builds on original idea]?"

"You're right, Pat. Your department could use another person [acknowledges merit of comment]. But Mr. Peters is really serious about this hiring freeze [balancing concern]. Let's try to come up with some ways we can get you more help without having to hire a new person [builds on original idea]."

CONCLUDING THE MEETING

The way a meeting ends can have a strong influence on how members feel about the group and how well they follow up on any decisions that have been made or instructions that have been given.[12]

When to Close the Meeting   There are three times when a meeting should be closed:

When the Scheduled Closing Time Has Arrived   When meetings run over their scheduled closing time, the cause is usually failure to follow the guidelines already mentioned in this chapter: off-the-track comments, digressions into personal attack and defense, and haphazard decision making. Even if the discussion has been a good one, it's often best to close on schedule to prevent members from drifting off to other commitments one by one or losing attention and becoming resentful. It's wise to press on only if the subject is important and the members seem willing to keep working.

When the Group Lacks Resources to Continue   If the group lacks the necessary person or facts to continue, adjourn until the resources are available. If you need to get cost figures for a new purchase or someone's approval for a new idea, for example, it is probably a waste of time to proceed until they have been secured. In these cases, be sure to identify who is responsible for getting the needed information, and set a new meeting date.

When the Agenda Has Been Covered   It seems obvious that a meeting should adjourn when its business is finished. Nonetheless, any veteran of meetings will testify that some discussions drag on because no one is willing to call a halt. Unless everyone is willing to socialize, it's best to use the techniques that follow to wrap up a meeting when the job is completed.

How to Conclude a Meeting   A good conclusion has three parts. In many discussions, the leader will be responsible for taking these steps. In leaderless groups or in groups with a weak leader, one or more members can take the initiative. (Table 9-4 is a checklist for concluding a meeting.)

TABLE 9-4   Checklist for Concluding a Meeting

- Concluding the Meeting
  - Does meeting run the proper length of time (versus ending prematurely or continuing after excessive length or wasted time)?
  - Is warning given shortly before conclusion to allow wrap-up of business?
  - Is summary of meeting's results and preview of future actions given?
  - Does leader acknowledge contributions of group members?
- Follow-up Activities
  - Does leader build agenda for next meeting upon results of previous one?
  - Does leader follow up on assignments of other members?
  - Do members follow through on their own assignments?

Signal When Time Is Almost Up   A warning allows the group to wrap up business and gives everyone a chance to have a final say:

> "We have about fifteen minutes before we adjourn. We still need to hear Bob's report on the Kansas City conference, so let's devote the rest of our time to that."

> "It's almost time for some of you to leave for the airport. I'd like to wrap up our meeting by putting the list of suggestions Mr. Moss has asked us to send him into its final form."

Summarize the Meeting's Accomplishments and Future Actions   For the sake of understanding, review what information has been conveyed and what decisions have been made. Just as important is reminding members of their responsibilities:

> "It looks like we won't have to meet again until the sales conference next Tuesday in San Juan. We'll follow the revised schedule that we worked up today. Chris will have copies to everyone first thing tomorrow morning. Nick will call the hotel to book the larger meeting room, and Pat will take care of having the awards made up. Let's all plan to meet over dinner at the hotel next Tuesday night."

Thank the Group   Acknowledging the group's good work is more than just good manners. This sort of reinforcement shows that you appreciate their efforts and encourages good performance in the future. Besides acknowledging the group as a whole, be sure to give credit to any members who deserve special mention:

> "We really got a lot done today. Thanks to all of you, we're back on schedule. Bruce, I really appreciate the work you did on the specifications. We never would have made it without you."

> "You were all great about coming in early this morning. The extra rehearsal will make a big difference in the presentation. Those charts are terrific, Julie.

And your suggestion about using the slide projector will make a big difference, Lou. Let's all celebrate after we get the contract."

FOLLOW UP THE MEETING

It's a mistake to assume that even a satisfying meeting is a success until you follow up to make sure that the desired results have really been obtained. A thorough follow-up involves three steps:

Build an Agenda for the Next Meeting   Most groups meet frequently, and they rarely conclude their business in one sitting. A smart leader plans the next meeting by noting which items need to be carried over from the preceding one. What unfinished business must be addressed? What progress reports must be shared? What new information should members hear?

Follow Up on Other Members   You can be sure that the promised outcomes of a meeting actually occur if you check up on other members. If the meeting provided instructions—such as how to use the new long-distance phone service—see if the people who attended are actually following the steps that were outlined. If tasks were assigned, check on whether they're being performed. You don't have to be demanding or snoopy to do this sort of checking. A friendly phone call or personal remark can do the trick: "Is the new phone system working for you?" "How's it going on those sales figures?" "Did you manage to get hold of Williams yet?"

Take Care of Your Own Assignments   Most homework that arises out of meetings needs continued attention. If you wait until the last minute before tackling it, the results are likely to be sloppy and embarrassing.

SUMMARY

Meetings are a common event in most organizations. They occupy large amounts of time and cost the business a great deal of money. Some meetings are aimed at sharing information; others are of a problem-solving nature; still others serve a ritual function that confers status on members, builds cohesiveness, and provides an informal channel of communication.

Meetings should be held only when the job at hand is beyond the capacity of one person to handle, requires a division of labor, and has more than one right answer. If misunderstandings or resistance to a decision are likely, it is also wise to hold a meeting to overcome these hazards. Well in advance of each meeting, members should receive an agenda that announces the time, length, and location of the session; those who will attend; background information on the topic; goals for the meeting; and any advance work members need to do.

Once the meeting is called to order, the chairperson should announce the goals of the session, review necessary background information, show how members can help, preview how the session will proceed, and identify any time constraints. The participation of quiet members can be encouraged by a variety of questioning techniques. When discussions wander off track, the chairperson and other members can regain focus by referring to time pressures, summarizing and redirecting the remarks of the members who have digressed, using relevancy challenges, and promising to deal with tangential issues after the meeting. The tone of meetings can be kept positive if members make an attempt to understand one another by asking questions and paraphrasing and if they enhance the value of one another's comments.

The meeting should be closed when its scheduled time is completed, when the group lacks resources to continue, or when the agenda has been completed—whichever comes first. The chairperson should give the group warning that time is almost up and then summarize the meeting's accomplishments and future actions. Group members should also be thanked for their contributions. The chairperson's activities after the meeting has concluded include building an agenda for the next session, following up on other members, and honoring his or her own commitments.

ACTIVITIES

1. Use the information in this chapter to decide which of these tasks would best be handled by a problem-solving group and which should be handled by one or more individuals working separately. Be prepared to explain the reasons for each choice.

    a. Developing procedures for interviewing prospective employees
    b. Tabulating responses to a customer survey
    c. Investigating several brands of office machines for possible purchase
    d. Choosing the most desirable employee health insurance program
    e. Organizing the company picnic
    f. Researching the existence and cost of training programs for improving communication among staff members

2. Your institution is considering restructuring its general education requirements. You have been selected by the administration to chair a committee to present the students' point of view. Decide whom to include on the committee, and draft an agenda for the group's first meeting.

3. Use the skills introduced in this chapter to describe how you would respond to the following comments in a meeting:

    a. "There's no way people will work Sundays without being paid double overtime."
    b. "No consultant is going to tell me how to be a better manager!"
    c. "I don't think this brainstorming is worth the time. Most of the ideas we come up with are crazy."
    d. "Talking about interest rates reminds me of a time in '79 when this story about Carter was going around. . . ."
    e. "Sorry, but I don't have any ideas about how to cut costs."

Communicator Profile

Brian O'Brien, Account Supervisor
Bloom FCA!
New York, New York

I recommend that someone starting out in the business world find a mentor and observe him or her conducting a meeting.

I am an account supervisor at Bloom FCA!, a New York advertising agency. I act as the liaison between the agency and the client, overseeing the client's business for the agency and working with them to develop marketing strategy. I represent the agency and the client's views to the agency's creative, media, and research teams. About 50 to 75 percent of my time is spent in meetings. A typical meeting might include the client's director of marketing, the client's brand manager, the agency's creative group, myself, and an account executive. A typical purpose for a meeting may be to evaluate how the desired message can best be communicated to the target audience.

Depending on the client, media budgets might range anywhere from $5–50 million. One of the accounts I'm working on now is St. Pauli Girl beer, an imported German beer; the other is a Japanese beer, Suntory. Determining the type of media (TV, radio, or magazines) we should use to advertise St. Pauli Girl is another good example of a reason for a meeting.

Since our industry is deadline driven, a good meeting is one in which something is definitively accomplished, for example, reaching agreement on the music to be used in a television spot or selecting the television programs on which the spot will appear. The account executive keeps a checklist of the issues to be discussed at the meeting and is responsible for writing up the "conference report," or minutes, of the meeting. The "conference report" is a written record of the decisions reached at the meeting and outlines the next steps to be taken for the project.

I recommend that someone starting out in the business world find a mentor and observe him or her conducting a meeting. A masterful leader speaks slowly and clearly, is well organized, hands out an agenda at the beginning of the meeting. The leader goes over the topics to be discussed first, and, at the end of the meeting, reviews the key agreements reached. He or she will be very good at keeping the discussion on track and the energy level of the meeting high.

Another tip to holding effective meetings: make sure everyone attending the meeting knows what the meeting is about beforehand. That sounds basic, but I can't stress how important it is. If possible, write a memo to "set the stage" for what will be discussed.

If you are *not* the one leading the meeting, it's very important to observe protocol; in a good meeting, everyone allows the others to present their point-of-view and no one jumps down anyone's throat. I don't agree with intimidation, though I have seen it used. I believe you should hear everyone out.

When someone dominates a meeting, you may have to speak up. If you strongly disagree with a point being presented, you should let the speaker know. You may not get the chance to speak your piece again. Recently, I disagreed with my boss in a meeting, and he later thanked me for speaking my mind.

By the same token, sometimes you have to admit when you're wrong. Have the integrity to recognize it when someone else has a better point than you do, but don't be intimidated by a person's age, sex, or title. Most good bosses hire people because they want their input. Make sure you give them yours.

As for someone who isn't participating in the discussion, you have to confront them directly and draw them out. There's an old saying, "You've got to dig a lot of coal to get to the diamond." In a meeting, the "gem of an idea" that you're looking for may be in the head of one of the shy parties, so be sure to get everyone's opinion on the subject.

In a meeting it is possible to disagree without being disagreeable. You must deal with facts, and it's very important not to get emotionally involved. If you can stay objective, and backup everything you say with a logical argument based on *facts*, you will be more valuable to the meeting.

PART IV

MAKING EFFECTIVE PRESENTATIONS

CHAPTER **10**

After reading this chapter, you should understand:

- The types of presentations common in business and professional settings
- The advantages of oral presentations over written documents
- The criteria for a clear, specific purpose statement
- The nature of a thesis statement
- The importance of analyzing a speaking situation in order to present material in a way that is suitable for yourself as speaker, for the audience, and for the occasion

You should be able to:

- List the types of presentations you are likely to give in your career
- Correctly define a specific purpose for a presentation you might deliver
- Conduct an analysis of the speaking situation for a specific presentation and describe how relevant situational factors should influence the approach of a presentation

DEVELOPING THE PRESENTATION

Whatever your field, whatever your job, you will need to give speeches or presentations. Sales representatives and account executives deliver presentations to potential customers. Brand managers propose ideas to management and explain new product lines to the sales force. Department heads and supervisors brief superiors on recent developments and their subordinates on new company policies. Computer specialists explain new systems and software to the people who will use them. Accountants give financial reports to their superiors and explain paperwork requirements to everyone else. Even engineers and research scientists report on their methods, progress, and results. Presentations are so pervasive that one expert estimates that every year speakers address audiences 5 million times.[1] Table 10-1 offers a sample of the kinds of presentations that most people deliver sooner or later in their careers.

While some business and professional presentations are formal, full-dress performances before large audiences, most are comparatively informal talks to a few people or even a single person. If you drop into your boss's office and say "Do you have a few minutes? I have some information that may help us cut down our travel expenses," you're arranging a presentation. You're also delivering a presentation when you teach the office staff how to use the new phone system, explain the structure of your department to a new employee, or explain to management why you need a larger budget.

Most people in business give planned presentations to small groups or even one person. Roger Enrico, now the chief executive officer of Pepsi-Cola, described a typical situation that arose when he was beginning his career:

> I started my Pepsico career at Frito-Lay as an associate brand manager on—get this—an onion-flavored snack called Funyons. My boss ran a bigger brand called Cheetos. Somewhere in the stratosphere was the guy in charge of Fritos.

TABLE 10-1   Common Types of Presentational Speaking

TYPE OF PRESENTATION	EXAMPLE
Briefing and informational announcements	New health-insurance procedure
Orientation sessions	New employee orientation
Training programs	How to operate new computer software
Research and technical reports	Description of market-research survey
Progress reports	Status report on monthly sales
Civic and social presentations	Speech to local service club
Convention and conference presentations	Report on company's technological breakthroughs
Television and radio interviews	Describing company's position on industrial accident or injury
Introductions	Introducing new employee to other workers
Sales presentations	Presenting product to potential customer
Project and policy proposals	Proposing new travel policy to management
Ceremonial occasions	Speaking at retirement celebration for longtime employee

But aside from the name, there were serious things wrong with Funyons. The product had survived lengthy test marketing. Frito-Lay had rolled it out nationally. Now, six months had passed. For reasons unknown, sales were rapidly heading south. . . .

So I went around to all the people responsible for every element of all the business. . . . And I found a correlation: Funyuns' sales turned down at about the same time that Frito-Lay introduced a new product, this one a potato snack. . . . I took this news to my boss. It seemed noteworthy to him, as well, so he passed me on to the VP of marketing. He brought the VP of sales in on it, and soon enough, people were telling me to get ready to present my findings to Harold Lilly, president of Frito-Lay.[2]

As your career progresses, presentational speaking skills become even more important. As one automobile executive explained:

As an executive rose in management, he had to rely less on his technical training and more on his ability to sell his ideas and programs to the next level of management. When I was just an engineer somewhere down the line working on a technical problem, everything affecting me was in my grasp. All I had to do was solve this particular problem, and I was doing my job. But now, as head of advanced engineering, I have to anticipate and predict product trends and then sell my programs for capitalizing on those trends.[3]

Most people who work in organizations eventually find that their effectiveness and success depend on their ability to organize their ideas and present them effectively. Sometimes a written memo or report will do the job, but there are often important reasons for presenting your ideas in person. For example, if people don't understand a point in a proposal, they may put it aside for weeks or simply veto it. Delivering your message in person provides immediate feedback that helps you clarify points and answer questions. Oral presentations are often more persuasive as well. A speaker's knowledge, enthusiasm, and apparent confidence can influence people to accept or reject an idea in a way that a written document cannot.

In practice, you'll rarely get approval for an important idea without explaining it in person. As one executive put it:

The people who have the power and responsibility to say *yes* or *no* want a chance to consider and question the proposal in the flesh. Documents merely set up a meeting and record what the meeting decided. Anyone serious about an idea welcomes the chance to present it himself—in person. We wisely discount proposals whose authors are unwilling to be present at the launching.[4]

A product manager at a major corporation reiterates the importance of face-to-face presentations when she explains how she approaches presenting new products to the sales force:

We provide all the information the sales force needs in writing, but information alone doesn't get salespeople *excited* in the product or feel confident about its potential. And if they aren't excited and confident about the product, they'll be less effective in selling it. So when I present a new product line at a sales meeting, I'm doing more than providing information; I'm letting the sales force know I, personally, stand behind the product. And when we're face to face, my own enthusiasm about the care and expertise we've put into development and manufacturing usually comes through in a way it can't in the printed literature.

The importance of face-to-face presentations is also apparent in one of the most common entry-level jobs in business: sales. You can see from the amount of "junk mail" you receive that businesses spend vast amounts on printed advertising. Yet most people who deal with direct-mail marketing agree that only about 3 percent of it results in sales, while 10 to 25 percent of face-to-face sales calls in many industries result in a sale. As you may have found in your own experience with salespeople, it's harder to say no in person.

Many people also give work-related speeches to audiences outside their organizations. Realizing that effective speakers carry their message to the public in ways that print and electronic media can't match, companies send representatives into the community to deliver speeches in a wide variety of settings.[5] Western Electric Company has over 100 speakers who make some 2,000 presentations each year. Standard Oil has between 50 and 100 representatives delivering some 500 speeches annually. Dow Chemical employees face 1,000 audiences each year, and 300 Georgia Pacific speakers made approximately 1,500 appearances in one twelve-month period. Don't get the idea that all these speakers are smooth-talking public relations experts. Over 90 percent of the 2,200 talks General Motors employees give each year are delivered by middle managers. Phillips Petroleum Company has sponsored what may be the most impressive speaking program in sheer numbers. In one year alone, 2,000 of its employees made between 8,000 and 10,000 presentations. If speaking publicly is this important to business, it's clearly worth your while to develop your own speaking skills.

Even people who seem to work in fairly solitary jobs give speeches to clubs, professional organizations, and community groups. The botany researchers at a national plant nursery regularly give speeches to garden clubs, textbook and journal editors speak to college and professional seminars about the requirements of writing for publication, and computer programmers conduct classes for small-business owners and individuals who buy computers.

Different kinds of presentations make different demands on the speaker. For example, a sales presentation to one customer may often seem more like a conversation because the customer may interrupt with questions, while a speaker addressing an audience of several hundred people may delay questions until the end. In spite of the differences, all presentations make many of the same demands on the speaker. The planning, structure, supports, and strategy of each of them are very important, and a good speaker follows approximately the same steps in planning and developing almost any presentation. The material we will discuss in the next five chapters applies to almost any presentation you will give in your career or profession.

ESTABLISHING A PURPOSE

Your first step in planning any presentation should be to define your purpose. A statement of purpose describes what you want to accomplish. Then, after you have spoken, the same statement helps you to know whether you have achieved your goal. There are two kinds of purpose to consider: general and specific.

GENERAL PURPOSE

As the name implies, a general purpose is a broad indication of what you're trying to accomplish. There are three types of general purposes.

To Inform   The goal of an informative presentation is either to expand your listeners' knowledge or to help them acquire a specific skill. Teaching a group of product managers about new developments in technology, training a new sales representative, or giving a progress report on regional sales to a senior sales manager are all typical examples of informative talks.

To Persuade   Persuasion focuses on trying to change what an audience thinks or does. Selling is the most obvious example, but there are others as well. A union organizer will try to persuade a group of employees to vote for a union, while a management representative might try to persuade them not to. An accountant might try to convince management to adopt a different procedure for reporting expenditures. A marketing manager might try to convince sales representatives to be more enthusiastic about a product that has not sold well.

To Entertain   Sometimes a speaker's goal is to help the audience have a good time. The welcoming speaker at a convention might concentrate on getting the participants to relax and look forward to the coming events. After-dinner speakers at company gatherings or awards dinners usually consider themselves successful if their remarks leave the group in a jovial mood.

SPECIFIC PURPOSE

If you think of a speech as a journey, your specific purpose is your destination. Stating the specific purpose tells you what you will have accomplished when you have "arrived." A good specific-purpose statement usually answers three questions:

Whom do I want to influence?

What do I want them to do?

How, when, and *where* do I want them to do it?

Giving a presentation without recognizing, focusing on, and remembering your objective is the equivalent of dumping the contents of your briefcase all over your boss's desk. You don't speak to fill time by reeling off fact after unorganized fact, nor to show beautiful pictures that take the breath away, nor to impress the audience with your wit and skill as a dramatic speaker. You don't give speeches to win speech-making awards. You are there to make the best of an opportunity, just as you do in every other aspect of your business activities.

Sandy Linver, *Speak and Get Results*

Your purpose statement should combine the answers to these questions into a single statement: "I want (who) to (do what) (how, when, where). Here are some examples of good purpose statements:

"I want all the salespeople to complete and submit form 2210 every time they grant a refund or adjustment."

"I want at least five people in the audience to ask me for my business card after my talk and at least one person to schedule an appointment with me to discuss my company's services."

"I want the graduates we've identified at our interviews to accept any jobs we offer them this spring."

"I want the boss to tell the committee that he's in favor of my proposal when they discuss it after my presentation."

"I want several people from the audience to tell me enthusiastically that they found my talk about money market funds interesting and useful."

Like these examples, your purpose statements should do three things: describe the reaction you are seeking, be as specific as possible, and make your goal realistic.

Describe the Reaction You Are Seeking   Your purpose statement should be worded in terms of the reaction you want from your audience. You can appreciate the importance of specifying the desired results when you consider a statement that doesn't meet this criterion: "I want to show each person in this office how to operate the new Dictaphone system correctly."

What's wrong with this statement? Most important, it says nothing about the desired audience response. With a purpose such as this, you could give a detailed explanation of the whole Dictaphone system without knowing whether anyone learned a thing! Notice the improvement in this statement: "I want everyone in this group to show me they can operate the Dictaphone correctly after my talk." With this goal, you can get an idea of how well you've done after delivering your presentation.

Be As Specific As Possible   A good purpose statement identifies the who, what, how, when, and where of your goal as precisely as possible. For instance, your target audience—the who—may not include every listener in the audience. Take one of the statements we mentioned earlier: "I want the boss to tell the committee that he's in favor of my proposal when they discuss it after my presentation." This statement correctly recognizes the boss as the key decision maker. If you've convinced him, your proposal is as good as approved; if not, the support of less influential committee members may not help you. Once you identify your target audience, you can focus your energy on the people who truly count.

The best purpose statements describe their goals in *measurable terms.* Consider these examples:

VAGUE	SPECIFIC
"I want to collect some donations in this meeting."	"I want to collect at least fifteen dollars from each person in this meeting."
"I want to get my manager's support for my idea."	"I want my manager to give me one day per week and the help of a secretary to develop my idea."

Knowing exactly what you want to accomplish dramatically increases the chances that you will reach your goal. Suppose you need to convince a group of subordinates to stay within their expense budgets. You already know that the following statement is no good: "I want to talk about the importance of our new budget limitations." (If you're not sure why, take another look at the preceding section on describing results.) A more result-oriented goal would be "I want this group to stay within its budget." A more result-oriented goal would be "I want this group to stay within its budget." But even this purpose statement has problems. Who are you going to encourage: people who are already holding the line on expenses or those who look like they might overspend? How many people do you hope to persuade? How will you appeal to them? (Each group might require a different approach.) When do you want them to do it: beginning immediately or when they get around to it? That may not be until after the fiscal year is over—too late to save this year's profits in your department. A more specific purpose statement can take care of questions such as these: "I want to convince the four people who had spent more than half their year's budgets by May 1 that the department's solvency depends on their cutting expenses and have them show me a revised plan by the end of the week that demonstrates how they intend to trim costs for the rest of the year." This statement gives you several ideas about how to plan your presentation. Imagine how much more difficult your task would be if you had settled for the first vague purpose statement.

Make Your Goal Realistic   Presentational speaking is like most other aspects of life: you usually don't get everything you want. The available time, characteristics of your audience, and the subject itself can limit what you can realistically hope to accomplish. Thus, your purpose statement should be attainable. For example, a sales representative selling expensive office equipment shouldn't expect to make a sale the first time she calls on a purchasing officer; instead, her purpose might be simply to get an appointment to make a presentation. Similarly, a department head training a group of new employees shouldn't expect to teach them the operations of the whole department in the first half hour (unless the operations are very simple); at the outset, he might select a few basic principles that he could expect them to learn and use for the first few days or weeks.

DEVELOPING THE THESIS

The thesis statement—sometimes called the central idea or key idea—is a single sentence that summarizes your message (see Table 10-2). Once you have a thesis, every other part of your talk should support it. The thesis gives your audience a clear idea of what you are trying to tell them:

> "We're behind schedule for reasons beyond our control, but we can catch up and finish the job on time."

> "Our new just-in-time order system helps us make sure that our supplies are not dated or shelf-worn, but we must monitor the inventory daily."

Presentations without a clear thesis leave the audience asking, "What's this person getting at?" And while listeners are trying to figure out the answer, they'll be missing much of what you're saying.

The thesis is so important that you will repeat it several times during your presentation: at least once in the introduction, probably several times during the body, and again in the conclusion.

Beginning speakers often confuse the thesis of a presentation with its purpose. Whereas a purpose statement is a note to *yourself* outlining what you hope to accomplish, a thesis statement tells your *audience* your main idea. Sometimes the two can be virtually identical. For example, a representative of an organization called Women in Business addressing a professional conference of

TABLE 10-2 *Methods for Identifying Your Thesis*

1. Imagine that you met a member of your audience at the elevator and had only a few seconds to explain your idea before the doors closed.	3. Ask yourself, "If my listeners heard only a small portion of my remarks, what is the minimum they should have learned?"
2. Imagine that you had to send a one- or two-sentence telegram that communicated your main ideas.	4. Suppose that a friend asked one of your listeners what you were driving at in your presentation. What would you want the audience member to say?

personnel officers might have the following purpose statement: "I want my listeners to understand that sexual harassment is a big problem for many working women." Her thesis would be "Sexual harassment is a big problem for many working women."

There are other cases, however, where purpose and thesis differ. A sales representative might approach a customer with this purpose: "I want Krakos Grocery to order Sun Valley bread." But his thesis will be "Mr. Krakos, Sun Valley bread is so popular that switching to it will increase your bread sales." This last example shows the difference between purpose and thesis: if the listeners accept the speaker's thesis, they'll behave in a way that accomplishes the speaker's purpose.

There are some cases in which purpose and thesis differ radically. For example, a representative of a microcomputer company, asked to address a group of local merchants about personal computer systems, might have this thesis: "Recent advances have changed my field dramatically in the past few years." Her purpose could be "I want to get at least five new customers as a result of this speech."

It may seem unethical to avoid mentioning one's purpose to an audience, but sometimes the omission is a matter of common sense and not deception. Mr. Krakos already knows the Sun Valley representative wants to sell him bread, but he's most interested in hearing *why* he should change suppliers. Similarly, an after-dinner speaker at a local service club might have the purpose of getting the audience to relax, but sharing that goal would probably seem out of place. There are other times, however, when hiding your purpose would clearly be unethical. A speaker who began his presentation by saying "I don't want to sell you anything; I just want to show you some aspects of home safety that every homeowner should know" and then went on to make a hard-sell pitch for his company's home fire alarms would clearly be stepping out of bounds. It usually isn't necessary to state your purpose as long as you are willing to share it with your audience, if asked. It's very rare, however, not to state the thesis at the beginning of a presentation.

ANALYZING THE SITUATION

A purpose statement describes the end you want to achieve, but it doesn't describe how you can reach your goal. The means is the presentation itself—the ideas you use and the way you express them.

Before you plan even one sentence of the presentation itself, you have to think about the situation in which you'll speak. A presentation that might fascinate you could bore or irritate the audience. You can make sure that your approach is on target by considering three factors: yourself as the speaker, the audience, and the occasion. Figure 10-1 shows how each of these factors narrows and focuses all the ways you could present a topic into the approach that best suits a particular situation.

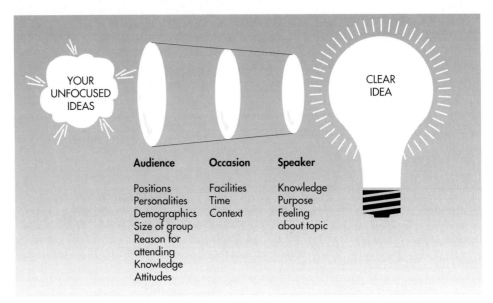

Figure 10-1 Analyzing the speaking situation. (Adapted from George Rodman, *Public Speaking*, 3rd ed. New York: Holt, Rinehart and Winston, 1986.)

ANALYZING THE AUDIENCE

The saying "Different strokes for different folks" is never more true than when delivering a presentation. Having good ideas isn't enough. You have to present those ideas in a way that your listeners will understand and appreciate. A number of factors will shape the way you adapt your material to a particular audience.

You should ask yourself a number of questions about your audience.

What Are Their Positions? Begin by considering the job titles of the members of your audience. If audience members are specialists—in engineering, finance, or marketing, for example—they'll probably be interested in those aspects of your talk. On the other hand, an audience of nonexperts or generalists would probably be bored by a detailed talk on a subject they don't understand. Surprisingly, most managers fall into this category. Even an executive who came up through the ranks as an engineer takes a different perspective upon becoming responsible for an entire job. The details that might once have been fascinating are now less important—perhaps still interesting, but not suitable for an overall view of a project. "Just give me a quick description, a schedule, and the dollar figures" is a common attitude.

What Are Their Personal Preferences? The personal idiosyncrasies of your listeners are just as important as their job titles. Some people insist on a formal presentation, while others are much more casual. Some audiences appreciate humor, while others are straitlaced. Some people hate to waste time on casual conversation and digressions, while others are willing to work at a more leisurely pace. Knowing these preferences can make the difference between success and failure in a presentation. One business consultant described how attitudes can vary from one set of listeners to another:

> We found . . . that in the same corporation engineers giving reports to different department heads were required to go about it in a totally different manner. One department head wanted every detail covered in the report. He wanted analyses of why the report was being done, complete background on the subject under discussion, and a review of the literature, and he expected the report to run twenty or thirty written pages. In addition, he wanted an oral presentation that covered almost every detail of the report. The man who ran the department right down the hall wanted just the opposite. He wanted short, comprehensive reports discussing only the elements that were new. He said he already knew what was going on in his department. He didn't want an analysis of the situation, and he didn't want any young engineer wasting his time. The reports that got an A in one department got an F in another and vice versa. Therefore, the first rule for anyone giving a report is to ask those who requested the report what form they would like it to take.[6]

One way to discover the attitudes of your audience—and to gain their approval of your idea—is to meet with them before your presentation. With this sort of preparation, you can make whatever adjustments are necessary to win over the key decision makers before you begin your formal presentation. A communication expert describes the value of this kind of advance work.

> At one of the largest publicly-owned utilities in the United States, senior officers of both Human Resources and Management Information Systems had prepared new program proposals for car pooling and a pilot electronic mail program. The research and development stages for each of these proposals had taken between four and six months. After extensive presentations, covering timeliness, costs both direct and indirect, and benefits to department heads and customers, the meeting participants were called upon for comment.
>
> Nearly everyone present at the meeting—between eight and ten other department heads—had suggestions for improvements and modifications. Why? Because they had not been given an opportunity to study the proposals in advance. Consequently, the discussion on these proposals alone took two or three times the allotted time for the entire meeting. So many changes were suggested by the other participants that the makers of the original proposals had to spend months revising them.
>
> . . . Obviously, if the chairman of the meeting (the chief executive officer) had been consulted before this meeting to help "bless" the projects, and other department heads had been briefed prior to the presentation to help buy them in, better results in a shorter period of time would have been achieved. My friend can attest to the effectiveness of this method because it's what he did before his own later presentation. The result was so fast that he had to hold himself back from suggesting that his proposal be further discussed before final acceptance.

Milo Frank, *How to Have a Successful Meeting in Half the Time*

What Demographic Characteristics Are Significant?   A number of measurable characteristics of your listeners might suggest ways to develop your remarks. One such characteristic is *sex*. What is the distribution of men and women? Even in this age of relative enlightenment, some topics must be approached differently, depending on your audience's sex. For instance, if you were trying to promote an equal opportunity program in your company, you might have to prove to male management that there was discrimination against women; the women in the company would probably already be aware of it.

A second demographic characteristic is *age*. A life insurance salesperson might emphasize retirement benefits to older customers and support for dependent children to younger ones with families. A speaker promoting a company health plan would discuss different activities with listeners in their twenties and thirties than she would with employees who were nearing retirement.

Cultural background is often an important audience factor. You would use a different approach with blue-collar workers than you would with a group of white-collar professionals. Likewise, the ethnic mix of a group might affect your remarks. According to one recent article, for instance, many companies unintentionally alienate Hispanic employees and customers by forbidding employees to speak any language but English.

Another demographic factor is the *economic status* of your audience. This factor is especially important in sales, where financial resources "qualify" potential customers as prospects for a product or service as well as suggest what features are likely to interest them. In real estate, for example, well-to-do customers would certainly be interested in different properties than less affluent ones. They might also be more concerned about the tax consequences of a sale and less concerned with monthly payments than with the interest rate at which the mortgage is written.

Not every variable is important in planning every speech. For instance, an engineer speaking about recent advances in the field should consider his audience's level of knowledge (about engineering and those advances) and occupations (that is, what those advances have to do with her listeners' work), but matters such as sex, age, and economic status probably wouldn't be important. On the other hand, a representative from Planned Parenthood speaking to a community organization would have to consider sex, age, and economic status as well as listeners' religious backgrounds and their attitudes toward the medical profession. The first step to good audience analysis is to recognize which dimensions of your listeners' background are important and to profile those dimensions accurately.

What Size Is the Group?   The number of listeners will govern some very basic speaking plans. How many copies of a handout should you prepare? How large must your visuals be to be seen by everyone? How much time should you plan for a question-and-answer session? With a large audience, you usually need to take a wider range of audience concerns into account; your delivery and choice of language will tend to be more formal; and your listeners are less likely to interrupt with questions or comments. A progress report on your current assignment would look ridiculous if you delivered it from behind a podium to four or five people.

You would look just as foolish speaking to a hundred listeners while reclining in a chair.

Why Is the Audience There?   Just like speakers, audiences have reasons for attending a presentation. Sometimes these reasons are straightforward; for example, a sales force will attend a sales meeting to learn about the company's new products and how to sell them and so increase their commissions. Not all audience purposes are as clear, though. If the sales meeting is being held in Miami or Hawaii, some attendees could be most interested in the idea of an expense-paid vacation. Many attendees might assume that all the information presented at the meeting will also be provided in written form and will not listen carefully to your presentation.

This doesn't mean that you should give up when you face an audience with ulterior motives. Rather, it means you need to find creative ways to achieve both their goal and yours. If the computer service representatives you're addressing are hostile to the new computer system, they may attend the training sessions only because they're required to do so. You will need to convince them that the system has advantages for them, such as saving them time and making their jobs easier, before they'll listen to your instructions on how to operate the system. If you don't do this, they may eventually make errors and blame them on the system.

Sometimes you can develop an approach that satisfies all your listeners. Like those teachers who reach the greatest number of students, you can learn to be entertaining and informative at the same time. But you can't please everyone all the time. If some of your listeners want to hear about the new product line and some want to hear, in detail, why last year's line failed, you will probably have to make a choice. At such times, your decision should be based on who you are most concerned about reaching.

What Does the Audience Know?   A group of experts doesn't need the background information that other audiences would require. In fact, these people would probably be bored and offended by your basic explanation. Likewise, people who are familiar with a project don't need to be brought up to date—

[Public speaking] . . . requires a lot of preparation. There's just no way around it— you have to do your homework. A speaker may be very well informed, but if he hasn't thought out exactly what he wants to say *today*, *to this audience*, he has no business taking up other people's valuable time.

It's important to be able to talk to people in their own language. If you do it well, they'll say "God, he said exactly what I was thinking." And when they begin to respect you, they'll follow you to the death. The *reason* they're following you is not because you're providing some mysterious leadership. It's because you're following them.

Lee Iacocca with William Novak, *Iacocca: An Autobiography*

---

unless they have missed some late-breaking developments. It's also important to ask yourself what your listeners do *not* know: uninformed people or nonexperts will be mystified (as well as bored and resentful) unless you give them background information.

Also ask yourself what misconceptions your listeners might have about the topic you're discussing. A potential customer might think that his current insurance coverage is perfectly adequate. Your boss may think that the obsolete equipment that's slowing your productivity is perfectly fine. When misconceptions like these exist, be sure to clear them up early in your presentation—or even beforehand, if possible.

What Are the Listeners' Attitudes?   You need to consider two sets of attitudes when planning your presentation. The first is your audience's attitude toward *you as the speaker.* If they feel hostile or indifferent ("Charlie is such a bore"), your approach won't be the same as if they are excited to hear from you ("I'm glad he says he's going to simplify the paperwork; last year, he did a great job of speeding up the process for getting repairs done"). You'll read more about how to deal with hostile audiences in Chapter 15.

In addition to their attitudes about you, the audience's feelings about *your subject* should influence your approach. Do your employees think the benefits of the new pension plan are too far in the future to be important? Does the sales force think the new product line is exciting or just the same old line in a new package? Do the workers think the new vice-president is a genius or just another figurehead? Attitudes such as these should govern your approach.

ANALYZING YOURSELF AS THE SPEAKER

No two presentations are alike. While you can learn to speak better by listening to other speakers, a good presentation is rather like a good hairstyle or sense of humor: what suits someone else might not work for you. One of the biggest mistakes you can make is to try to be a carbon copy of some other effective speaker. When developing your presentation, be sure to consider several factors.

Your Purpose   The very first question to ask yourself is why you are speaking. Are you especially interested in reaching one person or one subgroup in the audience? What do you want your key listeners to think or do after hearing you? How will you know when you've succeeded?

Your Knowledge   It's best to speak on a subject about which you have considerable knowledge. This is usually the case, since you generally speak on a subject precisely because you *are* an authority. Regardless of how well you know your subject, you may need to do some research—on the last three years' sales figures, the number of companies that have used the flexible-hours program you're proposing, the actual maintenance costs of the new equipment your company is buying, and so on. As you will read in Chapter 13, most presentations can be strengthened by supporting statistics, examples, quotations, and other material that you can find only with hard work. If you do need to gain more information, don't fool yourself into a false sense of security by thinking you know enough. It's better to overprepare now than to look like a fool later.

Your Feelings About the Topic   An old sales axiom says, "You can't sell a product you don't believe in." Research shows that sincerity is one of the greatest assets a speaker can have.[7] When you are excited about a topic, your delivery improves: your voice becomes more expressive, your movements are more natural, and your face reflects your enthusiasm. On the other hand, if you don't care much about your topic—whether it's a report on your department's sales, a proposal for a new program, a product you're selling, or a new method you're explaining—the audience will know it and think, "If the speaker doesn't believe in it, why should I?" A good test for your enthusiasm and sincerity is to ask yourself if you really care whether your audience understands or believes what you have to say. If you feel indifferent or only mildly enthusiastic, it's best to search for a new idea for your proposal or a new approach to your subject.

ANALYZING THE OCCASION

Even a complete understanding of your audience won't give you everything you need to plan an effective presentation. You also need to adapt your remarks to fit the circumstances of your presentation. Several factors contribute to the occasion.

Facilities   Will you be speaking in a large or small room? Will there be enough seating for all the listeners? Will the place be brightly or dimly lit? Will it be well ventilated or stuffy? Are chairs movable or fixed to the floor? Will there be distracting background noises?

Questions like these are critical, and failure to anticipate facility problems can trip you up. For example, the absence of an easel to hold your charts can turn your well-rehearsed presentation into a fiasco. Lack of a convenient electrical outlet can replace your slide show with an embarrassing blackout. Even the placement of doorways can make a difference. Most experienced speakers won't settle for others' assurances about facilities; they check out the room in advance and come prepared for every possible disaster.

Time   There are two considerations here. The first is the time you'll be speaking. A straightforward, factual speech that would work well with an alert, rested audience at 10:00 A.M. might need to be more entertaining or emphatic to hold everyone's attention just before quitting time. Besides the hour of the day, you also need to consider the length of time you have to speak. If you only have five minutes to give a progress report to management, for example, you can only outline the major aspects of your most recent product; whereas if you have half an hour, you might be expected to go into more detail and discuss some of the alternatives you have considered along the way. Sometimes the length of your talk won't be explicitly dictated; but that doesn't mean you should talk as long as you like. Usually, factors in the situation suggest how long it's wise for you to speak. Notice, for example, how well speaker Hugh Marsh adapted his remarks to the after-dinner setting of his summary business report to a group of association members:

> Good evening, ladies and gentlemen. Whenever I get on a podium this late, after a long day at the office, I remind myself of several immutable laws.
>
> First. There is Marsh's *First* Law of Oratory—on any platform, any speech will grow in length to fill the time available for its delivery. Well, take heart. I only have fifteen minutes.
>
> Then there is Marsh's *Second* Law of Oratory—the farthest distance between two points is a speech. Or, as we used to say in Texas, speeches too often are like a Longhorn steer—a point here and a point there and a lot of bull in between. Well, again, take heart. I will try to keep my two points close together.
>
> Another law I remind myself of is Marsh's *Third* Law of Oratory—no speech ever sounds as good at 7:00 P.M. as it did at noon.
>
> And, finally, there is Marsh's First Law of Meeting Attendance—everybody's gotta be someplace.
>
> As long as we're here, let's be friends. I'll be brief. You be attentive. I'll make my few points and get off so we can get back to the fun part of the meeting—socializing.[8]

Context   Events surrounding your presentation also influence what you'll say or how you say it. For example, if others are speaking as part of your program, you need to take them into account. ("I had originally planned to discuss the technical aspects of our new express delivery system, but I think Carol has covered them pretty thoroughly. Let me just bring your attention to two things.") Preceding speakers may have left your audience feeling bored or stimulated, receptive or angry, thoughtful or jovial. Since that state of affairs will affect how the audience receives your presentation, you should try to adjust to it.

Current events could also affect what you say or how you say it. For example, if you're presenting your new budget proposal just after the company has suffered a major financial loss, you should be prepared to show how your budget will cut costs. As you'll read in Chapter 11, one effective way to begin a speech is to talk about a recent occurrence: beginning your talk to the sales force by mentioning Steve's major new account, for instance, is a good way to get attention and motivate your audience.

SUMMARY

At one time or another, almost everyone makes on-the-job presentations. Some are formal and others informal, and some are directed at audiences within the firm, while others are aimed at external audiences. Even if presentations are not as frequent as other types of communication, they are important: the audience usually includes influential people, and the stakes are frequently high. In addition, the reputation you acquire as a good or bad speaker can affect the success of your career.

Presentations are often superior to written messages in several respects: presentations generate a quick response, allow the sender to adapt the message to the interests of an audience, and frequently are a more effective means of persuasion.

The first step in planning a presentation is to define your purpose. Is your general goal to inform or persuade? Specifically, you should define whom you want to reach, what you want them to do, how you want them to do it, and when and where it should be done. Your purpose statement should be worded in terms of the desired audience reaction, and it should be specific and attainable.

A second fundamental step in planning a presentation is to define your thesis, phrased as a single-sentence statement of your message. Your purpose and thesis should be based on an analysis of the speaking situation. This analysis consists of three parts. First, analyze yourself as a speaker. Consider your purpose for speaking, your knowledge of the subject, and the sincerity you can bring to the topic. Second, analyze the audience: who the listeners are, why they are listening to you, what they know, and what their attitudes are about you and your topic. Finally, analyze the speaking occasion. Consider the facilities in which you will be speaking, the time of day and length of time you have to speak, and the context in which your remarks will occur.

ACTIVITIES

1. What kinds of presentations are you most likely to give in your chosen career?

   You can understand the importance of presentational speaking by visualizing two or three of the situations you just listed. First imagine the consequences of your doing well in these situations; then picture yourself doing poorly. How would these different performances affect your career or your self-esteem?

2. Write a specific purpose and thesis statement for each of the following situations:

   a. A farewell speech honoring a not-too-popular manager at his retirement dinner
   b. A training session introducing a new telephone intercom system
   c. A kickoff speech for the United Way payroll deduction campaign
   d. An appeal to the boss for a new person in your department

   e. A proposal to your department head for changing course requirements for the major
   f. A banker's speech to an economics class on "The Changing Banking Industry"
   g. A request to your landlord for new carpeting

3. Imagine that you have been asked to give a fifteen-minute description of your department's functions. How would your purpose and approach differ if the speech were aimed at:

   a. A group of new employees from all over the company
   b. New employees within the department
   c. A group of managers from other departments
   d. Several of your superiors
   e. A supplier who is helping you update equipment

    f. A group of customers touring the company

4. Describe your approach if you were to ask one of your instructors for an incomplete grade in a course you are now taking.

5. List the most important factors to consider when planning a presentation to:

    a. Ask your boss for a raise

    b. Give instructions to a trainee

    c. Interview for a job

    d. Announce a cost increase in employee health-care benefits

    e. Brief a new supervisor on standard but informal operating procedures within your work group

Communicator Profile

Don Nichols, Trial Consultant
Courtroom Intelligence, Inc.
Odessa, Texas

The planning that goes into arguing a legal case is like an iceberg: only a small part is visible to the spectator. But the hours of work often make the difference between having a merely good case and a winning one.

Courtroom Intelligence is a consulting firm that helps attorneys and their clients develop and present the best possible case to a jury. When attorneys or witnesses speak to a jury, we help make sure that what those jurors hear helps present the case in a way that benefits the client. In other words, we don't practice law, we practice communication.

We offer a variety of services that help clients. We often begin with the process of jury selection. One expert said that 95 percent of a case may be decided during the picking of the jury, so this is a critically important step. We conduct community-opinion research polls and focus groups to get a sense of what potential jurors might feel about the issues that will come up in a case. This helps us recommend what kinds of jurors we ought to look for and what topics will be especially important to them during a trial.

When a case is especially important, we often conduct simulated trials to help our clients prepare for the real thing. We have associates take the role of opposing attorneys, the judge, and witnesses. By playing out the trial beforehand, we can prevent—or at least minimize—the kind of surprises that can shake our client's case.

Once a trial has started, we often spend time working with witnesses to prepare them for their day in court. The way witnesses answer questions can make a tremendous difference to a jury. So does their nonverbal behavior: a nervous witness who looks down when being questioned or sounds defensive can lose credibility even though his or her testimony is accurate and important. Based on our pretrial research, we rehearse the tough questions that are likely to be asked. This way witnesses are prepared when their time on the stand comes.

We also help our clients by preparing visual exhibits that present information clearly. We create charts and graphs, three-dimensional models, and audiovisual demonstrations. When time is of the essence, we often prepare these exhibits within twenty-four hours.

In important cases, we sometimes create a "shadow jury" of people who closely resemble the real jurors. They sit in on the entire trial, and every day we interview them to find out what's on their minds. If the shadow jurors find that something is unclear or if they have unanswered questions, we can come back the next day and present additional information at the real trial. Shadow juries are also a tremendous help when we're considering whether to settle a case before the trial is over. They can tell us whether we have a good chance at winning if we persist or if we can get a better result by settling.

The planning that goes into arguing a legal case is like an iceberg: only a small part is visible to the spectator. But the hours of work often make the difference between having a merely good case and a winning one.

11

After reading this chapter, you should understand:

- The reasons a presentation must be well organized
- The proper basic structure for a presentation
- The patterns of organizing a presentation described in this chapter
- The functions and types of introductions and conclusions
- The characteristics and placement of transitions

You should be able to:

- Develop the body of a presentation, choosing the most appropriate organizing pattern based on the guidelines in this chapter
- Develop an introduction that performs the necessary functions listed in this chapter
- Develop a conclusion that performs the functions listed in this chapter
- Use effective transitions at the appropriate points in a presentation

ORGANIZING YOUR IDEAS

Merrill Snyder, office manager of a midsized corporation, had assigned Tom Byrd, an assistant manager, the task of researching a new telephone system for the company. She asked Tom to report on his progress at the Monday-morning personnel-department meeting.

Tom arrived with a stack of letters, sample policies, and literature from several suppliers, and spread them out on the table as he began to speak.

"If we want to be able to transfer calls to our offices in Dayton and Carlisle, we should take a close look at Centrex. Some people say that AT&T has a better service record, though, which means we should probably consider the Merlin system, but I don't know about that for sure. Intertalk may be better for calls within the building than some other systems, and we can either buy or rent sets from them, although that doesn't do anything for our long-distance requirements. Any of the systems I've looked at will handle modem communication, but we really have to look at fax machines from different suppliers before we can make a decision about whether we also want to use them. Centrex offers a number of services, like call forwarding and call hunting. Although other systems do that, too, they don't all have the same services for the same price. Some other systems I think might be good are—"

"Wait a minute," Merrill said, "I'm having trouble following you. What's Intertalk? Do they offer the same system Centrex does, and how do they compare in price?"

"Intertalk is an intercom system," Tom explained. "If we go with that, it will be in addition to a phone system. But if we pick a phone system that includes intercom, we won't need Intertalk."

"Is Centrex the only system that offers call transferring? Surely not."

"I didn't say it *was*," Tom retorted. "Most systems offer that, but with Centrex you can do it with a regular no-frills phone. Merlin is good, though, and they'll replace sets if they break down so we won't lose time while they try to repair them on the spot."

"Tom," Merrill said, "the only way this will make sense to the rest of us is if you go back to your office and organize your material so that we can see all the features of each system, including prices and options, and how they compare. Draw up a chart. At our next meeting, I hope you'll be prepared to do that." By the tone of her voice, Tom understood that he had been reprimanded.

As this story shows, the organization of a message affects the listener's comprehension of the content. A garbled message isn't easy to follow—and it damages the speaker's credibility. By the time Merrill stopped Tom, she had serious doubts about how carefully he had thought about the systems; and when he finally makes a recommendation, she isn't likely to have much faith in his expertise unless his next presentation is much clearer. A poorly organized message is also frustrating to listeners—and probably the last thing Tom wants to do is frustrate Merrill, whose evaluation of him is likely to influence his future success in the company.

THE IMPORTANCE OF CLEAR ORGANIZATION

Most people will agree that clarity is important, but few realize just how critical it is. A substantial body of research indicates that organizing your remarks clearly can make your messages more understandable, keep your audience happy, and boost your image as a speaker.[1]

Despite the benefits of good organization, most presentations suffer from a variety of problems in this area:

- *Taking too long to get to the point.* Many speakers ramble, gush, or drone on about their topic long after their audience has lost interest. Tom Byrd's long-winded explanation of the telephone system was a waste of Merrill Snyder's time. Most businesspeople are in a hurry and have little patience for nonessential information. "What's the bottom line?" is their spoken or unspoken demand.

- *Including irrelevant material.* As a speaker, you probably know and care more about your topic than your audience does. Tom Byrd had immersed himself in the topic of telephone service providers and wanted to tell his boss everything on the subject. It's often hard to remember that your audience isn't likely to care as much about your topic as you do. Therefore, you need only include information that they must know.

- *Leaving out necessary information.* It's paradoxical that, in addition to talking too much about unimportant details, some speakers leave out the essentials. How much will a system cost? How much disruption would be involved in switching from the present carrier? How reliable will the new provider be? If you don't answer critical questions, your listeners won't be informed or impressed.

- *Getting ideas mixed up.* Poor speakers haven't taken the time to decide how to present their ideas in the clearest, most logical order. Byrd's disjointed summary was impossible for Snyder to sort out. When your audience isn't as familiar with the topic as you are, you must develop ideas in a way that leads audience members clearly from what they do know to the new information.[2]

No matter what the subject or the goal, almost every good presentation should follow the well-known pattern outlined in Figure 11-1: "First, tell them

---

If you want to "get in touch with your feelings," fine—talk to yourself, we all do. But if you want to communicate with another thinking human being, get in touch with your thoughts. Put them in order, give them a purpose, use them to persuade, to instruct, to discover, to advise.

William Safire, *Words of Wisdom*

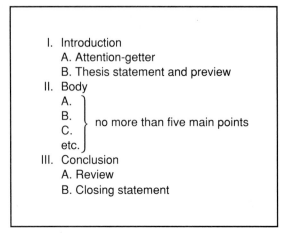

Figure 11-1   Outline format for presentation.

what you're going to tell them; then, tell them; then, tell them what you told them."

You have probably encountered this format many times. Despite its familiarity, many speakers act as if they have never heard of it. Like Tom Byrd, they launch into their subjects without any prefatory remarks about what they're about to say. Some finish their main ideas and then stop speaking without any summation or closing. Still others deliver what seems to be a model three-part talk but don't stop there; they continue tacking on new information after you have closed your mental files: "Did I mention that . . ." "We had the same problem, by the way, last year when . . ." or "Oh, another thing I should have mentioned. . . ." Even worse, many speakers don't seem to have *any* organizational plan in mind. Their remarks sound as if the speakers had dropped their note cards and shuffled them together in random order before addressing the group.

Chapter 10 described the first steps in developing a presentation: analyzing the situation and establishing a purpose. Once you have completed these steps, you need to decide what points you'll cover in your presentation and how to arrange them. You can do so by using the guidelines discussed in this chapter.

GATHERING IDEAS AND MATERIAL

Once you have figured out your thesis, you are ready to develop the information that will get your audience to accept it. Collecting this material usually requires research. If, for example, you want to sell potential customers on your product, you'll want to find out which competing products they are using now and how they feel about them. You'll also want to discover whether they are familiar with your product and what attitudes they have about it.

In other cases, the material you'll need to discuss may appear to be obvious. If you're giving a report on last month's sales, the figures might seem to form the bulk of your remarks. If you are explaining how to use a new piece of equipment, the operating steps appear to be the obvious body of your talk. Even in these cases, though, you'll probably need to do some digging. Last month's sales may take on more meaning if you compare them with those recorded in the same period in previous years, and getting those numbers may be worth the effort. Your instructions on the new equipment will be most successful if you find out whether and how accustomed your listeners are to operating similar equipment.

As these examples show, some research is almost always necessary. You should consider several sources for the information that will go into your presentation. The company's files—whether on paper or computerized—are often a good source of information. Interviews with knowledgeable people can provide both facts and insights. Library research is another source of information. Formal or informal surveys are still another way of gathering material.

Your research will produce a list of material from which you'll build your presentation. For example, suppose that you have been asked to address a group of employees about why you want them to use Mercury Overnight for letters and packages that need to be delivered quickly. Using your research on Mercury Overnight, you might make up a list that looks something like the one in Figure 11-2.

Notice that this list is a random assortment of points. In fact, your own collection of ideas probably won't even be neatly listed on a single piece of paper. More likely it will be scribbled on an assortment of index cards, check stubs, message pads, or whatever you had at hand when you came across a piece of promising information. Once you've assembled what seems like enough raw material, you're ready to organize it.

ORGANIZING THE BODY

Inexperienced speakers make the mistake of starting to plan a talk by beginning at the beginning, by first writing an introduction. This is like trying to landscape a piece of property before you've put up a building. Even though it doesn't come first in a presentation, the body is the place to start your organizing. Organizing the body of a talk consists of two steps: identifying the key points that support your thesis, and then deciding what organizational plan best develops those points.

IDENTIFY KEY POINTS

The list of ideas you've compiled by research and brainstorming probably contains more material than you'll want to use in your talk. So the next step is to figure out what key points best support your thesis and help you achieve your purpose. Your analysis of the speaking situation will also help you to pinpoint your key ideas.

Based on this analysis, you might decide that the major reasons that would convince listeners to sign up to use Mercury are:

1. Mercury Overnight will pick up the package at your office instead of your having to go through the mailroom.
2. It will also deliver right to your office if the label is marked properly, so you don't have to wait for the mailroom to process and deliver it to you.
3. When we experimented with different delivery services, Mercury delivered every single package we gave them within twenty-four hours.
4. Some of the companies we tried took two days or more about 25 percent of the time.
5. One company we tried got the package in on time about 90 percent of the time.
6. Other companies we've tried have held up packages for as much as a week for no good reason.
7. Mercury will deliver into the rural areas where many of our customers are, while some of the other companies only deliver in the urban areas.
8. Mercury will bill the departmental accounts, saving bookkeeping time.
9. Some companies charge a lot of extra money for the odd-sized packages we send sometimes, but Mercury just charges by weight.
10. Because we can't always count on overnight delivery with the delivery service we're using now, we often have to take time off to run a package across town.
11. Mercury charges less for heavy packages.
12. If we send several things at once to the same place, Mercury will give us a lower "group rate."
13. Mercury will come out any time to pick up a package.
14. Other companies will only make a regular daily stop, which doesn't do you much good if your package isn't ready when they come.
15. Mercury will make pickups from seven in the morning until midnight, which is nice if you're working early or late.
16. If you send the package through the post office and don't put enough postage on it, they'll send it back and the package won't get there in time.
17. The packages that we've sent through some other shippers sometimes get so badly damaged that the contents have to be replaced. The shipper will pay for contents if you insure the package, but that doesn't get it there in time.
18. Sometimes you have to ship a one-of-a-kind item, like a prototype for an advertisement, and if it gets lost or damaged it can take weeks to make a new one.
19. Mercury's basic shipping fee includes insurance.
20. It isn't easy to figure out which delivery service is best.
21. When the company was smaller, we used to just send things by mail.
22. We researched the idea of setting up our own delivery service, but management vetoed it because it cost too much.

Figure 11-2 Selling points produced by a brainstorming session.

A. Mercury is more reliable
B. Mercury is more convenient
C. Mercury's lower rates will save your budget for other matters

None of these points were on the brainstorming list in Figure 11-2, but they emerge as themes from that list. Each of the points that did appear on that list will fit into one of these categories, so the speech can be organized around these three points.

How do you identify your main points? One way is by applying the "one week later" test: ask yourself what main points you want people to remember one week later. Since most listeners won't recall much more than these few ideas, they logically should be emphasized during your talk.

The basic ideas that grow out of your audience analysis or brainstorming list might work well as the main points of your talk, but this doesn't always happen. As with the Mercury delivery-service example, there may be better ways to organize your material. Before you can decide, you need to think about the different ways the body of a presentation can be organized.

CHOOSE THE BEST ORGANIZATIONAL PATTERN

There are five basic ways to organize the body of a presentation. You should choose the one that best develops your thesis and thus helps you to achieve your purpose.

Chronological A chronological pattern arranges your points according to their sequence in time. You can use it to explain a process, such as the steps in putting an order through the order fulfillment and shipping departments or the schedule for developing a new product. One of its most common uses is to give instructions:

Thesis: Creating overhead transparencies is a simple process.

A. Make a photocopy of the image.
B. Place the photocopied image on the glass tray of the copier, as if you were going to make another copy.
C. Flip down the "single paper feed" tray on the side of the copier.
D. Insert face up a blank sheet of transparency film in the copier.
E. Press the "start" button on the copier.

Chronological patterns are also useful for discussing events that develop over time:

Thesis: We need to stay on schedule if we're to get the catalog out in time for the holidays.

A. A product list must be ready by March 1.
B. Photography and catalog copy have to be completed by May 6.
C. Page proofs have to be read and corrected by July 30.

D. Final proofs have to be reviewed by department heads by August 30.

E. Catalogs have to be shipped no later than October 5.

Chronological patterns may be used for discussing history:

Thesis: Guardian Insurance has had a long history of growth.

A. Guardian Insurance was founded in 1878 to cover small-business losses due to fire and theft.

B. In 1920, Guardian extended its coverage to homes and property, and began offering personal life insurance.

C. In 1945, Guardian began offering group health and life insurance policies.

D. In 1981, Guardian began offering dental plans to major policyholders.

Spatial Spatial patterns organize material according to how it is put together or where it is located physically. You might use a spatial pattern to show the parts in a model for a new product, the location of various departments in your building, or the safety requirements of a piece of equipment—where safety shields should be placed, the support required in the floor, and so on. You might sell a piece of real estate with a spatially organized presentation like this:

Thesis: This home is just what you need.

A. The upstairs has enough bedrooms for every member of the family plus a private study.

B. It has a large downstairs, with a large living room, a formal dining room, and an eat-in kitchen.

C. The basement has a finished playroom for the children and a utility room.

D. The yard has large trees and lots of space for a garden.

You can also show the geographical nature of a subject by citing examples from many places:

Thesis: Business is better in some areas than in others.

A. Northeast regional sales are 50 percent ahead of last year's.

B. Mid-Atlantic regional sales are 10 percent ahead of last year's.

C. Southern regional sales are about the same as last year's.

D. Midwest regional sales are down about 25 percent from last year's.

Topical A topical pattern groups your ideas around some logical themes or divisions in your subject. For example, you might organize a proposal for simplifying the expense-accounting procedures around the reasons for the change or a sales presentation for photocopiers around the three major types of copiers you think a customer might be interested in. An accountant might organize a proposal for a new inventory system this way:

Thesis: A just-in-time inventory system has three major benefits.

A. It eliminates excess inventory that may result from long-term ordering.
B. It cuts down on waste resulting from supplies becoming outdated or shopworn.
C. It saves on storage and computer-records costs.

You could also use a topical plan in a presentation explaining employee benefits—insurance, pension plans, and employee discounts:

Thesis: Consolidated Millworks Company offers many benefits to employees.

A. All employees are covered by free life, health, dental, and disability insurance.
B. All employees who have been with the company for ten years are eligible for the pension plan.
C. Employees are entitled to a 10 percent discount on all Consolidated Millworks products, plus discounts on products and services such as car rentals, books and records, and clothing from cooperating companies and merchants.

The topical approach is sometimes termed a "catchall approach" because people sometimes call a list of points *topical* if they can't think of another pattern that will work. However, a jumbled list of ideas isn't organized just because you call it topical. A genuine topical approach has elements that are logically related according to some scheme an audience can easily recognize. In the second example above, the three main divisions (insurance, pension plan, and discounts) are all parts of the entire employee benefits plan.

Cause-Effect   A cause-effect pattern shows that certain events have happened or will happen as a result of certain circumstances. For example, you might show prospective life-insurance customers how certain clauses will provide extra coverage if they are hospitalized or demonstrate how a new advertising program will help a product reach a wider market. You might also use it to demonstrate how certain circumstances are creating a problem:

Thesis: The problems in our order processing system (*cause*) are costing us sales and losing us customers (*effect*).

A. Orders are filled incorrectly, late, and sometimes not at all.
B. As a result, customers are delayed in their own plans; they become angry and go to our competitors.

An alternative form of the cause-effect structure is an effect-cause structure. When you use this structure, focus more on the results because you begin with the result and show how it came to pass or how you think it can be made to happen. For example, you might use an effect-cause pattern to explain why a company has a strict policy about absenteeism or to explain how you expect to accomplish a sales goal you have set. It may also be used to explain how a problem has been created:

Thesis: The decline in our car-rental profits (*effect*) is the result of several problems (*cause*).

A. Our profits have decreased 35 percent.
B. Several factors are responsible.
   1. Our competitors are offering better service at lower prices.
   2. Our maintenance costs have nearly doubled on newer cars.
   3. Our advertising is not effective.

Problem-Solution   A problem-solution pattern is usually used when the speaker is proposing some kind of change. When you use this pattern, you describe the problem, then show how your plan will solve it. You might use a problem-solution pattern to show a customer how your service contract will keep her from losing time and paying for expensive repairs when her personal computer breaks down or to demonstrate to management how a new procedure will avoid the problems of the current program. Here is an example:

Thesis: The new method I propose is better than the present method of partially automated machine drilling.

A. There are many problems with the current system.
   1. The handling time is almost five minutes per part.
   2. The rate of errors is about 4 percent.
   3. Our accident rate is very high.
B. The new system will solve these problems.
   1. The handling time is almost eliminated.
   2. The error rate is less than 1 percent.
   3. Workers are no longer involved in the most dangerous part of the process.[3]

RULES FOR MAIN POINTS

Whichever pattern of organization you use, your main points should meet the following criteria:

Main Points Should Be Stated in Complete Sentences   By stating your points in full, grammatical sentences, they will probably satisfy the "one week later" test and be remembered by your listeners. Notice how describing main points in complete sentences is clearer and far more effective than using simple three- or four-word statements.

FRAGMENT	COMPLETE SENTENCE
Choosing a physician	It's essential to choose a health-care provider from the list of approved doctors.
Sexual and ethnic discrimination	Allowing sexual or ethnic considerations to intrude into our hiring decisions isn't just bad judgment, it's illegal.
Demographic changes in market	Due to demographic changes, we can expect our market to shrink in the next ten years.
Updating computer files	Updating the computerized files every day is a simple four-step process.

All Points Should Develop the Thesis   Consider the following outline:

Thesis: Allowing employees more latitude in choosing their working hours is good for the company and for the workers.

A. Flexible scheduling is a relatively new idea.
B. Flexible scheduling improves morale.
C. Flexible scheduling reduces absenteeism.

The first point may be true, but the newness of flexible scheduling doesn't say anything about its value and, therefore, ought to be dropped.

A Presentation Should Contain No More Than Five Main Points   Your main points are, after all, what you want your listeners to remember, and people have difficulty recalling more than five pieces of information.[4] Even when you have a large amount of material, it's usually possible to organize it into five categories or less. For example, if you were preparing an analysis of ways to lower operating expenses in your organization, your brainstorming list might include these ideas:

Reduce wattage in lighting fixtures.

Hire outside data processing firm to handle seasonal billing rather than expanding permanent in-house staff.

Sell surplus equipment.

Reduce nonbusiness use of copying machines.

Reduce temperature in less-used parts of the building.

Pay overtime rather than add new employees.

Retrofit old equipment instead of buying new machinery.

Your outline could consolidate this list into three areas:

Thesis: We can reduce operating costs in three areas: energy, personnel, and equipment.

A. We can reduce our energy costs.
  1. Reduce wattage in lighting fixtures.
  2. Reduce temperature in less-used parts of the building.
B. We can save money by not hiring new employees.
  1. Hire outside data processing firm for seasonal billing.
  2. Encourage overtime instead of adding employees.
C. We can reduce our purchase and maintenance costs on equipment.
  1. Retrofit old equipment.
  2. Sell surplus equipment.
  3. Reduce personal use of copying machines.

This outline contains all the items in your list, but the three broad categories make your presentation much easier to comprehend than a seven-point presentation would be.

Each Main Point Should Contain Only One Idea Combining ideas or overlapping them will confuse audiences. Consider this outline:

Thesis: Many local businesses continue to discriminate against some job applicants.

A. Businesses discriminate on the basis of ethnic background.
B. Businesses discriminate on the basis of disability.
C. Businesses discriminate on the basis of age and sex.

Since discrimination can be related to either age or sex, there's no logical reason to put age and sex in the same category.

Main Points Should Be Parallel in Structure Whenever Possible Parallel wording can reflect your organization and dramatize your points. Consider how the repetition of "Businesses discriminate" in the last outline helps drive the point home far more forcefully than if your main points are worded this less effective way:

A. Most businesses discriminate against minorities.
B. Disability is another reason for discriminating against some job applicants.
C. Some businesses even refuse to hire employees who are over sixty-five.
D. Women often have extra trouble finding a job.

You won't always be able to state your main points using parallel construction, but a look at many of the examples in this chapter shows you that it can be used often.

PLANNING THE INTRODUCTION

The body of a presentation is important, but the introduction that precedes it needs just as much attention. Your introduction should take between 10 and 15 percent of the speaking time. During this short time—less than one minute of a five-minute talk—your listeners form their initial impression of you and your topic. That impression, favorable or not, will affect how they react to the rest of your remarks. To be most effective, an introduction should accomplish several purposes.

FUNCTIONS OF THE INTRODUCTION

As you have already learned, an introduction should have two parts: an attention-getter and a thesis statement/preview. These two parts should accomplish five things.

Capture the Listeners' Attention   As you learned in Chapter 4, audiences don't always approach a presentation ready to listen. The topic may not seem important or interesting to them. Your listeners may have been ordered to attend your presentation. Even when the presentation is obviously important, your listeners will usually have other matters on their mind. It's vital, therefore, to begin by focusing attention on you and your topic if there is any chance that the listeners' minds are elsewhere.

Give Your Audience a Reason to Listen   The best way to grab and hold your listeners' attention is to convince them that your message will be important or interesting to them. For example, if company employees are generally satisfied with the insurance program the company has been using, they won't be interested in hearing about a new health plan that will be cheaper for the company unless you can begin by enumerating its advantages to them—for instance, that it will provide them better emergency services. Similarly, management will be more interested in hearing your new ideas if you first say that the plans you're proposing will yield higher profits.

Set the Proper Tone for the Topic and Setting   If you want potential customers to buy more fire insurance, your opening remarks should prepare them to think seriously about the problems they would encounter if they had a fire in the house. If you want to congratulate your subordinates about their recent performance and encourage them to perform even better on the next assignment, your opening remarks should put them in a good mood—not focus on the problems you must face.

Establish Your Qualifications   If the audience already knows that you are an expert on the subject, if a previous speaker has given you an impressive introduction, or if your authority makes it clear that you're qualified to talk, establishing credibility isn't necessary. In other cases, however, you need to demonstrate your competence quickly so that the listeners will take your remarks seriously.

Introduce Your Thesis and Preview Your Presentation   In most cases, you need to state your main idea clearly at the beginning of your remarks so your listeners know exactly what you're trying to say. In addition to your thesis statement, a preview of your main points tells your listeners where you're headed.

Accomplishing these five goals in less than one minute isn't as difficult as it might seem because you can accomplish several functions at the same time. For example, notice how an insurance agent introduced a thirty-minute talk on an admittedly difficult topic:

Sets desired tone by establishing a bond with audience	Being an insurance agent gives me a lot of sympathy for tax collectors and dog catchers. None of us has an especially popular job. After all, it seems that with life insurance you lose either way: if the policy pays off, you won't be around to enjoy the money. On the other hand, if you don't need the policy, you've spent your hard-earned savings for nothing. Besides, insurance isn't cheap. I'm sure you have plenty of other things you could use your money for: catching up on bills, fixing up your house, buying a new car, or even taking a vacation.
Establishes qualifications	With all those negatives, why should you care about insurance? For that matter, why am I devoting my career to it? For me, the answer is easy: over the years, I've seen literally hundreds of people—people just like you and me—learn what a difference the right kind of insurance coverage can make. And I've seen hundreds more suffer from learning too late that insurance is necessary.
Thesis *Preview*	Well, tonight I want to give you some good news. I'll show you that you can win by buying insurance. You can win by gaining peace of mind, and you can even win by buying insurance that works like an investment, paying dividends that you can use here and now.

TYPES OF OPENING STATEMENTS

Of all parts of a presentation, the opening words are the hardest for many speakers. You have to be interesting. You have to establish the right tone. Your remarks have to relate to the topic that's being discussed. And, finally, the opening statement has to feel right for you.

The kind of opening you choose will depend on your analysis of the speaking situation. With familiar topics and audiences, you may even decide to skip the preliminaries and give just a brief background before launching into the thesis and preview:

> We've made good progress on Mr. Boynton's request to look into cost cutting steps. We've found that it is possible to reduce operating expenses by almost 10 percent without cutting efficiency. We'll be introducing six steps this morning. . . .

In most cases, you will want to preface your remarks with some sort of opening statement. Following are seven of the most common and effective ways to begin a presentation.

Ask a Question   Asking the right question is a good way to involve your listeners in your topic and establish its importance to them. Some questions call for an overt response. For example, a tax accountant explaining new tax legislation to a merchants' association might ask: "Is there anyone here who would feel all right about paying more taxes than the law requires? How many of you are *sure* you aren't doing just that?" This approach works well when you can be sure you'll get the response you want and when the question isn't too personal. In some cases, you should make it clear that you want each listener to respond mentally: "Answer this question for yourself. Are you sure that all of your expense reports would pass an Internal Revenue audit?"

Not all questions work as well as these. Some are uninteresting: "Have you ever wondered what the Sherman Antitrust Act means to you?" Others can be so

---

Eleanor Foa Dienstag, award-winning chief speech writer for the chief executive officer of a major financial services company, offers the following advice for an effective speech introduction:

> You do not—repeat, do not—need an opening joke to warm up the audience or calm your nerves. You do need to capture their attention. This can be done in a limitless number of ways—sometimes by the sheer force of personality, sometimes with a series of dramatic rhetorical questions or facts, such as "Do you know how many word processors are in today's offices? Do you know how many are projected to be there tomorrow?"
>
> Once you've captured their attention, you need to establish an immediate rapport with your audience. For example, if you're a computer expert and you know most businesspeople are terrified of computers, you might offer a brief anecdote that illustrates your sense of frustration when your word processor goes down. Or you might say, "Like you, I'm sometimes overwhelmed by the profusion of software." The point to get across is that you know where they're coming from and are sympathetic.

Eleanor Foa Dienstag, "The Fine Art of Speaking in Public"

thought-provoking that your audience will stop listening to you: "If you had to fire three of the people who report to you, how would you decide which ones to let go?" When you decide to begin with a question, be sure to avoid these mistakes.

Tell a Story   Since most people enjoy a good story, beginning with one can be an effective way to get audience attention, set the tone, and lead into the topic. This example, from the introduction to a speech on time management, accomplishes all these functions in a few sentences:

> Jean Fabre, the French naturalist, was one day observing processionary caterpillars. These are little fellows, about an inch long, that form up into long strings and move over trees eating leaves and insects. Fabre was able to get them onto the rim of an old red flower pot and had them close up their circle. As they moved around the rim in an unbroken circle, he figured that they would soon realize that they were going around in circles and would stop. Yet they starved to death within reach of food. They confused activity with accomplishment. They were as active as they could be, moving along staying busy. They just weren't getting anywhere.[5]

Give a Quotation   Quotations have two advantages. First, someone else has probably already said what you want to say in a very clever way. Second, quotations let you use a source with high credibility to back up your message.

Not every quotation has to come from a distinguished person. As long as the character you quote is appropriate for the audience and the topic, he or she can be almost anyone—even a fictional character:

> One of America's best-known philosophers—Charlie Brown of the comic strip Peanuts—once said—"There is no problem so big—no challenge so awesome—no dilemma so frustrating or complicated—that one cannot simply walk away from it." The problems of agriculture *are* big—awesome—frustrating *and* complicated . . . and can't be walked away from.[6]

Make a Startling Statement   An excellent way to get listeners' attention is to surprise them. Sales presentations often include startling facts in their openings: "Do you know that half of all business calls never reach the intended party?"

You won't achieve the desired result if your startling statement offends your audience. The remarks that might work perfectly at a football banquet could flop miserably in a church sermon. Illinois Bell spokesperson John R. Bonée succeeded in staying on the right side of appropriateness when he spoke to a group of administrators:

> You may have noticed that the title of my remarks this evening is "Making Love in Public" and you may have found it somewhat facetious. Believe me, it is not. Public relations is a widely misunderstood concept. It has been said that some people know so little about it that they think public relations means making love in public. In a certain sense, they are perfectly correct. It does mean, at the very least, making love *to* the public. That's what public relations is all about.[7]

Refer to the Audience   Mentioning your listeners' needs, concerns, or interests clarifies the relevance of your topic immediately and shows that you understand your listeners. For example, "I know you're all worried by rumors of cutbacks in staff. I called you here today to explain just what the budget cuts will mean to this department."

Former California governor George Dukmejian used the technique of referring to the audience in a talk to the Los Angeles Rotary Club. Dukmejian acknowledged the fact that people who listen to after-lunch speakers—even famous ones—appreciate brevity.

> I promise not to speak for too long this afternoon. It's worth noting that the Lord's Prayer is only 56 words long. The Gettysburg Address is 226. The Ten Commandments are 297. But the U.S. Department of Agriculture's order on the price of cabbage is 15,269 words. I'll try to finish somewhere in between.[8]

Refer to the Occasion   Sometimes the event itself provides a good starting point: "We're here today to recognize some very important people."

Sometimes you can begin by referring to some other aspect of the situation—for example, by relating your remarks to those of a previous speaker: "I was very interested in what Larry had to say about the way our expenses will rise in the next couple of years. Let's look at one way we can keep that increase as small as possible."

David M. Roderick of United States Steel used the technique of referring to a previous speaker in the introduction of his remarks to the National Press Club:

> Thank you, Don, for your introduction. I feel privileged to have this renowned forum as a platform for stating the case for our nation's steel industry—its plight and the importance of its survival.
>
> I just hope this issue is not too drab when compared to your two most recent luncheon presentations by gourmet James Beard and economist Arthur Laffer—pie on the plate and pie in the sky. And now steelmaking.
>
> Certainly what happens to the nation's fourth largest industry has to be important. Its demise would certainly be news—bad news for almost everyone. I think, then, its struggle to survive and regroup and prosper should be equally newsworthy.[9]

Tell a Joke   The right joke can be an effective way to get attention, make a point, and increase your audience's liking for you. The vice-president of an advertising agency, for example, might begin an orientation session for new management trainees with the following tale.

> I'm sure everyone has heard the story about the guy who smells awful all the time. When asked the reason for this he explains that it's because of his job—working in a circus giving enemas to elephants. The listener asks, "Why don't you get another job?" and the guy replies hotly, "What! And get out of *show business?*"[10]

Checklist for Organizing and Supporting a Presentation

- Introduction
  Captures attention of audience
  Gives audience reasons to listen
  Sets appropriate tone
  Establishes speaker's qualifications, if necessary
  Introduces thesis and previews content
- Body
  Uses clear, most effective organizational pattern
    Chronological
    Spatial
    Topical
    Cause-effect
    Problem-solution
  Main points should be stated in complete sentences
  All points help develop thesis
  Body contains no more than five main points
  Each main point contains only one idea
  Main points should be parallel in structure
- Transitions
  Refer to both recent and upcoming material, showing relationship between the two
  Clarify structure of speaker's ideas
    Exist in all necessary parts of presentation
    Between introduction and body
    Between main points within body
    Between body and conclusion
- Conclusion
  Reviews thesis and main points
  Concludes with effective closing statement

Well, that story has some truth in our business too. Lots of people view advertising as glamorous: three-hour expense-account lunches and big commissions. Advertising is certainly a kind of show business, but along with all the glamour comes a lot of hard, messy work. I want to begin this orientation program by telling you about both the clean, easy parts and the tough, grubby ones. Then you'll have a better idea what to expect in the next months and years.

Any humor you use should be appropriate to your topic and to the occasion. Telling a few knock-knock jokes before you launch into your financial report will draw attention—but not to your topic. The tone of your presentation could be ruined by a joke. For instance, you probably shouldn't tell a few jokes about smog and then say, "But seriously, folks, I want to talk about what we're doing to curb air pollution from our own factories."

Your jokes should also be appropriate for your audience. The in-jokes that work well with your office staff, for example, are likely to alienate clients at a contract negotiation because outsiders won't understand them.

PLANNING THE CONCLUSION

The conclusion of your presentation should be even shorter than the introduction: not much more than 5 percent of your total speaking time. Within those few moments, though, you must accomplish two important things.

FUNCTIONS OF THE CONCLUSION

As Figure 11-3 shows, a conclusion should have two parts: a review and a closing statement. Let's look at each of these parts in detail.

   I. Introduction
      A. Overnight delivery services certainly aren't cheap. But your own experience shows that the cost is even higher when those urgent shipments *don't* arrive on time. (*attention-getter*)
      B. Mercury Overnight is the quickest, most convenient, most affordable way to deliver your high-priority packages on time. (*thesis/preview*)
  II. Body
      A. Mercury is more reliable than other services.
         1. Mercury is the only shipper with a 100 percent trouble-free record for delivering our packages within twenty-four hours.
         2. Other services have caused us problems.
            a. They have failed to give twenty-four-hour service 25 percent of the time.
            b. In some cases they've held up packages for as much as one week.
            c. The post office has returned packages for insufficient postage.
            d. Some packages have been damaged in transit.
            e. In some cases packages have been lost.
      B. Mercury is more convenient than other services.
         1. They pick up and deliver items to individual offices, not just the mailroom.
         2. They'll pick up or deliver packages any time between 7:00 A.M. and midnight, instead of only coming by once a day.
         3. They'll bill departmental accounts, saving us bookkeeping time.
         4. Their dependability saves us from hand-delivering high-priority packages across town.
      C. Mercury is more economical than other services.
         1. They don't charge extra for oddly shaped packages.
         2. They charge less for heavy packages.
         3. We get a "group rate" when sending several packages at the same time.
         4. The basic shipping fee includes insurance.
 III. Conclusion
      A. Now you can see that Mercury Overnight is the best choice for your top-priority shipments. It's reliable, convenient, and economical. (*review*)
      B. With Mercury you won't just pay for the best service . . . you'll get it.

Figure 11-3   Sample presentation outline.

The Review   Your review should contain a restatement of your thesis and a summary of your main points. Sometimes these two elements will be virtually identical with their form on your outline:

> This afternoon, I've suggested that our merchandising approach needs changing to become more profitable. I've suggested three such changes: first, to increase our newspaper advertising; second, to feature higher-quality merchandise; and third, to expand our product line in all areas.

Your summary can also be a more subtle rewording of the same information: "By now I hope you agree with me that some basic merchandising changes can improve our balance sheet. When people find out that we have a broad range of high-quality products, I'm convinced that we'll have more customers who will spend more money."

The Closing Statement   A strong closing will help your listeners to remember you favorably; a weak ending can nullify many of your previous gains. Besides creating a favorable impression, the closing statement will give your remarks a sense of completion. You shouldn't leave your audience wondering whether you've finished. Finally, a closing statement ought to incite your listeners, encouraging them to act or think in a way that accomplishes your purpose. Let's look at several varieties of closing statements.

TYPES OF CLOSING STATEMENTS

Several of the techniques used for getting attention in your introduction will also work well as closing statements. To refresh your memory, they are:

Ask a question

Tell a story

Give a quotation

Make a startling statement

Refer to the occasion

Tell a joke

In addition, there are several other types of closing statements you might use.

Return to the Theme of Your Opening Statement   Coming back to the place you started gives a sense of completeness to your presentation. With this approach, you should refer to your opening statement, but add a new insight, further details, or a different ending: "At the beginning of my talk, I asked whether you might not be paying more tax than you need to. I suspect you discovered that you've been overly generous with Uncle Sam. I hope I have helped you to understand your real liability and to take advantage of some of the tax shelters available to you."

Appeal for Action   When your goal involves getting the audience to act in a certain way, you can sometimes close your presentation by asking for your desired result: "So now that you know what these workshops can do, the only question is when you ought to enroll. We have openings on August 19 and on September 23. I'll be available in a moment to sign you up for either date. I'm looking forward to seeing you soon."

End with a Challenge   Whereas an appeal asks for some action, a challenge almost demands it: "You can go on as before, not failing completely but not doing the best possible job. Or you can use the ideas you've heard this morning to become more creative, more productive, and more successful. Why be average when you can be superior? Why settle for a few hopes when you can reach your dreams? It's up to you."

ADDING TRANSITIONS

Transitions are words or sentences that connect the segments of a presentation. They work like bridges between the major parts of your remarks and tell your listeners how these parts are related. Transitions should occur between the introduction and the body, between the main points within the body, and between the body and the conclusion:

> "Those are big promises. Let me talk about how we can deliver on them. . . ."

> "Not all the news is bad, however. Let me tell you about some good things that happened at the conference. . . ."

> "After hearing about so many features, you may have trouble remembering them all. Let's review them briefly. . . ."

FUNCTIONS OF TRANSITIONS

Transitions like these serve three important purposes.

They Promote Clarity   Clarity in speech—especially one-way speechlike presentations—is more difficult to achieve than clarity in writing. The format of a letter, memo, book, or report makes its organization of ideas clear. Paragraphs, lists, different typefaces, and underlining can all emphasize how ideas are related to one another. In a presentation, however, listeners don't have the benefit of any of these aids to figure out how your ideas are put together. They only have what the verbal cues provide—transitional words and phrases.

They Emphasize Important Ideas   Transitions within presentations highlight important information the way italics and bold type emphasize it in print:

"Now let's turn to a third reason—perhaps the most important of all—for equipping your field representatives with electronic pagers."

"That's what company policy says about use of expense accounts. Now let's take a look at how things *really* work."

They Keep Listeners Interested   Transitions give momentum to a presentation. They make listeners want to find out what comes next.

"So we gave them the best dog-and-pony show you've ever seen. And it was perfect—just like we planned. What do you think they said when we were finished?"

"By now you're probably asking yourself what a product like this will cost. And that's the best news of all. . . ."

CHARACTERISTICS OF EFFECTIVE TRANSITIONS

Transitions that promote clarity, emphasize important ideas, and keep listeners interested possess two characteristics. First, they refer to both preceding and upcoming ideas. A transition is like a bridge: to get listeners from one point to another, it must be anchored at both ends. By referring to what you just said and to what you'll say next, you are showing the logical relationship among those ideas.

"Those are the problems. Now let's see what can be done about solving them."

"Now you see that the change makes sense financially. But how will it be received by the people that have to live with it?"

If you have trouble planning a transition that links preceding and upcoming material smoothly, the reason may be that the ideas aren't logically related and the organizational plan you've chosen is flawed. Review the organizing patterns on pages 301–304 and the rules for main points on pages 304–307 to be sure that the structure of your presentation's body is logically suited to the topic.

Transitions should also call attention to themselves. You should let listeners know that you're moving from one point to another so that they will be able to follow the structure of your ideas easily. Notice how the examples you have read so far all make it clear that the presentation is shifting gears. This sort of highlighting is often due to the use of key words:

"The next important idea is . . . "

"Another reason we want to make the change . . ."

"Finally, we need to consider . . ."

"To wrap things up . . ."

Phrases like these are not in themselves good transitions since they do not refer to both previous and upcoming material strongly enough. But when used as part of a transition like the ones illustrated in these pages, they do signal listeners that you are moving to a new part of your presentation.

SUMMARY

Presentations must be clearly organized for several reasons: well-organized presentations are more understandable; they boost the speaker's credibility; they are more persuasive; they reduce listener frustration.

All presentations ought to follow the same basic structure, containing an introduction, body, and conclusion. After developing a purpose and thesis, the first step in organizing a presentation is to develop a list of all the ideas that might possibly fit into the talk. The purpose statement and audience analysis then serve as devices for choosing the items that are appropriate for this specific presentation. These items ought to be arranged into a series of main and subpoints, following one of the patterns described in this chapter.

After developing the body of the presentation, the introduction, conclusion, and transitions should be added. The introduction should capture the attention of the audience, give the members a reason to listen, set the proper tone, establish the speaker's qualifications, and state the thesis and a preview of the main discussion points. The conclusion should review the thesis and main points and close with a strong statement. Transitions connect the parts of the speech, helping the material flow smoothly and keeping listeners oriented.

ACTIVITIES

1. What kinds of material would you gather for each of the following presentations? Where would you find your information?

   a. How changes in the telephone industry will affect consumers
   b. How to begin an investment program
   c. Changing trends in the popularity of various academic courses over the last ten years
   d. Why students should (should not) buy a personal computer
   e. Career opportunities for women in the field of your choice

2. Which organizational plan (chronological, spatial, and so on) would you use for each of the following presentations?

   a. Instructions on how to file a health-insurance claim form
   b. A request for time and money to attend an important convention in your field
   c. A comparison of products or services between your organization and a competitor
   d. A report on an industrial accident
   e. Suggestions on reducing employee turnover

3. Prepare an introduction and a conclusion for each of the following presentations:

   a. A talk to employees announcing personnel layoffs

   b. The last in a day-long series of talks to a tired audience on maintaining and operating equipment

   c. An appeal to co-workers for donations to the Community Christmas Relief Fund

   d. A visit to your class by the president of the local chamber of commerce, who will speak on "What Employers Look For in a College Graduate." Plan your concluding remarks to follow a question-and-answer period.

Communicator Profile

Fred W. Weingarten
Program Manager,
U.S. Congress Office
of Technology Assessment
Washington, D.C.

The worst thing we can do is to give our audiences a fuzzy or overly complicated picture of our work. If we fail to deliver a clear message, none of the work we've done will be understood or used by our clients.

The Office of Technology Assessment serves U.S. senators, members of the House of Representatives, and their senior staff members by analyzing long-term trends that might influence legislation. The subjects we deal with are extremely complex, and most of our professional staff have advanced degrees in economics, law, engineering, political science, and other technical fields.

We publish our findings in written reports, which can run up to four hundred pages in length. Because these reports are so long and complex, we almost always explain them in oral presentations. I give an average of two or three oral presentations a week, and the OTA as a whole delivers more than one thousand of them annually. It's probably no exaggeration to say that these presentations are the way most senators, representatives, and staff members come to understand our work. Some of our oral presentations occur as formal testimony in congressional hearings. Others consist of formal and informal briefings to members of Congress and their staffers. In addition, we also deliver frequent speeches to outside groups such as scientific organizations and lobbyists who have a strong interest in the information we produce that will shape legislation.

Presenting technical information to an audience of nonspecialists calls for careful organizing. We usually have a short time to explain very complicated information, and every word has to count. The worst thing we can do is to give our audiences a fuzzy or overly complicated picture of our work. If we fail to deliver a clear message, none of the work we've done will be understood or used by our clients.

We strive for clarity in a number of ways. First and most important, we explain our research in terms that our listeners care about. Rather than describe the research methods that fascinate us, we focus on the results those methods have produced. Instead of talking about the ins and outs of new technologies themselves, we explain how these technologies will affect subjects like unemployment, educational needs, and international trade—the real concerns of our clients, the senators and representatives. We keep this focus by working backward. First, we ask ourselves what questions our listeners will want to have answered. Will changing regulations cause consumer telephone bills to go up or down? Should the government fund research on supercomputers? Will growing uses of automation decrease jobs? Do current copyright laws adequately cover computer data? After framing these questions in ways that reflect audience concerns, we develop answers and try to arrange those answers in the clearest possible ways. Sometimes we'll state the problems and then list possible solutions. In other cases, we take a chronological approach, describing the history of an issue and projecting how it might unfold in the future. In still other presentations, we outline the key factors that influence a topic.

Another way we keep our material understandable is to discuss only a few key points in any presentation. A talk that's built around four or five points is easy to follow; one that touches more than that number will overwhelm even dedicated listeners. We often highlight these key ideas by listing them as "talking points" on a sheet of paper that's given to each listener before we begin. These lists of talking points are also a useful way to steer longwinded, tangential comments from our audiences back toward the points we're trying to make.

We also keep our talks clear and brief by ruthlessly weeding out any material that doesn't relate to the four or five key points we're trying to make. We often spend several years working on a problem, and it's tempting to ramble on about our findings during a presentation. We have to remember that our listeners don't care a great deal about the details of our professions: they're very busy people who want key facts and recommendations without any frills or even much background as long as they are confident the background exists.

12

After reading this chapter, you should understand:

- The functions that supporting material can serve
- When and how to use each type of verbal support—examples, factual and hypothetical stories, statistics, figurative and literal comparisons, and citations
- When and how to use lists and tables, pie charts, bar charts, pictograms, diagrams, photographs, objects, and models
- The proper uses for flip charts, poster-board displays, overhead transparencies, slides, chalkboard, handouts, computerized displays, and videotapes
- The guidelines for using visual aids in presentations

You should be able to:

- Develop and present the best support to add interest to a given point
- Develop the best support to clarify a given point
- Develop the best support to prove a given point
- Demonstrate your ability to use examples, stories, statistics, comparisons, and citations as necessary in a presentation
- Demonstrate your ability to use lists and tables, objects, models, photographs, diagrams, charts, handouts, computerized displays, and videotapes in presentations
- Select and use the most effective medium to present a given visual aid in a presentation

VERBAL AND VISUAL SUPPORT IN PRESENTATIONS

Leslie Hernandez, systems manager for an industrial-supply distributor, had spent months researching ways to reduce order-processing costs. She decided that the best way to do it was through a bar-coding system. The following was part of her oral presentation to management:

> If you shop at the local department store, you know that getting your order rung up can be time-consuming and frustrating. The cashier looks at the price tag on each item and punches the price and an elaborate inventory code into the cash register. That takes time. If the price tag is missing or smudged, the cashier has to call someone for the price—which takes more time. And if the cashier makes a mistake, correcting takes even more time—and if the mistake isn't caught, it costs either you or the store money.
>
> The local supermarket is a lot faster. The cashiers run the bar coding—those strange lines on each label—across a scanner, which automatically reads the price and the inventory number into the register and the store's computer system. That's faster for the store *and* the customer.
>
> We can use a similar bar-coding system for our internal order processing system and cut our order processing time by perhaps as much as 80 percent. F. W. Webb, a major industrial supplier in the Northeast, has been using bar coding for the past few years. It used to take an order clerk up to two hours to process internal requisition forms; now, it takes fifteen minutes.
>
> Webb's system has been so successful that they're thinking about using it for more of their inventory system. The systems manager there says the employees love it, too, because it's so easy to use.[1]

If Leslie had simply said "A bar-coding system would be faster and cheaper," her presentation wouldn't have been as effective. The managers listening to her presentation wouldn't have known whether that was her personal opinion, how much faster or cheaper the system might be, or possibly even what she meant by "bar coding." Because Leslie gave them specific figures ("as much as 80 percent") and examples and figures from a company that had used the system, however, her listeners knew the answers to those questions and felt she had done enough research to make a serious recommendation. In addition, comparing the system to one with which they were familiar—the pricing system at a local store—clarified what she meant by bar coding, showed how it saves time, *and* made the presentation more interesting because it related to the listeners' own experience.

FUNCTIONS OF SUPPORTING MATERIAL

Supporting material is anything that backs up the main points in a presentation—like the examples, statistics, and comparisons Leslie used in her presentation. As its name suggests, supporting material backs up or explains the claims that you make in your main and subordinate points. You can see the relationship between these claims and supporting material in the following examples:

> *Claim:* We could increase sales by staying open until 10:00 P.M. on weekday evenings.

Support: An article in *Modern Retailing* cites statistics showing that stores with extended evening hours boost profits by more than 20 percent of the direct overhead involved with the longer business day.

Claim: Replacing the toner cartridge on our copy machine isn't as complicated as it seems.
Support: Here's a diagram that shows how to do it. . . .

Claim: Taking the time to help customers will boost their loyalty and increase your commissions.
Support: Let me read you a letter written by one satisfied customer just last week. . . .

As these examples show, a presentation without supporting material would still be logical if it followed the organizational guidelines in Chapter 11. But it probably wouldn't achieve its goal because it would lack the information necessary to develop the ideas in a way that the audience would understand or appreciate. Carefully selected supporting material can make a presentation more effective by adding three things: clarity, interest, and proof.

CLARITY

Supporting material can make abstract or complicated ideas more understandable. Notice how the following example clarifies an idea that might otherwise be lost on an audience: that many computers are difficult to learn to operate because their commands are complicated and illogical.

Imagine driving a car that has no steering wheel, accelerator, brake pedal, turn signal lever, or gear selector. In place of all the familiar manual controls, you have only a typewriter keyboard.

Any time you want to turn a corner, change lanes, slow down, speed up, honk your horn, or back up, you have to type a command sequence on the keyboard. Unfortunately, the car can't understand English sentences. Instead, you must hold down a special key with one finger and type in some letters and numbers, such as "S20:TL:A35," which means, "Slow to 20, turn left, and accelerate to 35."

If you make typing mistakes, one of three things will happen. If you type an unknown command, the car radio will bleat and you will have to type the command again. If what you type happens to be wrong but is nevertheless a valid command, the car will blindly obey. (Imagine typing A95 instead of A35.) If you type something the manufacturer didn't anticipate, the car will screech to a halt and shut itself off.

No doubt you could learn to drive such a car if you had sufficient motivation and determination. But why bother, when so many cars use familiar controls? Most people wouldn't.

Most people don't bother to use a personal computer for the same reasons they wouldn't bother with a keyboard controlled car. Working on a computer isn't a natural skill, and the benefits hardly seem worth the hassle of learning how to get work done in an unfamiliar environment. If you make a typing mistake, the computer may do nothing, tell you it doesn't understand, do the wrong thing, shut itself down, or destroy all the work you've done and then shut itself down. Who cares if the machine is theoretically thousands of times more efficient than pencil and paper? If using the machine rattles you so much that you can't get anything done, it is in fact less efficient and may waste more time than it saves.[2]

INTEREST

Supporting material can enliven a presentation by making your main points more vivid or meaningful to the audience. Notice how one attorney added interest to a summary aimed at discrediting his opponent's restatement of evidence:

> It seems that when Abe Lincoln was a young trial lawyer in Sangamon County, Illinois, he was arguing a case with a lawyer whose version of the facts came more from his imagination than the testimony. Lincoln, in his argument, turned on him and said:
>
> "Tell me, sir, how many legs has a sheep got?" "Why, four, of course," the fellow answered. "And if I called his tail a leg, then how many legs would that sheep have?" Lincoln asked. The answer came, "Then he'd have five." "No!" Lincoln roared, pounding the jury rail; "he'd still have just *four* legs. *Calling* his tail a leg won't make it a leg. Now let's look at the actual testimony and see how many tails you've been calling legs."[3]

PROOF

Besides adding clarity and interest, supporting material can provide evidence for your claims and make your presentation more convincing. A speaker might use supporting materials this way to support the claim "Employer-sponsored day-care can boost productivity as well as helping parents":

> A survey of Union Bank employees in California showed the value of on-site, employer-sponsored day care. Turnover of employees using the bank's on-site center was only 2.2 percent, less than one quarter of the 9.9 percent turnover for workers who used other forms of day care. And that's not all: Employees using the day care center were absent from work an average of 1.7 days a year less than other parents of young children. This sort of center can even get parents back to work more quickly after a new baby is born: Mothers who used the bank's center took maternity leaves that were 1.2 weeks shorter than other parents.[4]

VERBAL SUPPORT

As Table 12-1 shows, many kinds of supporting material can be used to add interest, clarity, or proof to a presentation. The most common supports for business and professional presentations are examples, stories, statistics, comparisons, citations, and visual aids.

TABLE 12-1   Types of Verbal Support

TYPE	DEFINITION	USE	COMMENTS
Example	Brief reference that illustrates a point	Clarify Add interest (if sufficient number given)	Usually best in groups of two or more Precede or follow with story
Story	Detailed account of an incident	Clarify Add interest Prove (factual only)	Adapt to audience Must clearly support thesis Tell at appropriate length
Statistics	Numerical representations of point	Clarify Prove Add interest (when combined with other forms of support)	Link to audience's frame of reference Use sparingly Round off Supplement with visuals, handouts
Comparisons	Show how one idea resembles another	Clarify Add interest (figurative) Prove (literal)	Tailor familiar item to audience Make sure comparison is valid
Citations	Opinion of expert or articulate source	Clarify Add interest (sometimes) Prove	May be paraphrased or read verbatim Cite source Use sources credible to audience Follow up with restatement or explanation

EXAMPLES

Examples are brief illustrations that back up or explain a point. A recruiter trying to convince college graduates to hire on with her company might list several examples to support the claim that the organization has a generous personnel benefits program.

> The tangible rewards you'll receive as an employee go beyond your take-home salary. Consider the personnel benefits package: fully paid health insurance (medical, dental, and vision care), income protection plan that covers your salary in case of a disability, a completely paid life-insurance policy, generous vacations and paid holidays, and discounts at several local health clubs.

When they are used to prove a point, examples are most effective when several are given together. If you are supporting a claim that you are capable of taking on a more challenging job, it is best to remind your boss of several previous tasks you have handled well. After all, a single example could be an isolated instance or a lucky fluke.

STORIES

Stories illustrate a point by describing an incident in some detail. They come in two categories: hypothetical and factual. *Hypothetical* stories are fictional accounts that might easily have happened. They allow you to create material that perfectly illustrates the point you want to make. C. J. Silas, president of Phillips Petroleum Company, used this hypothetical story to illustrate his thesis that government regulation of natural gas is unfair:

> Put yourself in the place of a small gas producer. Imagine that you have an Uncle Harry who dies and leaves you a couple of gas wells in Kansas. If those are old wells—discovered before 1977—you might only be getting 40 cents an mcf for your gas.
>
> Your neighbor, on the other hand, might have a new well right across the fence—drilled just last year. Even though he's producing gas identical to yours, he can probably sell it for ten times as much. Both you and your neighbor may want to drill for more gas. But only one of you is in a good economic position to do so. That's how government controls discourage exploration.[5]

Hypothetical stories like this one are useful because they get the audience involved in the idea you are developing: "Imagine yourself . . .," "Suppose that you were . . .," "What would you do if . . . ." Besides being involving, hypothetical stories allow you to create a situation that illustrates exactly the point you are trying to make. You can adjust details, create dialogue, and use figures that support your case. But your account will be effective only if it is believable.

Notice how the following hypothetical story involves the listener while supporting the speaker's thesis that good advertisers know their markets:

> Imagine you are driving down a country road on a tour of the wine country and you come across the following sign: (*sign:* "LEMONADE." Handwritten in block letters, scrawled on a yellow background, as though written by a very young child.) Chances are, you are going to stop and get some lemonade. If I had kids and they asked me, as a professional designer, to make a sign for their lemonade stand, I would make it just like this one. After your glass of lemonade, you get back on the road and you come to this sign: (*sign:* "WINE." Same style as lemonade sign, but on a maroon background.) You'd be much less likely to stop. Not every style is right for every product. Rather, different styles of advertising are right for different kinds of products.[6]

Factual stories can also add interest and clarity. This story from a frustrated consumer illustrates the thesis that many businesses are more interested in making a sale than in supporting their products after the deal is closed. Notice how the last sentence restates the main idea so that the point of the story is clear.

> Last Tuesday I decided to call the automobile dealership. There were two numbers listed in the phone book, one for "Sales," the other for "Service." I asked the service

manager if I could bring my car in the following Saturday. Service managers always have a way of making you feel unwanted, and he seemed pleased to be able to tell me that they were closed Saturday and wouldn't be able to take me until a week from Thursday.

I didn't make a date. Instead I called the other number, under "Sales." "Are you open Saturday?" I asked. "Yes, sir," the cheery voice said at the other end of the phone. "We're here Saturdays from eight in the morning till nine in the evening, and Sundays from noon until six."

Now, if I can *buy* a car on Saturday, why can't I get one *fixed* on Saturday? What's going on here anyway? I think I know what's going on, of course. We're *selling* things better than we're *making* them, that's what's going on.[7]

While both factual and hypothetical stories can make a presentation clearer and more interesting, only the factual type can prove a point:

"Cutting the payroll by using temporary employees sounds like a good idea, but it has problems. Listen to what happened when we tried it at the place I used to work. . . ."

"I'm sure Wes can handle the job. Let me tell you what happened last year when we assigned him to manage the Westco account. . . ."

"You might think life insurance isn't necessary for a young, healthy person like you, but remember Dale Crandall, the linebacker from State? Well, he was about as healthy as they come, but. . . ."

Both hypothetical and factual stories gain effectiveness because they are interesting. You can add interest to your accounts by following several guidelines. First, the story should be suited to your audience. Will they be familiar with the situation you're describing? Will they care about it? Second, your story should support your point. An amusing story that doesn't support your thesis will just distract your listeners. Finally, be sure the story is the right length. Don't spin out a five-minute yarn to make a minor point, and don't rush through a story that will win your audience over.

STATISTICS

Statistics are numbers used to represent an idea. Most statistics are collections of examples reduced to numerical form for clarity. If you were arguing that there was a serious manufacturing problem with a new product line, describing one or two dissatisfied customers would not prove that the problem went beyond the usual "acceptable" rate of error in manufacturing or the usual rate of damage in shipping. The following statement, though, would constitute proof: "Our return rate on the new line is just over 40 percent—as opposed to the usual rate of 5 percent—and of all those returns, four-fifths are related to a flaw in the gear assembly."

Statistics are probably the most common form of support in business presentations. They are used to measure the size of market segments, sales trends, decreasing or increasing profits, changes in costs, and many other aspects of business. When handled well, statistics are especially strong proof because they are firmly grounded in fact and because they show that the speaker is well informed. John D. Ong of the B. F. Goodrich Company used statistics to back up his claim that the industrial capability of the United States is being overtaken by other countries:

> The rise of competition from Japan, Europe, Asia and Latin America has been so pervasive that I think many of us have lost sight of just how dramatic it's been. Less than 20 years ago, the United States manufactured about 50 percent of the world's television sets, 90 percent of the world's radios, 76 percent of the automobiles, and 47 percent of the world's steel. Now we produce barely 6 percent of the world's TV sets and radios combined, 28 percent of the cars, and 20 percent of the world's steel.[8]

Despite their potential effectiveness, poorly used statistics can spoil a presentation. One common mistake is to bury an audience under an avalanche of numbers like this speaker did at an annual stockholders' meeting:

> Last year was an exciting one for our company. We earned $6.02 per share on a net income of $450 million, up from $4.63 per share on income of $412 million in the preceding year. This increase came in part from a one-time gain of $13 million from the sale of common stock to New Ventures group, our research and development subsidiary. Excluding this one-time gain, we increased our earnings per share 5.8 percent in the recent year, and we increased our net income 6.5 percent.

These numbers would be very appropriate in a printed annual report, but when a speaker rattles them off to an audience one after another, there is little chance of following them. Rather than smothering your listeners with detail, you can provide a few key numbers. (If backup information is important, you can supply it in written materials accompanying your presentation.) Notice how the following appeal uses figures to highlight the most persuasive reasons for buying new equipment, while making details available for anyone who might be interested:

> Believe it or not, it's actually cheaper for us to buy a new half-inch video recorder for our training department than to replace the worn tapes on our old three-quarter-inch one. Eighty hours worth of the old-style tapes—that's a year's supply—will cost us about $1,750. But for less than $1,200 we can get a brand-new deck and the tapes to use with it. The savings are actually greater if we figure in the $200 or more we'd probably spend repairing the old machine if we kept it another year. The details are on the fact sheet, which I'll circulate now.

In addition to restricting the amount of statistical information you convey, it is usually best to simplify that information by rounding off numbers. It's easier to understand "almost two-thirds" than it is to absorb "64.3 percent," and "almost twice the cost" is easier to grasp than is "item A costs $65.18, while item B runs $127.15."

Besides having too many numbers, statistic-laden presentations are too dry for all but the most dedicated and involved audiences to handle. When you are speaking to a group of nonspecialists, it's important to link your figures to a frame of reference the group will understand. Notice how the following statistics (presented in the form of examples) give new impact to the old principle that "time is money":

> For a manager who is earning $30,000 a year, wasting one hour a day costs the company $3,750 a year.

> For a secretary at $20,000, fifteen minutes at each of two coffee breaks costs $1,427.50.

> And for a $100,000-a-year executive, a two-hour lunch costs the company an extra $12,500 annually.[9]

When a presentation contains more than a few statistics, you will probably need to use visual aids to explain them: numbers alone are simply too confusing to understand. As Bruce Joplin and James W. Pattilo point out in a manual for accountants, "Numbers confuse people. Numbers take longer to absorb and are often not remembered accurately. The hearer will recall that the profit for the West Coast Division was 'eight' but whether it was eight thousand dollars or eighty thousand dollars, he is not sure."[10]

COMPARISONS

Comparisons can make a point by showing how one idea resembles another. Some comparisons—called analogies—are *figurative*. They compare items from an unfamiliar area with items from a familiar one. By considering a few examples, you can appreciate the value of figurative comparisons to add clarity and interest to a presentation:

> We think that sending people to one company for loans, another for insurance, and a third for brokerage services makes about as much sense as sending them to one store for eggs, a second for meat, and a third for bread.[11]

> A fool in a high station is like a man on the top of a high mountain—everything appears small to him and he appears small to everybody.[12]

> The general-purpose home computer is a quaint anachronism and a totally bogus idea. It's like a Swiss Army knife. It may do a lot of things, but it does none of them very well.[13]

By linking the familiar with the unfamiliar, figurative analogies can help listeners understand concepts that would otherwise be mystifying. Consider how a series of familiar concepts can explain the potentially arcane differences between computer networks:

The physical layout of a computer network—the way various systems are connected—is called its topology. The most common network topologies are bus, ring, and star.

A bus topology is like a freeway with many on and off ramps. It has a common path (the bus) on which all data travels. Each device on the network can tap into this bus.

Ring topologies are similar to bus configurations, but the ends are tied together so that data travels in a circle unless it's diverted to one of the devices attached to the network.

Star configurations resemble a spider. The wires connecting the various devices with a central point represent the legs of the spider. The phone company's central office concept is an example of a star configuration.[14]

James M. Hay, chairman of Dow Chemical Canada, Inc., used a more extended figurative analogy to explain the importance of flexible planning in business. Notice how he compares the need for flexibility in a familiar setting (hockey) with the same need in a novel setting (business):

It's like football versus hockey. On the football field, offensive plays are conceived in the locker room. They are executed on signals from the quarterback to respond to relatively fixed circumstances. The similarity to a centrally planned economic development strategy is obvious.

In contrast, hockey reflects exactly the kind of high-speed adaptability to changing circumstances I'm suggesting. In hockey, plays are formulated and implemented in rapid succession. They are modified—adapted—almost instantly as the players move down the ice toward the goal, and as opposing players make their moves. Each player contributes positional play through training and experience. Hockey embodies the kind of adaptability we need in Canada if we are to fight for a strong recovery.[15]

Other comparisons are *literal,* linking similar items from two categories. An account executive might use this sort of comparison to argue that "we need to spend more of our advertising budget on direct mail. That approach worked wonders on the NBT campaign, and I think it can do the same for us here." One critic of the banking industry used literal comparisons to show the abysmal compensation for most bank tellers:

If the tellers at your local bank seem a little surly these days, they've got a good reason. They are among the worst paid workers around, according to a recent survey by the local consulting firm of Towers Perrin Foster and Crosby. Tellers earn about $16,200 annually: about $900 less than the take-home pay for mail clerks, $1,700 less than what the average custodian earns, and it's more than $6,000 less than what a computer operator brings home. When compared to secretaries, bank tellers' pay is pathetic: almost half of the $31,800 the average executive secretary earned in the 90 companies surveyed.

Whenever you propose adopting a policy or using an idea because it worked well somewhere else, you are using comparisons as proof. The strength of this proof depends on how clearly you can establish the similarity between the items you are comparing.

Comparisons are often an ideal way to clarify a potentially confusing idea. Notice in the following example how one attorney wisely invested several minutes developing an extended analogy to explain a medical point in a personal-injury suit:

> I asked my doctor, an orthopedic surgeon, to explain to the jury why, six months after the accident, when the lady is opening the oven, her disc blows out. He stated, "It's very simple. It is like when you park your car and hit the curb too hard. This may weaken the tire, it may cause an imperceptible weakness, crack, or fissure, and then with normal everyday wear and tear thereafter in the use of the vehicle, six months later the tire blows out. Well, this is what happened to this lady. This accident, this trauma, weakened her back and injured her back . . . and then, with her routine work . . . in this particular case when she bent down on the morning in question to open her oven—her back went out."[16]

Comparisons can be combined with other forms of support to clarify and prove. Dr. Luis Fernandes, chairman of Monsanto Company, used this technique to support his argument that government regulation of the chemical industry is excessive. Note how his analogy helps the audience to understand statistics that would otherwise have been difficult to comprehend:

> In the mid-60s, we were measuring chemicals in the environment in parts per million. Just last month, the Michigan Department of Natural Resources came to an agreement on waste disposal with Dow calling for waste products in quantities of parts per quadrillion. Let me say that again. I had to read it twice before I believed it. Parts per quadrillion. How can anyone understand that, which translates into one one-millionth of a gram of sugar in an Olympic-sized swimming pool—or measuring one second in 33 million years.[17]

Whether their purpose is to add clarity, interest, or proof, comparisons should possess two characteristics. First, the familiar part of comparisons should be well known to the audience. For instance, it would be a mistake to say "Jumbo certificates of deposit are similar to treasury bills in several ways" if your listeners do not know anything about treasury bills. In addition, you should be sure your comparisons are valid. You would be stretching a point if you tried to discourage employee abuse of the copying machine by claiming "Using the machine for personal papers is a crime, just as much as robbery or assault." A closer match is both more valid and effective: "You wouldn't help yourself to spare change from a cash register; everybody with a conscience knows that would be a case of petty theft. But using the copying machine for personal papers costs the company, just as surely as if the money came out of the cash register."

CITATIONS

Citations are a way to let others who are authoritative or articulate make a point more effectively than you could do on your own. Some citations add clarity and impact. You might, for example, add punch to a talk explaining the difficulties of cutting advertising costs by citing the famous remark of Alex Osborne, founder of one of the nation's largest advertising agencies: "Only half my advertising budget does any good. I just don't know which half." Likewise, you could emphasize the importance of getting agreements in writing by quoting movie producer Sam Goldwyn: "A verbal contract isn't worth the paper it's written on."

Other citations help build a persuasive case: "Nancy told me yesterday that we ought to add another 10 percent to our projected expenses" or "The June 28 issue of *Forbes* ran an article stating that the demand for home videotape rentals will triple in the next six years."

You can use citations most effectively by following these guidelines:

Cite the Source in a Way That Adds to the Credibility of Your Presentation   Notice how each of the citations in this section introduces the source, and consider how much less effective they would be without this sort of introduction.

Cite Sources That Have Credibility with Your Audience   Citing Karl Marx about the abuse of workers won't impress an audience of Republican manufacturers, while a similar message from a *Wall Street Journal* article might be effective.

Paraphrase Lengthy or Confusing Citations   Some citations are too long, boring, or confusing to read word for word. In these cases, you can still take advantage of the material by paraphrasing it:

> Before we go overboard on the idea of flexible scheduling, it's important to consider the research conducted recently by Professors Graham Staines of Rutgers University and Joseph Pleck of Wellesley College. In a survey of over a thousand employees, they found that people who worked modified schedules were not as happy with their family lives as were people who worked a traditional Monday through Friday, nine-to-five shift.

Restate the Point of Long Citations   If your citation has taken a minute or two to deliver, summarize the point it makes before moving on:

> "After hearing Roberta's figures, you can see that our advertising dollars are well spent."

Don't start with the idea, "I am going to give a slide talk; I am going to make a videotape; or I am going to put on a multimedia presentation."

You don't start there! You start with your aim, your goal, your objective. What do you want to do with the talk? If it calls for slides, fine. If television is the best medium to make the point, okay. But don't go for the medium first and the message later.

John R. Bonée, *A Few Age-Old Principles of Effective Oratory*

"You can see from this research that there are hidden costs in this proposal."

"Customer letters like those make it clear that we need to improve our service."

VISUAL AIDS

The old cliché is true: a picture often *is* worth a thousand words. That is why charts, diagrams, and other graphic aids are part of most business presentations.

Researchers have verified what good speakers have always known intuitively: Using visual aids makes a presentation more effective. In a recent study, two groups of business students watched videotaped presentations describing upcoming time management seminars. One group saw a version of the talk with no visual support, while the other saw the same talk with a number of high quality visuals. After the presentation, the audience was asked about their willingness to enroll in the time management course and about their opinion of the speaker they had just viewed.

Audiences who saw the presentation with visuals were clearly more impressed than those who saw the same talk with no visual support. They planned to spend 16.4 percent more time and 26.4 percent more money on the time management seminar being promoted. They also viewed the speaker as more clear, concise, professional, persuasive, and interesting.[18]

Well-designed graphics are also easier to understand than words alone. A chart listing a point-by-point comparison of two products is easier to follow than a detailed narrative. A plummeting sales curve tells the story more eloquently than any words. You can appreciate the value of visuals to make a point quickly and clearly by reading the following text alone and then seeing how the chart in Figure 12-1 makes the information so much clearer.

If not properly used and appropriately timed, visual aids (anything from charts and graphs to elaborate multimedia shows) can work against you.

First, people have opinions on everything. If you're not careful you can find the conversation deflected toward a critique of your visual aids rather than holding it to what you are there to sell in the first place.

Second, if introduced too early in the presentation it can be distracting. All of a sudden everyone's playing with your visual aids while your sales strategy and game plan go out of the window.

Until you are ready to get to the "show" part of the show and tell, keep your visual aids *out of sight*. You don't want people waiting and wondering what you've got in that little black box.

Mark H. McCormack, *What They Don't Teach You at Harvard Business School*

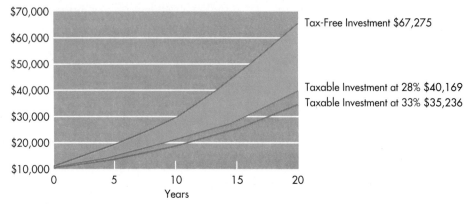

Figure 12-1 A visual aid is often clearer and more dramatic than words alone.

The power of tax-free accumulation is tremendous. Suppose you invested $10,000 at 10 percent. If you were taxed at a rate of 33 percent, your investment would grow to $35,236 over twenty years. If you were in the 28 percent tax bracket, your original nest egg would grow to $40,169. But with a tax-free investment, the original $10,000 would appreciate to a value of $67,275.

Visuals can help make complicated statistics easier for you to explain and easier for your listeners to understand. Besides increasing the clarity of your material, visuals will make your presentations more interesting. For example, investment brokers often use an array of well-prepared charts, tables, models, and so on to add variety to information that would be deadly dull without it.

Visuals can also boost your image in ways that extend beyond the presentation itself. A professional display of visuals labels you as a professional person—a candidate for recognition in the future by superiors and the public. Finally, visuals can make your information more memorable. Researchers have discovered that audiences recall far more information when it is presented both verbally and visually than when it is presented in only one way.[19]

METHOD	RECALL AFTER THREE HOURS	RECALL AFTER THREE DAYS
Verbal only	70%	10%
Visual only	72%	20%
Verbal and visual	85%	65%

Visual aids perform many useful functions. They can *show how things look*. An architect might use a model or an artist's sketch to describe a project to potential clients, and an advertising director could use photographs of a new product as part of a campaign.

Visual aids can also *show how things work*. An engineer could include diagrams as part of the instructions for a piece of equipment, and a sales representative could use a model to show how a boat is designed for speed and safety.

Visual aids also can *show how things relate to one another.* An organization chart provides a clear picture of the reporting relationships in a company; a flow chart pictures the steps necessary to get a job done.

Finally, visual aids can *emphasize important points.* You might use a chart to show customers the features of a new product or develop a graph to show the performance of a stock.

TYPES OF VISUAL AIDS

As a speaker, you can choose from a wide array of visual aids to make your presentations more effective. You won't use them all every time you speak, but sooner or later you will, in your presentations, use almost every type described in the following pages.

Objects and Models   Sometimes the object you are discussing or a realistic model is the best kind of support. This is especially true in training sessions and in some types of selling, where hands-on experience is essential. It's difficult to imagine learning how to operate a piece of equipment without actually giving it a try, and few customers would buy an expensive, unfamiliar piece of merchandise without seeing it demonstrated.

Photographs   Photographs can be the most effective way to illustrate a variety of images that need literal representation: an architectural firm's best work, a corporation's management team, or a stylish new product. Photographs also provide an excellent form of proof. For instance, an insurance investigator's pictures of a wrecked auto may be all that exists of a car months later, when a claim is argued in court.

Diagrams   Diagrams are abstract, two-dimensional drawings that show the important properties of objects without being completely representational. Types of diagrams you might use in presentations include floor plans (see Figure 12-2), drawings (see Figure 12-3), and maps (see Figure 12-4). Diagrams are excellent for conveying information about size, shape, and structure.

Lists and Tables   Lists and tables are an effective way of highlighting key facts and figures. They are especially effective when you list steps, highlight features, or compare related facts: advantages and disadvantages, current and past performance, your product versus a competitor's, and so on. The table in Figure 12-5 clearly lists the rate of return for several certificates of deposit offered by one bank. A sales manager might use a similar chart to compare this year's sales performance and last year's in several regions. A personnel officer explaining the advantages and disadvantages of two different health-insurance plans available to employees might use a list or table to help individual employees decide which plan might work best for them.

Amateur speakers often assume they need only enlarge tables from a written report in an oral presentation. In practice, this approach rarely works. Most

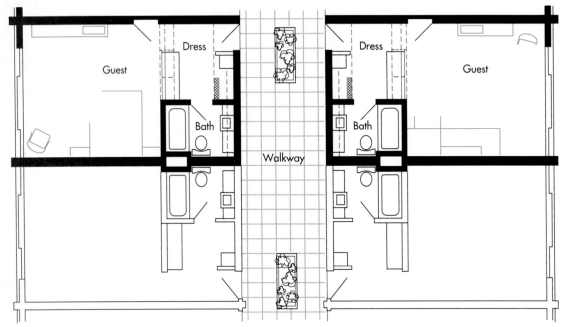

Figure 12-2 Floor plan.

written tables are far too detailed and much less understandable to be useful to a group of listeners. As you design lists and tables, remember the following points:

- Keep the visual aid simple. List only highlights. Use only key words or phrases, never full sentences.
- Use numbered and/or bulleted lists to emphasize key points. Numbered lists suggest ranking or steps in a process, while bullet lists work best for items that are equally important.

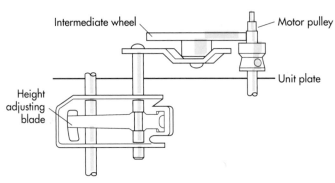

Figure 12-3 Drawing.

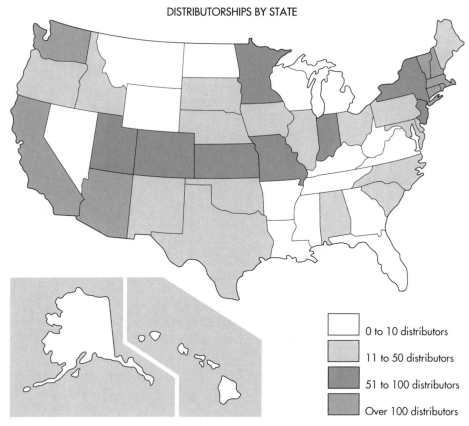

DISTRIBUTORSHIPS BY STATE

☐ 0 to 10 distributors

▨ 11 to 50 distributors

▨ 51 to 100 distributors

▨ Over 100 distributors

Figure 12-4 Map.

TWO-YEAR TERM
CERTIFICATES OF DEPOSIT

MINIMUM OPENING DEPOSIT	ANNUAL RATE	ANNUAL YIELD
$50,000	8.20%	8.66%
$15,000	8.15%	8.61%
$ 100	8.10%	8.55%

Figure 12-5 Table.

■ Use text sparingly. If you need more than eight lines of text, create two or more tables. Lines of text should never exceed twenty-five characters across, including spaces.

■ Use large type. Make sure that the words and numbers are large enough to be read by everyone in the audience.

■ Enhance the list's or table's readability. Careful layout and generous use of white space will make it easy to read.

Pie Charts   Pie charts like the ones in Figure 12-6 illustrate component percentages of a single item. Frequently, they are used to show how money is spent. They also can illustrate the allocation of resources. For example, a personnel director might use a pie chart to show the percentage of employees that work in each division of the company.

Many computer graphics programs make it easy to produce attractive and dramatic pie charts by tilting the figure or removing one segment. While this highlighting can attract interest, it also risks distorting the data.

Follow these guidelines when constructing pie charts:

■ Place the segment you want to emphasize at the top-center twelve o'clock position on the circle. When you are not emphasizing any segments, organize the wedges from largest to smallest, beginning at twelve o'clock with the largest one.

■ Label each segment, either inside or outside the figure.

■ List the percentage for each segment as well as its label.

Bar and Column Charts   Simple bar charts like the one shown in Figure 12-7 compare the value of several items: the productivity of several employees, the

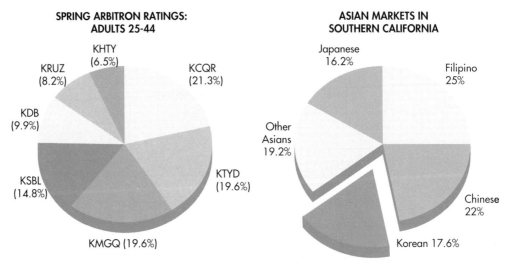

Figure 12-6   Simple and modified pie charts.

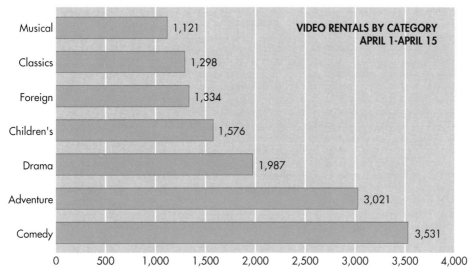

Figure 12-7   Simple bar chart.

relative amount of advertising money spent on different media, and so on. Subdivided charts like the one in Figure 12-8 compare the component amounts of several items, such as the relative amount of profit and cost for several products.

Simple column charts like the one in Figure 12-9 reflect changes in a single item over time. Multiple-column charts like the one in Figure 12-10 compare several items over time.

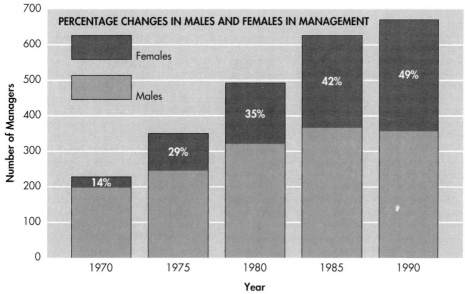

Figure 12-8   Subdivided column chart.

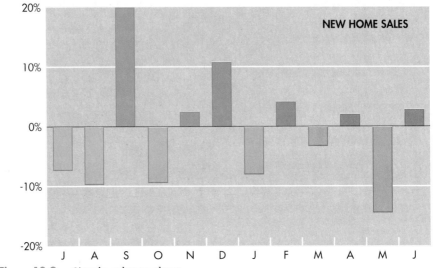

Figure 12-9 Simple column chart.

Several tips will help you design effective bar and column charts:

- Always represent time on the horizontal axis of your chart, running from left to right.
- Arrange the bars in a sequence that best suits your purpose. You might choose to order them from high to low, from low to high, in alphabetical order, or in order of importance.

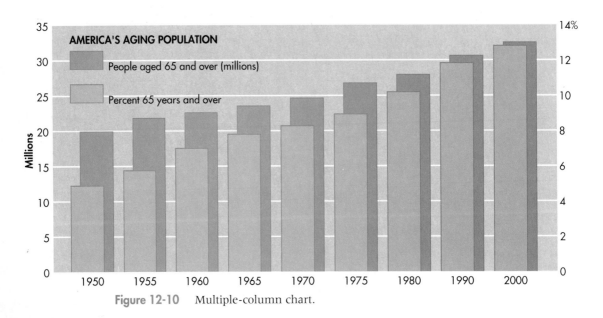

Figure 12-10 Multiple-column chart.

■ Make sure the numerical values represented are clear. This may mean putting the numbers next to bars or columns. In other cases, the figures will fit inside the bars. In a few instances, the scale on the axes will make numbering each bar unnecessary.

Pictograms Pictograms are artistic variations of bar, column, or pie charts. As Figure 12-11 shows, pictograms are more interesting than ordinary bars. This makes them useful in presentations aimed at lay audiences such as the general public. Pictograms are often not mathematically exact, however, which makes them less suited for reports that require precise data.

Graphs Graphs show the correlation between two quantities. They are ideally suited to showing trends, such as growth or decline in sales over time. They can also represent a large amount of data without becoming cluttered. Single-line graphs like the one in Figure 12-12 show trends. Multiple-line graphs like the one in Figure 12-13 show relationships among two or more trends. Notice in Figure 12-14 how identical data can be manipulated by adjusting the horizontal and vertical axes.

MEDIA FOR PRESENTING VISUAL AIDS

Choosing the most advantageous way to present your visual aids is just as important as picking the right type. The best photograph, chart, or diagram will flop if it isn't displayed effectively.

Figure 12-11   Pictogram.

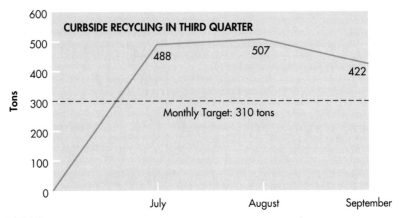

Figure 12-12   Single-line graph.

Flip Charts and Poster Board   Flip charts consist of a large pad of paper attached to an easel. You reveal visuals on a flip chart one at a time by turning the pages. You can also produce visuals on rigid poster board, which you can display on the same sort of easel.

Flip charts and poster-board displays are a common way of displaying visuals in business presentations. In fact, most conference and meeting rooms in business offices and convention hotels are equipped with an easel to show them. Sales-people use them to make presentations to clients. Marketing managers use them

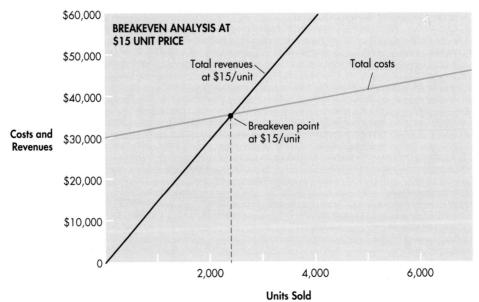

Figure 12-13   Multiple-line graph.

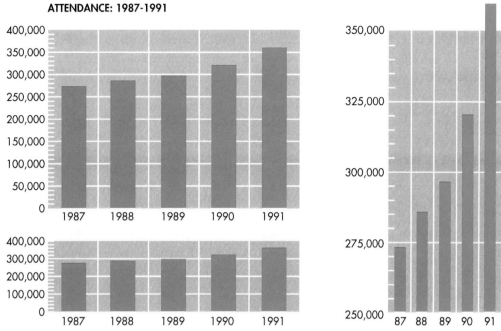

Figure 12-14 The same data can be distorted by varying the horizontal and vertical size and axes of a graph.

to present new plans to upper management. Production managers use them to map out schedules.

A major advantage of flip charts and poster displays is that they are relatively simple to prepare and easy to use. You can create them with familiar materials: pens, rulers, and so on. They are relatively portable (most easels collapse into a carrying case) and easy to set up. They don't require electrical equipment that can break down.

Despite these advantages, flip charts and poster boards have several potential drawbacks. First, they may be too small for some members of a large audience to see easily. Second, they are relatively fragile and can become shabby after being handled in presentations. Finally, posters and large charts are clumsy. They do not fit in a briefcase or under an airplane seat, and they make it awkward to perform simple maneuvers like shaking hands or catching a taxi.

Transparencies Transparencies are clear sheets that are used with an overhead projector to cast an image on a screen. They are frequently the visual aid of choice when the audience is too large for flip charts or poster displays. You can create original images with special pens or reproduce visuals from other sources using a standard office copying machine equipped with special acetate sheets. (Most copy shops are equipped for this job.) Color copying machines can even transform a glossy magazine photo or slide into an 8 1/2" x 11" transparency, allowing you to mix photos and other types of print exhibits without forcing you to use a slide projector as well as an overhead machine.

Transparencies have several advantages. They can be produced quickly—in seconds with the right copying machine. They are often easier to create than other types of visuals since you can copy professional-looking visuals from other sources instead of creating images from scratch. They can be projected to a large size for all members of a large audience to see. They are visible in a lighted room. Using special pens, you can draw on them as you speak, underlining key words, circling important numbers, completing graphs, and so on. After the presentation, you can erase your additions and reuse the same sheets in future presentations. They are easy to store and don't wear out like flip charts and poster boards.

Transparencies also suffer from several drawbacks. Most important, they require a bulky projector that isn't always easy to find and may not work on the day of your presentation. (Many speakers have been thwarted by a burned-out lightbulb.) In addition, the audience or speaker may have to be positioned in a

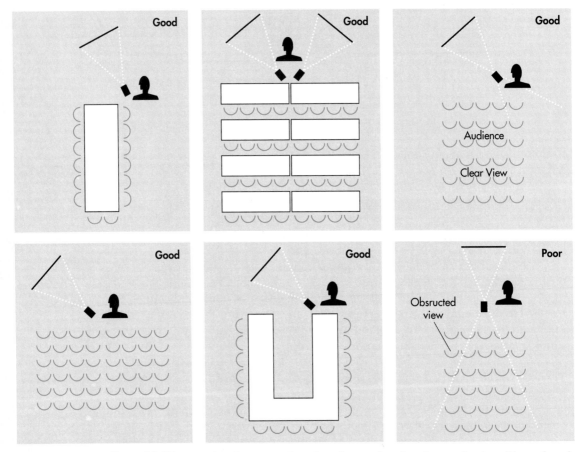

Figure 12-15   Good and poor seating plans for overhead projector viewing. (Reproduced with permission from 3M Audio Visual Division.)

special way so the projector doesn't block anyone's view. (See Figure 12-15 for room layouts.) Finally, the projection screen may need to be mounted at an angle to prevent a "keystone" distortion of the image. (See Figure 12-16.)

Presentations using an overhead projector will be most effective when you remember several points:

- Show transparencies only when you are discussing them. Between transparencies, shut off the projector.
- Never remove or replace images while the projector is on. Position a transparency, and then turn on the machine. Turn it off, and then remove the sheet.
- Use a piece of paper or cardboard to cover the parts of a sheet you haven't discussed yet. As you come to each point, move the cover to reveal the new information. This technique prevents your audience from getting ahead of you.
- Face the audience as you speak. Use a pointer to refer to the transparency as it rests on the glass stage of the projector; don't turn your back on the audience and point to the screen.

Slides　Although they are projected on a screen like overhead transparencies, slides have different uses and properties. They work best when you want to show

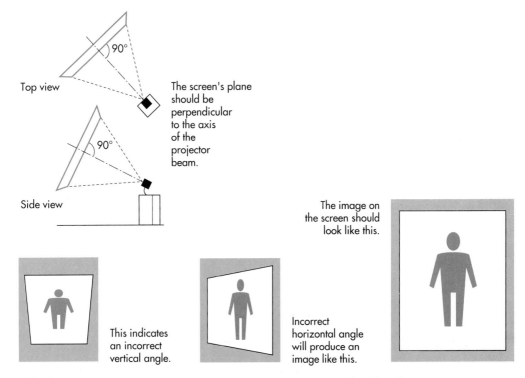

Figure 12-16　Proper viewing angles for overhead projector. (Reproduced with permission from 3M Audio Visual Division.)

an actual photographic image. In fact, they are often far superior to photos printed on paper since they can be easily seen by even a large audience. They are cheap and can be produced quickly—in an hour or a couple of days. They are easy to edit: you can add, delete, and rearrange them to suit the needs of a particular presentation.

New software programs and services make it easy to transfer computer-generated visuals onto slides so that they can be mixed with traditional photographs in a presentation. Companies with a high demand for this service can purchase slide recorders, which connect to a computer and produce transparencies almost immediately. Low-volume users who can't justify the cost of a slide recorder can send floppy disks containing their files to services that will convert the files into slides.

The biggest drawback of slides is the need for a darkened room. While the slides are being shown, the speaker is only a shadowy figure to the audience. This setup makes it easy for minds to wander or for listeners to doze off. If you do use slides:

- Keep the show brief. The distraction factor will be smallest if you don't keep the room dark for a long time. Don't dwell on each slide. Everyone has suffered through a seemingly endless narrative of boring vacation slides, and the same abuses can occur in business presentations.
- Use a remote-control device with a long cord so you can stand next to the screen during your show. When you become a disembodied voice at the back of the room, you are inviting the audience to drift off.
- Talk to your listeners, not to the screen. Stand to one side, and use a pointer to direct their attention. Never turn your back on your audience.

Handouts Handouts provide a permanent record of your ideas. The more intricate features of a product, names and phone numbers, or "do's and don'ts" are easier to recall when your listeners have a printed record of them. Handouts are also a way to give your audience more details than you want to talk about in your presentation. You might, for instance, mention the highlights of a sales period or briefly outline the technical features of a new product and then refer your listeners to a handout for further information.

You can use handouts to reduce or eliminate your listeners' need to take notes. If you put key ideas and figures on a handout, their attention will be focused on you instead of on their notebooks—and you'll be sure their notes are accurate. Some speakers use an "electronic blackboard," a plastic write-and-wipe board that can also produce handout-sized copies of what you've written on the board.

The biggest problem with handouts is that they can be distracting. The activity that accompanies passing around papers interrupts the flow of your presentation. Once the handout is distributed, you'll have to compete with it for your audience's attention. For this reason, it's better to distribute handouts *after* you've finished speaking. If printed material has to be introduced during your presentation, tell your listeners when to begin referring to it and when to stop: "Let's take a look at the budget on the pink sheet in your folders." "Now that we've examined the budget, let me direct your attention to the chart up here."

Computerized Displays   Liquid crystal display panels (LCDs) connect to a computer and fit on an overhead projector. They allow the user to project images from the computer onto a large screen, where these images can be seen easily by an audience. The price of LCDs is steadily dropping, even for color displays. As they become affordable, LCDs are likely to become a familiar and useful fixture in business presentations.

With graphics software, computerized visuals have several advantages. They allow users to prepare and modify sophisticated images with relative ease. Impressive techniques like animation and fades from one image to another are possible. Live, computer-generated "slide shows" illustrating a sequence of images are the strong suit of LCD-equipped computers. These shows can be controlled by a speaker using a remote control, giving the speaker freedom to move away from the keyboard and focus on the audience.

Videotape   As the price of camcorders and videocassette players falls, the possibility of including videotape in presentations grows. Everyone is familiar with the attention-grabbing potential of television, and it is tempting to use that technology to boost the impact of your talks.

There are times when videotaped support is a plus. If you are illustrating action—the performance of an athletic team or the gestures of a speaker, for example—video may do the job better than any other medium. But despite the benefits of video, including televised segments can be risky. There is an enormous gap between the production quality you can achieve with a hand-held camcorder and the kind of sophistication that is possible with professional editing equipment. Common problems include segments that last too long, that lack the kind of narration and musical accompaniment that add continuity, and that are full of jerky images and awkward cuts between shots. The risk of using amateur videos containing flaws like these is that they will cast the rest of your message in an unprofessional light. This is why most business-communication experts only use video programs that have been professionally prepared—usually at considerable expense.

COMPUTER-ASSISTED DESIGN OF VISUAL AIDS

Less than a decade ago, most business speakers had few choices about how to design visuals. They could rely on their own talent and create them by hand— usually with amateurish results—or they could turn the job over to a professional graphic artist, who would produce impressive displays—usually at great cost. Now any businessperson with a personal computer, relatively inexpensive software, and a decent printer can produce charts and graphs that approach the quality that used to be possible only by experts.[20] As Table 12-2 shows, there are many ways to

TABLE 12-2   Computer-Assisted Design Options

Methods of creating images
    Word-processing software
    Drawing software
    Charting software (usually combined with spreadsheet)
    Presentation-design software
    Scanning of pictures, charts, or text
Output
    Paper handouts
    Overhead-projection transparencies
    35-millimeter slides
    On-screen displays

create and display computer-generated images. Figure 12-17 illustrates how computer graphics can enhance the display of information.

The range of computerized graphic displays is great. At its most basic, a beginner can use software programs like Lotus 1-2-3 and Microsoft Excel to turn spreadsheet numbers into a variety of charts—pie, bar, column, line, and so on. Specialized presentation software like Aldus Persuasion or Microsoft Power Point make it especially easy to produce customized color transparencies, slides, handouts, and on-screen slide shows that are closely linked to a set of speaker's notes.

Businesses with more resources have the equipment and staff to produce elaborate displays.[21] For example, General Motors' Environmental Activities Department has an on-staff presentation graphics designer who produces 35-millimeter slides, overhead transparencies, posters, and paper handouts for all 160 employees in the department. Besides turning out visually impressive exhibits, this specialist can work quickly. It is not uncommon for department members to give the designer a script in the morning for a presentation they plan to give later that day.

Occasionally designers seem to seek credit merely for possessing a new technology, rather than using it to make better designs. Computers and their affiliated apparatus can do powerful things graphically. . . . But at least a few computer graphics only evoke the response "Isn't it remarkable that the computer can be programmed to draw like that?" instead of "My, what interesting data. . . ."

The purpose of decoration varies—to make the graphic appear more scientific and precise, to enliven the display, to give the designer an opportunity to exercise artistic skills. Regardless of its cause, it is all non-data-ink or redundant data-ink, and it is often chartjunk. Graphical decoration . . . comes cheaper than the hard work required to produce intriguing numbers and secure evidence.

Edward R. Tufte, *The Quantitative Display of Visual Information*

First Quarter Sales
($00)

	Store #1	Store #2	Store #3
Jan	425	248	125
Feb	298	224	150
Mar	322	148	109

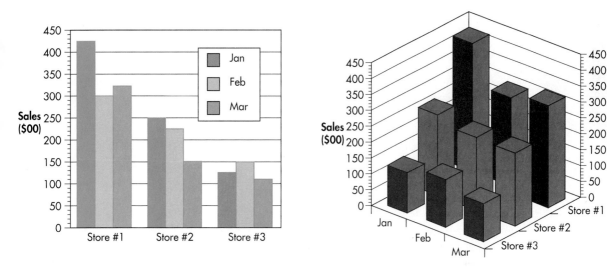

Figure 12-17   Computer graphics can increase sophistication and clarity of displays. The same information becomes more understandable and visually interesting when it is enhanced by use of charting software. Tables can be created with most word processing programs. Two-dimensional charts can be generated from most programs with spreadsheet and charting capabilities, such as Microsoft Excel and Lotus 1-2-3. The three-dimensional chart was created with Delta Graph, a sophisticated charting program.

Computer-assisted designs can often impress audiences in ways that low-tech exhibits cannot. One Southern California real-estate development company wanted to convince a slow-growth-oriented city council that its proposed seven-story office building would not overwhelm its surroundings. The developers knew that the traditional architect's rendering would not convince the city council, so they hired a design consultant who used a set of computerized drawing, painting, and animation tools to create a more realistic vision of the completed product. Besides producing a better image, the computerized design proved more flexible. For example, the developers created customized versions of the drawing that showed the name of potential lessees on a sign across the building. As one of the building's planners put it, "I can show that image to Company X and ask, 'How would you like to have your company's name up there?' That's a very strong marketing tool."

Although computer-assisted design can be very effective, it isn't foolproof. Even basic charting programs—like their word-processing and spreadsheet cousins—do take time to learn. If you are using one for the first time, prepare to invest an hour or two of study and practice before turning out a finished product. It's even better to get the help of a friend or fellow worker who already is skilled with a design program. Being able to ask someone familiar with the software can save you a great deal of the time and frustration you would otherwise experience in trial-and-error experimenting or leafing through an instruction book.

Once you have mastered a charting program, it is important to resist the temptation to overuse it. In most presentations, simplicity is a virtue. Just because it is *possible* to produce an elaborate visual full of detail, it doesn't mean that this sort of display will communicate your message effectively. For example, the three-dimensional chart in Figure 12-17 is probably as complex as a visual display should be—at least in an oral presentation. If it were any more complex, it would make the figure hard to understand in the limited time available for viewing. Detailed visuals may be appropriate for written reports. But in oral talks, simplicity is usually the best approach.

RULES FOR USING VISUAL AIDS

Whether you are using handouts, poster boards, flip charts, transparencies, slides, or a chalkboard, be sure to follow these basic rules:

Strategy As with any part of your presentation, visual exhibits must be chosen with care.

Be Sure You Have a Reason for Using a Visual Aid If your image doesn't explain a point better than words alone, don't use it. Visuals used for their own sake will distract your audience from the point you're trying to make.

Match the Sophistication of Your Visuals to the Audience Presentations to important audiences—top bosses, key customers, and so on—usually require polished graphics. For more routine talks, you can probably produce perfectly adequate exhibits on your own. Thanks to advances in computer graphics, you may even be spared the trouble of having to create figures from scratch. In any case, you shouldn't mix informal images with more formal ones any more than you would wear tennis shoes with a dressy outfit.

Design Confusing or sloppy exhibits will be counterproductive. These simple guidelines will help you create clear, neat images.

Make Sure the Visual Is Large Enough to See   The visual that looks so clear on the desktop in front of you might be almost microscopic from where your listeners are seated. Avoid using items, drawings, or photographs that are so small you have to describe them or pass them around. Remember, a distracting or unclear visual is worse than no support at all.

Keep the Design of Your Visuals Simple   Show only one idea per exhibit and avoid unnecessary details. If an exhibit needs further explanation, supply it verbally. Remember that you are giving an oral presentation, not showing your audience a written report.

Use Only a Few Words   Most exhibits are visual images, so you should avoid excessive text. Captions should contain only key words or phrases, not sentences. Omit subtitles. Never use more than twenty-five characters in a single line. If a visual needs more explanation, supply it orally.

Use Only Horizontal Printing   Avoid vertical or diagonal wording. If necessary, place captions in margins to allow you to use a horizontal format.

Label All Items for Clear Identification   Make sure each exhibit has a descriptive title. Label each axis of a chart, each part of a diagram, and so on.

Presentation   The way you present your exhibits is as important as their design.

Don't Display a Visual Until You Are Ready for It   Once you have revealed an exhibit, the audience will try to make sense of it, whether or not you are ready to discuss it. This sort of preview invites confusion and lessens the impact of the point you want to make with the exhibit. In addition, it also distracts your listeners from what you are saying now.

Remove a Visual After Discussing It   Leaving a visual on display after its usefulness is over draws away the attention of your audience. If you are using a flip chart, put blank sheets between the visuals. With an overhead projector, turn off the light between exhibits. Erase chalkboard visuals after you have referred to them.

Make Sure Your Visuals Will Work in the Meeting Room   Double-check the availability of easels, screens, and other equipment you'll need. Be sure that electrical outlets are available in the right locations. Check sight lines from all audience seats. Be sure you can easily control lighting levels as necessary.

Practice Using Your Visuals   Rehearse setting up and removing visuals smoothly and quickly. Review the comments you'll make with each one. Be sure exhibits are arranged in the right order and lined up properly so you can avoid the embarrassment of mixed-up charts or upside-down slides.

SUMMARY

Supporting material is vital in any presentation. It serves three purposes: to clarify the speaker's ideas, to make the material more interesting, and to offer proof. Several types of verbal support are available to a speaker: examples, stories (factual and hypothetical), statistics, comparisons (figurative and literal), and citations.

Visual aids are a common and important type of support in most business presentations. They can make a point more quickly and clearly than can words alone, add variety and interest, and boost a speaker's professional image. Visuals serve several functions: they can show how things look, how they work, or how they relate to one another, and they can highlight important information.

Speakers can use several visual aids: objects, models, photographs, diagrams, lists and tables, pie charts, bar and column charts, pictograms, and graphs. These visuals can be presented via a number of media: flip charts and poster-board displays, overhead transparencies, slides, chalkboard, handouts, computerized displays, and videotapes. Whatever the medium, all visuals should follow the same basic rules. They should be easy to understand, purposeful, well suited to the point they illustrate and to the audience, and workable in the presentational setting. Speakers should be familiar with the visuals they use to avoid any unpleasant surprises when the time for delivery comes.

ACTIVITIES

1. What types of support introduced in this chapter would you use to add interest, clarity, and proof to the following points?

   a. Tuition costs are keeping promising students out of college.
   b. Textbooks are (are not) overpriced.
   c. Timely payment of bills is in the customer's best interest.
   d. Companies are helping themselves as well as employees by sponsoring and subsidizing exercise programs during working hours.
   e. A liberal-arts education can benefit one's career—better in many ways than technical training.

2. Imagine that you have been assigned to develop a sales presentation to promote the product or service of your choice.

   Develop three main points that would be most impressive to a specific audience and list the types of support you would use with each point.

3. Develop a chart or graph showing the overall changes in the demographic characteristics (age, sex, and so on) of your student body over the past ten years.

4. The local chamber of commerce has hired you to compile graphic exhibits that will be used in presentations to encourage people to visit and settle in your area. Design materials reflecting the following information:

   a. Average monthly rainfall
   b. Month-to-month variations in temperature
   c. Days with sunshine

If you believe that these figures would *discourage* an audience, you may choose data that paint an appealing picture of a different area.

5. Develop three visual aids that could be used to introduce new students to registration procedures used in your school.

6. Collect examples of each type of verbal and visual support described in this chapter. Comment on how effectively each example follows the guidelines in the text. Describe how each piece of support should be adopted for use in an oral presentation.

Communicator Profile

Eugene Weston III, A.I.A., Partner
Liebhardt, Weston & Associates, Architects
La Jolla, California

We use as few mechanical gadgets as possible since they multiply the number of things that can go wrong.

Liebhardt, Weston & Associates is an architectural firm specializing in commercial, institutional, and recreational projects. Some of our recent jobs include work for the San Diego Wild Animal Park, the master plan for the Kuwait National Zoo, the research library for the Scripps Institution of Oceanography, and San Diego's Old Globe Theatre. Projects we design generally range from $1 million to $10 million in construction costs.

We make formal presentations for virtually every new client we seek. The most obvious goal of these presentations is to show our talents as designers, but this isn't the only thing we try to accomplish. We also try to demonstrate that we can deliver our work on time, that we're experienced at the kind of work the potential client is seeking, and that we can work within the client's budget. That a firm makes good presentations doesn't guarantee that they'll be good architects, but without good presentations they wouldn't get most jobs in the first place.

We always use visuals of one sort or another in our presentations. Since we are dealing with a three-dimensional product, our business relies especially heavily on illustrations. The amount and type of visuals we use depends on the size of the job, the nature of the client, and the kind of project. A simple job with an unquestioning client might only call for a set of informal sketches. On the other hand, a large job with specialized challenges for clients who are very demanding or unsure of what they want might call for a full-scale "dog and pony show."

We use many different types of visuals.

While slides are among the easiest kinds for us to produce, we've found they don't work especially well since so many architects use them these days. As soon as the lights go down, some clients tend to lose attention—and the last thing we want to do is put anyone to sleep! Since we usually address just a few listeners, eight-by-ten–inch mounted color photographs often are a good way to show buildings we have designed in the past. When we want to illustrate an idea that hasn't been built yet, we rely on artists' renderings. They are especially effective since they allow us to emphasize features that make our ideas unique and downplay distractions like surrounding buildings. We often use plans to show relationships between various systems or areas. For instance, floor plans are the best way to show how several rooms relate to one another or to illustrate how an electrical or plumbing system fits into a design.

We also use charts containing words and images. One very useful type is a time line showing a proposed schedule. Displaying the deadlines and milestones graphically makes them far easier to understand than simply putting them in a list. Another type of chart that has proved useful lists the members of a design team: architects, engineers, consultants, and others. Clients are very concerned about whom they'll actually be dealing with, and seeing specific names on these charts helps to address their concerns.

In addition to the visuals we use during a presentation, we often give each member of an interview committee a handout at the end of our talk. This packet contains reproductions of many of the visuals we introduced during the presentation itself. It serves as a tangible reminder of who we are and what we've said. We have learned never to distribute these handouts until we've finished the prepared part of our talk. If we give these papers out early, people start looking at them instead of us.

We have found three principles that help us use visuals most effectively. First, we always rehearse our presentation before delivering it to clients. Things rarely work the way we expect them to, and practice sessions cut down on the surprises. Second, we use as few mechanical gadgets as possible since they multiply the number of things that can go wrong. We once were embarrassed when we couldn't begin an elaborate slide-tape presentation because the $8,000 machine we'd just bought wouldn't start. After some time, we found the one switch that needed to be thrown, but that delay left us looking foolish. Finally, we have learned that presentations that involve visuals work best when two people are involved. One can set up and take down exhibits while the other talks. This prevents long silences while a lone presenter juggles visuals and tries to speak to the listeners.

A good presentation can make the difference between getting the job and losing it. So can a bad one! Do everything you can to prepare a talk that focuses on your listeners' interests and concerns, and make sure that it's delivered as smoothly and professionally as possible.

13

After reading this chapter, you should understand:

- The merits and drawbacks of manuscript, memorized, impromptu, and extemporaneous forms of delivery
- The guidelines for using speaking notes
- The procedure for delivering effective impromptu remarks
- The visual elements that contribute to effective delivery
- The vocal elements that contribute to effective delivery
- The factors that should influence whether to invite audience questions during or after a presentation
- The irrational myths that contribute to speaking anxiety

You should be able to:

- Develop and use a set of speaking notes that enhance your delivery
- Deliver brief, impromptu remarks effectively
- Deliver an extemporaneous presentation that follows the guidelines for visual, verbal, and vocal behavior
- Invite and respond effectively to audience questions arising from a presentation you have delivered
- Apply the guidelines for overcoming speech anxiety to a presentation you will deliver

DELIVERING THE
PRESENTATION

In an age of instantaneous communication via telephone, computer, and fax, face-to-face presentations might seem like an anachronism. After all, presentations are enormous consumers of time: just scheduling a date when everyone can attend can be a major chore. Then the audience members have to travel to the location of the talk—sometimes across the hall, but just as often much farther afield. After the message is delivered, the speaker and audience have to finish up their business and get back to work. With all this effort, even a ten-minute talk to a five-person audience takes at least an hour of working time—much more than it would take to send the same message in writing or even over the telephone.

Despite their apparent inefficiency, presentations are still an important part of doing business—and with good reason. The potential advantages of speaking with an audience face to face are tremendous. You can control the attention of your audience instead of risking the chance that your message will be shuffled aside. You can share your enthusiasm about the message in a way that words on paper or spoken over the telephone can't match. If your listeners have questions or objections, you can address them directly.

In order to take advantage of these strengths, a presentation has to be well delivered. If you look sloppy, speak in a way that is hard to understand, or seem unenthusiastic, the face-to-face medium changes from an asset to a liability. Instead of leading the audience to accept your message, poor delivery can cause them to doubt or even reject it. As communication consultant Roger Ailes puts it, "You become the message. People cannot distinguish between the words and who speaks them."[1]

The following pages will offer suggestions that can help you deliver your remarks in a way that makes your message clearer, more interesting, and more persuasive. They describe the various styles of delivery, offer tips for improving your visual and vocal performance, explain how to deal with questions from the audience, and give advice for dealing with the nervousness that often accompanies an important presentation.

TYPES OF DELIVERY

There are four ways to deliver a presentation. In most situations, though, two of these approaches are so disastrous that only uninformed speakers use them.

MANUSCRIPT PRESENTATIONS

You have probably heard speakers read their remarks word for word from a prepared statement. Manuscript speaking is common at annual companywide meetings, conventions, and press conferences. Yet few experiences are so boring as the average manuscript presentation.

The most dynamic and personable managers often try to conceal their nervousness at facing a large audience by reading from a script—and they turn into lifeless drones. Since most speakers are not trained at reading aloud, their delivery is halting and jerky. Even worse, a nervous speaker who relies too heavily on a manuscript can make serious mistakes without even knowing it. Management consultant Marilyn Landis describes one such disaster:

> I remember the president of a large corporation who followed his usual pattern of asking his public relations director to write a speech for him. Due to a collating error, the script contained two copies of page five. You guessed it. The president read page five twice—and didn't even realize it.[2]

Even when a speaker reads a report flawlessly, the presentation often sounds mechanical and lifeless. It may be possible to read an adventure story or an interesting newspaper article enthusiastically, but almost anyone's voice and manner will be flat when reading a financial report or a market analysis. One important ingredient of a speaker's credibility is sincerity, and it's difficult to seem sincere when reading.

To make things worse, the text of a manuscript presentation is often a copy of a written report—usually far too long and detailed for effective oral presentation. "I don't know why we have to sit through people reading a report that's been copied and distributed," one manager complained. "I can read it myself a lot faster."

In legal or legislative testimony, diplomatic speeches, or other situations in which a slight misstatement could have serious consequences, manuscript speaking may be your best means of delivery. Most presentations, however, do not fall into this category. A simple but important rule for most cases, then, is *don't read your presentation*.

MEMORIZED PRESENTATIONS

If speaking from a script is bad, trying to memorize that script is even worse. You probably have been subjected to a door-to-door salesperson's obviously memorized pitch for encyclopedias or carpet cleaning. If so, you know that the biggest problem of a memorized presentation is that it *sounds* memorized.

It might seem that memorizing a presentation would help with your nervousness, but memorizing almost guarantees that "stage fright" will become a serious problem. Speakers who spend great amounts of time simply learning the words of a talk are asking for trouble. During the presentation, they must focus on remembering what comes next instead of getting involved in the meaning of those remarks. One worker described a personnel manager's habitual problems with memorized presentations:

> He'd start *reciting*, like a kid reciting a poem in school. If you interrupted him to ask a question, he'd stumble all over himself. Then he couldn't pick up again where he'd left off. He had to start over.

Sometimes it's necessary to memorize parts of a presentation since referring to notes at a critical moment can diminish your credibility. A salesperson is usually expected to know the major features of the product—how much horse-

Never memorize! You cannot communicate with your audience if you're struggling to remember each word of a speech. And what happens if you forget?

"Studio One" was one of the most popular shows in the golden days of live television. During one memorable broadcast, the scene was the interior of an airplane cabin. The plane was at an altitude of 30,000 feet, flying over the mountains of Tibet. Three men were in the cabin talking when suddenly there was silence. One of the actors had forgotten his lines. There were no retakes, no stopping of the action. That was it. Millions of eager viewers were glued to their black-and-white screens, waiting to see what would happen next. What did the actor do? He got to his feet, in an airplane cabin 30,000 feet over the mountains of Tibet, and voiced this immortal line: "Well, here's where I get off." He left the set and walked into history.

If *you* memorize a speech and forget it anywhere along the line, you'll have to get off that plane at 30,000 feet over Tibet—and there's no parachute. But even if you do find your way back, when you memorize, the material controls you, rather than you controlling the material. *Master* your material, but don't memorize. Memorizing robs you of being natural.

Milo Frank, *How to Get Your Point Across in Thirty Seconds or Less*

power, how much it costs, or how many copies per minute it delivers. A personnel manager might be expected to know, without referring to a brochure, the value of the employee's life insurance (if each employee's is the same) and how much the employee contributes to the premium. You would also look foolish at a retirement dinner if you said, "Everybody knows about Charlie's contributions—" and then had to pause to refer to your notes. For such situations, you can memorize essential *parts* of a presentation.

EXTEMPORANEOUS PRESENTATIONS

An extemporaneous presentation is planned and rehearsed, but not word for word. If you prepare carefully and practice your presentation several times with a friend, a family member, or even a group of co-workers or subordinates, you have a good chance of delivering an extemporaneous talk that seems spontaneous and even effortless. Virtually every presentation you plan—a sales presentation, a talk at the local high school, a progress report to a management review board, a training lecture, an annual report to employees or the board of directors—should be delivered extemporaneously.

A good extemporaneous presentation should be carefully rehearsed, but it will never be exactly the same twice. The words will differ each time. The speaker might respond to an audience's nonverbal cues to explain a point more fully or to move on when the point seems clear. The important points, though, remain the same. The speaker uses notes for reminders of the order and content of ideas.

There is no single best format for speaking notes. Some speakers prefer abbreviated outlines, while others find that index cards with key words or phrases work best. Whatever form you use, speaking notes should possess these characteristics:

Notes Should Be Brief   Overly detailed notes tempt a speaker to read them. Inexperienced salespeople who rely on a brochure, for instance, often wind up reading to their prospective customers. More experienced salespeople might be able to use the brochure's boldface headings as a guide.

Notes Should Be Legible   Your words shouldn't turn into meaningless scribbles when you need them. The writing on your notes should be neat and large enough to be read at a glance.

Notes Should Be Unobtrusive   Most audiences won't be offended if you speak from notes, as long as the notes aren't distracting. A sheet of 8 1/2 by 11-inch paper flapping in your hand can become a noisy irritation, as can shuffling several sheets of paper on a lectern. Some speakers avoid such problems by providing their listeners with a guide and then using the guide for their own notes.

IMPROMPTU PRESENTATIONS

Sooner or later you will be asked to give an impromptu talk—an unexpected, off-the-cuff presentation. A customer might stop in your office and ask you to describe the new model you'll have next spring. At a celebration dinner, you may be asked to "say a few words." A manager might ask you to "give us some background on the problem" or to "fill us in on your progress." You may suddenly discover at a weekly meeting that your subordinates are unaware of a process they need to know about in order to understand the project you were about to explain.

While you may feel anxious at the thought of impromptu speaking, the experience needn't be as threatening as it seems. Most of the time, you will be asked to speak about a subject within your expertise—such as a current project, a problem you've solved, or a technical aspect of your training—which means you have thought about it before. Another reassuring fact is that most listeners won't expect perfection in off-the-cuff remarks.

Your impromptu presentations will be most effective if you follow these guidelines.[3]

Predict When You May Be Asked to Speak   Most impromptu speaking situations won't come as a complete surprise. You may be an "expert" on the subject under discussion or at least one of the people most involved in a situation. Or perhaps your knowledge of the person in charge suggests that impromptu remarks are to be expected. In any case, if you prepare yourself just in case you're asked to speak, your remarks will be better planned and delivered.

Accept the Invitation with Assurance   Try to look confident, even if you're less than delighted about speaking. If you stammer, stall, or look unhappy, your audience will doubt the value of your remarks before you say a word. Once asked, you're going to speak whether or not you want to. You might as well handle the situation well.

Present a Definite Viewpoint Early   Let the audience know your thesis at the outset: "I see several problems with that idea" or "From my experience with the Digitech project, I think our cost projections are low." If you aren't sure what your opinion is, present that thesis: "I'm not sure which approach we ought to take. I think we need to look at both of them closely before we decide."

Present Reasons, Logic, or Facts to Support Your Viewpoint   As with any presentation, your points will be clearer and more persuasive when you back them up with supporting material: statistics, examples, comparisons, and so forth. Of course, this information won't be as detailed as if you had been able to prepare it in advance; but provide some evidence or explanation to support your points: "As I recall, the Digitech job ran 10 percent over estimate on materials and 15 percent over on labor."

Don't Apologize   Nobody expects a set of impromptu remarks to be perfectly polished, so it is a mistake to highlight your lack of knowledge or preparation. Remarks like "You caught me off guard" or "I'm not sure whether this is right" are unnecessary. If you really don't have anything to contribute, say so.

Don't Ramble On   Many novice speakers make the mistake of delivering their message—and then continuing to talk: "So that's my point: I think the potential gains make the risk worthwhile. Sure, we'll be taking a chance, but look what we stand to win. That's why I think it's not just a matter of chance, but a calculated risk, and one that makes sense. We'll never know unless we try, and . . ."

The speaker needed only one sentence: "I think the risk is worth taking." Instead, he probably left the audience feeling bored and resentful. The safest way to avoid rambling is to use the few moments before you speak to sketch a mental outline of your main points. Then stick to it.

GUIDELINES FOR DELIVERY

Choosing the best method of delivery will help make your presentations effective, but it is no guarantee of total effectiveness. Your speeches will be better if you also consider the visual and vocal elements of delivery: words, how you look, and how you sound.[4]

VISUAL ELEMENTS

A major part of good delivery is how a speaker looks. One manager illustrated this fact dramatically by commenting on the appearance of a trainer she had hired.

I read an article on personnel management this guy had published in a trade journal. The ideas were terrific, and I thought he would be the ideal person to lead our annual retreat for top managers. I spoke with him over the phone, and he sent me a written plan for the weekend that looked as good as the article.

That's why I was so surprised when I finally met this trainer. He couldn't look anybody in the eye, and he kept fidgeting and stammering all weekend long. What he said was fine, but he looked so bad that nobody took him seriously. I looked bad for choosing him, but I sure learned a lesson. I'll never put my reputation behind anybody again before I see how they operate in person.

You can improve your visual effectiveness by following several guidelines.

Dress Effectively   Appearance is important in any setting. How you dress is even more important when you get up to speak, however. You may be able to hide a rumpled suit behind your desk sometimes or get away with wearing clothes more casual than usual office norms dictate the day you move your office furniture, but not when you get up to give your financial report at the annual meeting or present your latest proposal to top management.

Dressing effectively doesn't always mean dressing up. If the occasion calls for casual attire, an overly formal appearance can be just as harmful as underdressing. Automotive consultant Barry Isenberg found that an informal appearance contributed to his success as a leading speaker. While waiting to speak to an audience of hundreds of auto wreckers at a day-long seminar, Isenberg looked on as an attorney dressed impeccably in a three-piece suit gave an organized talk on warranties. Despite the importance of the topic, the audience was obviously bored silly. Isenberg rushed upstairs to his hotel room and changed out of his business suit and into the attire of his listeners—casual pants and an open-neck shirt. When his turn to speak arrived, Isenberg moved out from behind the lectern and adopted a casual speaking style that matched his outfit. Afterward, a number of listeners told Isenberg he was the first speaker who seemed to understand their business.[5]

Step Up to Speak with Confidence and Authority   Employees are often surprised to discover their forceful, personable superiors completely lose their effectiveness when they have to address a group of people—and show this before they say a word. Speakers who fidget with their hands or their clothing while waiting to speak, approach the podium as if they were about to face a firing squad, then fumble with their notes and the microphone send the nonverbal message "I'm not sure about myself or what I have to say." An audience will discount even the best remarks with such a powerful nonverbal preface.

Your presentation begins the moment you come into the view of your listeners. Act as if you are a person whose remarks are worth listening to.

Get Set Before Speaking   If you need an easel or projection screen, move it into position before you begin. If a lectern needs repositioning, do it before you begin your talk. The same goes for the other details that come with so many presentations: adjust the microphone, close the door, reset the air conditioner, rearrange the seating.

Just as important, be sure to position yourself physically before beginning. Usually out of nervousness, some speakers blurt out their opening remarks before they are set in their speaking position. A far better approach is to stand or walk to the position from which you will talk, get set, wait a brief moment, and then begin speaking.

Establish and Maintain Eye Contact   A speaker who talks directly to an audience will be seen as more involved and sincere. Whether you're proposing an innovative new product line, reassuring your employees about the effects of recent budget cuts, or trying to convince a group of local citizens that your company is interested in curbing pollution, your impression on the audience can ultimately determine your success.

This kind of immediacy comes in great part from the degree of eye contact between speaker and listeners. Use the moment before you speak to establish a relationship with your audience. Look around the room. Get in touch with the fact that you are talking to real human beings: the people you work with, the potential customers who have real problems and concerns you can help with, and so on. Let them know by your glance that you are interested in them. Be sure your glance covers virtually everyone in the room. Look about randomly: a mechanical right-to-left sweep of the group will make you look like a robot. Many speech consultants recommend taking in the whole room as you speak. If the audience is too large for you to make eye contact with each person, choose a few people in different parts of the room, making eye contact with each one for a few seconds.

Begin Without Looking at Your Notes   Make contact with the audience as you begin speaking. You can't establish a connection if you are reading from notes. You can memorize the precise wording of your opening statement, but it isn't really necessary. Whether you say "I have a new process that will give you more reliable results at a lower cost" or "My new process is more reliable and costs less" isn't critical: the important thing is to make your point while speaking directly to your listeners.

Stand and Move Effectively   The best stance for delivering a presentation is relaxed but firm. The speaker's feet are planted firmly on the ground, spaced at shoulder width. The body faces the audience. The head is upright, turning naturally to look at the audience.

Using good posture doesn't mean standing rooted to the ground. Moving about can add life to your presentation and help release nervous energy. You can approach and refer to your visual aids, walk away from and return to your original position, and approach the audience. Your actions should always be purposeful, though. Nervous pacing might make a speaker feel better, but turn listeners into distracted wrecks.

If you're addressing a small group such as four or five employees or potential customers, it may be more appropriate to sit when you're delivering a presentation. Generally, the same rules apply in such cases. You should sit up straight and lean forward—lounging back in your chair or putting a foot up on the desk indicates indifference or even contempt. Sit naturally; your behavior should be as direct and animated as it would be if you were conversing with these people—which, in a way, you are.

Don't Pack Up Early   Gathering your notes or starting for your seat before concluding is a nonverbal statement that you're anxious to get your presentation finished. Even if you are, advertising it will only make your audience see the presentation as less valuable. Keep your attention focused on your topic and the audience until you are actually finished.

Move Out Confidently When Finished   When you end your remarks (or finish answering questions), move out smartly. Even if you are unhappy with yourself, don't shuffle off dejectedly or stomp away angrily. Most speakers are their own greatest critics, and there is a good chance the audience rated you more favorably than you did. If you advertise your disappointment, however, you might persuade them you really were a flop.

VERBAL ELEMENTS

The words you choose are an important part of your delivery. As you practice your presentation, keep these points in mind.

Use an Oral Speaking Style   Spoken ideas differ in structure and content from written messages. The difference helps explain why speakers who read from a manuscript sound so stuffy and artificial. When addressing your audience, your speech will sound normal and pleasing if it follows some simple guidelines.

- *Keep most sentences short.* Long, complicated sentences may be fine in a written document, where readers can study them until the meaning is clear, but in an oral presentation your ideas will be easiest to understand if they are phrased in brief statements. Complicated sentences can leave your listeners confused: "Members of field staff, who are isolated from one another and work alone most of the time, need better technology for keeping in touch with one another while in the field as well as with the home office." The ideas are much clearer when delivered in briefer chunks: "Members of the field staff work alone most of the time. This makes it hard for them to keep in touch with one another and with the home office. They need better means of technology to stay in contact."
- *Use personal pronouns freely.* Speech that contains first-person and second-person pronouns sounds more personal and immediate. Instead of saying "People often ask . . .," say "You might ask . . ." Likewise, say "Our sales staff found . . .," not "The sales staff found . . ."
- *Use the active voice.* The active voice sounds more personal and less stuffy than passive use of verbs. Saying "It was decided . . ." isn't as effective as saying "We decided . . ." "Do not say "The meeting was attended by ten people"; say "Ten people attended the meeting."
- *Use contractions often.* Instead of saying "We do not expect many

changes," say "We don't expect many changes." Rather than saying "I do not know. I will find out and give you an answer as soon as possible," say "I don't know. I'll find out and give you an answer as soon as possible."

■ *Address your listeners directly.* Using direct forms of address makes it clear that you are really speaking to your listeners and not just reading from a set of notes. Personalized statements will keep an audience listening: "Frank, you and your colleagues in the payroll office are probably wondering how these changes will affect you"; "Ms. Diaz, it's a pleasure to have the chance to describe our ideas to you this morning."

Don't Emphasize Mistakes Even the best speakers forget or bungle a line occasionally. The difference between professionals and amateurs is the way they handle such mistakes. The experts simply go on, adjusting their remarks to make the error less noticeable.

Usually, an audience won't even be aware of a mistake. If they don't have a copy of your speaking outline, they won't know about the missing parts; even if they notice that you have skipped a section in a brochure you're going over with your listeners or in a prepared outline you've distributed after your speech for your listeners' reference, they'll assume you did it on purpose, perhaps to save time. If you lose your place in your notes, a brief pause will be almost unnoticeable—as long as you don't emphasize it by frantically pawing through your notes.

What about obvious mistakes—citing the wrong figures, mispronouncing a name, or trying to use equipment that doesn't work, for example? The best response here is again the least noticeable. "Let me correct that. The totals are for the first quarter of the year, not just for March," you might say and then move on. When equipment fails, adapt and move on. "The chart with those figures seems to be missing. Let me summarize it for you."

Use Proper Vocabulary, Enunciation, and Pronunciation The language of a board of directors' meeting or a formal press conference is different from that of a factory workers' meeting or an informal gathering of sales representatives at a resort. It is important to choose language that is appropriate to the particular setting.

It is also important to pronounce your words correctly. Few mistakes will erode your credibility or irritate an audience as quickly as will mispronouncing an important term or name: the word is *scenario*, not "screenario," and the author of this book likes to be called "Adler," not "Alder." Enunciation—articulating words clearly and distinctly—is also important. "We are comin' out with a new data processin' system" makes the speaker sound ignorant to many people, even if the ideas are good.

VOCAL ELEMENTS

As Table 13-1 shows, how you sound is just as important as what you say and how you look. Speakers' voices are especially effective at communicating their atti-

TABLE 13-1   Checklist for Effective Delivery

- Visual Elements
  Dresses effectively
  Steps up to speak with confidence and authority
  Gets set before speaking
  Establishes and maintains eye contact
  Begins without looking at notes
  Stands and moves effectively
  Doesn't pack up early
  Moves out confidently when finished
- Verbal Elements
  Uses an oral speaking style
  Doesn't emphasize mistakes
  Uses proper vocabulary, enunciation, and pronunciation
- Vocal Elements
  Speaks with enthusiasm and sincerity
  Speaks loudly enough to be heard
  Avoids dysfluencies

tudes about themselves, their topics, and their listeners: enthusiasm or disinterest, confidence or nervousness, friendliness or hostility, respect or disdain. The following guidelines are important elements in effective communication.

Speak with Enthusiasm and Sincerity   If you don't appear to feel strongly about the importance of your topic, there's little chance the audience will. Yet professionals often seem indifferent when they present ideas they're deeply committed to.[6]

The best way to generate enthusiasm is to think of your presentation as sharing ideas you truly believe in. In the stress of making a presentation, you might forget how important your remarks are. To prevent this, remind yourself why you are speaking in the moments before you speak. Thinking about what you want to say can put life back into your delivery.

Speak Loudly Enough to Be Heard   At the very least, a quiet voice makes it likely that listeners won't hear important information. In addition, listeners often interpret an overly soft voice as a sign of timidity or lack of conviction. ("She just didn't sound very sure of herself.") Shouting is offensive, too ("Does he think he can force his product down our throats?"), but a speaker ought to project enough to be heard clearly and to sound confident.

Avoid Dysfluencies   Dysfluencies are those stammers and stutters ("eh," "um," and so forth) that creep into everyone's language at one time or another. Other "filler words" are "ya know," "so," "okay," and so on. A few dysfluencies will be virtually unnoticeable in a presentation; in fact, without them, the talk might seem overly rehearsed and stilted. An excess of jumbles, stumbles, and fillers, however, makes a speaker sound disorganized, nervous, and uncertain.

The truth is, no one can manufacture an image for anyone. If you want to improve or enhance yourself in some way, the only thing a consultant can do for you is to advise and guide you. We can point out assets and liabilities in your style and we then offer substitutions and suggestions to aid you. You have to want to improve and work at it. Most importantly, whatever changes you make have to conform to who you really *are*—at your best. All the grooming suggestions, all the speech coaching, all the knowledge about lighting, staging, and media training—everything popularly associated with "image-making"—won't work if the improvements don't fit comfortably with who you essentially are.

Roger Ailes, *You Are the Message*

Dysfluencies can be overcome with some concentration. One manager who found that her presentations were marred by "okays" asked an associate to tally the number of "okays" in her conversation. She then agreed to contribute a dime for each one to the Friday-afternoon happy-hour fund, hoping the financial penalty would break her bad habit. The first week she was astonished to find her bill was over twenty dollars, but after only a month her "okay" rate had dropped to a level where counting was hardly worth the effort. Once she was aware of the "okays" in her everyday conversation, she found she could control them in her more formal presentations, too.

QUESTION-AND-ANSWER SESSIONS

The chance to answer questions on the spot is one of the biggest advantages of oral presentations. Where a written report might leave readers confused or unimpressed, your on-the-spot response to questions and concerns can win over an audience.

Audience questions are a part of almost every business and professional talk from sales presentations and training sessions to boardroom meetings. Sometimes question-and-answer sessions are a separate part of the presentation. In other cases, they are mingled with the speaker's remarks. In any case, a skillful response to questions is essential.

WHEN TO ANSWER QUESTIONS

Sometimes you have no choice about when to answer questions from your listeners. If the boss interrupts your talk to ask for some facts or figures, you're not likely to rule the question out of order. Nonetheless, as a speaker, you can control much of the timing of audience questions.

During the Presentation   Speakers often encourage their listeners to ask questions during a talk. This approach lets you respond to the concerns of your listeners immediately. If people are confused, you can set them straight by expanding on a point; if they have objections, you can respond to them on the spot.

Dealing with your listeners' questions during a talk does have its drawbacks. Some questions are premature, raising points you plan to discuss later in your talk. Others are irrelevant and waste both your time and your listeners'. If you decide to handle questions during a talk, follow these guidelines.

Allow for Extra Time   Answering questions sometimes occupies as much time as your planned talk. A fifteen-minute report can run a half hour or longer with questions. If your time is limited, keep your remarks brief enough to leave time for the audience to respond.

Promise to Answer Premature Questions Later   Don't feel obligated to give detailed responses to every question. If you plan to discuss the information requested by a questioner later in your talk, say, "That's a good question; I'll get to that in a moment."

After the Presentation   Postponing questions until after your prepared remarks lets you control the way your information is revealed. You don't have to worry about someone distracting you with an irrelevant remark or raising an objection you plan to answer. You also have much better control over the length of your talk, lessening the risk that you'll run out of time before you run out of information.

On the other hand, when you deny listeners the chance to speak up, they may be so preoccupied with questions or concerns that they miss much of what you say. For instance, you might spend half your time talking about the benefits of a product while your listeners keep wondering whether they can afford it. In addition, since most of the information people recall is from the beginning and the end of presentations, you risk having your audience remember the high price you mentioned during the question-and-answer session or the sticky question you couldn't answer rather than the high quality you proved in your presentation.

HOW TO MANAGE QUESTIONS

Whether you handle them during or after a presentation, questions from the audience can be a challenge. Some are confusing. Others are thinly veiled attacks on your position: "How much time have you New York folks spent out here in the Midwest?" Still other questions are off the topic you're discussing: "Your talk about film projectors was very interesting. I wonder, do you ever teach classes on making films?" You can handle questions most effectively by following these suggestions.

Start the Ball Rolling   Sometimes listeners may be reluctant to ask the first question. You can get a question-and-answer session rolling with your own remarks: "One question you might have is . . ." or "The other day someone asked whether . . ."

Anticipate Likely Questions   Put yourself in the position of your listeners. What questions are they likely to ask? Is there a chance that they will find parts of your topic hard to understand? Might some points antagonize them? Just as you prepare for an important exam by anticipating the questions that are likely to be asked, you should try to prepare responses to the inquiries you're likely to receive.

Clarify Complicated or Confusing Questions   Make sure you understand the question by rephrasing it in your own words: "If I understand you correctly, Tom, you're asking why we can't handle this problem with our present staff. Is that right?" Besides helping you understand what a questioner wants, clarification gives you a few precious moments to frame an answer. Finally, it helps other audience members to understand the question. If the audience is large, rephrase every question to make sure that it has been heard: "The gentleman asked whether we have financing terms for the equipment."

Treat Questioners with Respect   There's little to gain by antagonizing or embarrassing even the most hostile questioner. You can keep your dignity and gain the support of other listeners by taking every question seriously or even complimenting the person who asks it: "I don't blame you for thinking the plan is farfetched, Nora. We thought it was strange at first, too, but the more we examined it, the better it looked."

Keep Answers Focused on Your Goal   Don't let questions draw you offtrack. Try to frame answers in ways that promote your goal: "This certainly is different from the way we did things in the old days when you and I started out, Steve. For instance, the computerized system we have now will cut both our costs and our errors. Let me review the figures once more."

You can avoid offending questioners by promising to discuss the matter with them in detail after your presentation or to send them further information: "I'd be happy to show you the electrical plans, Peggy. Let's get together this afternoon and go over them."

Buy Time When Necessary   Sometimes you need a few moments to plan an answer to a surprise question. You can buy time in several ways. You can *rephrase the question:* "It sounds like everything about the project looks good to you except the schedule, Gene." You can *turn the question around:* "How would you deal with the situation and still go ahead with the project, Mary?" You can also *turn the question outward:* "Chris, you're the best technical person we have. What's the best way to save energy costs?"

Follow the Last Question with a Summary   Since listeners are likely to remember especially well the last words they hear you speak, always follow the question-and-answer session with a brief restatement of your thesis and perhaps a call for your audience to act in a way that accomplishes your purpose for speaking. A typical summary might sound like this:

I'm grateful for the chance to answer your questions. Now that we've gone over the cost projections, I think you can see why we're convinced that this proposal can help boost productivity and cut overhead by almost ten percent overnight. We're ready to make these changes immediately. The sooner we hear from you, the sooner we can get started.

SPEAKING WITH CONFIDENCE

If the thought of making a presentation leaves you feeling anxious, you are in good company. According to Irving Wallace and David Wallechinsky's *Book of Lists,* a sample of three thousand Americans identified "speaking before a group" as their greatest fear, greater even than death.[7] This doesn't mean most people would rather die than give a speech, but it does show which event makes them more anxious.

Stage fright—or communication apprehension, as communication specialists call it—is just as much a problem for businesspeople as it is for the general population. Communispond, a New York communications consulting firm, surveyed five hundred executives and found that nearly 80 percent listed stage fright as their greatest problem in speaking before a group, putting it ahead of such items as "handling hostile interrogators."[8]

If you get butterflies in your stomach at the thought of giving a speech, if your hands sweat and your mouth gets dry, if you feel faint or nauseated or have trouble thinking clearly, you might be comforted to know that most people, including famous performers, politicians, and business executives who frequently appear before audiences, experience some degree of nervousness about speaking. Although it is common, communication apprehension doesn't have to present a serious problem.

It is reassuring to know that, however anxious you feel, your apprehension isn't as visible as you might fear. In several recent studies, communicators have been asked to rate their own level of anxiety.[9] At the same time, other people gave their impression of the speaker's level of nervousness. In every case, the speakers rated themselves as looking much more nervous than the observers thought they were. Even when the anxiety is noticeable, it doesn't result in significantly lower evaluations of the speaker's effectiveness.

These research findings are good news for anxious speakers. It's reassuring to know that, even if you are frightened, your listeners aren't likely to recognize the fact or find it distracting. And knowing that the audience isn't bothered by your anxiety can actually reduce a major source of nervousness, leading you to feel more confident.

ACCEPT A MODERATE AMOUNT OF NERVOUSNESS

A certain amount of anxiety is not only normal, but desirable. When the success of your new product line depends on how well you explain it to the sales force, the future of a new proposal depends on how convincingly you can present it to management, or your next promotion or raise depends on how successful your speech is at the annual meeting of the company board of directors, it is natural to feel nervous.

A certain amount of anxiety can even be an asset. One consultant says, "If I had a way to remove all fear of speaking for you, I wouldn't do it. The day you become casual about speaking is the day you risk falling on your face."[10] The threat of botching your presentation can lead to what Edward R. Murrow once called "the sweat of perfection," spurring you to do your best. And the adrenaline rush that comes as you stand up—your body's response to a threatening situation—can make you appear more energetic, enthusiastic, and forceful than if you were more relaxed and casual.

A proper goal, then, is not to eliminate nervousness, but to *control* it. As one experienced speaker put it, "The butterflies never go away; it's just that after a while they begin to fly in formation."

SPEAK MORE OFTEN

Like many unfamiliar activities—ice skating, learning to drive a car, and interviewing for a job, to mention a few—the first attempts at speaking before a group can be unnerving. The first attempts at any new activity are bound to be awkward. One source of anxiety is lack of skill and experience. In addition, the very newness of the act is frightening. What is new is unknown, and we assume the unknown always contains some risk.

Since newness generates anxiety, one way to become a more confident speaker is to speak more. As with other skills, your first attempts should involve modest challenges with relatively low stakes. Speech courses and workshops taught in colleges, corporations, and some community organizations provide opportunities for a group of novices to practice before one another and a supportive instructor. Once on the job, it's a good idea to make a number of beginning presentations to small, familiar audiences about noncritical matters. One corporate executive who anticipated having to give a number of important speeches and presentations began calling small meetings of his subordinates more frequently. At these meetings, he presented new information and problems to them as a group rather than following his usual habit of dropping in on each of them individually. On one occasion, when he was preparing his department's strategic plan for the following year to top management, he called his subordinates together for a rehearsal: "My success at presenting the strategic plan will affect our budget and staff allowances for a full year," he told them, "so I want you to give me all the help you can."

REHEARSE YOUR PRESENTATION

Rehearsal will ensure that you are familiar with your material by the time you face your audience. As you practice your talk, follow these guidelines.

Rehearse on your feet, before an audience. Mental rehearsal has its place, but you won't know if your ideas sound good or if they fit into the available time until you say them aloud.

Expect your talk to run 20 percent longer. Presentations almost always run longer in real time than during rehearsals. If you are speaking for ten minutes, rehearse for about eight. Even if your talk ultimately runs a bit short, nobody will mind.

Rehearse three to six times. Fewer than three times may leave you feeling shaky about your content. More than six times can make your talk sound canned.

Pay special attention to your introduction and conclusion. Audiences remember the opening and closing of a talk most clearly. The first and last moments of your presentation have special importance, so make sure you deliver them effectively in a way that makes every word count.

Rehearse in a real setting. If possible, rehearse in the room where you will actually speak. Make sure you have all the equipment you will need and that it all works. The checklist in Table 13-2 can help you keep track of the materials you need.

THINK RATIONALLY ABOUT YOUR PRESENTATION

Some speakers feel more apprehensive because of the way they *think* about the speech than because of the act of speaking.[11] This is why the executive mentioned above felt little fear about speaking before friends, co-workers, or subordinates but felt very anxious about delivering the same speech to top management—an audience of powerful strangers. In such cases, we think of the event differently. In the first case, the thought is "I know I'll be accepted," while in the second instance, the speaker thinks "They might not like what I'm saying."

Researchers have identified a number of irrational but powerful beliefs that lead to unnecessary apprehension.[12] Among these mistaken beliefs are these:

Table 13-2 Speaking-Materials Checklist

EQUIPMENT NEEDED		SUPPLIES
Overhead projector	Audio or videotapes (blank	Paper
Slide projector (with remote	or prerecorded)	Pencils, pens
control)	Video monitor	Name cards
Projection screen	Extension cord(s)	Chalk, marking pens
Audio cassette recorder	Chalkboard	Handouts
Video recorder (proper format)	Flip chart	Attendance list
Video camera (with connecting	Easel	
cable)	Podium	

Myth: A Presentation Must Be Perfect   Whether you're addressing a meeting of potential clients worth millions of dollars to your company or a small group of trainees, your presentation must be clearly organized, well documented, and effectively delivered. Expecting it to be perfect, though, is a surefire prescription for nervousness and depression. A talk can be effective without being flawless. The same principle holds for other types of speaking errors. Most listeners won't notice if you omit a point or rearrange an idea or two.

Myth: It Is Possible to Persuade the Entire Audience   Even the best products don't sell to everyone, and even the most talented people don't win the full support of their audiences. Instead of expecting to persuade everyone, strive for and be satisfied with the support you need.

It is a mistake to expect one presentation to achieve everything you are seeking. Your first sales presentation might only convince a prospective customer to consider buying the furniture for a new office building from your company, and you may have to convince management to let you hire ten more staff members over five years, rather than all at once. If you think of your remarks as one step in a campaign to achieve your long-term goals, you will feel less pressure.

Myth: The Worst Will Probably Happen   Some pessimistic speakers make themselves unnecessarily nervous by dwelling on the worst possible outcomes. They imagine themselves tripping on the way to the podium, going blank, or mixing up their ideas. They picture the audience asking unanswerable questions, responding with hostility, or even laughing. Even though such disasters are unlikely, these daydreams take on a life of their own and may create a self-fulfilling prophecy: the fearful thoughts themselves can cause the speaker to bungle a presentation.

One way to overcome the irrational fear of failure is to indulge your catastrophic fantasies. Picture yourself fainting from terror, everyone falling asleep, or the boss firing you on the spot. Now imagine the best possible outcome: receiving a standing ovation or an immediate promotion to the vice-presidency. After thinking about these extremes, ask yourself how likely each is. Then think about what might *really* happen and realize that you have the ability to determine the outcome within that range of realistic possibilities.

SUMMARY

There are four types of presentational delivery: manuscript, memorized, extemporaneous, and impromptu. With rare exceptions, an extemporaneous style is the most effective, combining the enthusiasm that comes with spontaneity and the accuracy that comes from rehearsal. When an impromptu talk is necessary, it will be most effective if the speaker presents a clear thesis; supports it with reasons, logic, or facts; speaks without apologizing; and does not ramble on.

Good delivery involves a number of elements, including visual, verbal, and vocal ones. Most of these involve looking enthusiastic and confident and sounding well rehearsed and committed to both the topic and the audience.

Question-and-answer sessions are part of almost every presentation. They allow a speaker to respond to the concerns of an audience more quickly and completely than is possible in written documents. A speaker needs to decide whether to invite questions during or after the prepared part of a presentation. Handling questions during a talk permits a speaker to clarify points as they arise, although there is a risk of getting sidetracked by discussing irrelevant points or information that will come up later in a presentation. Responding to questions after the prepared segment of a talk lets the speaker keep control of both the available time and the way information is introduced. On the other hand, listeners who have to hold their questions may be too distracted to follow the speaker's other points carefully.

Anxiety about speaking is common and not always a problem. A manageable amount of anxiety causes a speaker to prepare carefully and contributes to an energetic presentation. A speaker can keep anxiety within tolerable limits by accepting it as a normal occurrence, being well prepared, and thinking rationally about the event. Rational thinking involves the realization that one need not be perfect in order to be effective, that no single presentation will fully persuade an entire audience, and that catastrophes are unlikely to occur.

ACTIVITIES

1. With two or more classmates, try the various styles of delivery for yourself.

    a. Begin by choosing a paragraph of text on an appropriate business or professional topic. You can write the copy yourself or select an article from a newspaper, magazine, or some other publication.

    b. Read the text to your listeners verbatim. Pay attention to your feelings as you deliver the comments. Do you feel comfortable and enthusiastic? How do your listeners describe your delivery?

    c. Try to memorize and then deliver the segment. How difficult is it to recall the remarks? How effective is your delivery?

    d. Now deliver the same remarks extemporaneously, rephrasing them in your own words. See whether this approach leaves you more comfortable and your listeners more favorably impressed.

2. Scan a current television guide, and select a program in which a speaker is making some sort of oral presentation. The subject matter is not important: the show can be educational, religious, political, or news-related.

    a. Turn down the volume, and observe the speaker's visual delivery. Notice the effects of dress, posture, gesture, facial expression, and eye contact.

    b. What do these aspects of delivery suggest about the speaker's status, enthusiasm, sincerity, and competence?

3. Locate a television or radio program that involves an oral presentation on some subject. The content is not important.

a. Notice the speaker's volume, rate of speaking, pitch, and presence or absence of dysfluencies. What do they tell you about his or her sincerity, enthusiasm, and confidence?

b. What do the speaker's vocabulary, enunciation, and pronunciation tell you about his or her competence?

4. Think about at least five effective speakers you have known. Which of the delivery styles outlined in this chapter did each use?

Communicator Profile

Teresa Garcia, Human Resources Administrative Coordinator Transamerica Insurance Group Los Angeles, California

Find a speaking approach that feels natural and works for you, and then polish that approach. Trying to speak like someone else just won't work.

As a human-resources coordinator, a major part of my job has been to design and deliver training programs to teach our employees a variety of "people" skills. Our workshops deal primarily with management and supervisory development as well as presentational speaking.

In the last few years, I have given well over one hundred presentations. In addition, I've sold life insurance myself. Selling, of course, always involves making a presentation. I've spoken to groups ranging in size from one to fifty. These audiences have consisted of everyone from potential customers to new entry-level employees to senior corporate executives.

I've learned that the way a presentation is delivered can make the difference between success and failure. The same material that sounds clear and exciting from one speaker can be tedious and unimportant from someone else. Experts have said that the first thirty seconds of a talk are critical, and most of that first impression comes from how you speak, rather than from what you say.

There's no single correct style of delivery. In the first place, you have to speak and move in a way that's right for you. For instance, some people are just naturally more animated or humorous than others, and it would look foolish to act excited or tell jokes if that's not your style. Also, the approach that's right for one audience would be wrong for another group. For example, when I conduct an impromptu staff meeting, it feels comfortable to perch myself on a table and talk informally. I would never be so casual briefing a group of vice-presidents.

Despite differences like these, there are two musts for every important presentation. First, I've found that it's always necessary to prepare and practice for a talk. I've often spent as much as twelve hours planning a brief but important talk. First I jot down the key ideas in a rough outline form. Then, at another sitting, I try to organize the ideas into a smooth form. Then I rehearse my talk, first alone and then to one or more "practice" listeners. These trial runs usually uncover some changes I need to make, and that calls for a new round of planning and practicing. This sort of preparation takes time, but the results are worth it.

Another "must" is always to speak *to* an audience, not *at* them. I'd call it being personable. I greet them with a "Good morning" or "Good afternoon" before starting to speak. I use language that sounds personal instead of reading from a written report, and I look at them during my talk. I always invite questions, either during or after the talk. In other words, my delivery isn't too different from what it would be in a one-to-one conversation. In my mind, that's what distinguishes a face-to-face presentation from a piece of writing. If you lose that personal contact, you'd be better off sending a letter. I think it offends an audience when a speaker rattles off a set of remarks as if they weren't really there.

When it's time for you to make a presentation, keep four points in mind. First, learn and follow the basic organizing plan for a talk: introduction, body, and conclusion. You can't go wrong with that approach. Second, *always* prepare and practice your talk. Third, know your audience, and develop a presentation that is appropriate for them. And finally, be yourself. Find a speaking approach that feels natural and works for you, and then polish that approach. Trying to speak like someone else just won't work.

CHAPTER 14

After reading this chapter, you should understand:

- The four types of informative presentations commonly delivered in business and professional settings
- The importance of designing an informative presentation appropriate for the speaking occasion
- The range of strategies that can be used to deliver an informative message clearly and effectively

You should be able to:

- Develop an informative presentation that appeals to the interests and needs of a given audience
- Use comparisons to explain an unfamiliar topic
- Use repetition, transitions, signposts, and interjections to clarify a presentation
- Translate a complex, unfamiliar idea into simple terms
- Develop and use strategies to involve an audience in a presentation

INFORMATIVE PRESENTATIONS

The office manager explains to employees how to use the company's new voice mail system.

A human-resources specialist explains federal and state laws governing nondiscrimination in hiring to a committee that will be interviewing job candidates.

The foreman of a construction job gives the client a report on the progress of the project.

A corporate recruiter speaks to an audience of college students on the opportunities in his industry.

Informative presentations like these are a common and important part of doing business. Some of these informative messages are delivered informally, with the speaker and a few listeners gathered around a conference table or piece of equipment. These messages might be brief ones: to help people catch up on late-breaking developments or to explain simple procedures like a how to operate the new fax machine. At other times, the audience might be large and the planning extensive. Management might explain how the acquisition of the company by a large corporation will affect operations. A professional trainer might lead a three-day workshop on new accounting procedures.

Whatever the setting, topic, and audience, delivering informative material in an effective way is important. Recent college graduates recognize this fact: when a group of alumni were asked to rate the importance of a wide array of speaking skills, informative speaking wound up at the top of the list.[1] Perhaps the reason that businesspeople see the value of good speaking skills is because many of the presentations they hear are awful. Almost half of the vice-presidents surveyed at the nation's top 1,000 corporations reported that they found the majority of business presentations "boring," and 40 percent admitted that they have dozed off at least once during a presentation.[2]

Applying the techniques of effective speaking that you have already learned in Chapters 10 through 13 will help keep your audience awake, alert, and informed. The material in the following pages offers even more advice about how to make sure your informative presentations are successful.

The trickiest report to give is a technical one for nontechnical people. A key industry problem today is that everyone is a specialist—at least everyone seems to be. Both society and industry have become so complicated that the generalist is obsolete. All of us who are technicians in our own field are now obliged to communicate our expertise to nontechnical people. . . . Today's executive must package his technical information in a way that can be understood by nontechnical people.

John T. Molloy, *Molloy's Live for Success*

TYPES OF INFORMATIVE PRESENTATIONS

Most informative presentations fall into one of four categories: reports, briefings, explanations, and training.

REPORTS

Reports describe the state of an operation. They are usually (but not always) given by subordinates to their superiors to keep them informed and help them make decisions. Some reports are frequent and informal, such as the daily accounting of sales volume that department heads give a sales manager. Others are more formal, such as the financial accounting that senior management presents at a stockholders' meeting or the final report that a project manager gives his superior. In between fall a range of reports, including a sales representative's progress report, a secretary's report to her boss on events that occurred while he was on a business trip, a market researcher's profile of a market segment, or a plant supervisor's report on workers' reaction to a new machine.

BRIEFINGS

A briefing is a short speech that informs a generally knowledgeable audience about a specific area in which new knowledge has been gleaned.[3] The executive chef of a restaurant might brief waiters about the details of a new menu. The account representative handling an advertising account might brief the agency's team about a client before an important meeting. Nurses and police officers attend briefings before each shift to bring them up to the moment on the current situation.

EXPLANATIONS

Explanations increase listeners' understanding of a subject. An orientation session for new workers falls into this category as does a meeting in which a new employee benefits package is introduced or a purchasing policy explained. When a firm faces a major change in its business fortunes—whether this means growth or cutbacks—wise managers gather their employees and explain how the changes will affect each one of them. Sometimes explanations are aimed at audiences outside the company. A utility-company representative describing the future of electrical rates to the Rotary Club meeting and a community official explaining the effects of new zoning ordinances on local industry are also giving explanations. The sample speech at the end of this chapter explains to employees how the company's tax-reduction plan will increase their real income.

TRAINING

Training teaches listeners how to do something. It can be informal or highly structured, from the simple advice an experienced employee gives a newcomer about how to transfer a telephone call to a week-long seminar on accounting principles for managers of a company.

Successful businesses recognize the value of training. One measure of its importance is the amount of time and money that firms invest in training their employees. For example, at McDonalds, every person who takes an order or prepares food has received eighty hours of instruction.[4] On any given day, International Business Machines Corporation is training 22,000 of its employees somewhere in the world. This sort of training doesn't come cheap. The annual cost of this training for IBM is $1.5 billion, not counting the participants' time.[5]

STRATEGIES FOR EFFECTIVE INFORMATIVE SPEAKING

Whether you're explaining how you want your office organized, how your division solved a problem, or how your organization works, getting your audience to listen and understand can be one of the hardest communication tasks to face. You can use the following techniques to make your presentations interesting and clear.

COVER ONLY NECESSARY INFORMATION

As an informative speaker, you will usually be far more knowledgeable about the topic than the audience to whom you speak. This knowledge is both a blessing and a potential curse. On the one hand, your command of the subject means that you can explain the topic thoroughly. On the other hand, you may be tempted to give listeners more information than they want or need.

If you cover your topic in too much detail, you are likely to bore—or even antagonize—your listeners. One personnel specialist made this mistake when briefing a group of staffers about how to file claims with a new health-insurance carrier. Instead of simply explaining what steps to take when they needed care, he launched into a twenty-minute explanation of why the company chose the present carrier, how that company processed claims at its home office, and where each copy of the four-part claims form was directed after it was filed. By the time he got to the part of his talk that was truly important to the audience—how to get reimbursed for out-of-pocket expenses—the group was so bored and restless that they had a hard time sitting still for the information. Don't make a mistake like this in your presentations: as you plan your remarks, ask yourself what your listeners need to know, and tell them just that much. If they want more information, they will probably ask for it.

Besides boring listeners, there is always the danger that when you overwhelm them with information, they'll become so confused that they'll give up trying to understand the material you are explaining. One office manager created this sort of short circuit in the minds of her staff when she explained the features of a new word-processing system. "It will do everything," she gushed. For the next hour she described the wonders of the program: its ability to handle footnotes, prepare indexes, offset page margins for bound books, hyphenate words, create tables of contents, number paragraphs, outline ideas, perform mathematical functions, and print documents in over thirty-five typefaces. As her talk stretched on, the staff grew more distressed. As one worker later put it, "You have to walk before you can run. I wish she had started by showing us how to type up simple letters and memos. After we could do that, then maybe we would have been ready to learn about all the bells and whistles."

LINK THE TOPIC TO THE AUDIENCE

People will most likely listen to a speaker when they have a reason for doing so. Sometimes the intrinsic interest of the subject is reason enough to listen; for instance, most people would listen carefully to a session on the fringe benefits of their jobs because they know the benefits are worth something to them personally. On the other hand, most people probably aren't interested in a discussion of "how we design the financial structures for new projects."

What can you do with a subject that isn't intrinsically interesting? One way to boost interest is to show that listening will help the audience avoid punishment. ("Don't try to charge the company for anything you're not entitled to. If you do, you'll be put on probation, or you could lose your job.") A more pleasant and effective alternative, however, involves demonstrating the payoffs that come from listening. Some important needs are physical health, safety from danger, financial security, friendship, job advancement, recreation, and respect from others.

A financial officer explaining new expense-account procedures, for instance, might begin by saying, "I want to make sure you get the company to reimburse you for all expenses you're entitled to. I also don't want you to spend your own money, thinking the company will pay you back, and then find out it won't." Expense reporting might be a tedious subject to many people, but the chance to save money (or to avoid losing money) would also interest most listeners.

LINK THE FAMILIAR TO THE UNFAMILIAR

Research has shown that people have the best chance of understanding new material when it bears some relationship to information they already know.[6] Without a familiar reference point, listeners may have trouble understanding even a clear definition. Two examples illustrate how comparisons and contrasts with familiar information help make new ideas more understandable:

Confusing: "Unlike magnetic media, a CD-ROM computer disk is a storage medium that can be read optically by a laser scanner."

More familiar: "The best way to understand the difference between CD-ROM and floppy computer disks is to compare the two most common ways we can buy music recordings these days: audiotape cassettes and CDs. A floppy disk works much like an audiotape, while a CD-ROM disk is more like the CDs you can buy at the local music store." (If the listeners understand the difference between audiotapes and CDs, they will find it easier to understand the computer storage media.)

Confusing: "Money-market funds are mutual funds that buy corporate and government short-term investments." (In order to understand this definition, the audience needs to be familiar with money-market funds and with corporate and government short-term investments.)

More familiar: "Money-market funds are like a collection of IOUs held by a middleman. The funds take cash from investors and lend it to corporations and the government, usually for between 30 and 90 days. These borrowers pay the fund interest on the loan, and that interest is passed along to the investors." (If the audience understands IOUs and interest, they can follow this definition.)

INVOLVE THE AUDIENCE

Listeners who are actively involved in a presentation will understand and remember the material far better than will passive listeners.[7] There are three ways to involve the audience: direct participation, using volunteers, and using question-and-answer formats.

Of these three methods, *direct participation* creates the greatest involvement. This approach is especially effective when you want the listeners to develop a skill or firsthand understanding. People will learn how to operate a particular machine, fill in a particular form, or perform a procedure much better with hands-on experience than if they are only told what to do. Sales training often involves simulated experiences in addition to hearing lectures and reading books. Many programs that train employees to deal with the public include role-playing exercises.

Using *volunteers* can create interest and let even the nonparticipating listeners get a sense of how they might have responded if they had been chosen. For example, a sales representative who is demonstrating a new computer system might ask a member of the audience to provide a specific problem, which the speaker would then use to demonstrate how the system operates.

These methods are highly entertaining and very appropriate for training and explaining sessions, especially with a large audience. For day-to-day reports and briefings, they probably would be too much. In the latter cases, however, question-and-answer sessions are desirable, if not absolutely necessary.

ORGANIZING INFORMATIVE MESSAGES

The way you structure your message will affect how well the audience understands it. All the principles you learned in Chapter 11 apply for reports, briefings, explanations, and training. Beyond these basic guidelines, two strategies will help make your ideas easy to follow.

START WITH AN OVERALL PICTURE

Every presentation needs an introduction. But when the goal is to inform listeners, a clear preview is especially important. Without an overview, your listeners can become so confused by your informational trees that they won't be able to see the conceptual forest. Orient the audience by sketching the highlights of your message in enough detail to help them see what they are expected to know and how you will explain it to them. In the following example, the vice-president of a corporation facing a major change began her remarks with a preview that addressed the biggest concern of her listeners and outlined the information she would be presenting.

> As you probably know by now, management has decided to move all our manufacturing operations to the new Texas plant. There have been a lot of rumors floating around about what that will mean for us here, and we want you to know the facts.
>
> The most important fact is that *no employee*—not a single person—will lose his or her job as a result of this move. There will, however, be some changes in what many of us will be doing and where we'll be doing it. That's what I'll be explaining here today. Specifically, everyone here will fit into one of three categories. Some of us will keep doing the same work at the same place. Others will be staying here, but will be retrained in new jobs. And some of us will be offered our same jobs in Texas— along with some pretty generous incentives to make the move.
>
> You're probably wondering which of these categories you fit in, so let me explain.

An overview is also important when you're giving instructions or describing a process. This orientation helps listeners see where you're headed:

> This morning, we're going to learn about the new E mail system. I'll start by spending a little time explaining how the system works. Then we'll talk about the four ways you can use the system. First I'll show you how you can send messages to any person or group of people in the company—instantly. Then we'll talk about how you can get messages others have sent you. After that you will learn how you can put items on the company-wide bulletin board. Finally, I'll show you how you can take part in company-wide electronic conversations about topics that interest you.
>
> I'll spend about ten minutes describing each of these steps in detail, and after each description you'll get a chance to try out the system yourself. By the time we break for lunch, you should be able to use the system in a way that will save you time and hassles and keep you better informed about what you need to know to get your job done. You won't be an expert, but you'll know enough to make the system work.

EMPHASIZE IMPORTANT POINTS

Since an oral presentation doesn't allow listeners to stop the flow of information and review what's been said—which they could do if they were reading a report or listening to a tape—it is especially vital to highlight key points. You can use several techniques to emphasize important points.

Number Items   If you are covering several points in a presentation or listing steps in a process, identifying each one by number will keep listeners aware of where you are:

> "The first advantage of the new plan is . . ."

> "A second benefit the plan will give us is . . ."

Use Signposts   As their name implies, signposts tell listeners how a new piece of material relates to your topic. Transitions are a kind of signpost:

> "We've talked about the problems that are facing the office products division; now let's look at some solutions."

Individual words or phrases can also let an audience know how your next remarks fit into a presentation:

> "*Another* important cost to consider is our overhead."

> "*Next*, let's look at the production figures."

> "*Finally,* we need to consider changes in customer demand."

Use Interjections   Interjections are words or phrases thrown into a commentary to highlight the importance or placement of an idea:

> "So what we've learned—*and this is important*—is that it's impossible to control personal use of office telephones."

> "Now here's another feature—*perhaps the best of all*—that makes this such a terrific plan."

Use Repetition and Redundancy   Repeating words (repetition) or delivering an idea two or more times in slightly different words (redundancy) intensifies the message and increases the odds that your point will get across:

> "Under the old system it took three weeks—*that's fifteen working days*—to get the monthly sales figures. Now we can get the numbers in just two days. That's right, *two days.*"

Add Internal Summaries and Previews   Unlike readers of a written document, people who listen to a presentation don't have the luxury of scanning a table of contents or rereading a paragraph to figure out how one part of your message relates to another. A way to help your audience stay oriented is to offer periodically an internal summary reviewing the important points you've covered:

> "Now you can see that the problem grew from several causes: a shortage of parts, inexperienced maintenance people, and the overload of opening the new warehouse."

Like internal summaries, internal previews orient an audience—this time by alerting them to the upcoming points:

> "You're probably wondering how all these changes will affect you. Well, some of them will make life much easier, and others will present some challenges. Let's look at three advantages first, and then we'll look at a couple of those challenges I mentioned."

In many cases, you can maximize the clarity of a presentation by combining an internal summary and a preview:

> "You can see that we've made great progress in switching to the new inventory system. As I've said, the costs were about ten percent more than we anticipated, but we see that as a one-time expense. I wish I could be as positive about the next item on the agenda—the customer service problems we've been having. Complaints have increased. We do believe we've finally identified the problem, so let me explain it and show you how we plan to deal with it."

USE MULTIPLE CHANNELS

Listeners are likely to understand and remember a message when you deliver it via more than one channel. You can present figures on an overhead projector or flip chart while you introduce them orally. You might then represent those numbers visually, using a chart or graph. If you're discussing a physical object, you might display photos of it on slides or even bring in the object itself to show your listeners. If you are illustrating a process, you might decide to play a brief videotape of it.

Using multiple channels has two advantages. First, it allows you to pick the most efficient medium to represent your ideas. Some concepts are best expressed in words, but others are much clearer when the audience can see, hear, or even touch them. Talking about a new line of clothing or the taste of a new food product isn't nearly as effective as giving your audience a firsthand look or taste, for example. Likewise, telling listeners in a training session how to deal with customer objections isn't nearly as effective as demonstrating it for them or letting them handle a situation themselves.

Besides being clearer, multiple channels have the advantage of keeping your

There are only three means of description available to us—words, pictures, and numbers. The palette is limited. Generally, the best instructions rely on all three, but in any instance one should predominate, while the other two serve and extend. The key to giving good instructions is to choose the appropriate means.

If I were going to describe my office, I could tell you in words, but it would take forever. I could tell you in numbers, but you would be left without a sense of the texture of the environment; you would have statistics without context. Clearly, the most appropriate way to describe my office would be in pictures, with a few dimensions and words of explanation.

If I were going to describe a person, a picture could never convey the complexities of personality. Only words might possibly do this, with a picture to enhance the description.

If I were going to describe the tangible assets of a company, I would probably rely on numbers, i.e. gross sales, profitability, market share, because these would be the easiest to compare, and would help you understand a company in terms relative to others of its kind.

Richard Saul Wurman, *Information Anxiety*

listeners interested. The variety of seeing images, hearing recordings, handling a sample is likely to make an audience eager to learn more, while hearing even a good speaker talk for an extended period can lead to fatigue.

SAMPLE INFORMATIVE PRESENTATION

The following presentation is typical of informative talks given every business day. The personnel specialist in a medium-sized company has gathered a group of staff members together to describe the features of a tax-reduction plan covering employee benefits. Notice how the speaker uses most of the strategies covered in this chapter to make her ideas clearer and to increase the attention of her audience.

The speaker's goal here is to help listeners decide whether they're interested enough in the benefits plan to attend a much longer meeting on the subject. She wisely chooses this approach to avoid going into great detail about the plan when some people might not be interested. By giving a short description of how the plan works, she can keep this introductory talk brief and simple.

The promise of increasing take-home pay is a guaranteed attention-getter.

I know you're busy, but I don't think you'll mind taking a few minutes away from work this morning. You see, I'm here today to show you a way that you can increase the amount of money you take home every month.

No, I'm not going to announce an across-the-board raise. But increasing your salary isn't the only way to boost your income. Another way that works just as well is to reduce your taxes. After all, every dollar less you pay in taxes is like having a dollar more in your pocket.

An overall view of the plan is presented here.

In the next few minutes, I'll explain the company's Flexible Benefits Plan. It's a perfectly legal option that lets you increase your real income by cutting the amount of taxes you pay, so that your income will grow even without a raise. I know this sounds too good to be true, but it really works! I've already signed on, and figure it will save me almost two thousand dollars a year. It can probably save a lot for you, too.

A brief transition alerts listeners to the first main point in the body of the presentation: the difference between before- and after-tax dollars.

Before you can appreciate how the Flexible Benefits Plan works, you have to understand the difference between *before-tax* and *after-tax* dollars. [Show Exhibit 1 here.] Before-tax dollars are the amount that show up every month in the "Gross Amount" box on our paychecks. But we don't get to spend our full salaries. There are several deductions: federal income tax withholding, Social Security (the amount in the "F.I.C.A." box), state tax withholding, and disability-insurance premiums (the amount in the "S.D.I." box). What's left in the "Net Amount" box is our pay in after-tax dollars.

The enlarged display of a familiar paycheck stub clarifies the unfamiliar concepts of before- and after-tax dollars.

Exhibit 1 Paycheck stub

90-2176
1222

7209

PAY _____ One thousand four hundred twenty nine and 60/100 _____ DOLLARS

TIME WK'D	DATE	TO THE ORDER OF	GROSS AMOUNT		FED. W/H	F.I.C.A.	STATE W/H	S.D.I.	CREDIT UNION	NET AMOUNT
	7/31/92	J. Doe	1958.33		293.74	78.33	68.54	88.12		1429.60

DISCRIPTION

G.U. Horton

The speaker wisely avoids a complicated discussion of before- and after-tax dollars in different tax brackets.

Once all those deductions are taken away from our pay, every before-tax dollar shrinks in value to about 73 cents. [Show Exhibit 2 here.] And that's in a low tax bracket. If your income is higher, then the difference between before- and after-tax dollars is even bigger. This means that it takes at least $136.33 in after-tax dollars to buy something that costs $100 in before-tax dollars.

Visual display increases the clarity and impact of the difference between before- and after-tax dollars.

Exhibit 2   Value of Before- and After-Tax Dollars

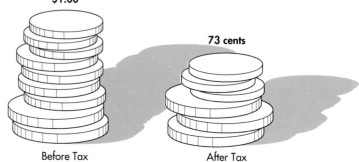

Transition here makes movement to the second part of the body clear.

You can probably see now that it's better to buy things in before-tax dollars whenever you can. And that's what the Flexible Benefits Plan lets you do. Let me explain how it works.

The Flexible Benefits Plan is so great because it allows you to pay for some important items in before-tax dollars. The plan lets you set aside pay in two categories: medical costs and dependent care. Let's cover each of these in detail so you can see which expenses are covered.

An internal preview orients the audience to the next two points.

Speaker generates audience involvement by inviting them to consider their own expenses in the following areas.

A look at the chart entitled "Allowable Medical Expenses" shows which items you can use under the Flexible Benefits Plan. [The speaker points to each item on Exhibit 3 as she discusses it.] As I cover these expenses, think about how much *you* spend in each area.

The chart helps listeners understand which expenses are covered.

Exhibit 3   Allowable Medical Expenses

- Health-insurance deductibles
- Health-insurance copayments
- Drugs and prescriptions
- Vision care and equipment
- Psychologists and psychiatrists
- Dental care and orthodontia

The hypothetical example helps show how the plan works in real life.

A citation helps prove that the cost of medicines is considerable.

Examples of typical vision-care fees illustrate the potential costs in this area.

Comparing the unfamiliar benefits plan to the familiar notion of a discount helps make the advantages clear.

Transition uses signposting to mark a shift to the second type of expense covered by the plan.

First we'll talk about health-insurance deductibles and copayments. Under our company's policy, you pay the first $300 of expenses for yourself and each dependent. You also make a $10 copayment for each visit to a doctor. Let's say that you and one dependent have to pay the $250 deductible each year, and that you made five visits to the doctor. That's a total of $650 per year you could have covered under the plan.

Drugs and prescriptions include every kind of medicine you buy, even if you buy it over the counter without a prescription. And, don't forget, the plan covers payments you make for everyone you claim as a dependent: your kids, maybe your spouse, and maybe even an older parent whom you're caring for. Here's an article from *Changing Times* magazine that says that a family of three spends an average of $240 per year on drugs. Maybe you spend even more. Whatever you do spend on medicine can be included in the plan, which means you will pay less for it than if you used after-tax dollars.

Vision care and equipment include eyeglasses and contact lenses as well as any fees you or your dependents pay to optometrists or ophthalmologists. With a pair of reading glasses costing at least $45 and a new set of contact lenses costing over $80, the money could really mount up.

Psychologists and psychiatrists are also covered, which means that any counseling you receive will cost a lot less.

Dental care and orthodontia are covered, too. If you or your dependents need major dental work, this can mean a lot. And if you're paying for your kids' braces, you can really save a bundle. We did some checking, and the average orthodontic treatment today runs about $3,500 over three years—or over $1,000 per year.

Nobody likes to spend money for medical expenses like these, but paying for them with before-tax dollars under the Flexible Benefits Plan is like getting a discount of 20 percent or more—clearly, a great deal.

But medical costs aren't the only expenses you can include in the Flexible Benefits Plan. There's a second way you can boost your take-home pay: by including dependent care in the plan.

For most people, dependents are children. Any costs of caring for your kids can be paid for in before-tax dollars, meaning you'll pay a lot less. You can include

The example of potential savings under the plan is a guaranteed attention-getter for working parents.

day-care services, preschool fees, even in-home care for your child. We did some checking and found that keeping a child in preschool or day care in this area from 8:30 in the morning until 5:00 P.M. averages about $5,000 per year. By shifting this amount into the Flexible Benefits Plan, the real cost drops by over $1,000. Not bad for filling out a few forms!

A restatement of the thesis is combined with introduction of an example to support its claim.

When you combine the savings on health care and dependents, the potential savings that come from joining the Flexible Benefits Plan are impressive. Let's take a look at a typical example of just how much money the Flexible Benefits Plan can save. Your personal situation probably won't be exactly like this one, but you can still get a feeling for how good the plan is. [Show Exhibit 4.]

Exhibit 4 Savings with Flexible Benefits Plan

	WITHOUT PLAN	WITH PLAN
GROSS SALARY	$23,500	$23,500
SALARY REDUCTIONS		
Health care	0	650
Prescriptions and drugs	0	240
Vision care	0	60
Dental care	0	180
Dependent care	0	1,800
	$23,500	$20,570
TAXES		
Federal income tax @ 15%	3,525	3,085
State income tax @ 3.5%	764	720
FICA and SDI @ 8.15%	1,915	1,676
	$6,204	$5,481
AFTER-TAX EXPENSES		
Health care	650	0
Prescriptions and drugs	240	0
Vision care	60	0
Dental care	180	0
Dependent care	1,800	0
NET PAY	$14,366	$15,089
ANNUAL SAVINGS	$723	

The chart provides a visual outline of the example. Without the exhibit, the dollar amounts would be too confusing to follow.

Let's suppose your salary is $23,500 and you have a spouse and one child. Let's say that your health and dependent expenses are pretty much like the ones we've been discussing here today. [Point to "Salary Reductions" section of chart.] Your health-insurance deductibles and copayments amount to $650, and you spend $240 over the year on prescriptions and drugs. Let's say that one person in your family needs one set of eyeglasses. You all get dental checkups, and you don't even have cavities! You spend $1,800 on child care—not bad these days.

If we look at the top third of the chart, it might seem that following the plan costs you more. After all, your salary without the plan would be $23,500, but it would be only $20,570 with your expenses from the plan deducted.

As the speaker points to the "Annual Savings" line on the chart, the audience sees in real dollars the potential advantage of the plan.

But look what happens once we start to figure taxes. [The speaker points to "Taxes" section of chart.] Since your pay with the plan is less, you pay less in taxes. A little subtraction shows that the difference between the $6,204 you'd pay without the plan and the $5,481 you'd pay with it amounts to a savings of $723.

This is just a small example of how much you can save. If your expenses are higher—if you have more medical costs, for example—the advantage is even greater. As your salary goes up and you move into a higher tax bracket, the advantages grow, too. And don't forget that the savings I've been talking about are just for one year. As time goes by, your earning power will grow even more.

In a restatement of the thesis the speaker returns to the main advantage of the plan.

Now you can see why we are so glad to offer the Flexible Benefits Plan. It can boost your take-home pay even before you get a raise. And keep in mind, it costs you nothing.

Listeners are told what to do next, if they are interested in the plan.

If you're interested in learning more, we encourage you to read the booklet I'll hand out in a moment. It contains a worksheet that will help you estimate how much you stand to save under the plan. If the idea still interests you, please attend the workshop we'll be holding next Friday during the lunch hour in the third-floor meeting room. At that time, we can answer your questions and make an appointment for each of you to sign up at the personnel office. In the meantime, I'll be happy to answer any questions you have now.

SUMMARY

Informative presentations fall into one of four categories: reports, briefings, explanations, and training. In addition to following the guidelines for effective presentational speaking described earlier in this book, an informative speaker can benefit by using several techniques described in this chapter.

Covering only necessary information ensures that the audience cannot be distracted by extraneous material. Linking the topic to the interests and concerns of the audience offers listeners a reason to heed the presentation. Linking new or unfamiliar concepts to ideas that are familiar to the audience makes the material easier to understand. Finally, involving the audience is a way to keep attention high and increase understanding.

Following several organizational principles can increase comprehension. Beginning the presentation with an overall picture of the ideas to be covered gives listeners a frame of reference. Emphasizing important points helps achieve the speaking goal. Numbering items, signposting, repetition and redundancy, and internal summaries and previews all add emphasis. Using multiple channels to convey a message increases understanding.

ACTIVITIES

1. What needs or interests could you appeal to in each of the following presentations?

   a. A briefing for employees on new performance-appraisal procedures
   b. A training program on listening skills for managers
   c. A speech to local high-school students on "Careers in _____" (you choose the topic)
   d. A report to the administration of a college on student attitudes toward business courses
   e. A presentation promoting a one-day fifty-dollar "Dress for Success" seminar to students

2. Covering only necessary information can increase understanding in an informative presentation. Identify the key points in each of the following presentations:

   a. A report you might make to a financial-aid advisor on your academic progress in the current school year
   b. A briefing to a co-worker returning from an absence or to fellow students who missed a recent class meeting
   c. An explanation of the formal and informal communication pattern in an organization where you have worked
   d. A training session on how to deliver a presentation to a group of listeners who have never spoken to a group

3. Describe how you could use familiar concepts to help introduce one of the following topics to a group of listeners who did not understand it. (If you are not familiar with any of the following, choose a concept that you do understand, and explain it in terms an audience will find familiar.)

   a. Depreciation of business equipment
   b. Computer operating system commands
   c. Etiquette at a business meal
   d. Stagflation
   e. The life cycle of a product
   f. A corporate balance sheet
   g. Chapter 11 bankruptcy

4. Describe how you could involve the audi-

ence in each of the following training sessions:

a. How to deal with customer complaints
b. Learning to use a new voice mail phone system
c. Deciding whether to lease or buy a piece of equipment
d. How to fill out a new expense-account form

Communicator Profile

Stephanie Dollschnieder
Regional Marketing Manager
Pacific Bell Directories
Anaheim, California

My audiences are mostly adults, which poses a special challenge. Studies show that adults will tune you out after about thirteen minutes unless you change your method of presentation.

A big part of my work involves informing people about our products and services. I conduct training seminars and present marketing information and special proposals to in-house audiences. I also spend a great deal of time speaking to various community groups. This week, for example, I spoke to the Sales and Marketing Executives of Los Angeles about Pacific Bell Directories' marketing strategies. In the last few months, I've spoken to other groups, such as the Vietnamese, Chinese, and Korean Chambers of Commerce—all large and important groups in the ethnically diverse Los Angeles area.

In-person presentations work better than any other form of communication, I have found. A conference call or memorandum isn't as effective because it lacks the human element: the body language, and the feedback of immediate questions and responses. There is synergy created in an effective presentation. The same message written out and mailed to several people may well be received by each one in a slightly different way. If I'm not there to explain, there's no chance for immediate clarification.

My audiences are mostly adults, which poses a special challenge. Studies show that adults will tune you out after about thirteen minutes unless you change your method of presentation. So you must switch to slides or an overhead projector, for example, or stop and discuss a handout. Your visual aids will depend on the complexity of your information and the size of your audience. I recommend at least using a handout, something the listener can take away after the presentation.

It is extremely important not to come across as condescending. I had a near disaster once because I tilted my head back ever so slightly so that my voice would carry to the back of a large room. One of my associates told me at the lunch break that I was turning people off but we didn't know why. We replayed the videotape and noticed my "stuck up" posture. Sure enough, when I changed it, everything went much better.

My advice to students who want to give effective presentations is always to practice in front of a friend or a mirror, or at least a wall. Never practice "just in your head" because it simply will not work. You won't feel prepared, and you won't do a good job.

If your message is potentially unpleasant—bad news, say, or very detailed and perhaps boring—make your voice dynamic. Humor is excellent if you can use it well and it's in good taste. Eye contact and minimal notes are important. Move about with ease among the audience, and speak slightly faster than normal to gain credibility. Yes, and all of these skills can be learned by any motivated person. And remember, it's normal to be nervous. They say even Johnny Carson still gets nervous sometimes.

15

After reading this chapter, you should understand:

- The differences among persuasion, coercion, and manipulation
- The types of persuasive presentations most common in business and the professions
- The various strategies available to maximize the persuasiveness of a message
- The elements that contribute to a speaker's credibility
- Four ways to organize a persuasive message

You should be able to:

- Define an effective goal and audience for a persuasive message
- Choose the best position for the thesis of a persuasive message
- Identify the audience needs that should form the basis of a persuasive appeal
- Identify the evidence necessary to support a persuasive claim
- Determine whether or not to cite opposing ideas when presenting a persuasive message
- Maximize your credibility as a speaker
- Choose the best organizational plan for a given persuasive message

PERSUASIVE PRESENTATIONS

Two partners are convinced that they have a winning idea for a new restaurant. They meet with a commercial loan officer from a local bank to seek financing for their project.

Faced with a wave of injuries, the foreman of a construction crew convinces his team members that they need to observe safety practices more carefully.

A local real-estate brokerage has merged with a nationwide chain. Ever since the news became public, rumors have swept the office about how the changes will affect pay, policies, and even job security. The owner has called a companywide meeting to reassure employees that the change will benefit them.

As part of a community-relations program, the electric company has started a community speakers' bureau. The bureau's director is speaking to a group of employees to recruit them as volunteers for the service.

A group of employees has grown increasingly disgruntled with the boss's policy on vacation scheduling. They have chosen a three-person delegation to present their grievances.

As these examples show, salespeople are not the only persuaders in business. At one time or another, everyone in an organization needs to influence the thinking or actions of others. When an issue is especially important, though, the persuasion frequently takes place in a presentation.

This chapter will give you information that can help you succeed in the persuasive presentations you will give in your career. It begins with a definition of persuasion, contrasting this form of communication with other methods of seeking change. After demonstrating that persuasion can be valuable and ethical, the chapter describes the types of persuasive presentations that commonly occur in business and professional settings. It then outlines a variety of strategies that can be used to present a message effectively. The chapter offers ways that speakers can maximize their credibility. Finally, the chapter presents four organizational patterns for developing persuasive messages.

ETHICAL PERSUASION DEFINED

Since persuasion often conjures up images of unscrupulous salespeople peddling worthless products to gullible consumers, it is important to begin our discussion with a definition of persuasion as an ethical and honorable form of communication. *Persuasion* is the act of motivating an audience, through communication, to voluntarily change a particular belief, attitude, or behavior.[1] This definition might seem long-winded, but it helps distinguish persuasion from other ways of influencing an audience.

To understand the nature of persuasion, imagine that the city council has announced its intention to turn a local athletic field and playground into a parking lot. The area's residents are understandably upset. Faced with this situation, the residents have four choices. First, they could accept the decision and do nothing to change it. This alternative is neither persuasive nor satisfying.

A second alternative would be to use coercion—forcing the council against its will to reverse its decision. The group could try to coerce a change by invading and disrupting a council meeting, demanding that the council promise to keep the park or face more demonstrations. Threatening to mount a recall campaign against any members who insist on supporting the parking lot would be another coercive approach. Although threats and force can change behavior, they usually aren't the best approach. The recipient of the threats can counterattack, leading to an escalating cycle of hostility. Threatened parties often dig in their heels and resist changing to save face or as a matter of principle, responding, "I'll be damned if I'll change just because you threaten me." Coercion also makes the instigator look bad.

A different approach to getting someone to change his or her mind involves manipulation—tricking the other party into thinking or acting in the desired way. A deceptive approach to the park-versus-parking-lot problem might be to present the council with a petition against the lot containing forged signatures to inflate the petition's size or to gain public sympathy by exaggerating the adverse effects of the project on certain groups—children, the elderly, and small business owners, for example.

It is reassuring to know that, besides being ethical, honesty is also the most effective policy when it comes to changing the mind of an audience. A "boomerang effect" often occurs when receivers learn that they have been the target of manipulative communication. Faced with this discovery, they will often change their attitudes in the direction opposite that advocated by a speaker.[2] In other cases, speakers are viewed as more credible when they openly admit that they are trying to persuade an audience.

In mass communication, manipulation takes the form of propaganda: messages that use concealed means to sell the public an ideology.[3] The ideology can be religious, political, or economic. Regardless of the subject, propaganda uses a wide array of techniques to impose a uniform system of beliefs on the public. The municipal-parking-lot issue is probably not big enough to generate a propaganda campaign by either the city or the neighbors. But when an issue is larger and more ideological, propaganda might come into play. The real-estate industry might, for instance, try to persuade the residents of the city that growth is good for them. Likewise, conservationists could promote the message that "small is beautiful." No matter what position one takes on an issue, propaganda can be used to gain converts. The key to this approach is manipulation of the audience.

A final way to achieve change is persuasion—communication that convinces the other person to act voluntarily in the desired way. The citizens' group could organize an appeal showing that the community sees keeping the park as more important than increasing the amount of available parking. It could describe the benefits of the park, bringing in local residents to testify about its importance to the community.

This chapter focuses on teaching the principles of persuasion. It doesn't instruct you on accepting the status quo: no guidance is needed for that alternative. You'll have to look elsewhere for advice on how to coerce others—at least blatantly. Finally, this isn't a chapter on how to deceive others into following your wishes. Manipulation can get results, but it raises serious ethical questions. What you'll learn in the following pages is how to make the best possible case for your position so that others will voluntarily choose to accept it.

The line between persuasion and coercion is sometimes fuzzy.[4] While bald threats are clearly coercive, what about implied warnings? Consider the example of the city park. Speakers could remind the council that unhappy voters might remember the decision to close the park and choose other candidates in the next election. Approaches like this seem to have a coercive element even if you give the other party a choice of whether to comply.

On the other end of the scale, the boundary between persuasion and manipulation is also vague. If speakers compliment council members on their past concern for the environment and responsiveness to the voters before trying to persuade them to cancel the parking facility, are the speakers being persuasive or deceitful? If they stage an emotional but accurate series of pleas by children who will be forced to play in the street if the lot is built, are they being manipulative or merely smart?

By now, it should be clear that manipulation, persuasion, and coercion don't fall into three distinct categories. Rather, they blend into one another, like colors of the spectrum:

Coercion	*Persuasion*	*Manipulation*

The point where one method of gaining compliance stops and another begins will vary from situation to situation. Perhaps the best measures of whether a particular message is genuinely persuasive are (1) whether the recipient feels truly free to make a choice, and (2) whether the originator would feel comfortable if he or she were the recipient of the message instead of its sender.

TYPES OF PERSUASIVE PRESENTATIONS

Most persuasive presentations in business fall into one of four categories: sales presentations, proposals, motivational speeches, and goodwill speeches.

SALES PRESENTATIONS

Television commercials and direct-mail advertising might sell spaghetti sauce or commemorative medallions, but few people will spend large amounts of money without being sold personally. Salespeople make presentations about such diverse goods and services as real estate, insurance, merchandise packaging, telephone systems, advertising space, office furniture, heavy machinery, car-rental contracts, restaurant franchises, and many more.

PROPOSALS

In an organization, the goal of most proposals is to persuade higher management. Many involve plans for a new program such as a new product line or an advertising campaign. Others involve requests for resources: additional staff, larger budgets, new equipment. Still others involve changes in policy or procedures: a new compensation plan or a change in the way a job is handled. Still others are personal requests for changes: a raise, involvement in a particular project, or a promotion. A developer seeking a zoning variation from the local planning committee, an account executive presenting a new campaign to a customer, or an executive proposing contract revisions to a union leader are also making proposals.

MOTIVATIONAL SPEECHES

At their worst, motivational speeches can combine the most oppressive elements of a bad sermon and a high-school pep rally. On the other hand, when delivered effectively and at the proper time, such presentations can produce good results. A manager trying to persuade her subordinates to fill out a lengthy, time-consuming financial report by telling them it is essential for the good of the company will only arouse resentment if everyone knows that management reads only two lines on the reports (the gross margin and the pretax profit). The manager would probably be more successful at the same task if she agreed that the form is largely useless but said, "Look, you know how those financial guys are. They don't know anything about the market—they only know whether your numbers add up. We'll get a lot less interference from above if we give them the numbers they need to look good."

GOODWILL SPEECHES

Representatives of organizations frequently speak to audiences to promote interest or support for their organizations. A corporate recruiter addressing graduating seniors and a bank economist explaining economic forecasts are making speeches of goodwill. So is the utility company's representative addressing the press after an accident in a nuclear power plant.

These goodwill speeches may seem informative, but they also try to change the attitudes or behavior of their listeners. The corporate recruiter is trying to encourage some students to apply for jobs with his company; the economist is trying to build the image of her institution as a leading business bank; and the utility-company representative is trying to soften negative reactions.

PERSUASIVE STRATEGIES

Whatever its nature and audience, a persuasive presentation should follow most of the guidelines described in Chapters 10 through 13 of this text. In addition, the presentation's effectiveness will be increased if it takes advantage of the following principles.

APPEAL TO THE NEEDS OF YOUR AUDIENCE

Asking for a promotion because you need the money isn't nearly as effective as demonstrating that you can help the company better in the new position. Asking for an assistant because you feel overworked isn't as likely to impress your boss as showing how the help will increase productivity or allow you to take on more business.

Perhaps the most important key to effective selling is identifying the prospect's needs and showing how the product can satisfy them. One organization's success at implementing this principle was featured in *Fortune* magazine:

> A word-processing machine salesman does not merely sell hardware. He goes into an office, asks to see how the paperwork is handled, makes himself an overnight expert about the business involved, then prepares a plan for increasing its productivity by using a specific Lanier machine and disc. When he gives a demonstration, he programs the machine to churn out that prospect's actual paperwork.[5]

Even if the audience is not interested in or is unsympathetic to an idea, there is usually some way to link a proposal to the listeners' needs or values. A representative of an oil company speaking to residents of a coastal town where offshore drilling is being proposed could defend the move by showing how the local economy would benefit and how drilling platforms increase the abundance of marine life in the oceans, which in turn improves fishing.

Whenever possible, base your appeal on several needs. Listeners who are not reached by one appeal can still be persuaded by another. If you were trying to persuade co-workers to vote for separate smoking and nonsmoking areas in your building, for example, you might identify several needs for both smokers and nonsmokers and show how your proposal would fill each need:

NEED	SATISFACTION
Physical health	Separating smoking and nonsmoking areas will protect nonsmokers from cigarette smoke and may even help smokers cut down or quit smoking.
Comfort	Isolated smoking lounges will keep less ventilated parts of the building from getting unpleasantly smoky.
Friendship	Smokers won't annoy nonsmokers, and nonsmokers won't bother smokers about smoking in the separate lounges.

Grant G. Gard tells salespeople "Don't start talking about yourself, your likes, your dislikes, or your achievements. Your prospect cares only about himself or herself and the things that affect him or her. Talk only in terms of the prospect's interests." The same principle applies to all persuasive communication; it's better to build an argument around the listener's needs than your own.

Doug Harper, "Honing Your Professional Image," *Industrial Distribution*

HAVE A REALISTIC GOAL

Even the best presentation can't accomplish miracles. The oil-company representative defending his company's proposal to start offshore drilling doesn't expect his arguments about business growth and increasing marine wildlife to turn opponents into enthusiastic supporters. Rather than asking for their support, his purpose was simply to have them recognize that offshore drilling "was not all that bad." Similarly, a sales representative trying to sell furnishings for a new office building would not expect to make a $2 million sale on her first call; she might try only to make an appointment to present her proposal to the planning committee.

A human-resources assistant at a medium-sized company used the strategy of choosing an appropriate goal to promote her belief that the corporation should sponsor day care for the children of employees. Recognizing that management, after hearing a single presentation, would not accept her arguments proving the advantages for the company of providing this service, she decided that the goal for her first presentation on the subject should be to receive authorization to spend six hours per week for two months conducting a feasibility study on how well child-care services had operated in other companies. She was confident that, once she had the proof that programs had worked elsewhere, management would be more open to sponsoring one.

FOCUS APPEALS ON CRITICAL AUDIENCE SEGMENT

Sometimes one or two listeners have the power to approve or reject your appeal. Abraham Lincoln made this point clearly when his cabinet unanimously opposed one of his ideas. "The vote is eight to one against the plan," the president stated. "The motion carries." In cases such as this, it is important to identify the interests, needs, attitudes, and prejudices of those key decision makers and then focus your appeal toward them. For instance, if the office-furnishings sales representative finds that most of the members of the planning committee vote with the president, her presentation to the committee will be aimed at his apparent needs and interests. If she finds that the president doesn't meet with the planning committee, she might try to get an appointment to speak with the president.

DEFER THESIS WITH HOSTILE AUDIENCES

Usually, you state your thesis during the introduction of a presentation, but this rule may not be effective with skeptical or hostile listeners. If a manager seeking acceptance of changes in staffing thinks that the audience will respond favorably to her thesis ("Increased business has led us to open up several new positions, and we'd like you to apply for them"), she'll put the idea in the introduction of the speech. If she believes the thesis will not be received enthusiastically ("Declining business requires us to defer pay raises for the upcoming year") or if she believes an audience that hears the news too early will be too upset to accept—or even hear—the rationale behind the decision, she will present the thesis later in the speech.

A presentation with a deferred thesis still needs an introduction to capture the attention of the audience, demonstrate the importance of the topic, and orient the listeners to what will follow. In talks with a deferred thesis, the part of the introduction containing the preview carries the extra burden of setting up the thesis without stating it directly.

> It's no secret that the recession and our industrywide slump in general have hurt the company. Today I want to tell you how management has tried to cope with these problems in a way that will protect our livelihoods as much as possible.

After the preview, the body of the presentation leads the audience, step by step, to the point at which they are ready to understand and accept the speaker's thesis:

> As you can see, given the problems we've faced, management's choice has been to either lay off personnel or defer pay raises. We hope you agree that our decision to defer raises is the best one under the circumstances and that you'll realize we still consider you valuable members of our team.

PRESENT AMPLE EVIDENCE TO SUPPORT CLAIMS

Chapter 12 outlined the types of support that can help you prove your claims: examples, stories, statistics, comparisons, and citations. When your goal is to persuade an audience, the generous use of support is especially important.

Research demonstrates that when an audience hears persuasive evidence backing up a persuasive claim, the chances increase that the influence of the message will last long after the presentation has concluded.[6] Furthermore, evidence supporting a claim makes listeners less likely to accept opposing viewpoints that they may hear after you have finished speaking.

The best evidence comes from credible sources. If your credibility on the subject is not high, be sure to cite others whose expertise and impartiality your listeners respect. For example, a prospective customer would expect a sales representative to praise a product he or she is trying to sell. But if the salesperson cites others who know the product and who don't have an interest in its sale, the message ("This product is excellent") becomes more persuasive. In this case, the testimony of other customers or of an independent testing service such as Consumers Union would be excellent sources of evidence.

CONSIDER CITING OPPOSING IDEAS

Research indicates that it is generally better to mention and then refute ideas that oppose yours.[7] There are three situations when it is especially important to forewarn listeners about opposing ideas:

When the Audience Disagrees with Your Position   In such cases, it's wise to compare their position and yours, showing the desirability of your thesis. If management has previously opposed products similar to the one you are about to propose, for instance, you'll need to bring up their objections ("It's too risky, the capital outlay is too big, and the sales force can't sell it") and show how your proposal will meet their objections. ("We can minimize the risk and the initial costs by limiting the first production run; if we put extra emphasis on advertising and show the sales force how other companies have sold similar products very successfully in the last few years, they'll be more enthusiastic and more effective.") Similarly, if you're trying to sell an out-of-the-way plant location to a company that has planned to build the new plant in a more central location, you might show how transportation is as cheap and available in your location as at the one they've planned or that savings on real-estate taxes and labor will allow the company to pay higher transportation costs. If you don't mention arguments that are already on their minds, your listeners may consider you uninformed.

When the Audience Knows Both Sides of the Issue   Well-informed listeners, even if they haven't made up their minds about an issue, will find a one-sided appeal less persuasive than a presentation that considers opposing arguments. Discussing these ideas shows that you are not trying to avoid them. Even if you refute the competition, considering it at all is more evenhanded than focusing exclusively on your plan and never acknowledging that alternatives exist.

An account executive at a full-service stock brokerage showed that he respected the knowledge and judgment of his listeners at an investment seminar when he discussed the alternatives to using the services of his firm.

> I know that most of you are familiar enough with the financial marketplace to be asking yourself "Why don't I save money and use a discount brokerage?" And that's a fair question. After all, discount firms charge you a much smaller commission for each transaction than full-service houses like mine. I'd like to suggest that the answer to the question of which kind of brokerage to use lies in the old saying "You get what you pay for." If you use a discount firm, you'll get limited service. Now, that may be all you want and all you need. But if you're looking for a source of financial support and attention, you'll get it at a full-service brokerage. Let me explain.

When the Audience Will Soon Hear Your Viewpoint Criticized or Another One Promoted   You will be better off defusing your opponents' thesis by bringing up and refuting their arguments than by letting them attack your position and build up theirs in its place. For example, a union organizer speaking to a group of plant workers might anticipate an argument from management this way:

The company representative will tell you that after we organized the Oregon plant, the people were out of work, on strike, for four months the next year. That's true. What the company probably won't tell you is that the people got strike pay from the union. They also won't tell you that the people there were losing money every year before that because their wages weren't keeping up with inflation, and the strike got them guaranteed cost-of-living raises, plus life, health, and disability benefits and improved safety conditions.

MAXIMIZING SPEAKER CREDIBILITY

Winston Churchill once said that, when it comes to persuading, what matters most is who you are, then how you say what you want to say, and, finally, what you say. Even without taking this assertion literally, it is true that credibility is a powerful factor in persuasion. Research shows that credibility can be enhanced in a variety of ways.[8]

DEMONSTRATE YOUR COMPETENCE

Listeners will be most influenced by a speaker who they believe is qualified on the subject. You are more likely to believe career advice from a self-made millionaire than from your neighbor who has been fired from four jobs in three years. Similarly, the department staff is more likely to accept the direction of a new manager who seems knowledgeable about the specific work of that department. Management is more likely to agree to take a risk on a new manufacturing material if the product manager seems to know the market very well. These are all examples of trusting someone's competence.

There are three ways to build your perceived competence. The first is by demonstrating your *knowledge of the subject.* For example, the product manager might help to establish her credibility by citing statistics ("Our market research showed that 85 percent of the potential market is more concerned with maintenance costs than the initial cost of the product. A study published in the trade journal last month demonstrated that maintenance costs are often 80 percent of the cost of the equipment"). She could also remember facts ("Dorwald Associates tried something like this, although only in government markets, and it was pretty

---

The bigger the prospect, the more likely they are to expect professionalism. My experience has been that when you don't get the business you are rarely, if ever, told the real reason or the complete reason you lost. The easy out is to tell you that it was price. But often the real reason is that you did a sloppy, disorganized, disjointed, and unprofessional job of telling your story. In the prospect's mind, the quality of your presentation is a mirror image of the quality of your company, your product, your service, and your people.

David A. Peoples, *Presentations Plus*

---

successful") and recount appropriate examples ("I was checking the records last week, and I realized that we could afford to replace the machines every five years on what we'd save on maintenance if we used plastic instead of metal").

A second way to demonstrate competence is by making your *credentials* known. These credentials could be academic degrees, awards and honors, or successful experiences ("I helped set up Hinkley's very profitable system a few years ago").

A third way to show your competence is through *demonstration of your ability*. A junior manager who bungles his figures will have a hard time convincing his superiors that he ought to be given more financial responsibility. A sales representative who reminds a customer that she has often solved problems by arranging emergency shipments will establish credibility for her claim that her company provides good service.

EARN THE TRUST OF YOUR AUDIENCE

The most important ingredient of trustworthiness is *honesty*. If listeners suspect you are not telling the truth, even the most impressive credentials or grasp of the subject will mean little. For instance, a union leader gets little support from union members if they think that he's made a private agreement with management.

Impartiality is a second element of trustworthiness. We are more likely to accept the beliefs of impartial speakers than of those who have a vested interest in persuading us. A sales representative is hardly a neutral source of information about her product or her competition's. She could, however, cite an independent journal's evaluation of a product.

EMPHASIZE YOUR SIMILARITY TO THE AUDIENCE

Audiences are most willing to accept the ideas of a speaker whose attitudes and behaviors are similar to their own. This persuasive ability exists even when the similarities are not directly related to the subject at hand. Thus, a subordinate may get a better hearing from the boss when both are golfers, have children of the same age, come from the same part of the country, or dress similarly. Customer-service representatives for farm machinery generally wear casual clothing and open-necked shirts to fit in with the people they visit. Many sales representatives begin conversations with prospects by expressing a common interest—gardening, baseball, or a recent event that affects the customer's business.

Similarity in areas related to the speaker's topic is even more persuasive. This fact has led to the strategy of establishing *common ground* between speaker and listeners early in a presentation. A speaker who shows he and the audience have similar beliefs will create goodwill that can make listeners willing to consider more controversial ideas later on. Notice, for example, how a business owner seeking a zoning variance bases her appeal to the local architectural review board:

> Like you, I'm a strong believer in preserving the character of our town. As a businesswoman and a long-time resident, I realize beauty and lack of crowding are

our greatest assets. Without them, our home would become just another overgrown collection of shopping malls and condominiums.

Also, like you, I believe that change isn't always bad. Thanks to your efforts, our downtown is a more interesting and beautiful place now than it was even a few years ago. I think we share the philosophy that we ought to preserve what is worth saving and improve the town in whatever ways we can. I appreciate the chance to show you how this project will make the kind of positive change we all seek.

This speaker's chances of gaining acceptance for her proposal were increased by her demonstrated support for the principles the board promotes. Of course, the board has to believe that the speaker is sincere. If they suspect she is just telling them what they want to hear, her credibility will shrink, not grow.

INCREASE YOUR APPEAL TO THE AUDIENCE

Illogical as it may seem, listeners are more persuaded by speakers they find appealing in some way. One source of attractiveness, of course, is *appearance.* Listeners are also attracted to speakers who are *complimentary.* Letting an audience know you respect their accomplishments, value their judgment, or like them personally will predispose them toward accepting your viewpoint. An account executive addressing the marketing staff of a new company client, for instance, might begin by saying, "It's a great honor to work with you. I'm especially excited about working at Nordik because I know this staff has been primarily responsible for building Nordik's reputation for innovative, creative marketing campaigns."

DEMONSTRATE SINCERITY

Speakers perceived as believing strongly in their subjects are more persuasive than unenthusiastic ones. The audience reaction is usually "If this person cares so much about the idea, there must be something to it." Sincerity is only impressive if the audience *detects* it, however; unfortunately, some speakers don't show their enthusiasm and so reduce their effectiveness. A plant superintendent delivering a glowing report about the progress that his staff is making in solving an important problem, for example, could really be concerned about his job, which is dependent on the problem being solved quickly. If his tension shows more than his enthusiasm, his superiors might suspect that the problem is still more serious than he claims.

These are the fundamental selling truths. If you don't know your product, people will resent your efforts to sell it; if you don't believe in it, no amount of personality and technique will cover that fact; if you can't sell with enthusiasm, the lack of it will be infectious.

Mark H. McCormack, *What They Don't Teach You at Harvard Business School*

ORGANIZING PERSUASIVE MESSAGES

Credibility may be important, but the way you structure your message also plays a major role in determining how successful you will be at persuading an audience. Chapter 11 discussed several patterns for organizing the body of a presentation. Of these, the problem-solution pattern is often appropriate in persuasive situations. The other plans described in the following pages can also work well. As Table 15-1 shows, there is no single best plan. The one you choose will depend on the topic and your audience's attitudes toward it.

PROBLEM-SOLUTION

This plan works especially well when your audience does not feel a strong need to change from the status quo. Since listeners have to recognize that a problem exists before they will be interested in a solution, showing them that the present situation is not satisfactory is essential before you present your idea.

> **Thesis:** Establishing a system of employee incentives can boost productivity.
>
> **A.** Our level of productivity has been flat for over two years while the industrywide rate has climbed steadily in that period. (*Problem*)
> **B.** Establishing an incentive system will give employees a reason to work harder. (*Solution*)

A problem-solution pattern might also be used to show how updating a computer system will solve problems with inventory monitoring, why a potential customer needs a personal financial advisor, or why a department needs additional staff.

The problem-solution approach is often effective, but it is not the best strategy for every situation. If your listeners already recognize that a problem exists, you may not need to spend much time proving the obvious. In these

TABLE 15-1 Considerations for Choosing a Persuasive Organizational Plan

ORGANIZATIONAL PLAN	CONSIDERATIONS
Problem-solution	Most basic persuasive pattern. Use when audience needs convincing that a problem exists.
Comparative advantages	Use when audience is considering alternatives to your proposal. Show how your plan is superior to other(s). Defer thesis if audience will object to idea before hearing your reasoning.
Criteria satisfaction	Use when audience is not likely to consider alternative plans. Choose criteria important to your audience, and show how your plan meets them. If audience may be hostile to your plan, introduce criteria before discussing the plan.
Motivated sequence	Use when problem and solution are easy to visualize. Effective when seeking immediate audience reaction.

circumstances, you might touch on the problem in the introduction to your talk and devote the entire body to suggesting a solution. In this case, a topical plan might be the best approach—especially if the audience is likely to accept your recommendation without considering other alternatives. If you are competing against other ideas, however, a comparative-advantages plan may be a better organizational strategy.

COMPARATIVE ADVANTAGES

This approach puts several alternatives side by side and shows why yours is the best. This strategy is especially useful when the audience is considering an idea that competes with the one you're advocating. Under these circumstances, ignoring alternative plans is a bad idea. A head-on comparison that supports your case is a far more effective plan. The manager of a health club used a comparative-advantages approach to encourage new members.

I. Introduction: When you decide to join a health club, you have several choices in the area. You might be tempted by the special introductory rates at some other clubs in town, but a feature-by-feature look shows that Nautilus 2000 is your best choice.
II. Body
   A. The club is open longer every day than any other club in town.
   B. The club has more exercise machines than any other in town.
   C. The club has a wider variety of activities than any other in town: aerobics classes, swimming, saunas, massage, racquetball, and a snack bar.
   D. The club's staff are all licensed fitness counselors—a claim no other club in town can make.
III. Conclusion: When it comes to value for your dollar, Nautilus 2000 is your best health-club choice.

In the preceding example, the speaker made her thesis clear at the beginning of her presentation. A comparative-advantages approach also works well when you choose to defer your thesis. In this instance, you can build a case showing how your proposal is superior to the alternatives and then present your thesis as a conclusion. An insurance agent used this strategy to convince an audience to buy coverage.

I. Introduction: How should you spend your discretionary income?
II. Body: There are several alternatives.
   A. You can spend it all on recreation, but that won't buy financial security for your family if anything happens to you.
   B. You can make investments to plan for the future, but there is always the risk of losing that money.
   C. More expensive housing is an option, but it risks placing you even more in debt.

D. Insurance guarantees your family an income if you die or are disabled.

III. Conclusion: At least some of your disposable income ought to be devoted to insurance. (*Deferred thesis*)

In this situation, deferring the thesis was a smart idea. If the speaker had started by praising the virtues of buying insurance, most listeners would have tuned out. Since very few people relish the thought of spending their discretionary income on something as intangible as more insurance coverage, they'd probably reject the idea unless they are led to the conclusion that it is the best choice.

CRITERIA SATISFACTION

This strategy sets up criteria for a plan that the audience will accept and then shows how your idea or product meets them. Unlike a comparative-advantages approach, a criteria-satisfaction plan does not consider alternative ideas. For this reason, it is a good approach when your audience isn't likely to think of alternative plans.

A venture capitalist used a criteria-satisfaction plan when seeking investors for a business project. Notice how he introduced each criterion and then showed how his project would satisfy it.

I. Introduction: Being in the right place at the right time can be the key to financial success. I'm here today to offer you a chance to reap substantial benefits from an extremely promising project. Like any investment, this project needs to be based on the sound foundation of a solid business plan, a talented management team, and adequate financing. Let me show you how the project meets all of these important requirements.

II. Body
A. The first criterion is that the business plan must be solid. Extensive market research shows the need for this product. . . .
B. The second criterion is a talented management team. Let me introduce the key members of this management team and describe their qualifications. . . .
C. The third criterion is a solid, realistic financial plan. The following plan is very conservative yet shows strong potential for a substantial profit. . . .

III. Conclusion: Because it meets the conditions of a solid business plan, this project is worth your serious consideration.

In this example, the speaker introduced each criterion and then immediately showed how his plan satisfied it. A different approach is to present all the criteria first and then present your proposal. The strategy here is to gain the audience's acceptance first and boost your credibility. Having done this, you go on to show how your plan meets those conditions. With this approach, the thesis is deferred—which is especially smart when the audience may not be inclined to accept it without some powerful arguments.

A manager used a criteria-satisfaction plan with a deferred thesis to announce a wage freeze to employees—hardly a popular plan. If she had announced her thesis first ("A wage freeze is in your best interests"), the employees probably would have been too upset to listen thoughtfully to her arguments. By leading her audience through the reasons leading up to the freeze, she increased the chances that they would understand management's reasoning. Notice how the thesis is first presented in the middle of the body and is restated in the conclusion.

    I. Introduction: You know that we've faced declining revenues for the past year. During these hard times, we need a policy that is best both for the company and for you, the employees. That's the only way we will be able to survive.

    II. Body
        A. There are three important criteria for selecting a policy. (*Introduces criteria first*)
            1. It should be fair.
            2. It should cause the least harm to employees.
            3. It should allow the company to survive this difficult period without suffering permanent damage.
        B. A wage freeze is the best plan to satisfy these criteria. (*Satisfaction of criteria*)
            1. It's fair.
                a.⎫
                   ⎬ evidence
                b.⎭
            2. It causes minimal harm to employees.
                a.⎫
                   ⎬ evidence
                b.⎭
            3. It will enable the company to survive.
                a.⎫
                   ⎬ evidence
                b.⎭

   III. Conclusion: A wage freeze is the best plan at this difficult time.

MOTIVATED SEQUENCE

The motivated-sequence approach is a five-step organizing scheme designed to boost the involvement and interest of the audience.[9] Regardless of the topic, the sequence of steps is the same:

    1. *Attention:* Capture the attention of the audience by introducing the problem in an interesting manner.

    2. *Need:* Explain the problem clearly and completely. Use a variety of supporting material to back up your claim, proving that the problem is serious. Ideally, make your listeners feel that the problem affects them in some way. Make them eager to hear a solution.

3. *Satisfaction:* Present your solution to the problem. Provide enough support to prove that the solution is workable and that it will, indeed, solve the problem.

4. *Visualization:* Describe clearly what will happen if your proposal is adopted so that the audience has a clear mental picture of how your proposal will solve the problem. You may also paint a verbal picture of what will happen if your proposal is *not* adopted. In either case, the key to success in this step is to paint a vivid picture of the outcomes, showing how your proposal will make a real difference.

5. *Action:* Call for a response by your audience. Explain what they can do to solve the problem.

The motivated-sequence plan provides a step-by-step approach for organizing a speech. It builds on the basic problem-solution plan: step 1 arouses the interest of listeners so that they will be more receptive to the topic; step 4 goes beyond simply providing a solution and helps the audience picture what a difference it will make; step 5 guides the audience on how to bring the solution about, making it easier for them to take the necessary steps and arousing them to act.

The motivated sequence works best when the problem that you present and the solution that you propose are easy to visualize. If your listeners can imagine the problem and see themselves solving it by following your plan, they'll be motivated to accept your reasoning. Recognizing this fact, a travel agent used the motivated sequence to capture the interest of an audience and show them the joys of cruising:

Attention	Imagine yourself cruising in tropical waters . . . visiting foreign ports . . . dancing all night . . . dining on gourmet cuisine without worrying about the size of the check. These are just a few of the joys of cruising.
Need	I'm sure everyone here would take a cruise if they could. But you're probably saying to yourself, "I can't afford it." You may be resigned to taking a vacation that costs plenty but doesn't give you the kind of special experience that's only possible on a vacation cruise.
Satisfaction	I'm happy to say that you *can* afford it. Let me show you that cruising can be no more expensive than other, much-less-exciting vacations. . . .
Visualization	What would a cruising vacation be like? Imagine yourself sailing on our ten-day "Sun and Sea Odyssey." Your trip would begin with a champagne bon voyage reception. . . .

Action   A few reservations are still available for this winter's cruises. If you let me know that you are interested today, I'll send you a brochure describing the cruises in detail. Then we can discuss how to plan the vacation of your dreams at a price you can afford.

Because the motivated-sequence approach closes with an appeal to action, it is especially well suited to getting an immediate response to your proposal. Recognizing this fact, a fund-raiser used it to generate pledges for an urgent appeal.

Attention   Here's a picture of the Myer family. Ted, the father, is a trained stonemason and proud of it. Anne, the mom, is a registered nurse. Little Chris is a normal kid who loves baseball and pizza. His teachers say he has a gift for math and languages.

Need   Since this photo was taken, the Myers have had a run of terrible luck. Last year, Ted fell at work and wrenched his back. He's been unable to work ever since, and his disability insurance has almost run out. Three months after Ted's accident, Anne was diagnosed as having leukemia. She's undergoing treatment, and the doctors are optimistic; but she can't work now, and there's no telling when she will be able to return to her job. The Myers lived on their savings for six months, but now all the money is gone. Last week they had to move out of their apartment, and they have nowhere to go. Nowhere, that is, except Transition House.

Satisfaction   You can help provide temporary housing for the Myers and other neighbors who are in trouble by contributing to Transition House. Your donations will give these good people a safe place to stay while they get back on their feet and save them from life on the street.

Visualization   We're hoping to raise enough money tonight to give the Myer family a month at Transition House. During that time, Ted can finish training for a new career as a bookkeeper and get back to work. He hopes to become a CPA. Once he's on the job, the Myers will be able to find a new apartment so that Anne can fight for her health and Chris can stay in his same school, where he's doing so well.

Action   What we need from you tonight is a donation. We're asking for anything you can afford: the price of an evening on the town or maybe a postponement of that new outfit you were thinking of buying. In just a moment, I'll be passing out pledge cards. . . .

At first glance, the motivated-sequence approach seems to depart from the basic introduction-body-conclusion pattern of organizing a presentation. A closer look shows that the plan does follow the same pattern:

I. Introduction
   A. Attention
   B. Thesis/Preview
II. Body
   A. Need
   B. Satisfaction
   C. Visualization
III. Conclusion
   A. Review
   B. Action

By now, you can see that all of the organizational plans described in this chapter follow the same basic principles you learned in Chapter 11. Each has an introduction that captures the attention of your audience and gives members reasons to listen. Each has a body that is arranged in a pattern that is easy to follow and helps achieve the purpose of the presentation. Each has a conclusion that reinforces the thesis of the talk and leaves the audience motivated to accept it.

SAMPLE PERSUASIVE PRESENTATION

The following presentation demonstrates most of the persuasive principles covered in this chapter as well as the general guidelines about speaking to an audience introduced in Chapters 10 through 13. The purpose and approach are based on a sound audience analysis. As Figure 15-1 shows, the talk has a clear thesis and a clear, logical organizational structure. A variety of verbal and visual support adds interest, clarity, and proof.

The speaker's company, Ablex Technologies, manufactures sophisticated electronic components. One of its best customers is BioMedical Instruments (BMI), which produces a wide variety of sophisticated medical diagnostic instruments. The company's biggest contracts with BMI are for kidney-dialysis and blood-analyzer parts, which total almost $1 million per year.

Ablex also supplies BMI with parts for an x-ray unit. This is a much smaller and older contract. BMI doesn't make this model of x-ray machine anymore but is committed to furnishing current users with replacement parts until the machines drop out of use, and Ablex is obliged to supply BMI. Producing these x-ray parts is usually a problem: orders are small and sporadic, leading to delays and headaches for everyone concerned. The speaker has a plan about how to handle the x-ray parts in a better way.

The audience is Mary Ann Hirsch, the buyer at BMI, and one or two production engineers. It's unlikely that the purchasing director or the chief

Thesis
The proposed forecasting and purchasing agreement will allow both BMI and Ablex to better supply x-ray parts in a timely, affordable, and trouble-free manner.

I. Introduction
  A. Our basically positive relationship with BMI has only one problem: the x-ray parts.
  B. While a problem does exist, there is a solution.
    1. The problem involves erratic orders for x-ray parts.
    2. Our solution has several benefits.

II. Body
  A. Supplying x-ray parts has been a continuing headache.
    1. Orders for x-ray parts are irregular and unpredictable. *(line graph)*
    2. These irregular orders make it tough for us to ship orders to BMI in a timely way. *(example)*
    3. These delays are bad for Ablex, BMI, and customers. *(example)*
  B. Fortunately, there is a solution to the x-ray problem.
    1. Here's an outline of our plan.
    2. This plan has several advantages.
      a. Orders can be delivered more quickly. *(comparison chart)*
      b. Ordering is more flexible. *(examples)*
      c. Time can be saved in ordering and follow-up. *(example)*
      d. The unit cost is less than that under current plan. *(column chart, comparison chart)*

III. Conclusion: By now you can see that there's a solution to the x-ray problem.
  A. The plan has advantages for everyone involved.
  B. We look forward to putting it into action soon.

Figure 15-1   Outline of sample presentation.

project engineer will be there, since they usually rely on their subordinates to gather the information. But ultimately, the purchasing director and chief product engineer will be the ones to approve or reject this idea. So in a way, they're part of the audience, too.

This introduction emphasizes the positive aspects of the relationship with the customer.

This brief sketch of the problem establishes common ground: "We're in this together, and it's no good for either of us."

We've been involved in a long, positive relationship with BMI. The only troubles we've ever encountered have come from the x-ray parts. Even though they are only a small part of our business with you, they seem to involve the greatest headaches for you and us. The timing of these orders is impossible for you to predict, which makes it hard for us to get parts from our suppliers and deliver the product to you quickly. This leads to all sorts of problems: unhappy customers who have to wait for the equipment they ordered and time spent by people at both of our companies keeping in touch.

A preview of the main advantages of the plan that will be proposed.

Transition to the "Problem" section of the presentation.

The visual exhibit clearly demonstrates the unpredictable nature of customer orders.

We think there's a better way to handle the x-ray problem. It'll reduce frustration, cut costs, and let all of us spend our time on more productive parts of our jobs. But before we talk about this new plan, let me review why the present arrangement for handling x-ray orders is such a headache.

The main problem we face is irregular orders. A look at the order history for the last year shows that there's no pattern—and no way to predict when customers will order replacement parts for their x-ray units. [Show Exhibit 1 here.]

Exhibit 1   X-Ray Ordering Pattern

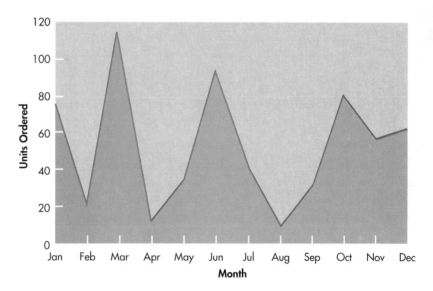

Example illustrates the problems flowing from irregular orders.

Transition leads to second consequence of irregular orders: wasted time.

This unpredictable pattern makes it tough for us to serve you quickly. We have to order parts from our suppliers, which often can take a long time. For instance, in the February 17 order, it took six weeks for our supplier to get us the parts we needed to manufacture the x-ray components you needed. Once we had the parts, it took us the usual four weeks to assemble them. As you said at the time, this delay kept your customer waiting almost three months for the components needed to get their equipment up and running, and that's poison for customer relations.

Delays like this aren't just bad for your relationship with customers, they also waste time—yours and ours.

Example highlights the amount of time wasted.

Mary Ann, do you remember how many phone calls and letters it took to keep track of that February order? In fact, every year we spend more time on these x-ray orders that involve a few thousand dollars than we do on the dialysis and blood-analyzer parts that involve around a million dollars annually. That's just not a good use of time.

Transition to "Solution" part of presentation.

So we clearly have a situation that's bad for everybody. Fortunately, we believe there's a better way—better for you, us, and your customers. The plan involves your giving us an annual purchasing forecast for x-ray parts. Instead of waiting for your customers to place individual orders, you'd estimate the total sales likely to occur in a year. Then we would acquire enough parts from our suppliers to assemble those items so that we could have them ready quickly as your customers place orders.

Solution summarized concisely.

Advantages of solution introduced and summarized in chart.

This simple plan has several advantages. They're summarized on this chart, but let me explain them in a little more detail. [Show Exhibit 2 here.]

Exhibit 2 Advantages of Annual Forecasting for X-Ray Parts

- Quicker delivery
- Flexible ordering
- Fewer problems
- Lower cost

Strongest advantage to listeners is introduced first to get positive impression early.

The first advantage is that advance purchasing will speed up delivery of your orders. Instead of waiting for our suppliers to ship parts, we can begin to assemble your order as soon as you send it. You can get an idea of the time savings by looking at how much time this plan would have saved on the order you placed in February. [Show Exhibit 3.]

Bar chart graphically demonstrates time saved.

Exhibit 3   Annual Forecasting Speeds Delivery Time

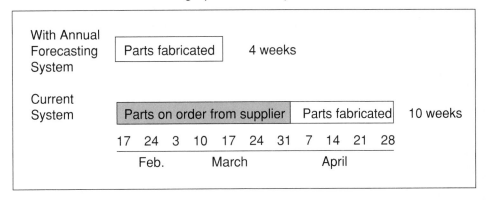

Transition leads to second advantage of the plan: flexibility.

Transition leads to anticipation of possible listener objection: What if orders decrease?

Credible authority cited to support this point.

Internal review reminds listeners of previously introduced advantages and leads to identification of a third benefit: less wasted time.

Besides being quick, the plan is flexible. If you wind up receiving more orders than you anticipated when you made your original forecast, you can update the plan every six months. That means we'll never run out of parts for the x-ray units. Suppose you projected 1,400 units in your original forecast. If you've already ordered 1,000 six months later, you could update your forecast at that point to 2,000 units and we'd have the parts on hand when you needed them.

This semiannual revision of the forecast takes care of *increases* in orders, but you might be wondering about the opposite situation—what would happen if orders are *less* than you expected. The plan anticipates that possibility, too. We're willing to extend the date by which you're obliged to use your annual estimate of parts to eighteen months. In other words, with this plan you'd have eighteen months to use the parts you expected to use in twelve. That's pretty safe, since Ted Forester [BMI's vice-president of sales and marketing] predicts that the existing x-ray machines will be in use for at least the next six or seven years before they're replaced with newer models.

Flexibility and speed are two good advantages, but there are other benefits of the plan as well. It can save time for both you and us. You know how much time we spend on the phone every time there's a surprise x-ray order, and I imagine you have to deal with impatient customers, too. Talking about delays is certainly no fun, and with this annual purchasing plan it won't be necessary since we can guarantee delivery within four weeks of receiving your order. Think of the aggravation that will avoid!

By now, you can see why we're excited about this plan. But there's one final benefit as well: the plan will save you money. When we order our parts in larger quantities, the unit price is less than we face with smaller orders. We're willing to pass along those savings to you, which means that you'll be paying less under this plan than you are now. Notice how ordering a year's supply of parts drops the unit price considerably. [Show Exhibit 4.]

Second-most-important advantage is introduced last, where it is likely to be remembered by listeners.

Exhibit 4   Annual Forecasting Reduces Unit Price

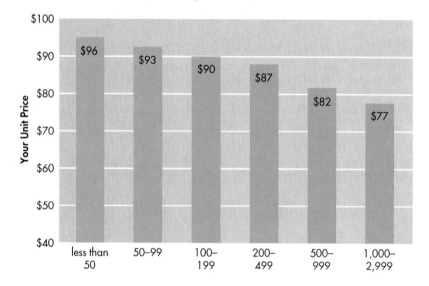

Chart visually highlights cost savings.

You can see that this plan is a real money saver. Compare the savings you could have realized on last year's order of 597 units if this plan had been in effect. [Show Exhibit 5.]

Exhibit 5   One Year's Savings with Annual Forecasting Plan

597 units at higher unit price...$55,506
597 units at volume unit price 45,969
First year savings ....$ 9,537

Review of the plan's advantages and appeal to adopt it.

So that's the plan. It's simple. It's risk-free. It's convenient. It's flexible. And along with all these advantages, it can cut your costs. We're prepared to start working with you immediately to put this plan into action. If we start soon, we'll never have to deal with x-ray headaches again. Then we can put our energy into the larger, more satisfying projects that are more rewarding for both of us.

SUMMARY

Persuasion is the act of motivating an audience, through communication, to voluntarily change a particular belief, attitude, or behavior. Unlike coercion on the one hand or manipulation on the other, it presents a message to an audience and allows the members to choose whether or not to accept it. Persuasive presentations are common in business and professional settings. Most take the form of sales presentations, proposals, motivational speeches, or goodwill speeches.

A variety of strategies maximize the chances of achieving a persuasive goal. Focusing the message on a key audience segment and defining a realistic goal are important. Demonstrating how the message can meet the needs of the audience is essential. Choosing the optimal placement for the thesis and deciding whether or not to discuss opposing ideas are important considerations. In all cases, citing ample evidence to support claims can make the message both persuasive and memorable.

Speakers can enhance their credibility by demonstrating their competence, trustworthiness, and sincerity. Credibility is also enhanced when the speaker establishes common ground with the audience and when the audience views the speaker as personally attractive.

Four organizational plans are well suited to persuasive presentations: problem-solution, comparative advantages, criteria satisfaction, and motivated sequence. The choice of which organizational plan to use should be governed by the nature of the message and the attitudes of the audience toward the idea being proposed as well as whether listeners are aware of and inclined to support opposing ideas.

ACTIVITIES

1. Contrast an ethical persuasive approach to each of the following situations with coercive and manipulative alternatives:

   a. A boss tries to get volunteers to work weekend hours.

   b. A union representative encourages new employees to join the union.

   c. A representative of the fire department asks residents of a rural area to clean up the brush around their property.

d. The head of a department seeks authorization to add a new secretary to the staff to handle a backlog of paperwork.

2. What persuasive strategies described in this chapter might a speaker use in each of the following situations?

   a. Persuading the loan officer at a local bank to lend you money for your proposed business venture
   b. Encouraging local businesspeople to join a service club to which you belong
   c. Convincing your boss to authorize a two-week leave of absence so that you can attend a relative's wedding across the country.
   d. Arguing that your suggestions for cutting costs are better than those proposed by your supervisor.

3. Credibility is a function of perceived competence, trustworthiness, similarity, and sincerity. How could a speaker's credibility be enhanced in each situation that follows?

   a. A group of business students appeals to the Chamber of Commerce to sponsor an internship program for students seeking experience in local firms.
   b. A sales representative proposes a telecommunications system for an organization made up of one thousand people.
   c. A manager encourages subordinates to share their suggestions or complaints with her.

4. What organizational plan would be best suited to each of the following messages:

   a. Showing a customer why leasing a car is a better choice than buying one
   b. Convincing a charitable foundation to grant money to your job-training program for disadvantaged teenagers
   c. Persuading a group of cost-conscious consumers of the advantages of shopping at a top-quality department store
   d. Demonstrating the features of an expensive computer system
   e. Persuading a group of longtime employees to accept a new affirmative-action hiring program

5. Use the information in this chapter to outline the most persuasive introduction, body, and conclusions for each of the following messages:

   a. *Purpose:* Have salary increased
      Audience: Boss concerned with keeping costs down
   b. *Purpose:* Sell accounting and payroll services
      Audience: Owner of a twenty-five–person business
   c. *Purpose:* Persuade audience to enroll in classes at local community college
      Audience: Clerical workers
   d. *Purpose:* Request funds to develop and run on-site day-care center for employees
      Audience: Top management of five-hundred–employee company

Communicator Profile

R. Terence Budden
District Exploration Geologist
Unocal Corporation
Houston, Texas

Don't make a presentation without having the best possible command of the facts. The worst mistake you can make is to misstate a fact, either mistakenly or by bluffing when you don't really know the answer. After you've been proved wrong on one item, everything else you say will be suspect.

My job is to supervise the geological aspects of Unocal's exploration for oil and gas offshore along the Gulf Coast. My team generates ideas for drilling projects, and we monitor the geological data during drilling to see if we are on target.

Presentations are a big part of my job. Most of these presentations are aimed at the managers who have to give approval before we can lease a drilling tract or start a well. The money involved for these projects is significant—between $800,000 and $20 million—so management wants to be sure that our drilling has a good chance of producing results before they authorize that kind of expenditure. I also make presentations each year when we propose our region's budget to management. The challenge here is to convince my bosses that we deserve to have the $20 million or so in operating expenses we need to run a successful exploration effort.

Most of the presentations I give are a combination of informing and persuading. The informative part involves giving the audience enough background to understand why we're proposing a particular project. For instance, we usually give an overview of an area's geology and describe the activities of other companies operating in the area. Once we've given this background, we go on to the persuasive part of the talk—showing why the project we're proposing makes economic sense.

Probably the biggest speaking challenge I face is to simplify and condense tremendous amounts of information into the brief speaking time available. Our drilling proposals are based on months, or even years, of work and tens of thousands of pieces of data. It's often hard to boil down all this information into a package that won't overwhelm or bore the managers who are in the audience. We rely heavily on visual exhibits to help make our points, but even here we work hard to make our maps simple enough for our audience to follow, while still being comprehensive enough to illustrate the points we are trying to make.

There are three pieces of advice that every business speaker ought to follow. First, know your listeners, and adapt your message to them. On the most basic level, this means knowing their level of understanding so you won't make your presentation too complicated or too simple. It also means knowing your listeners' personal biases and attitudes. Are they sympathetic to or skeptical of your idea? Do they like a serious, formal approach, or are they more relaxed and informal?

My second suggestion is to be concise. Time is the most valuable commodity for most businesspeople, and you'll win their respect and appreciation by making your points in the quickest, clearest way possible.

The third piece of advice is to know your material. Don't make a presentation without having the best possible command of the facts. The worst mistake you can make is to misstate a fact, either mistakenly or by bluffing when you don't really know the answer. After you've been proved wrong on one item, everything else you say will be suspect. If you don't know the answer to a question, say so. Then either ask a team for the answer or promise to uncover the facts and get back to the questioner soon.

APPENDIX

FORMAT AND DESIGN OF WRITTEN BUSINESS MESSAGES

Just as your style of dress and grooming creates a first impression when you meet others face-to-face, the appearance of your written messages makes a powerful statement. A well-designed, well-executed piece of correspondence makes your message easier to understand and paints a flattering picture of you. Likewise, a shabby report, letter, or memo has the same effect as stained clothes or bad breath.

Because written messages are so important, entire books and academic courses are devoted to their study. This appendix is no substitute for a thorough study of written communication. What it does, however, is provide some guidelines about the accepted design of typical business messages. The following suggestions reflect the most common standards for written communication. Many organizations have their own styles that may vary in one or more ways from these basic rules. When you are writing on behalf of an organization, you will probably choose to follow its conventions.

GENERAL APPEARANCE

Regardless of the format and type of messages, most business correspondence should follow some basic guidelines.

TYPING

Most business documents should be typewritten or created by a computer printer that has at least typewriter-quality output. There are two reasons for this rule. First, typewritten copy is easier to read than most handwriting, and the least you can do for your readers is to make your ideas legible. In addition to legibility, typing also creates a businesslike impression that will serve you well in most situations. A typewritten message conveys more psychological weight than a handwritten one, just as a business suit creates more credibility than a casual outfit.

There are exceptions to the typing rule. A personal message—a letter of congratulations or condolence, for example—should probably be handwritten. It is usually acceptable to jot down a quick note to a colleague and perhaps even your boss, rather than taking time to type it up. A longer or more formal message, however, ought to be typed. The culture of an organization usually offers clues about when handwritten notes are acceptable, so pay attention to how the successful people around you communicate. When in doubt, use a typewriter.

All the benefits of a typewritten message will be lost if you do a sloppy job. A crisp, clear typeface is essential. This means using an electric or electronic typewriter, ideally with a carbon or plastic ribbon. Cloth ribbons and manual typewriters produce type that is fuzzy and uneven. Dot-matrix characters on lower-quality computer printers should be avoided whenever possible. The copy they produce can look rough and be difficult to read. Erasures on an important message are a taboo; they create the same impression as food stains on your clothes.

A word processor with a good printer is the best way to produce neat messages since it allows you to check and adjust your work before putting it on paper. Most business typewriters now have a key that will remove typographic errors quickly and easily. Even if your machine lacks this feature, you can buy correction film that will lift off or neatly cover up mistakes. Whatever equipment you use, make sure your work is meticulous.

The typeface you use also sends a message. The most common faces, like Courier or Letter Gothic, are usually the best to use. Other businesslike, easily readable type styles may be useful to distinguish your message, but you should avoid using informal ones (for example, script) or radically different typefaces that call more attention to the medium than the message.

PAPER

The traditional paper dimensions for most business correspondence are 8 1/2 ×11 inches, although some memorandum forms are smaller; legal documents are usually printed on 8 1/2 × 14-inch paper. White is the standard color for business paper, although neutral colors like light gray, cream, or beige are sometimes used. In some organizations, memos are typed on colored paper to make them easily identifiable. It is best to avoid brightly colored papers since it is hard to read or photocopy messages printed on them. It is also best to avoid slick or highly textured paper since it can result in blurred type.

High-quality paper makes your messages look better and ensures that they will stand up under the reading, routing, filing, photocopying, faxing, and other punishment many documents receive. Choosing the right paper weight is also important. Weight is measured in pounds (the weight of four 500-sheet reams). For reports and memos, it is safest to use at least 20-pound paper, although 16-pound stock may do in a pinch. Stationery and résumés create the best effect when they are printed on at least 24-pound paper. The cotton content of paper is also a measure of its quality. Stock of at least 25 percent cotton has a better look and feel than the noncotton variety.

SPELLING AND GRAMMAR

The content of your correspondence should match its high-quality appearance. Even a single error can stand out, drawing readers' attention away from all the effective aspects of your message. A glaring mistake in an otherwise perfect document can have the same effect as a piece of food stuck between the teeth of an impeccably dressed and groomed person.

Most spelling errors are easily caught with spell-checker programs that now accompany word processing computer software as well as many electronic typewriters. Don't assume that technology will correct all mistakes, however. If you carelessly type a word that is wrong for the situation but exists in the dictionary ("principle" instead of "principal," for example), the spell-checker will not catch the error. Spell-checking software is also of no help with most names. You will have to be sure that the letter to Ms. MacGregor doesn't leave your desk addressed to Ms. McGregor.

Grammar is just as important as spelling. Incorrect constructions can make you look ignorant or sloppy, leaving the reader to speculate about whether you may be as incompetent in other areas as you are in writing.

GENERAL FORMATTING RULES

Most documents should be laid out on the page so that they are easy to read and understand. Margins should be generous—at least an inch all around. The copy should be centered on the page, not crammed toward the top, bottom, or one side. Again, word-processing software can make this task much easier than it would be on a manual typewriter.

Length of typed lines should be short enough to make the copy easily readable. If your typeface is large (12 points), each line should have a maximum of 60 characters. If you are using smaller (9 point or 10 point) type, the line should be no more than 70 characters. On shorter pieces of correspondence, you can shorten the number of lines and increase the margins to create a better-looking layout.

LETTERS

Business custom dictates the standard parts of business correspondence. The elements of a business letter aren't just a social nicety: each has a good reason for existing. Some elements should be included in every letter, while others are included if they are appropriate.

STANDARD ELEMENTS

No matter what the business or topic, every business letter should contain the following:

1. Heading

2. Date

3. Inside address

4. Salutation

5. Body

6. Complimentary close

7. Signature block

Heading   The heading of a letter shows its source: the organization's name, address, and telephone number. Most organizations have printed letterheads that contain the heading. For personal correspondence, type this information (excluding your name) about two inches from the top of the first page.

Date   The date the letter is written should be typed at least one blank line beneath the bottom of the heading. The month should be spelled out completely, not abbreviated. The number of the day should be typed, and the full year should be included. The general format is month-day-year (January 15, 1992), although in the military and some other organizations the customary format is day-month-year (3 February 1992), without a comma separating the month and year. It is usually not considered correct to abbreviate a date by just typing its numerals.

Inside Address   This information identifies the recipient of the letter. It should be separated from the date by at least one blank line. The amount of space separating the inside address from the date should be adjusted to suit the length of the letter.

   A courtesy title should precede the recipient's name. For men, "Mr." is correct unless the addressee merits a professional title such as "Doctor" or "Captain." Note that all professional titles should be spelled out, not abbreviated. For women who do not have a professional title, "Ms." is generally the safest form of address. If, however, you know that the addressee prefers to be identified as "Mrs." or "Miss," you should use that title. It is always best to address your letter to a specific person. You can usually get the name of the person you are seeking by making a telephone call to the company and saying, "I will be sending some correspondence to the director of your customer support division. Can you give me that person's name?" If you do not know the name of a specific person, it is acceptable to address the letter to the department or to a job title (for example, "Director, Department of Human Resources").

   If the addressee's organizational title is short, it can be included on the same line as his or her name: "Ms. Miranda Cortez, General Manager." If the recipient has a longer title or if the title includes a department, this information can be displayed on a single line below the name.

Salutation   The way you address the recipient should be governed by your relationship with that person. If you have not met or if the relationship is a formal one, you should use his or her title and last name: "Dear Mr. Cooper." If you are on a first-name basis with the recipient, it is probably appropriate to use that form of address in your salutation: "Dear Marianne."

There is no agreed-upon salutation for letters when you do not know the recipient. The old-fashioned "Gentlemen" may be inaccurate and sexist, so the alternative "Ladies and Gentlemen" is a better choice. Another option is "Dear Sir or Madam," although the formality suits some messages better than others. Generalized types of address such as "Dear Customer" are best for multiple mailings since they sound impersonal. The old standby "To Whom It May Concern" is best suited to formal messages. Another alternative when you do not know who the recipient will be is to omit the salutation entirely, assuming that the title in the heading will be sufficient to convey your message.

Body   The body of your letter will usually occupy the greatest space. It should be typed single-spaced, with a blank line separating it from the preceding and following parts of the letter. You should also separate each paragraph of the letter by a blank line.

Depending on the contents of the body, you may want to format some of the information it contains in a distinct manner—as a list, indented from the regular margins, or in underlined or bold type. Just be sure that the format you use is consistent within the letter. If an organization has its own style sheet for letter elements, be sure to follow it.

Complimentary Close   The complimentary close is a single word or phrase, separated from the body by a blank line. Your choice of close provides a way to create just the desired tone: there is a noticeable difference between the casual "Best regards" and the more formal "Very truly yours." Other traditional closes include "Sincerely" and "Cordially."

Signature Block   The signature block should be typed four lines below the complimentary close. At this point you should type your name, unless it is included on the letterhead. Your title, if any, can be included on the same line as your name or immediately below. If your name might leave doubt about your gender, you may include a title in the signature block. Women who also prefer to be addressed by a specific title (for example, "Mrs.") can add the desired title here.

ADDITIONAL LETTER PARTS

Some letters require additional information that is not included in the standard format. There are ways of formatting this information that allow you to convey specific messages without cluttering up the body of the letter. It is unlikely that you will ever send a letter containing all of these elements, but sooner or later each of them will find its way into your correspondence.

Addressee Line   This line should be printed above the heading, separated by two blank lines. It provides a way to indicate any special handling the letter should receive. Common notifications include "URGENT," "CONFIDENTIAL," and "PERSONAL." The entire addressee notification should be typed in capital letters to emphasize its importance.

Attention Line   The attention line provides a way to direct your letter to a specific department or position title when you do not know the name of the person you want to receive the message. It is also a useful way to personalize a letter when you only know the last name of the recipient (See Figure A-1). Common attention lines take the following form:

ATTENTION: CREDIT DEPARTMENT

ATTENTION: Food Services Director

ATTENTION: Ms. James

The attention line may be placed within the inside address just below the name of the company or it may be typed two lines below the inside address. In either case, the form you use on the mailing envelope should match the form you use on the letter itself.

Subject Line   The subject line provides a clear indication of the topic of a letter, which is especially important when you are writing to an office that receives a high volume of mail. The subject line will increase the chances that your message will get the right sort of attention and that it will be easy to file and locate.

There are two possible positions for the subject line. It may be typed just below the salutation, separated by a blank line. Alternatively, it can be typed above the salutation, assuming the position that an addressee notation might be given in another type of correspondence.

Reference Initials   When the person who types the letter is different than its composer, the initials of the typist are usually included below the signature block. If the writer's name is included in the signature block, only the typist's initials need appear as a reference. If the letter is written on behalf of a company without the signature of an individual sender being identified, then the initials of both the writer (in capitals) and typist (in lowercase type) should be included. Either of the following forms is acceptable:

SWA:gh   SWA/gh

Enclosure Line   An enclosure line indicates that materials accompany the letter itself. This provides a useful check to make sure that anything that was supposed to be included in the mailing was, indeed, enclosed. It also provides a permanent record about any enclosed material.

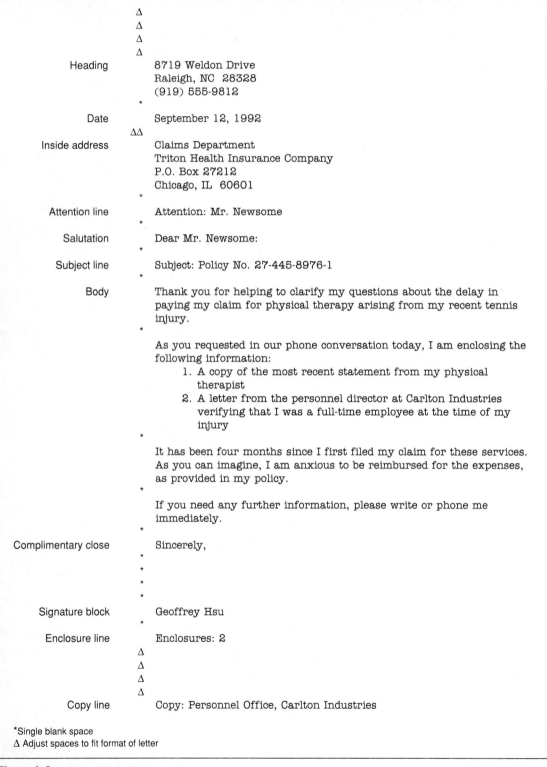

	Δ
	Δ
	Δ
	Δ
Heading	8719 Weldon Drive
	Raleigh, NC 28328
	(919) 555-9812
	*
Date	September 12, 1992
	ΔΔ
Inside address	Claims Department
	Triton Health Insurance Company
	P.O. Box 27212
	Chicago, IL 60601
	*
Attention line	Attention: Mr. Newsome
	*
Salutation	Dear Mr. Newsome:
	*
Subject line	Subject: Policy No. 27-445-8976-1
	*
Body	Thank you for helping to clarify my questions about the delay in paying my claim for physical therapy arising from my recent tennis injury.
	*

As you requested in our phone conversation today, I am enclosing the following information:

1. A copy of the most recent statement from my physical therapist
2. A letter from the personnel director at Carlton Industries verifying that I was a full-time employee at the time of my injury

It has been four months since I first filed my claim for these services. As you can imagine, I am anxious to be reimbursed for the expenses, as provided in my policy.

If you need any further information, please write or phone me immediately.

Complimentary close	Sincerely,
Signature block	Geoffrey Hsu
Enclosure line	Enclosures: 2
Copy line	Copy: Personnel Office, Carlton Industries

*Single blank space
Δ Adjust spaces to fit format of letter

Figure A-1   Block letter format.

The enclosure notation appears at the bottom of the letter and one or two spaces below the signature block and reference initials, if any. The notation may simply state "Enclosures," if the specific contents are described in the body of the letter. Or it may specify either the number of enclosures ("Enclosures: 2") or their actual contents ("Enclosure: Rate schedule").

Copy Line   A copy notation lets the addressee know who else will be receiving the letter. The notation should be set flush with the left margin and below any reference initials and enclosure notations. The following forms are common ways of identifying a copy notation:

cc: Rebecca Haynes   pc: Rebecca Haynes
c: Rebecca Haynes   Copy: Rebecca Haynes

Mailing Line   If the letter is sent by a means other than first-class mail (for example, certified mail, special delivery, facsimile), it may be desirable to indicate this fact. The notation may be placed in two locations: either at the top of the letter just above the inside address, or below the signature block and any other notations described in this section.

Postscript   A postscript is an afterthought that occurs to the sender after the body of the letter is written but before the letter is sent. When taken in this sense, postscripts should be avoided: if a message is important enough to dignify with a letter, you should compose it thoughtfully. A second use for postscripts is to emphasize or separate an idea from the body of the letter. You might, for example, append personal congratulations for an accomplishment or thanks for a favor to the body of a businesslike message. Because of their "by the way" nature, postscripts are more appropriate when the sender and addressee have a familiar relationship than in a letter to a stranger.

Second-Page Heading   If a letter is longer than one page, a heading at the top of the second and following sheets will help make your correspondence easy to identify. Subsequent pages should contain the name of the addressee, the page number, and the date. Each of these elements may be typed on its own line at the left margin,

Mr. Eldon Press
July 22, 1992
Page 2

or they may be combined on a single line set flush with the left margin,

Mr. Eldon Press, July 22, 1992, Page 2

or they may be separated by tabs and centered on the page,

Mr. Eldon Press   -2-   July 22, 1992

LETTER FORMATS

Most business letters follow one of two formats: the block format (see Figure A-1) and the modified block format (see Figure A-2). The main differences between these styles are the placement of elements and the way they are indented. Either format is acceptable for a business letter, although some organizations may have a standard style that should be followed in any correspondence mailed on its letterhead.

In the block format, each element and paragraph is set flush with the left margin. In the modified block format, the date, complimentary close, and signature block appear just to the right of the center of the page. In this format the first line of each paragraph in the body may also be indented five spaces, although this feature is not required.

ENVELOPES

Since the envelope that contains your letter will be the first thing the receiver sees, it should look just as professional as the correspondence it contains. In addition, a clearly addressed envelope minimizes the chances that your message will be lost on its way to the addressee.

The address on the envelope should match the content and style of the inside address on the letter it contains. Since the postal service routes mail by reading from the bottom of the address upward, your letter should start with the more specific information and add increasingly more general information on each succeeding line:

1. Name of the addressee

2. Department or group

3. Name of the organization

4. Name of building or mail stop number

5. Street address and suite number or post office box number

6. City, state or province, and ZIP code or Postal Code

7. Country (if the letter is being mailed overseas)

Most envelopes for business correspondence are number 10 size, which measures 9 1/2 × 4 1/4 inches—just right to hold an 8 1/2 × 11-inch piece of stationery folded in thirds. If your correspondence is too bulky to fit easily into such an envelope, mail the correspondence in a larger envelope. Standard manila envelopes of varying sizes are available for this purpose at stationery stores. These oversized envelopes give you the advantage of sending your message without folding the paper. The address on a larger piece of correspondence will look most professional if you type it on a separate mailing label, which can then be attached to the envelope. If you use an envelope that does not already have the

DAVIS, DOYLE, ANSON ASSOCIATES
300 Constance Street, Suite 1600
Ft. Worth, Texas 76102

Δ
Δ
Δ
Δ
Δ

Date   June 18, 1992
           *
Addressee line   CONFIDENTIAL
           *
           *
Inside address   Ms. Rebecca Hovarth
                         Managing Partner
                         Batnett, Prince and Horton Advertising
                         1197 Century Avenue, Suite 479
                         Ft. Worth, TX   76102
           *
Salutation   Dear Rebecca:
           *
Body   Our search of the Dallas-Ft. Worth area revealed a large number of
                         candidates for the creative director's position you intend to fill. The
                         enclosed report profiles those we believe to be the top six candidates.
           *
                         I have spoken with each of the people on the list, and all of them are
                         interested in talking further about a career move. As you requested, I
                         have not disclosed the name of your agency to any of them, and I
                         assured them that their interest in changing positions would be kept
                         confidential.
           *
                         Once you have looked over the profiles, we can set up a meeting with
                         the candidates who look promising. Please let me know as soon as you
                         are ready to take the next step.
           *
Complimentary close   Best regards,
           *
           *
           *
           *
Signature block   John W. McNair
           *
Reference initials   mjp
           *
Enclosure line   Enclosure
           *
Postscript   P.S. Thanks for sending the information about rafting in the Grand
                         Canyon. If it isn't too late to make a reservation, I'm going to give it a
                         try this summer!

Δ
Δ
Δ
Δ
Δ

*Single blank space
Δ Adjust spaces to fit format of letter

Figure A-2   Modified block letter format.

organization's return address printed on it, type the necessary information neatly, as indicated in Figure A-3.

FOLDING THE LETTER

While the recipient isn't likely to notice a properly folded letter, a poorly folded one can create an unwelcome impression. For standard 8 1/2 × 11-inch station–ery, fold the sheet (or sheets) in thirds. Begin by folding the bottom third upwards, creasing it neatly. Then fold the top third downward, leaving a quarter inch or so of space between the top of the page and the first crease. Finally, insert the letter with the open end at the top and the loose flap facing out. When enclosing sheets in a large envelope, place the side with the type facing the rear of the envelope so it is immediately visible when the receiver opens his or her mail.

MEMOS

It isn't necessary to type up an official memo for every message. When you need to send a quick note to an officemate, jotting a few words on a memo form, a Post-it Note, or even a piece of scratch paper will probably do the job. But if your message is to be filed for future reference or if it will be read by a boss, who may be judging the quality of your ideas, you should invest the time to type up a memo.

FORMAT

Because they are internal messages, memos are usually not sent on the kind of top-quality paper used for letters. They may be typed on regular 8 1/2 × 11-inch

```
Jennifer Grasso
752 Crossfield Street
Denver, CO   80221




                          Mr. Gregory Larsen
                          Capitol Services Corporation
                          111 Dearborn Street
                          Orlando, FL   32805
```

Figure A-3   Envelope format.

paper or half-sized sheets measuring 5 1/2 × 8 1/2 inches. The paper size is usually standardized within the organization.

Every memo should contain the same basic elements:

1. Heading

2. Date

3. Addressee's name

4. Sender's name

5. Subject

Since many businesses have preprinted memo forms, adding this information is simply a matter of filling in the spaces. If you are creating a memo from scratch, it is acceptable to use either the format in Figure A-4 or to center the heading and set the date, addressee's name, sender's name, and subject line flush with the left margin.

Heading   Every memo should be identified by the word "MEMO" or "MEMO-RANDUM," typed in capitals and centered at the top of the page.

Date   The date should indicate when the memo was sent, not the date it was written. If the information in the memo changes between the time it was composed and when it was typed and delivered, the content should be adjusted. As with letters, the date should not be abbreviated.

The Addressee's Name   It is usually not necessary to use a courtesy title like "Mr." or "Dr." with the addressee's name. The only exception to this rule is when you speak to the addressee in person. In many organizations, the accepted format is simply to list the addressee's first initial and last name (for example, "J. Banducci").

If the memo is being sent to an entire group of people (for example, department heads, sales representatives), simply indicate the category on the name line. If the memo is addressed to a large number of people who do not fit into an easy category, the words "See distribution list" or simply "Distribution" accompanied by an asterisk should go on the address line with the names of the addressees below (see Figure A-4).

The Sender's Name   Use the same format for your name as you do for the addressee's name, minus any courtesy title. If the recipient does not know you or if it would be helpful to add the weight of your position in the organization, include your department and/or your personal title (see Figure A-4). A memo doesn't contain a signature line, but you may add your initials next to your name on the "FROM" line.

The Subject of the Memo   This line helps the receiver identify the nature of your message quickly and makes it easier to file the memo. Try to keep the subject

MEMORANDUM

TO: Distribution*   DATE: April 6, 1992
FROM: K. Osgood   SUBJECT: Voice mail training
           Director of Support Services

The new voice mail system is scheduled for installation on May 11. In order to have a smooth transition from our present phone system, all employees should receive training before installation day.

The following dates and times are available for training. All training will be conducted in the second-floor conference room. Please arrange to have everyone in your department attend one session.

Only 15 employees can be accommodated at each meeting, so please write or call Jane Finney at extension 327 to reserve spaces. Personnel who have not reserved times by April 19 will be scheduled into available slots.

Date	Time
April 27	9:00-10:30
	11:00-12-30
	1:00- 2:30
April 28	8:30-10:00
	10:30-12:00
	1:00- 2:30
May 4	9:00-10:30
	11:00-12:30
	1:00- 2:30
May 8	1:00- 2:30
	3:00- 4:30

* Department heads
  K. Fernandez
  E. Washington

c: H. Wylie, Key Communications Corp.

Figure A-4   Memo format.

line brief. Instead of saying "Results of the survey you requested on customer satisfaction," simply type "Results of customer-satisfaction survey."

STYLE

The style of most memos is short and to the point, although memos should never be so brusque as to seem rude. Memos don't contain a salutation or complimentary close, and it isn't necessary to begin or conclude with the kind of niceties ("It was good to see you yesterday . . . ") you might use when writing a letter. It is likely that the recipient of your memo is a busy person who will appreciate receiving just the necessary facts.

The body of a memo should resemble a letter in appearance: single-spaced with a line space separating paragraphs. The same sort of lists and headings that are appropriate in letters can be used in memos. Ideally, the memo will be no longer than one page since lengthier memos may not get the kind of full reading you want. If your memo does require a second page, it should be headed just like a letter. Other elements that can be used in business letters (reference initials, copy lines, enclosure line, etc.) are also appropriate in memos.

REPORTS

Written reports are an essential part of most organizations since reports are a natural way to convey large amounts of detailed information. Even if you present your ideas in person, it is likely you will back them up with a written document. The range of reports is broad. Some reports are purely informational, while others provide recommendations. Yet other reports are analytical: instead of simply presenting information, they interpret it. Still others are persuasive in nature, calling for a specific course of action.

Reports come in many lengths. The simplest and briefest—a weekly sales report, for example—is a periodic listing of information. This is often a computer printout with little or no commentary. Other reports come packaged in letters or memos. Despite their familiar appearance, these reports are different from most ordinary correspondence. Because they usually contain more facts and figures, they are typically organized into sections, each identified by heading. They also frequently use lists, tables, and even graphics to clarify the data they present. Figure A-5 illustrates a typical letter/memo report. At the other end of the spectrum are extensive formal reports. These are usually large enough to bind and resemble books in their length and features.

ELEMENTS

There are no clear borders between "short" and "long" reports or between "formal" and "informal" ones. As a writer, your goal should be to choose the right form and length for the job at hand. All but the longest, most detailed reports can be organized by using the following elements. As you plan your report, choose the ones that are appropriate for the complexity of your document.

January 27, 1992

TO: M. J. Farrell
FROM: D. L. Ward
RE: 1991 Sales Results

Here are the final figures for last year:

	Q1 (000)	Q2 (000)	Q3 (000)	Q4 (000)
East	$1,230	$1,243	$1,267	$ 1,286
North	410	416	423	428
West	959	973	1,003	3,923
South	1,570	1,593	1,641	6,422
Totals	$4,169	$4,225	$4,334	$12,059

Each region exceeded its annual quota by the following margins:

	Quota (000)	Sales (000)	Excess
East	$ 4,650	$ 5,026	8.1%
North	1,900	2,112	11.1%
West	5,800	6,858	18.2%
South	10,000	11,226	12.1%

Conclusions and Recommendations

1. Quarter-to-quarter sales increased throughout the year in every division, despite the steadily weakening economy. This suggests our products are gaining strength--more than the figures suggest at first glance.

    Based on this strength, we might consider introducing the expanded line in the next year, rather than waiting for an economic recovery, as we had planned. The demand seems to exist, especially at the top end of our present line.

2. Fourth quarter sales in the West and South jumped dramatically. This increase justifies our decision to expand operations in both areas.

    While opportunities are more limited in the East and North, it may be cost-effective to try a limited expansion there. If you're interested in the possibility, I can show you some figures on the subject.

3. Each division exceeded its quota, all of them by a greater degree than we had hoped for. As a result, everyone's morale is high. Given the present enthusiasm of our personnel and the promising market conditions, we could probably establish next year's quotas at a level slightly above this year's sales. This would present a challenge for everyone, but the challenge would almost certainly be well received.

Figure A-5   Memo report.

Cover   Most long reports have a heavy cover of cardboard, plastic, or even leather. A cover not only protects the document inside, it also makes a nonverbal statement about the importance of the message. The cover should contain the title and author's name as well as the name and title of the recipient.

Letter of Transmittal   This letter may precede or follow the title page. It describes the purpose of the report and its audience. It may also summarize key information in the report.

Title Page   The title page contains the report title (usually in capital letters); the name, title, and company of both the writer and recipient; and the date of submission. This information is centered on the page.

Table of Contents   A table of contents will help readers find their way around long reports. It should include a list of tables, charts, and other graphics, unless these elements are detailed in a separate table of illustrations. The table of contents should be laid out so that major sections are aligned with the left margin, while subordinate headings are indented.

Executive Summary   The summary (sometimes called "abstract," "synopsis," or "précis") describes the major findings in the report. It should be brief—ideally a page or less, although more length may be necessary in extremely large reports. The summary is a critical part of the report since not all readers may take the time to study the more detailed contents thoroughly.

Body   The body of the report should be organized into sections appropriate to the length and nature of the document. Some or all of the following sections may be appropriate: purpose, background, procedures, findings, and recommendations. There are no firm rules about section titles. The key is to display your information in the clearest, most effective way by means of organizational elements.

The report should be laid out with plenty of white space to make reading easy. Either single or double spacing is acceptable. At least one inch of space should be visible at the top, bottom, and both sides of each page. If the report will be bound, leave extra space to compensate for the loss of viewing area. Headings should be displayed prominently, following a consistent pattern such as the one in Figure A-6. Pages should be numbered consistently. Lowercase Roman numerals are used for any material preceding the body of the report. Although the title page is counted, it should not contain a numeral. Begin the first page of the body with the Arabic number 1. Numbers should go either at the top right corner or centered at the bottom of each page.

Addenda   It may be clearest, especially in long reports, to place all supplementary material after the body. Charts, graphs, tables, supporting correspondence, maps, questionnaires, and references all fall into this category. Give each item a separate number (for example, Figure 1, Exhibit 2, Table 3), and refer to this number in the body of the report to guide readers.

```
                         FIRST  LEVEL  HEADING

    xxxxxxxxxxxxxxxxxxxxxxxxxxxxxxxxxxxxxxxxxxxxxxxxxxxxxxxxxxxxxxxxxxxx
    xxxxxxxxxxxxxxxxxxxxxxxxxxxxxxxxxxxxxxxxxxxxxxxxxxxxxxxxxxxxxxxxxxxx
    xxxxxxxxxxxxxxxxxxxxxxxxxxxxxxxxxxxxxxxxxxxxxxxxxxxxxxxxxxxxxxxxxxxx
    xxxxxxxxxxxxxxxxxxxxxxxxxxxxxxxxxxxxxxxxxxxxxxxxxxxxxxxxxxxxxxxxxxxx

                         Second Level Heading

    xxxxxxxxxxxxxxxxxxxxxxxxxxxxxxxxxxxxxxxxxxxxxxxxxxxxxxxxxxxxxxxxxxxx
    xxxxxxxxxxxxxxxxxxxxxxxxxxxxxxxxxxxxxxxxxxxxxxxxxxxxxxxxxxxxxxxxxxxx
    xxxxxxxxxxxxxxxxxxxxxxxxxxxxxxxxxxxxxxxxxxxxxxxxxxxxxxxxxxxxxxxxxxxx
    xxxxxxxxxxxxxxxxxxxxxxxxxxxxxxxxxxxxxxxxxxxxxxxxxxxxxxxxxxxxxxxxxxxx
    xxxxxxxxxxxxxxxxxxxxxxxxxxxxxxxxxxxxxxxxxxxxxxxxxxxxxxxxxxxxxxxxxxxx

    Third Level Heading

    xxxxxxxxxxxxxxxxxxxxxxxxxxxxxxxxxxxxxxxxxxxxxxxxxxxxxxxxxxxxxxxxxxxx
    xxxxxxxxxxxxxxxxxxxxxxxxxxxxxxxxxxxxxxxxxxxxxxxxxxxxxxxxxxxxxxxxxxxx
    xxxxxxxxxxxxxxxxxxxxxxxxxxxxxxxxxxxxxxxxxxxxxxxxxxxxxxxxxxxxxxxxxxxx
    xxxxxxxxxxxxxxxxxxxxxxxxxxxxxxxxxxxxxxxxxxxxxxxxxxxxxxxxxxxxxxxxxxxx

        Fourth Level Heading  xxxxxxxxxxxxxxxxxxxxxxxxxxxxxxxxxxxxxxxxxx
    xxxxxxxxxxxxxxxxxxxxxxxxxxxxxxxxxxxxxxxxxxxxxxxxxxxxxxxxxxxxxxxxxxxx
    xxxxxxxxxxxxxxxxxxxxxxxxxxxxxxxxxxxxxxxxxxxxxxxxxxxxxxxxxxxxxxxxxxxx
    xxxxxxxxxxxxxxxxxxxxxxxxxxxxxxxxxxxxxxxxxxxxxxxxxxxxxxxxxxxxxxxxxxxx
    xxxxxxxxxxxxxxxxxxxxxxxxxxxxxxxxxxxxxxxxxxxxxxxxxxxxxxxxxxxxxxxxxxxx
    xxxxxxxxxxxxxxxxxxxxxxxxxxxxxxxxxxxxxxxxxxxxxxxxxxxxxxxxxxxxxxxxxxxx
```

Figure A-6 Standard report headings.

RÉSUMÉS

At some point during the employment process, you will almost certainly be asked to submit a résumé. Like an interview, your résumé has to do more than just present your credentials. Most of your serious competitors will also have the right qualifications: you have to present these qualifications in an attractive way. A résumé is important because, along with the letters you write your potential employer, it is the only tangible clue to the type of person you are. After you have left the interview, your résumé will remain behind as a reminder of the way you tackle a job and of the kind of employee you are likely to be.

The most effective résumés are tailored to the interests and needs of a particular position and employer. This is not always practical, however, if you are applying to several firms at the same time. At the very least, your résumé should reflect the requirements of a field. For example, a medical technician should stress laboratory skills when applying for a job in a lab; but when the job opening is in a clinic, it is better to emphasize experience that involves working with people. A résumé that encourages job offers focuses on the employer's needs—how you can help the employer.

APPEARANCE

Like every important business document, your résumé should be impeccable. Any mistakes or sloppiness here could cost you the job by raising doubts in an employer's mind. Because the design of résumés can be complicated, many candidates hire professional services to create them.

Whether you type the résumé yourself or have it done for you, the final product should reflect the professional image you want to create. It should be neat and error-free; it should contain plenty of white space to avoid crowding; it should be printed on heavy paper, either white or a light neutral color; it should avoid the mass-produced look that comes from reproduction on poor-quality copying machines.

Although you want to make yourself stand out from the crowd, be cautious about using unusual kinds of paper or typefaces. A novel approach may capture the fancy of a prospective boss, but it may be a turnoff. The more you know about the field and the organization itself, the better your decisions will be about the best approach to take.

Your résumé should almost never exceed two pages in length—and one is better. Employers are often unimpressed with longer résumés, which are hard to read and can seem padded—especially when they come from people with comparatively little job experience. A long résumé may even get you disqualified altogether. One magazine editor admitted that when he was overwhelmed by 150 applicants for a job as his assistant, he laid out all the résumés on a table to sort. When he got tired of lifting the first pages to see what was on the second page, he threw out all the résumés that were longer than one sheet. Later, when his boss asked him how he was progressing, he was able to say, "Very well! I've already eliminated half of the applicants."

ELEMENTS

While résumés can be organized in more than one way, they will almost always contain the same basic information.

Name, Address, and Phone Number   Make sure that the information allows an interested employer to reach you easily. If necessary, list both a permanent home address and a school address. If you are currently employed, list either that phone number or another one where you can be reached during business hours.

Job or Career Objective   Most employers agree that a statement of professional objective should be part of a résumé. An effective statement should consist of two sentences. The first should announce your general goal and mention some important "demonstrated skills"—talents that will qualify you for the job. The second statement should detail one or more specific areas in which you want to work. For example,

> A position in public relations using proven skills in writing, researching, and motivating. Special interests in radio and television programming.

> Entry-level position in design and development of microprocessor circuitry. Eventual advancement to position as project leader or technical manager.

Education   Employers are usually interested in learning about your academic training, especially education and training since high school, degrees earned, major fields of study, and dates you attended. Begin with your most recent education and work backward. If the information will be helpful and if space permits, you may consider listing notable courses you have taken. If your grade-point average is impressive, include it. Finally, note any honors you have earned. If you received awards for other accomplishments, consider listing all your achievements in a separate section entitled "Awards and Honors."

Experience   Every employer wants to know what kinds of work you have performed. By using the general title "Work Experience" instead of the more limited "Employment History," you can highlight a summer internship, delete a dishwashing job, group minor or similar jobs together, and include volunteer work or club activities that taught you marketable skills.

While you should list your former job titles, employers are really most interested in the kinds of duties you performed. They search this category for the answers to two questions: What can you do? What are your attributes as an employee? You can provide answers to these questions by accompanying your job title, name of employer, and city with a list of the duties you performed. There is no need to use complete sentences—phrases will do. Be sure to use very concrete language, including technical terminology, to describe the work you performed (see Figure A-7). Place this section either before or following the section on education, depending on which will be most important to an employer.

Susan Noji

Home Address and Phone   University Address (until 6/7/92)

1117 Palm Avenue   876 Wicker Avenue
Tucson, Arizona 85712   Redlands, California 92373
(602) 555-8957   (714) 682-4787

JOB OBJECTIVE	An entry-level position in broadcast media production using proven skills in videotape and film. Special interest in news, educational, and documentary programming.
EDUCATION	B.S., Western University (1989–91). Major in Broadcasting and Film, minor in Speech Communication.
	A.S. in General Studies, Pima Community College (1984–87). Degree granted "with honors."
WORK EXPERIENCE	1990–91: Technical director, Western University media productions: "Chumash Memories: An Oral History," "Women at Work," "Cocaine: Dreams and Nightmares."
	1990: Production supervisor, Western University Media Services. Assisted in production of over forty instructional film and videotape programs for university faculty.
	1989: Student summer intern, KRER-TV, Phoenix, Arizona. Assisted in production of news and public-affairs programming.
	1988-89: Camera operator, sound technician, film editor, lighting technician, and prop crew for Pima College Media Services department.
SPECIAL SKILLS AND INTERESTS	Experienced in videotape productions and editing, including use of studio and portable cameras, remote broadcasting, and 3/4-inch splicing and editing.
	Familiar with super-8mm and 16mm filming, including sound recording. Experienced in editing and splicing footage for productions and archival storage.
CERTIFICATION	F.C.C. Third Class Operator Permit.
REFERENCES	Available upon request.

Figure A-7   Standard résumé featuring education and work experience.

Special Interests and Aptitudes   Most employers want to know about special abilities that will make you a more valuable employee. These include community-service activities (cite offices you have held), languages you can write or speak, special equipment you can operate, hobbies, and so on. The key here is to include only information that the employer will find useful and that casts you in a favorable light.

Memberships   If you belong to any organizations in your field, list them here. Be sure to include any offices or committee appointments you have held. Membership in service and civic groups is usually less important, so include them only if you have held a major office.

Certification   Many professions and skilled trades offer people the opportunity to become officially certified by taking a competitive examination or by completing an advanced course of study. If you are certified or licensed in any occupational field, create a category in which to display that fact, even if it has only one entry.

References   This section always should be the last one in a résumé. Many experts suggest that you simply include the phrase "References available upon request" and supply the names only when and if you are asked. Employers rarely investigate references until you are under serious consideration, and including them on your résumé may waste precious space.

   If you decide that your references will be impressive enough to merit listing, be sure to follow some basic guidelines. Choose only the three or four people who combine the best elements of familiarity with your work and a credible position. Recommendations from high-status people carry more weight, but a reference from a celebrity who barely knows you is not as good as one from an unknown who has worked closely with you. In any case, be sure to get permission from these people first.

TYPES OF RÉSUMÉS

There are two approaches to organizing a résumé. The standard approach (see Figure A-7) emphasizes your education and work experience. The functional approach (see Figure A-8) features the skills you bring to the job (organizer, researcher, manager, etc.) and provides examples of the most significant experiences that demonstrate these abilities. When you write a functional résumé, follow the "Skills and Experience" category immediately with a chronological "Work Experience" and a scaled-down "Education" category that lists only institutions, degrees, and dates. Either of these categories may come first, depending on whether you gained most of your skills and experience in school or on the job.

JONATHAN L. PANOWSKI
665 Meadowlark Ln.
Woburn, Massachusetts 01803
(617) 453-0411

CAREER OBJECTIVE	A position using proven skills in writing, research, and public communication. Special interest in employee training.

SKILLS AND EXPERIENCE

Writing and Editing

- Transformed detailed job descriptions in fields including electronics, manufacturing, and computer sciences into narrative comprehensible to lay readers.
- Wrote training manual for new employees at Country Stores, Inc.
- Assisted in writing and editing grant proposals for paraprofessional training at Hollyfield Voc-Tech Center.

Research

- Designed and conducted labor market analysis study for training program at Hollyfield Voc-Tech Center.
- Assisted in computerization of statistical data gathered in this study.
- As a medical library assistant, compiled research file for a hypertension study conducted by physicians at the University of Tennessee Medical School.

Public Communication

- Delivered numerous presentations to area employers to promote Hollyfield Voc-Tech Center.
- Spoke to various audiences, including the Eastern Massachusetts Private Industry Council, about outcomes of Hollyfield labor market analysis study.
- As a teacher in Kinshasa, conducted demonstration teaching sessions for Zairean teachers and administrators in conjunction with the United States Information Service.

WORK EXPERIENCE

1985 to present — Labor market analyst, with additional responsibilities in job development. Hollyfield Voc-Tech Center, Hollyfield, Mass.

1983 to 1985 — Manager/training supervisor, County Stores, Inc., Des Moines, Iowa.

1981 to 1983 — Director of English as a Second Language program, American School of Kinshasa, Kinshasa, Zaire.

1979 to 1981 — Research assistant, University of Tennessee Medical School, Memphis, Tennessee (temporary during college).

EDUCATION — M.A. in Education, University of Tennessee at Knoxville, 1985. B.A. in American History, Memphis State University, Memphis, Tennessee, 1983.

ORGANIZATIONS — Member of Society for Technical Communication. Member, American Society for Training and Development

REFERENCES — Available upon request.

Figure A-8 Functional résumé focusing on demonstrated skills.

NOTES

CHAPTER 1

1. Dan B. Curtis, Jerry L. Winsor, and Ronald D. Stephens, "National Preferences in Business and Communication Education," *Communication Education* 38 (January 1989): 6–14.
2. B. Murray, "The Practicality of the Liberal Arts Major," *Innovation Abstracts* 9 (March 1987): 1–2.
3. B. W. Bowman, "What Helps or Harms Promotability?" *Harvard Business Review* 42 (January–February 1964): 14.
4. T. W. Harrell and M. S. Harrell, "Stanford MBA Careers: A 20 Year Longitudinal Study," Graduate School of Business Research Paper No. 723 (Stanford, Calif., 1984).
5. T. Bailey, "Changes in the Nature and Structure of Work: Implications for Skill Requirements and Skill Formation," Columbia University Conservation of Human Resources Technical Paper No. 9 (November 1989).
6. J. Flanigan, "The Nation's Educational Crisis Is Also a Business Crisis," *Los Angeles Times* (January 21, 1990): D1.
7. G. Goldhaber, *Organizational Communication*, 5th ed. (Dubuque, Iowa: Wm. C. Brown, 1990), p. 143.
8. A. S. Bednar and R. J. Olney, "Communication Needs of Recent Graduates," *Bulletin of the Association for Business Communication* (December 1987): 22–23.
9. See, for example, A. Petofi, "The Graphic Revolution in Computers," in *Careers Tomorrow: The Outlook for Work in a Changing World*, ed. E. Cornish (Bethesda, Md.: World Future Society, 1988), pp. 62–66.
10. J. D. Wyllie, "Oral Communications: Survey and Suggestions," *American Business Communication Association Bulletin* (June 1980): 14–15.
11. A. K. Gulezian, "Does the Non-Business Major's Background Matter? Employers Say Yes!" *Journal of College Placement* 39 (1978): 67–68.
12. F. S. Endicott, *The Endicott Report: Trends in the Employment of College and University Graduates in Business and Industry 1980* (Evanston, Ill.: Placement Center, Northwestern University, 1979).
13. See R. S. Ross, *Understanding Persuasion*, 3rd ed. (Englewood Cliffs, N.J.: Prentice-Hall, 1990), pp. 88–105.
14. R. H. Lengel and R. L. Daft, "The Selection of Communication Media As an Executive Skill," *Academy of Management EXECUTIVE* 11 (1988): 225–32.
15. Lengel and Daft, p. 229.

CHAPTER 2

1. For a discussion of the characteristics of networks, see P. R. Monge, "The Network Level of Analysis," in *Handbook of Communication Science,* ed. C. R. Berger and S. H. Chafee (Newbury Park, Calif.: Sage, 1987), pp. 239–70.
2. For a review of research on formal networks, see F. M. Jablin, "Formal Organization Structure," in *Handbook of Organizational Communication,* ed. F. Jablin, L. Putnam, K. Roberts, and L. Porter (Newbury Park, Calif.: Sage, 1987), pp. 389–419.
3. D. Katz and R. Kahn, *The Social Psychology of Organizations,* 2nd ed. (New York: Wiley, 1978).
4. "Managers' Shoptalk," *Working Woman* (February 1985): 22.
5. Katz and Kahn, *The Social Psychology of Organizations,* p. 239.
6. T. J. Peters and R. H. Waterman, Jr., *In Search of Excellence: Lessons from America's Best-Run Companies* (New York: Harper & Row, 1982), p. 267.
7. Quoted in G. M. Goldhaber, H. S. Dennis, G. M. Richetto, and O. A. Wiio, *Information Strategies: New Pathways to Management Productivity,* rev. ed. (Norwood, N.J.: Ablex, 1984), p. 19.
8. L. Schuster, "Wal-Mart Chief's Enthusiastic Approach Infects Employees, Keeps Retailer Growing," *Wall Street Journal* (April 20, 1982): 21.
9. Adapted from Katz and Kahn, *The Social Psychology of Organizations,* p. 245.
10. L. Berkowitz and W. Bennis, "Interaction Patterns in Formal Service-Oriented Organizations," *Administrative Science Quarterly* 5 (1961): 210–22.

11. J. Mann, "Group Relations in Hierarchies," *Journal of Social Psychology* 54 (1961): 283–314.

12. G. Goldhaber, *Organizational Communication*, 5th ed. (Dubuque, Iowa: Wm. C. Brown, 1990), p. 160.

13. Adapted from *Goldhaber*, pp. 174–75.

14. For a description of the nature of informal communication networks, see P. R. Monge and E. M. Eisenberg, "Emergent Networks," in *Handbook of Organizational Communication*, pp. 137–53.

15. T. E. Deal and A. A. Kennedy, *Corporate Cultures: The Rites and Rituals of Corporate Life* (Reading, Mass.: Addison-Wesley, 1982), p. 86.

16. T. J. Murray, "How to Stay Lean and Mean," *Business Month* (August 1987): 29–32.

17. J. P. Kotter, "What Effective Managers Really Do," *Harvard Business Review* 60 (November–December 1982): 156–67.

18. K. Davis, "Management Communication and the Grapevine," *Harvard Business Review* 31 (September–October 1953): 43–49.

19. Deal and Kennedy, *Corporate Cultures*, p. 85.

20. Goldhaber, *Organizational Communication*, p. 162.

21. Deal and Kennedy, *Corporate Cultures*, pp. 16–17.

22. E. C. Ravlin and C. L. Adkins, "A Work Values Approach to Corporate Culture: A Field Test of the Value of Congruence Process and Its Relationship to Individual Outcomes," *Journal of Applied Psychology* 74 (June 1989): 424–33.

23. M. H. Brown, "Defining Stories in Organizations: Characteristics and Functions," in *Communication Yearbook 13*, ed. J. A. Anderson (Newbury Park, Calif.: Sage, 1990), pp. 162–90.

24. Peters and Waterman, *In Search of Excellence*, p. 240. See also J. M. Byer and H. M. Trice, "How an Organization's Rites Reveal Its Culture," *Organizational Dynamics* (Spring 1987): 15.

25. Peters and Waterman, *In Search of Excellence*, pp. 244–45.

26. A. Kennedy, "Back-Yard Conversations: Net Tools for Quality Conversations," *Communication World* (November 1984): 26.

27. Adapted from S. P. Robbins, *Organizational Behavior*, 4th ed. (Englewood Cliffs, N.J.: Prentice-Hall, 1990), p. 468, and A. J. DuBrin, *Foundations of Organizational Behavior* (Englewood Cliffs, N.J.: Prentice-Hall, 1984), p. 411.

28. "MBA: Short Takes on Management/Business/Administration," *Working Woman* (August 1984): 34.

29. Adapted from Deal and Kennedy, *Corporate Cultures*, pp. 129–33.

30. F. Steele, *Physical Settings and Organization Development* (Reading, Mass.: Addison-Wesley, 1973), p. 46.

31. E. Klein, "Tomorrow's Work Force," *D&B Reports* (January–February 1990): 30–35, and M. Riche, "America's New Workers," *American Demographics* (February 1988): 33–41.

32. L. Copeland, "Making the Most of Cultural Differences at the Workplace," *Personnel* (June 1988): 53.

33. J. Schacter, "Firms Begin to Embrace Diversity," *Los Angeles Times* (April 17, 1988): A1.

34. G. Hofsteide, *Culture's Consequences: International Differences in Work-Related Values* (Newbury Park, Calif.: Sage, 1980), and G. Hofsteide, "The Cultural Relativity of Organizational Practices and Theories," *Journal of International Business Studies* (Fall 1983): 75–89. For a summary of Hofsteide's research, see Robbins, *Organizational Behavior*, pp. 487–90.

35. G. Hofsteide, "Motivation, Leadership, and Organization: Do American Theories Apply Abroad?" *Organizational Dynamics* (Summer 1980): 55–60. See also Robbins, *Organizational Behavior*, p. 487.

36. See, for example, J. Dreyfuss, "Get Ready for the New Work Force," *Fortune* (April 23, 1990): 165–81.

37. M. Marby, "Pin a Label on a Manager—and Watch What Happens," *Newsweek* (May 14, 1990): 43.

38. Copeland, p. 60.

39. J. C. Pearson, L. Turner, and W. Todd-Mancillas, *Gender and Communication*, 2nd ed. (Dubuque, Iowa: Wm. C. Brown, 1991), pp. 153–157.

40. "Past Tokenism," *Newsweek* (May 14, 1990): 37–43.

CHAPTER 3

1. E. M. Eisenberg and S. R. Phillips, "Miscommunication in Organizations," in *"Miscommunication" and Problematic Talk*, ed. N. Coupland, H. Giles, and J. Wiemann (Newbury Park, Calif.: Sage, 1991), pp. 244–58.

2. J. W. Gilsdorf, "Executive and Managerial Attitudes Toward Business Slang: A Fortune-List Survey," *Journal of Business Communication* 20 (1983): 29–42.

3. J. S. Armstrong, "Unintelligible Management Research and Academic Prestige," *Interfaces* 10 (1980): 80–86.

4. "Up in Smoke," *Accountant's Journal* 66 (April 1987): 10.

5. See, for example, J. B. Bavelas, A. Black, N. Chovil, and J. Mullett, *Equivocal Communication* (Newbury Park, Calif.: Sage, 1990), and E. M. Eisenberg and M. G. Witten, "Reconsidering Openness in Organizational Communication," *Academy of Management Review* 12 (1987): 418–26.

6. J. A. DeVito, *Human Communication: The Basic Course* (New York: Harper & Row, 1988), pp. 87–88.

7. See, for example, C. E. Johnson, "An Introduction to Powerful and Powerless Talk in the Classroom," *Communication Education* 36 (1987): 167–72; B. Erickson, E. A. Lind, B. C. Johnson, and W. M. O'Barr, "Speech

Style and Impression Formation in a Court Setting: The Effects of Powerful and Powerless Speech," *Journal of Experimental Social Psychology* 14 (1978): 266–79; and W. O'Barr and B. K. Atkins, "'Women's Language' or 'Powerless Language'?" in *Women and Language in Literature and Society*, ed. S. McConnell-Ginet, R. Borker, and N. Furman (New York: Praeger, 1980), pp. 93–110.

8. See C. E. Johnson, "Powerful and Powerless Talk: An Overview," *Communication Education* 36 (1987): 167–72, and E. M. Notarantonio and J. L. Cohen, "The Effects of Open and Dominant Communication Styles on Perceptions of the Sales Interaction," *Journal of Business Communication* 27 (1990): 171–84.

9. Summarized in J. K. Burgoon, D. B. Buller, and W. G. Woodall, *Nonverbal Communication: The Unspoken Dialogue* (New York: Harper & Row, 1989), pp. 155–56.

10. J. B. Stiff, J. L. Hale, R. Garlick, and R. G. Rogan, "Effect of Cue Incongruence and Social Normative Influences on Individual Judgments of Honesty and Deceit," *Southern Speech Communication Journal* 55 (1990): 206–29.

11. For a discussion of the principle "You can't not communicate nonverbally," see M. T. Motley, "On Whether One Can(not) Communicate: An Examination via Traditional Communication Postulates," *Western Journal of Speech Communication* 54 (1990): 1–20, and J. B. Bavelas, "Behaving and Communicating: A Reply to Motley," *Western Journal of Speech Communication* 54 (1990): 593–602.

12. P. Ekman, "Cross-Cultural Studies of Facial Expression," in *Darwin and Facial Expression*, ed. P. Ekman (New York: Academic Press, 1973).

13. N. Sussman and H. Rosenfeld, "Influence of Culture, Language and Sex on Conversational Distance," *Journal of Personality and Social Psychology* 42 (1982): 67–74.

14. See J. D. Rothwell, *In Mixed Company* (Ft. Worth, Tex.: Holt, Rinehart and Winston, 1992).

15. S. Roan, "Overweight and Under Pressure," *Los Angeles Times* (December 18, 1990): E1, E4.

16. D. Nye, review of L. Fenton, *Dress for Excellence*, in *Across the Board* 24 (February 1987): 61.

17. S. Forsythe, M. F. Drake, and C. E. Cox, "Influence of Applicant's Dress on Interviewer's Selection Decisions," *Journal of Applied Psychology* 70 (1985): 374–78.

18. Nye, n. 16, above.

19. C. Pogash, "Mayor Dianne Feinstein's Twelve Rules for Getting Ahead," *Working Woman* (January 1986): 85.

20. H. Twidale, "The Triumph of Executive Chic," *Working Woman* (November 1985): 140.

21. W. Wells and B. Siegel, "Stereotyped Somatypes," *Psychological Reports* 8 (1961): 1175–78.

22. B. Hunter, "Are You Ready to Face '60 Minutes'?" *Industry Week* (March 8, 1982): 74.

23. "Memos," *Industry Week* (January 11, 1982): 11.

24. A. Mehrabian, *Silent Messages*, 2nd ed. (Belmont, Calif.: Wadsworth, 1981).

25. E. Hall, *The Hidden Dimension* (New York: Doubleday, 1969), pp. 113–25.

26. M. Knapp, *Nonverbal Behavior in Human Interaction*, 2nd ed. (New York: Holt, Rinehart and Winston, 1978), pp. 127–30.

27. Knapp, p. 129.

28. Mehrabian, *Silent Messages*, p. 51.

29. D. Ogilvy, *Principles of Management* (New York: Ogilvy & Mather, 1968), p. 2.

30. J. E. McGrath and J. R. Kelly, *Time and Human Interaction* (New York: Guilford, 1989).

31. R. J. Schoenberg, *The Art of Being a Boss* (New York: New American Library, 1978), p. 36.

32. "Are You Really Ready to Change Jobs?" in "Fall Job Market," advertising supplement to the *Washington Post* (September 28, 1986): 22.

33. "Coaching Football—Italian Style," *Thousand Oaks* (Calif.) *News Chronicle* (January 4, 1990): 1, 20.

34. W. Griffitt, "Environment Effects of Interpersonal Affective Behavior: Ambient Effective Temperature and Attraction," *Journal of Personality and Social Psychology* 15 (1970): 240–44.

35. T. Allen, "Meeting the Technical Information Needs of Research and Development Projects," MIT Industrial Liaison Program Report No. 13-314 (Cambridge, Mass., November 1969).

36. F. Steele, *Physical Settings and Organizational Development* (Reading, Mass.: Addison-Wesley, 1973).

37. Steele, p. 65.

38. P. Manning, *Office Design: A Study of Environment* (Liverpool, Eng.: The Pilkington Research Unit, 1965), p. 474.

39. Steele, *Physical Settings and Organizational Development*, p. 38.

CHAPTER 4

1. J. Beels, "It's Time to Get Back to Basics," *Industrial Finishing* (May 1987): 28.

2. B. L. Harragan, "Career Advice," *Working Woman* (December 1985): 32.

3. K. K. Murphy, *Effective Listening: Hearing What People Say and Making It Work for You* (New York: Bantam, 1987), p. 74.

4. P. T. Rankin, "The Measurement of the Ability to Understand Spoken Language," *Dissertation Abstracts* 12 (1952): 847–48.

5. J. D. Weinrauch and J. R. Swanda, Jr., "Examining the Significance of Listening: An Exploratory Study

of Contemporary Management," *Journal of Business Communication* 13 (February 1975): 25–32.

6. J. P. Kotter, "What Effective General Managers Really Do," *Harvard Business Review* 60 (November–December 1982): 156–67.

7. H. Mintzberg, "The Manager's Job: Folklore and Fact," *Harvard Business Review* 53 (July–August 1975): 49–61.

8. S. L. Becker and L. R. V. Ekdom, "That Forgotten Basic Skill: Oral Communication," *Association for Communication Administration Bulletin* 33 (1980): 12–15.

9. V. DiSalvo, D. C. Larsen, and W. J. Seiler, "Communication Skills Needed by Persons in Business Organizations," *Communication Education* 25 (1976): 269–75.

10. *U.S. News & World Report* (May 26, 1980): 65.

11. B. D. Sypher, R. N. Bostrom, and J. H. Siebert, "Listening, Communication Abilities, and Success at Work," *Journal of Business Communication* 26 (1989): 293–303.

12. D. P. Rogers, "The Development of a Measure of Perceived Communication Openness," *Journal of Business Communication* 24 (1987): 53–61.

13. S. Zurier, "Strictly for Salesmen," *Industrial Distribution* (August 1987): 47.

14. R. G. Nichols, "Listening Is a 10-Part Skill," *Nation's Business* 75 (September 1987): 40.

15. R. G. Nichols, *Are You Listening?* (New York: McGraw-Hill, 1957), pp. 1–17.

16. See, for example, S. Golan, "A Factor Analysis of Barriers to Effective Listening," *Journal of Business Communication* 27 (1990): 25–36, and J. E. Hulbert, "Barriers to Effective Listening," *Bulletin for the Association for Business Communication* 52 (1989): 3–5.

17. A. Vangelisti, M. L. Knapp, and J. A. Daly, "Conversational Narcissism," *Communication Monographs* 57 (1990): 251–74.

18. P. F. Drucker, "Management Communications," in *Management—Tasks, Responsibilities, Practices* (New York: Harper & Row, 1974).

19. *Industrial Marketing* (April 1982): 108.

20. B. Fine, "Ten Lessons I Learned at Bloomingdale's," *Working Woman* (September 1985): 44.

21. D. J. Schwartz, *The Magic of Thinking Big* (New York: Simon & Schuster, 1980), p. 78.

22. Ibid., p. 77.

23. C. T. Brown and P. W. Keller, "A Modest Proposal for Listening Training," *Quarterly Journal of Speech* 48 (1962): 395, and B. Markgraf, "Listening Pedagogy in Teacher-Training Institutions," *Journal of Communication* 12 (March 1962): 64.

CHAPTER 5

1. D. B. Curtis, J. L. Winsor, and R. D. Stephens, "National Preferences in Business and Communication Education," *Communication Education* 38 (1989): 6–14.

2. L. Iacocca and W. Novak, *Iacocca: An Autobiography* (New York: Bantam, 1984), p. 58.

3. Quoted by H. Sutton, "The CEO As Syndicated Columnist," *Across the Board* 24 (July–August 1987): 62.

4. C. E. Larson and F. M. J. LaFusto, *Teamwork: What Must Go Right/What Can Go Wrong* (Newbury Park, Calif.: Sage, 1989), p. 85.

5. E. Sieburg, "Confirming and Disconfirming Communication in an Organizational Setting," in *Communication in Organizations*, ed. J. Owen, P. Page, and G. Zimmerman (St. Paul, Minn.: West, 1976), pp. 129–49; and E. Sieburg and C. Larson, "Dimensions of Interpersonal Response," paper presented to the International Communication Association, Phoenix, Arizona, 1971.

6. J. Gibb, "Defensive Communication," *Journal of Communication* 11 (September 1961): 141–48.

7. Thomas L. Quick, *Managing People at Work Desk Guide* (New York: Executive Enterprises, 1983), in *Working Woman* (November 1975): 31.

8. "Nineteen Eighty-Nine Turkeys of the Year," *San Jose Mercury News*, November 23, 1989, p. 1D.

9. S. Terkel, *Working* (New York: Pantheon, 1972), p. xxxii.

10. L. Coser, *The Functions of Social Conflict* (New York: Free Press, 1956).

11. For more detailed descriptions of the following approaches to conflict, see A. Frank and J. Brownell, *Organizational Communication and Behavior* (New York: Holt, Rinehart and Winston, 1989), pp. 498–503.

12. M. McCormack, *What They Don't Teach You at Harvard Business School* (New York: Bantam, 1984), pp. 152–53.

13. R. J. Burke, "Methods of Resolving Superior-Subordinate Conflict: The Constructive Use of Subordinate Differences and Disagreements," *Organizational Behavior and Human Performance* 5 (1970): 393–411.

14. Ibid.

15. R. Fisher and W. Ury, *Getting to Yes: Negotiating Agreement Without Giving In* (Boston: Houghton Mifflin, 1981), p. 45.

16. S. R. Wilson and L. L. Putnam, "Interaction Goals in Negotiation," in *Communication Yearbook 13,* ed. J. A. Anderson (Newbury Park, Calif.: Sage, 1990), pp. 374–406.

CHAPTER 6

1. C. J. Stewart and W. B. Cash, Jr., *Interviewing: Principles and Practices*, 6th ed. (Dubuque, Iowa: Wm. C. Brown, 1991), p. 5.

2. S. Nelton, "Getting It All Done," *Working Woman* (December 1985): 93.

3. Stewart and Cash, *Interviewing,* p. 1.

4. D. Harper, "Strictly for Salesmen," in a review of G. Gard, *Championship Selling,* in *Industrial Distribution* (May 1987): 122.

5. Stewart and Cash, *Interviewing,* p. 59.

6. L. B. Andrews, "Mind Control in the Courtroom," *Psychology Today* 16 (March 1982): 70.

7. L. Zunin and N. Zunin, *Contact: The First Four Minutes* (Los Angeles: Nash, 1972), pp. 8–14.

8. D. Deaver, in Shirley J. Shepherd, "How to Get That Job in 60 Minutes or Less," *Working Woman* (March 1986): 118.

9. H. A. Medley, *Sweaty Palms: The Neglected Art of Being Interviewed* (Belmont, Calif.: Wadsworth, 1978), p. 12.

10. Adapted from G. L. Wilson and H. L. Goodall, Jr., *Interviewing in Context* (New York: McGraw-Hill, 1991), p. 291.

CHAPTER 7

1. S. Moramarco, "What You Should Say About Yourself in a Job Interview," *Redbook* (August 1979): 50.

2. H. D. Tschirgi, "What Do Recruiters Really Look For in Candidates?" *Journal of College Placement* (December 1972–January 1973): 75–79.

3. "The Hidden Hurdle: Executive Recruiters Say Firms Tend to Hire 'Our Kind of Person,' " *Wall Street Journal* (May 12, 1979): 1.

4. R. N. Bolles, *What Color Is Your Parachute: A Practical Manual for Job-Hunters and Career-Changers* (Berkeley, Calif.: Ten Speed Press, 1991), pp. 20–21.

5. M. S. Granovetter, "The Strength of Weak Ties," *American Journal of Sociology* 78 (1973): 1360–80.

6. E. M. Rogers, *Diffusion of Innovations,* 3rd ed. (New York: Free Press, 1983), p. 297.

7. J. Giambanco, "Taking Off in a Fast-paced Industry," *Working Woman* (April 1985): 133.

8. S. S. Fader, "Start Here: Finding 'Hidden' Jobs," *Working Woman* (June 1984): 45.

9. Fader, p. 42.

10. T. H. Willard, "Computers Could Soon Tackle Personnel Tasks," *Los Angeles Times* (May 16, 1990): D3.

11. A. Fooner, "Three Ways to Break Out of a Dead-End Job," *Working Woman* (February 1986): 82–83.

12. R. W. Eder and G. R. Ferris (eds.), *The Employment Interview: Theory, Research, and Practice* (Newbury Park, Calif.: Sage, 1989).

13. H. A. Medley, *Sweaty Palms: The Neglected Art of Being Interviewed* (Belmont, Calif.: Wadsworth, 1978), p. 1.

14. R. S. Wyer and T. K. Srull, "Human Cognition in Its Social Context," *Psychological Review* 93 (1990): 322–39; and R. Guilford, C. F. Ng, and M. Wilkinson, "Nonverbal Cues in the Employment Interview: Links Between Applicant Qualities and Interviewer Judgment," *Journal of Applied Psychology* 70 (1985): 735.

15. D. B. Goodall and H. L. Goodall, Jr., "The Employment Interview: A Selective Review of the Literature with Implications for Communications Research," *Communication Quarterly* 30 (Spring 1982): 116–22.

16. Medley, *Sweaty Palms,* p. 19.

17. C. J. Stewart and W. B. Cash, *Interviewing: Principles and Practices,* 6th ed. (Dubuque, Iowa: Wm. C. Brown, 1991), p. 137.

18. Medley, *Sweaty Palms,* p. 164.

19. M. Z. Sincoff and R. S. Goyer, *Interviewing* (New York: Macmillan, 1984), p. 80.

20. J. K. Springston and J. Keyton, "So Tell Me, Are You Married?: When the Interviewee Knows You're Asking an Illegal Question," *Proceedings of the 1988 Annual National Conference of the Council of Employee Responsibilities and Rights* 2 (1988): 177–86.

21. Medley, *Sweaty Palms,* pp. 164–65; Stewart and Cash, *Interviewing: Principles and Practices,* pp. 163–65.

22. P. H. Bradley and J. E. Baird, Jr., *Communication for Business and the Professions* (Dubuque, Iowa: Wm. C. Brown, 1980), p. 117.

23. C. W. Downs, G. P. Smeyak, and E. Martin, *Professional Interviewing* (New York: Harper & Row, 1980), p. 167.

24. Kenneth Blanchard, "Rating Managers on Performance Reviews," *Today's Office* 22 (August 1987): 6–11.

25. C. O. Longenecker, "Truth or Consequences: Politics and Performance Appraisals," *Business Horizons* 27 (November–December 1989): 169–82.

26. G. L. Wilson and H. L. Goodall, *Interviewing in Context* (New York: McGraw-Hill, 1991), p. 181.

27. L. Iacocca and W. Novak, *Iacocca: An Autobiography* (New York: Bantam, 1984).

28. N. R. F. Maier, *The Appraisal Interview: Objectives, Methods, and Skills* (New York: Wiley, 1958).

29. J. L. Pearce and L. W. Porter, "Responses to Formal Performance Appraisal Feedback," *Journal of Applied Psychology* 71 (1986): 211–18.

CHAPTER 8

1. R. Reich, *Tales of a New America* (New York: Time Books, 1987), p. 126.

2. M. V. Redmond, "A Plan for the Successful Use of Teams in Design Education," *Journal of Architectural Education* 17 (May 1986): 27–49.

3. T. J. Peters and R. H. Waterman, Jr., *In Search of Excellence: Lessons from America's Best-Run Companies* (New York: Harper & Row, 1982), p. 211.

4. Peters and Waterman, pp. 13–14.

5. S. Nelton, "Management: Getting to a Decision," *Working Woman* (August 1984): 25.

6. M. E. Shaw, *Group Dynamics: The Psychology of Small Group Behavior*, 3rd ed. (New York: McGraw-Hill, 1981), pp. 61–64.

7. Marjorie E. Shaw, "A Comparison of Individuals and Small Groups in the Rational Solution of Complex Problems," *American Journal of Psychology* 44 (1932): 491–504.

8. D. J. Rachman and M. H. Mescon, *Profile Kit for Business Today*, 4th ed. (New York: Random House, 1990), Profile 2.

9. D. Mortensen, *Communication: The Study of Human Interaction* (New York: McGraw-Hill, 1972), pp. 267–68.

10. J. D. Rothwell, *In Mixed Company* (Ft. Worth, Tex.: Holt, Rinehart and Winston, 1992), pp. 60–61.

11. Peters and Waterman, *In Search of Excellence*, p. 32.

12. Rothwell, *In Mixed Company*, pp. 57–58.

13. E. Bormann, *Small Group Communication: Theory and Practice* (New York: Harper & Row, 1990).

14. See R. Y. Hirokawa, "Group Communication and Problem-Solving Effectiveness: An Investigation of Group Phases," *Human Communication Research* 9 (1983): 291–305; Edward R. Marby and Richard E. Barnes, *The Dynamics of Small Group Communication* (Englewood Cliffs, N.J.: Prentice-Hall, 1980), p. 78; Norman R. F. Maier and Robert A. Maier, "An Experimental Test of the Effects of 'Developmental' vs. 'Free' Discussions on the Quality of Group Decisions," *Journal of Applied Psychology* 41 (1957): 320–23; Ovid L. Bayless, "An Alternative Model for Problem-Solving Discussion," *Journal of Communication* 17 (1967): 188–97.

15. J. Dewey, *How We Think* (New York: Heath, 1910).

16. B. A. Fisher, "Decision Emergence: Phases in Group Decision Making," *Speech Monographs* 37 (1970): 53–66. See also M. S. Poole and J. Roth, "Decision Development in Small Groups IV: A Typology of Group Decision Paths," *Human Communication Research* 15 (1989): 232–56.

17. M. S. Poole and J. Roth, "Decision Development in Small Groups V: Test of a Contingency Model," *Human Communication Research* 15 (1989): 549–89.

18. R. Husband, "Leading in Organizational Groups," in *Small Group Communication*, ed. R. Cathcart and L. Samovar, 5th ed. (Dubuque, Iowa: Wm. C. Brown, 1988), p. 494.

19. Rothwell, *In Mixed Company*, pp. 200–1.

20. K. Lewin, R. Lippitt, and R. K. White, "Patterns of Aggressive Behavior in Experimentally Created Social Climates," *Journal of Social Psychology* 10 (1939): 271–99.

21. L. L. Rosenbaum and W. B. Rosenbaum, "Morale and Productivity Consequences of Group Leadership Style, Stress, and Type of Task," *Journal of Applied Psychology* 55 (1971): 343–58.

22. R. R. Blake and J. S. Mouton, *The New Managerial Grid* (Houston: Gulf, 1985).

23. F. E. Fiedler, *A Theory of Leadership Effectiveness* (New York: McGraw-Hill, 1967).

24. P. Hersey and K. Blanchard, *Management of Organizational Behavior*, 4th ed. (Englewood Cliffs, N.J.: Prentice-Hall, 1982); K. Blanchard, "Selecting a Leadership Style That Works," *Today's Office* 23 (September 1988): 14.

25. P. Hersey and K. Blanchard, "So You Want to Know Your Leadership Style?" *Training and Development Journal* (February 1974): 22–37.

26. B. Dumaine, "Who Needs a Boss?" *Fortune* (May 7, 1990): 52–60.

27. Dumaine, p. 52.

28. M. Z. Hackman and C. E. Johnson, *Leadership: A Communication Perspective* (Prospect Heights, Ill.: Waveland Press, 1991), p. 76.

29. The discussion of the first five types of power is adapted from the work of J. R. P. French and B. Raven, "The Bases of Social Power," in *Studies in Social Power*, ed. D. Cartwright (Ann Arbor: University of Michigan, Institute for Social Research, 1959). Information power was introduced by B. Raven and W. Kruglanski, "Conflict and Power," in *The Structure of Conflict*, ed. P. G. Swingle (New York: Academic Press, 1975), pp. 177–219. Connection power is introduced by Hersey and Blanchard, *Management of Organizational Behavior*, p. 179.

30. Bormann, *Small Group Communication*. For a succinct description of Bormann's findings, see Rothwell, *In Mixed Company*, pp. 191–94.

31. Adapted from Hackman and Johnson, *Leadership*, pp. 125–26.

32. L. Iacocca and W. Novak, *Iacocca: An Autobiography* (New York: Bantam, 1984), p. 52.

33. R. Witkin, "FAA Says Delta Had Poor Policies on Crew Training," *New York Times* (September 19, 1987): 1; reported in C. E. Larson and F. M. J. LaFusto, *Teamwork: What Must Go Right/What Can Go Wrong* (Newbury Park, Calif.: Sage, 1989), p. 37.

34. Some sequences of escalating penalties for nonconformity have been described in the literature. See, for example, J. R. Wenberg and W. Wilmot, *The Personal Communication Process* (New York: Wiley, 1973), and T. D. Daniels and B. K. Spiker, *Perspectives on Organizational Communication*, 2nd ed. (Dubuque, Iowa: Wm. C. Brown, 1991), p. 237.

35. Shaw, *Group Dynamics*, pp. 398–99.

36. A. S. Tannenbaum, *Social Psychology of the Work Organization* (Monterey, Calif.: Brooks/Cole, 1966), p. 66.

37. Adapted from E. G. Bormann, *Discussion and Group Methods,* 2nd ed. (New York: Harper & Row, 1975), pp. 176–95. See also P. Adler and P. Adler, "Intense Loyalty in Organizations: A Case Study of College Athletics," *Administrative Science Quarterly* 33 (1988): 401–18.

38. D. W. Johnson and F. P. Johnson, *Joining Together: Group Theory and Group Skills* (Englewood Cliffs, N.J.: Prentice-Hall, 1975), p. 59.

39. A. L. Delbercq, A. H. Van de Ven, and D. H. Gustafson, *Group Techniques for Program Planning: A Guide to Nominal Group and Delphi Processes* (Glenview, Ill.: Scott, Foresman, 1975), pp. 7–16.

40. I. L. Janis, *Victims of Groupthink* (Boston: Houghton Mifflin, 1972), p. 9.

41. D. G. Myers and H. Lamm, "The Group Polarization Phenomenon," *Psychological Bulletin* (July 1976): 602–27.

42. S. P. Robbins, *Organizational Behavior: Concepts, Controversies, and Applications,* 4th ed. (Englewood Cliffs, N.J.: Prentice-Hall, 1990), p. 289.

43. A. Osborn, *Applied Imagination* (New York: Scribner's, 1959).

CHAPTER 9

1. D. Colemon, "The Electronic Rorschach," *Psychology Today* 17 (February 1983): 35–43.

2. P. L. Blocklyn, "Consensus on Employee Communications," *Personnel* (May 1987): 62.

3. D. Cole, "Meetings That Make Sense," *Psychology Today* 23 (May 1989): 14–15.

4. D. Tyson, "Meetings Cited as Time Wasters," *Los Angeles Times* (Sept. 4, 1989, pt. 4): 2–3.

5. In J. H. Boren, *The Bureaucratic Zoo: The Search for the Ultimate Mumble* (McLean, Va.: EPM Publications, 1976).

6. F. Williams, *Executive Communication Power: Basic Skills for Management Success* (Englewood Cliffs, N.J.: Prentice-Hall, 1983), p. 65.

7. N. Qubein, "The Fine Art of Leading a Meeting," *Working Woman* (August 1987): 68.

8. *Leading Meetings* (Great Neck, N.Y.: Xerox Learning Systems), vol. 1, pp. 15–17.

9. L. N. Loban, "Questions: The Answer to Meeting Participation," *Supervision* (January 1972): 11–13.

10. M. McMaster and J. Grinder, *Precision: A New Approach to Communication* (Beverly Hills, Calif.: Precision Models, 1980), pp. 70–73.

11. *Leading Meetings,* vol. 1, p. 50.

12. *Leading Meetings,* vol. 2, pp. 41–45.

CHAPTER 10

1. L. Fletcher, *How to Design and Deliver a Speech,* 3rd ed. (New York: Harper & Row, 1985), p. 3.

2. R. Enrico, "Follow Me! The Path of a Leader," *Across the Board* 24 (January 1987): 25–26.

3. J. P. Wright, *On a Clear Day You Can See General Motors* (New York: Avon, 1979), p. 96.

4. H. M. Boettinger, *Moving Mountains, or The Art of Letting Others See Things Your Way* (New York: Collier, 1969), p. 6.

5. "The Conference Board," *Across the Board* 24 (September 1987): 7.

6. J. T. Molloy, *Molloy's Live for Success* (New York: Bantam, 1985), p. 16.

7. B. E. Bradley, *Fundamentals of Speech Communication: The Credibility of Ideas,* 3rd ed. (Dubuque, Iowa: Wm. C. Brown, 1981), pp. 58–61.

8. Hugh L. Marsh, "Summary Membership Remarks." Aluminum Company of America, delivered at New York Chapter, Institute of Internal Auditors, New York City, May 13, 1983.

CHAPTER 11

1. For a discussion of research supporting the value of organization, see B. E. Bradley, *Fundamentals of Speech Communication: The Credibility of Ideas,* 6th ed. (Dubuque, Iowa: Wm. C. Brown, 1991), pp. 181–83.

2. Adapted from C. L. Bovée and J. T. Thill, *Business Communication Today,* 2nd ed. (New York: Random House, 1989), pp. 89–90.

3. Based on an outline in W. A. Mambert, *Presenting Technical Ideas: A Guide to Audience Communication* (New York: Wiley, 1968), pp. 163–64.

4. J. L. Haynes, *Organizing a Speech: A Programmed Guide,* 2nd ed. (Englewood Cliffs, N. J.: Prentice-Hall, 1981), p. 44.

5. P. Preston, *Communication for Managers* (Englewood Cliffs, N. J.: Prentice-Hall, 1979), p. 24.

6. N. L. Reding, "Leading American Agriculture into the 21st Century," speech delivered at College of Agriculture commencement, University of Missouri, Columbia, May 14, 1983; reprinted in *Executive Speaker* 4 (September 1983): 6.

7. J. R. Bonée, "Making Love in Public: Bank Marketing and Public Relations," speech delivered at Bank Administrative Institute, Elgin, Ill., April 12, 1983; reprinted in *Executive Speaker* 4 (August 1983): 7.

8. Quoted in J. W. Robinson, *Winning Them Over* (Rocklin, Calif.: Prima Publishing, 1987), p. 279.

9. D. M. Roderick, "A Most Ingenious Paradox," speech delivered at National Press Club, Washington, D.C.; reprinted in *Executive Speaker* 5 (January 1984): 4.

10. J. Quick, *Short Book on the Subject of Speaking* (New York: Washington Square Press, 1978), p. 47.

CHAPTER 12

1. Information based on an article by S. Zurier, "Bar Coding Slashes Order Processing Time 88%," *Industrial Distribution* (July 1987): 52–55.
2. L. Poole, "A Tour of the Mac Desktop," *Mac World* 1 (February 1984): 16.
3. C. Spangenberg, "Basic Values and the Techniques of Persuasion," *Litigation* (Summer 1977): 64.
4. H. Anderson, "Day Care: Big Hit at the Office," *Los Angeles Times* (May 21, 1989): 30–33.
5. C. J. Silas, "Natural Gas: The Bureaucratic Muddle," January 1983; reprinted in *The Executive Speaker* 4 (May 1983): 6.
6. Mimi Sheiner, "Excellence in Advertising—Why Your Advertising Should Make Your Palms Sweat," delivered at Commonwealth Club, San Francisco, September 16, 1986; reprinted in *The Executive Speaker* 8 (February 1987): 1.
7. A. Rooney, "Sales vs. Service," *Executive Speechwriter Newsletter* 14 (May 1989): 5.
8. J. D. Ong, "Workplace 2000: Managing Change," delivered at National Alliance of Business Conference, Atlanta, March 25, 1988; reprinted in *The Executive Speaker* 8 (November 1988): 6.
9. "Making Time and Money Real," *Executive Communication Report* 3 (March 1987); developed by *Small Business Report*, 203 Calle del Oaks Mount, Monterey, CA 93940.
10. B. Joplin and J. Pattilo, *Effective Accounting Reports* (Englewood Cliffs, N.J.: Prentice-Hall, 1979), p. 104.
11. T. G. Labrecque, "A Radical Approach to Banking Reform: Legalize Competition," delivered at University of Richmond Business School, February 12, 1987; reprinted in *The Executive Speaker* 8 (August 1987): 5.
12. T. L. Martin, Jr., *Malice in Blunderland* (New York: McGraw-Hill, 1973), p. 40.
13. P. Saffo, "Compute: IBM Is Refocusing on Revising Home PCs," *Los Angeles Times* (June 25, 1990): D4.
14. J. Levy and R. Miller, "Taking the Guesswork Out of Networking," *Today's Office* 24 (January 1990): 9–10.
15. J. M. Hay, "Business Recovery in the Canadian Chemical Industry," delivered at Business Outlook Conference, Toronto, September 28, 1983; reprinted in *The Executive Speaker* 4 (November 1983): 5–6.
16. R. E. Cartwright, "Winning Psychological Principles in Summation," *Trial Diplomacy Journal* 1 (Spring 1978): 34.
17. L. Fernandes, delivered at the Chemical Council of Missouri Luncheon, St. Louis, May 10, 1984; re- printed in *The Executive Speaker* 5 (June 1984): 14.
18. "Paper Work Is Avoidable (If You Call the Shots)," *Wall Street Journal* (June 17, 1977): 24.
19. D. R. Vogel, G. W. Dickson, and J. A. Lehman, "Driving the Audience Action Response," *Computer Graphics World* 5 (August 1986): 25–28. See also D. R. Vogel, G. W. Dickson, and J. A. Lehman, "Persuasion and the Role of Visual Presentation Support: The UM/3M Study," 3M Corporation (1986): 1–20.
20. E. P. Zayas-Baya, "Instructional Media in the Total Language Picture," *International Journal of Instructional Media* 5 (1977–78): 145–50.
21. For a detailed description of how to create graphics with computers, see *The Presentation Design Book: Projecting a Good Image with Your Desktop Computer*, ed. M. Y. Rabb (Chapel Hill, N.C.: Ventana Press, 1990).
22. For a survey of sophisticated graphics presentations, see *Presentation Products* (September 1990).

CHAPTER 13

1. R. Ailes, "You Are the Message," *Executive Communications* (January 1988): 1.
2. M. Landis (Houser), "Taking the Butterflies out of Speechmaking," *Creative Living* 9 (Spring 1980): 19.
3. Adapted from L. Fletcher, *How to Design and Deliver a Speech,* 4th ed. (New York: Harper & Row, 1990), pp. 347–51.
4. Ibid., chs. 2 and 3.
5. J. Grossman, "Resurrecting Auto Graveyards," *Inc.* (March 1983): 73–80.
6. W. L. Haynes, "Public Speaking Pedagogy in the Media Age," *Communication Education* 38 (1990): 89–102.
7. I. Wallace and D. Wallechinsky, *Book of Lists* (New York: Bantam, 1977), p. 469.
8. "The Speaker May Look Calm but Survey Confirms Jitters," *Los Angeles Times* (September 13, 1981): Pt. V, p. 13.
9. See, for example, R. R. Behnke, C. R. Sawyer, and P. E. King, "The Communication of Public Speaking Anxiety," *Communication Education* 36 (April 1987): 138–39; J. Burgoon, M. Pfau, T. Birk, and V. Manusov, "Nonverbal Communication Performance and Perceptions Associated with Reticence," *Communication Education* 36 (April 1987): 119–30; K. L. McEwan and G. Devins, "Increased Arousal in Emotional Anxiety Noticed by Others," *Journal of Abnormal Psychology* 92 (November 1983): 417–21.
10. J. C. Humes, *Talk Your Way to the Top* (New York: McGraw-Hill, 1980), p. 135.
11. M. J. Beatty and M. H. Friedland, "Public Speaking State Anxiety As a Function of Selected Situational

and Predispositional Variables," *Communication Education* 38 (1990): 142–47.

12. See, for example, A. Ellis, *A New Guide to Rational Living* (North Hollywood, Calif.: Wilshire Books, 1977), and A. Beck, *Cognitive Therapy and the Emotional Disorders* (New York: International Universities Press, 1976).

CHAPTER 14

1. J. R. Johnson and N. Szczupakiewicz, "The Public Speaking Course: Is It Preparing Students with Work Related Public Speaking Skills?" *Communication Education* 36 (1987): 133.

2. Reported in *Presentation Products* 2 (August 1989): 8.

3. R. Verderber, *Essentials of Informative Speaking: Theory and Contexts* (Belmont, Calif.: Wadsworth, 1991), p. 201.

4. R. E. Wilkes, "Mortgage Megatrends," speech delivered at Austin Association of Professional Mortgage Women, Austin, Texas, September 15, 1987; reprinted in *The Executive Speaker* 9 (1988): 9.

5. E. Graham, "High-Tech Training," *Wall Street Journal* (February 9, 1990): R16.

6. Research summarized in T. H. Leahey and R. J. Harris, *Human Learning,* 2nd ed. (Englewood Cliffs, N.J.: Prentice-Hall, 1989), p. 203.

7. K. Blanchard, "Managers Must Learn to Teach," *Today's Office* 22 (October 1987): 8–9.

CHAPTER 15

1. Adapted from Ronald B. Adler and George Rodman, *Understanding Human Communication,* 4th ed. (Ft.

Worth, Tex. Holt, Rinehart and Winston, 1991), pp. 426–27.

2. M. Burgoon and M. D. Miller, "Communication and Influence," in *Human Communication: Theory and Research,* ed. G. L. Dahnke and G. W. Clatterbuck (Belmont, Calif.: Wadsworth, 1990), pp. 233–34.

3. C. J. Larson, *Persuasion: Reception and Responsibility,* 5th ed. (Belmont, Calif.: Wadsworth, 1989), p. 360.

4. See P. Kearney, T. G. Plax, V. P. Richmond, and J. C. McCroskey, "Power in the Classroom IV: Alternatives to Discipline," in *Communication Yearbook 8,* ed. Robert N. Bostrom (Beverly Hills, Calif.: Sage, 1984), pp. 724–46.

5. "At Lanier a Better Mousetrap Isn't Quite Enough," *Fortune* (February 26, 1979): 74, 76.

6. M. Burgoon and J. K. Burgoon, "Message Strategies in Influence Attempts," in *Communication and Behavior,* ed. G. J. Hanneman and W. J. McEwen (Reading, Mass.: Addison-Wesley, 1975), p. 153.

7. M. Allen, J. Hale, P. Mongeau, S. Berkowitz-Stafford, S. Stafford, W. Shanahan, P. Agee, K. Dillon, R. Jackson, and C. Ray, "Testing a Model of Message Sidedness: Three Replications," *Communication Monographs* 57 (1990): 275–91.

8. For a detailed review of credibility, see S. Trenholm, *Persuasion and Social Influence* (Englewood Cliffs, N. J.: Prentice-Hall, 1989), pp. 179–201, and R. N. Bostrom, *Persuasion* (Englewood Cliffs, N.J.: Prentice-Hall, 1983), pp. 64–86.

9. B. E. Gronbeck, R. E. McKerrow, D. Ehninger, and A. H. Monroe, *Principles and Types of Speech Communication,* 11th ed. (Glenview, Ill.: Scott, Foresman/ Little, Brown, 1990), pp. 180–218.

ACKNOWLEDGMENTS

TEXT

Page 6: From Saul D. Alinsky, *Rules for Radicals.* New York: Vintage, 1972.

Page 15: Gordon A. Craig, *Force and Statecraft: Diplomatic Problems of Our Time,* second edition. New York: Oxford University Press, 1990.

Page 17: Cynthia F. Mitchell, "Firms Seek Cure for Dull Memos," *Wall Street Journal,* October 4, 1985.

Page 39: Thomas J. Peters and Robert H. Waterman, *In Search of Excellence: Lessons from America's Best-Run Companies.* New York: Harper and Row, 1982.

Page 43: "Stairway to Success," *Newsweek,* April 19, 1979.

Page 53: Barbara Mandrell and Susan Kohler-Gray, "Digital Equipment Corporation: A Pioneer in Diversity," *Personnel,* January 1990.

Page 67: From Norman R. Augustine, *Augustine's Laws.* Copyright © 1983, 1986 by Norman R. Augustine. All rights reserved. Reprinted by permission Viking Penguin Inc.

Page 69: Deborah Tannen, *"That's Not What I Meant! How Conversational Style Makes or Breaks Your Relationships with Others."* New York: William Morrow, 1986.

Page 75: David A. Ricks, *Big Business Blunders: Mistakes in Multinational Marketing.* Homewood, Ill.: Dow Jones-Irwin, 1983.

Page 78: George Lee Walker, *The Chronicles of Doodah.* Boston: Houghton Mifflin, 1985.

Page 92: From *What They Don't Teach You in Harvard Business . . .* by Mark McCormack. Copyright © 1984 by Book Views, Inc. Used by permission of Bantam Books, a division of Bantam Doubleday Dell Publishing Group, Inc.

From *Iacocca: An Autobiography* by Lee Iacocca with William Novak. Copyright © 1984 by Lee Iacocca. Used by permission of Bantam Books, a division of Bantam Doubleday Dell Publishing Group, Inc.

Page 98: Ralph Nichols, "Listening Is a 10-Part Skill," *Nation's Business,* September 1987.

Page 101: Tom Peters, *Thriving on Chaos.* New York: Knopf, 1987. York: Harper and Row, 1982.

Page 138: Roger Fisher and Scott Brown, *Getting Together: Building a Relationship That Gets to Yes.* Boston: Houghton Mifflin, 1988.

Page 146: From *What They Don't Teach You in Harvard Business . . .* by Mark McCormack. Copyright © 1984 by Book Views, Inc. Used by permission of Bantam Books, a division of Bantam Doubleday Dell Publishing Group, Inc.

Page 137: Art Parrish, "A Little Understanding Goes a Long Way," *Industrial Distribution,* May 1987.

Page 178: Richard Bolles, *What Color Is Your Parachute: A Practical Manual for Job-Hunters and Career-Changers.* Berkeley, Calif.: Ten-Speed Press, 1986.

Page 180: Reported in *American Business,* Winter 1987.

Page 186: Martin Yate, *Knock 'Em Dead: With Great Answers to Tough Interview Questions.* Holbrook, Mass.: Bob Adams.

Page 187: Jane Ciabattari, "When It's Your Turn to Be Boss," *Working Woman,* March 1987.

Page 168: Robert Townsend, *Further Up the Organization.* New York: Knopf, 1984, p. 161; Alan Mameyer in *Training,* October 1986; Kenneth Blanchard, "Rating Managers on Performance Reviews," *Today's Office,* August 1987, pp. 6–8.

Page 227: Brian Dumaine, "Who Needs a Boss?" *Fortune,* May 7, 1990, p. 52.

Page 238: Carl F. Larson and Frank M. J. LaFusto, *TeamWork: What Must Go Right/What Can Go Wrong.* Newbury Park, Calif.: Sage, 1989.

Page 240: Reported in *Executive Speechwriter,* September 1990.

Page 253: Harold Geneen and Alvin Moscow, *Managing.* Garden City, N.Y.: Doubleday, 1984.

Page 255: From Roger K. Mosvick, *We've Got to Start Meeting Like This: A Guide to Successful Business Meeting Management.* Glenview, Ill.: Scott, Foresman, 1987.

Page 262: Robert Townsend, *Further Up the Organization.* New York: Knopf, 1984.

Page 280: Sandy Linver, *Speak and Get Results.: The Complete Guide to Speeches and Presentations That Work in Any Business Situation.* New York: Summit Books, 1983.

Page 285: Milo O. Frank, *How to Run A Successful Meeting—In Half the Time.* New York: Simon and Schuster, 1989.

Page 288: From *Iacocca: An Autobiography* by Lee Iacocca with William Novak. Copyright © 1984 by Lee Iacocca. Used by permission of Bantam Books, a division of Bantam Doubleday Dell Publishing Group, Inc.

Page 297: William Safire and Leonard Safir, *Words of Wisdom: More Good Advice.* New York: Simon and Schuster, 1989.

Page 309: Eleanor Foa Dienstag, "The Fine Art of Speaking in Public," *Working Woman,* February 1986.

Page 333: From *What They Don't Teach You in Harvard Business* . . . by Mark McCormack. Copyright © 1984 by Book Views, Inc. Used by permission of Bantam Books, a division of Bantam Doubleday Dell Publishing Group, Inc.

Page 348: Edward R. Tufte, *The Visual Display of Quantitative Information.* Cheshire, Conn.: Graphics Press, 1983.

Page 360: Milo O. Frank, *How to Get Your Point Across in 30 Seconds—or Less.* New York: Simon and Schuster, 1986.

Page 368: Roger Ailes, *You Are the Message: Secrets of the Master Communicators.* Homewood, Ill.: Dow Jones-Irwin, 1988.

Page 380: John T. Molloy, *Molloy's Live For Success.* New York: Morrow, 1981.

Page 388: Richard Saul Wurman, *Information Anxiety.* New York: Doubleday, 1989.

Page 402: Doug Harper, "Honing Your Professional Image," *Industrial Distribution,* May 1987.

Page 406: David A. Peoples, *Presentations Plus: David Peoples' Proven Techniques.* New York: Wiley, 1988.

Page 408: From *What They Don't Teach You in Harvard Business* . . . by Mark McCormack. Copyright © 1984 by Book Views, Inc. Used by permission of Bantam Books, a division of Bantam Doubleday Dell Publishing Group, Inc.

PHOTOS

Chapter 1: Ron Chapple/FPG

Chapter 2: Peter Menzel/Stock, Boston

Chapter 3: Deborah Kahn/Stock, Boston

Chapter 4: Steve Payne

Chapter 5: Susan Lapides/Design Conceptions

Chapter 6: FPG

Chapter 7: Joel Gordon

Chapter 8: Jeffry W. Myers

Chapter 9: FPG

Chapter 10: Ron Chapple/FPG

Chapter 11: Joel Gordon

Chapter 12: William D. Adams/FPG

Chapter 13: Susan Lapides/Design Conceptions

Chapter 14: Spencer Grant/The Picture Cube

Chapter 15: Alexander Lowry/Photo Researchers

INDEX